"WARHAWK"

This Warhawk, the 15,000th fighter built by the Curtiss-Wright Corporation, was emblazoned with the insignia of the 28 Air Forces using Curtiss fighters!
  The Tiger-Shark teeth marking it bears was used by a Royal Air Force Squadron in the Middle East and also by the American Volunteer Group in China, but, as one pilot explained in the latter case, with larger teeth markings because the Japanese were reputedly short-sighted!

AIRCRAFT CAMOUFLAGE AND MARKINGS 1907-1954

Written and Compiled by

BRUCE ROBERTSON

Text Copyright © *Bruce Robertson*

Paintings by

WILLIAM F. HEPWORTH, *M.S.I.A.*

Produced by

D. A. RUSSELL, *M.I.Mech.E.*

First Published Autumn 1956

Sixth Impression
1966

HARLEYFORD PUBLICATIONS LIMITED

LETCHWORTH, HERTS., ENGLAND

Library of Congress Card No.
58-11940

Published in the
UNITED STATES OF AMERICA
by
AERO PUBLISHERS, INC.

MADE AND PRINTED IN THE U.S.A. BY

AERO PUBLISHERS, INC. 329 AVIATION ROAD FALLBROOK, CALIF.

A F2B flying boat in dazzle-painting to render it conspicuous in the event of a forced landing at sea. The F2B differed from the better known F2A by having open cockpits. This particular aircraft, N4545, built by May, Harden and May, was delivered to Felixstowe Air Station in July, 1918, where it was based until the Armistice in November, 1918.

AUTHOR'S PREFACE

Aircraft markings like everything else are made for a purpose whether it be official, functional or merely self-expression. My object has been to show the nature of these markings to the modeller and to explain their significance to those interested in aircraft. This is not a book of aircraft, but a book of aircraft *markings*. The reader must not therefore expect a balanced survey of aircraft types, although he is entitled to anticipate a representative survey of markings applicable to all well-known service aircraft. In the same way, he must not expect all illustrations to be of complete aircraft, for the very title requires the magnification of markings that might form a very small part of an aircraft as a whole.

Particular attention has been paid to identification markings, and where a simple rule by serial number can be used to identify a particular mark number, this has been given. The modeller may only be concerned with such basic information, in this respect, as the identity of the prototype, first production model or a service example; the enthusiast on the other hand can rarely be satisfied, and the subject is vast. I have therefore given him (or her) such examples or notes, as far as possible, that have not previously appeared in print.

My greatest difficulties have been in deciding upon the constitution of a general rule and the extent of the inevitable exceptions. It was, too, with some apprehension I realised that the varied markings in a particular unit might well deserve a lengthier description than a whole command, where the strict standardisation enforced could be expressed in a few words.

I have not applied retrospectively the present systems of aircraft designations, but have used the nomenclature contemporary to the period under review. As far as the R.A.F. was concerned, role-prefix letters to mark numbers were introduced in 1942, and from 1948 these numbers changed from Roman to Arabic figures.

It has been said that the best books do not use abbreviations. That may be so, but in the reader's interest, to gain extra space for the presentation of photographs, abbreviations have been used. Their full meanings are explained on the last page of this book.

My task has been immeasurably eased by the close and helpful editing of Mr. D. A. Russell, who also put me in touch with some of his world-wide circle of aviation enthusiasts, for drawing upon information. I have too, derived much pleasure in partnering Mr. W. F. Hepworth as the colour artist of this book, who also produced most of the sketch pages. To Mr. M. J. F. Bowyer I am particularly indebted for contributing 'United States Air Forces in Britain', pages 143-6 and for his compilation of 'R.A.F. Unit Codes 1939-45', as well as for much useful information from his famous records. Mr. W. A. Bacon made many valuable suggestions, and Mr. N. D. Johnston of New Zealand, filled in many blanks in my knowledge of markings in the Pacific Areas, 1941-45.

I am very grateful for the assistance rendered by the Staffs of Government Departments; The Naval Information Department of the Admiralty; the Information Division and Air Historical Branch of the Air Ministry; and the Imperial War Museum. In particular I would wish to assure A. J. Charge Esq., M.B.E., J. L. Golding Esq. and Miss R. Coombs, of the Imperial War Museum, that their help has been much appreciated.

Information has been sought from many sources, and I consider myself fortunate in being able to approach many experts who have willingly answered my questions. Others have helped in may ways by making documents available, or searching records on my behalf; several serving officers, too, have given me the benefit of their wide experience I wish to thank Squadron Leader J. H. Adcock, M.B.E., G. E. Banwell Esq., Squadron Leader B. Bardega, D.F.M., J. M. Bruce Esq., M.A., 'Chronicler', Mrs. M. Corden, Wing Commander D. J. Evans, D.F.C., R. W. Hall Esq., Miss A. M. Holmes, Brian Lamb (whose youth was no handicap to his ability), John D. R. Rawlings Esq., Flight Lieutenant P. H. Renkin, Flight Lieutenant W. McR. Sinclair, Squadron Leader K. Taylor, D.F.C., Miss W. E. Thompson and C. J. Thoms Esq. (of Canada).

Since the publication of the first edition of this book in 1956, I have been indebted to many readers from their suggestions including, in particular, the following: Peter G. Cooksley Esq., Bryan Gibbins Esq., W. M. Lamberton Esq., William T. Larkins Esq., Peter G. Masefield Esq., James Oughten Esq., Eric Taylor Esq. and Frank Yeoman Esq.

Finally and specially, I thank the 'Air Britain' Organisation for their many facilities; and the printers' operatives, who have so patiently co-operated in my object of having the text presented, where applicable, in a manner as close as possible, to that of the actual aircraft markings.

London, 1961.   BRUCE ROBERTSON.

ACKNOWLEDGEMENTS

The Editor and Author gratefully acknowledge the following sources (listed alphabetically) for photographs used in this book: Air Ministry, pages 21-2, 24, 30, 65 (bottom), 66, 67 (bottom), 68-73, 74 (top), 76, 77 (top), 79-80, 82, 83 (bottom), 84, 168, 171-2, 177, 181, 196 and 210; Mr. M. J. F. Bowyer Esq., pages 166 (bottom), 167, 169, 173 (bottom), 174, 175 (bottom two), 176 and 178-180; Colin Bruce Esq., page 173 (top); 'Flight', pages 74 (bottom), 75, 77 (bottom), 81, 164-6 and 182; William Green Esq., pages 183 and 191; Imperial War Museum, pages 2, 4, 8-10, 12-13, 15-20, 23, 25, 26 (top), 28-9, 31, 32, 36-41, 47, 48 (top), 53-4, 57-8, 60 (top and bottom left), 61 (top), 62, 63 (bottom), 65 (top), 67 (top), 94-101, 105-111, 112 (bottom), 114-120, 123-127, 129-130, 134-138, 142-145, 153 (bottom), 156, 159, 160 (top), 190, 192, 193, 198, 200 and 201; Colonel G. B. Jarratt, page 175 (top six); Legion Condor, pages 92 and 93; J. Nieto, page 63 (top); Herr H. Nowarra, pages 60 (bottom right), 61 (bottom) and 154 and 155 (top); Merle C. Olmsted pages 148-9; John D. R. Rawlings, Esq., pages 91 (top), 113 and 128; Royal New Zealand Air Force, page 131; 'Real Photographs' Ltd., pages 11, 14, 26 (bottom), 27, 35, 88-90, 112 (top), 153 and 194 (top); Dr. Wallace Teed, page 140 and to several 'unknown' contributors for pages 15 (top), 46, 48 and 162.

About This Book

By **D. A. RUSSELL**, *M.I.Mech.E.*

This Sopwith Pup, presented to the United Kingdom in 1917 by the peoples of Kashmir, is shown by its inscription to be the twelfth aircraft donated by the Indian Punjab. The number B1778 reveals that this machine was of the batch serialled B1701-1850 built by the Standard Motor Company Ltd., Coventry.

To meet a popular demand, 'Camouflage, 1914-18 Aircraft' was published in 1943. Most of the information used in that work has been incorporated in this book. Following its success, 'Camouflage 1939-42 Aircraft' was published in 1946; with the intention of producing a further book to cover the years 1943-45—but the latter work was never completed.

At that time of writing, during the Second World War, the Admiralty, Air Ministry and Ministry of Aircraft Production were much too preoccupied to give their full co-operation, and our National Museums, being understaffed, could not give these two books the full support they deserved.

Now, after some fifteen years, under happier conditions enjoying the full support from Official Sources, and drawing on many comprehensive records privately accumulated; it has been possible to completely revise both of these books and to introduce a very large amount of new and hitherto unpublished information.

It is fitting that before many valuable records are lost or destroyed, the markings and insignia of Service Aircraft be permanently recorded, not only for the two World Wars, but also for those intermediate years of uneasy peace. Whereas the Navy's history concerns naval engagements with the ships participating, and the Army's traditions stem from battles and the regiments engaged; the Royal Air Force, our youngest Service, but now our first line of defence, has its pageantry in its aircraft and the squadrons to which they belonged.

The warpaint of camouflage, the red-white-blue roundel familiar as the Union Jack, the insignia of units and the emblems of individual pilots have given aircraft a fascination that appeals to young and old alike. It has also become a study to which many thousands of Aviation enthusiasts have given, and will continue to give, many hundreds of thousands of hours' attention.

The scale modeller should find this book of particular interest; there is little point in scale modelling unless the finished product is truly representative, which it cannot be if it is not accurate in detail. A model is often judged by its appearance—its finish. The old maxim of not 'spoiling the ship for want of a ha'peth of tar' is worthy of note. With the information in this book no modeller need have any further worry as to whether his models are appropriately camouflaged, and carry the correct markings.

After each new film on Aviation, documentary or otherwise, a spate of correspondence appears, not only in the Aeronautical Press, but even in *The Times*, with criticisms that show a lack of attention to detail in the matter of markings. The readers of this book can now become as critical as anyone else; and the Film Companies themselves might be well advised to note the information here.

It is hoped that the Aircraft Enthusiast will find in this book much new useful information. It goes much further than any previous books to show what aircraft markings were; it aims also to explain their significance. Markings are all indicative; a serial number relates to an aircraft's inception, code letters and devices are a guide to the unit, the mode of camouflage to a theatre of operations and many other, smaller markings, reveal much of interest to the enthusiast.

This book is the first to show how aircraft types and their variants may be distinguished by their markings. For example: Sopwith 1½ Strutters were made in both fighter and bomber versions; B.E.2Cs were used by both the R.F.C. and R.N.A.S.; the Hawker Hurricane was one of several types made both in this country and in Canada. In all cases, their origin, service and type can be ascertained from their markings, and their individual service numbers.

It is in this matter that the aircrew veterans of both World Wars can get out their log-books and perhaps find mention of the very machines in which they flew; they may learn too of their subsequent service. Ground staff of those stirring days may recognise the markings of aircraft they serviced, perhaps finding their own handiwork recorded!

It is said that a camera cannot lie; but a negative can be re-touched! Indeed, during the two World Wars, a number of photographs were so treated for security reasons, often to obscure markings. In the 1914-18 War, this

A Martin B-26B of the United States Twelfth Army Air Force presented by the New York Central Railroad Employees. The names of the crew members appear by the appropriate position, a practice discouraged by the R.A.F., who took the view that if the crew evaded capture after a forced landing in enemy territory, the enemy would thus be presented with a nominal roll of those they were seeking.

was done rather crudely by scratching the negative, but in the late War alterations were made much more subtly and are not always apparent. The reader is assured that photographs used in this book have been carefully vetted for such 'doctoring'. Many of them have been obtained from private sources, and have never before been published; they are all authentic, and none has been retouched in any way.

An exhaustive search has been made for suitable new illustrations which constitute a unique collection in themselves. A few reproductions that have appeared elsewhere are included because they are classic and authentic examples.

Markings cover many aspects apart from a general finish which might vary from the bright red and cream practice guided missile of to-day to the drab wartime nightfighter of yesterday. There are those markings required by international Convention, markings by which famous units may be identified and individual insignia reflecting the tenor of the times. Our late enemies are shown to have had a grim, but almost unsuspected sense of humour in some of their markings. The characters created by Walt Disney

rise above the enmity of nations, being used by friend and foe alike. Sex plays a not inconspicuous part, some aircraft were decorated with the most brazen of females, indeed there was rivalry to produce the most outrageous compositions; others were grotesque, humorous or poignant.

The greatest care has been taken to achieve accuracy. Many official documents have been made available, dope and paint specimens examined and even strips of fabric from wartime aircraft in the Pacific Area were obtained.

In this, the fourth edition, much additional information has been incorporated: an official chart of wartime colour schemes, many extra pages featuring squadron and unit badges on an unprecedented scale, additional tables and others extended, and more photographs, together with a dust cover in full colour.

In these varied respects, as also in regard to many of the 'Tables', and much of the text, this book is unique in that never before has such a mass of information on all aspects of Aircraft Camouflage and Markings, covering such a long period—1907 to 1954—been gathered together between the covers of one book.

Another Railway Gift. A Spitfire VC, EE602, built by Westland Aircraft bearing the presentation details — 'Central Railways Uruguayan Staff,' being presented by the Uruguayan Ambassador to No. 237 (Rhodesia) Squadron.

Aircraft Camouflage

CONTENTS

	Page
Frontispiece Dazzle Painting	2
Author's Preface by Bruce Robertson	3
Editor's Foreword by D. A. Russell, M.I.Mech.E	4 to 5
Part 1 1907-1918 The Great War and Before	9 to 64
Part 2 1919-1939 The Years between the Wars	65 to 93

	Page
Part 3 1939-1945 The Second World War	94 to 161
Part 4 1945-1954 The Post-War Years	162 to 191
Appendices 1914-1954	192 to 230
Index of Aircraft Types	231 to 232
Abbreviations	232

CHAPTERS

PART 1

Chapter		Page
1	*British Service Markings*	9
2	*The Single-Seat Fighters*	13
3	*The Two-Seat Fighters*	19
4	*Corps Reconnaissance Aircraft*	22
5	*Bombing Aircraft*	25
6	*Training Aircraft*	28
7	*British Naval Aircraft*	35
8	*Experimental and Miscellaneous Aircraft Markings*	39
9	*Aircraft of the Empire (Australia, Canada, South Africa and New Zealand)*	41
10	*British Aircraft Markings in the Theatres of the War*	46
11	*French Service Markings*	47
12	*United States Aircraft*	53
13	*Aircraft of the Allies (Belgium, Italy, Portugal, Rumania, Russia, and Serbia)*	57
14	*Germany and the German Allies*	60

PART 2

Chapter		Page
1	*British Service Aircraft Markings*	65
2	*Fighter Aircraft of the Royal Air Force*	68
3	*R.A.F. General Purpose 1919-1936*	71
4	*Bomber and Transport Aircraft in the R.A.F. 1919-1936*	74
5	*Training and Communications Aircraft 1919-1939*	76
6	*British Naval and Coastal Aircraft*	79
7	*Prelude to War*	82
8	*Commonwealth Air Forces 1919-1939*	88
9	*Service Aircraft of the U.S.A. 1919-1939*	90
10	*Markings in the Campaigns of the Inter-War Years*	92

PART 3

Chapter		Page
1	*R.A.F. General Markings 1939-1945*	94
2	*R.A.F. Fighter Command and A.D.G.B.*	97
3	*R.A.F. Bomber Command*	105
4	*Coastal Command*	109
5	*Training in the United Kingdom*	112
6	*Tactical and Support Aircraft—European Theatre*	114
7	*Transport, Communications and Miscellaneous Aircraft*	117
8	*The R.A.F. in Middle East and Mediterranean Areas*	119
9	*The R.A.F. in the Far East*	123
10	*Aircraft of the British Fleet*	125
11	*Commonwealth Air Forces*	128
12	*Aircraft of the Allies*	134
13	*American Air Forces*	137
14	*Germany and the German Satellites*	153
15	*Italian and Japanese Aircraft*	159

PART 4

Chapter		Page
1	*Markings of the Royal Air Force 1945-54*	162
2	*Markings of Service Aircraft at Home 1945-54*	164
3	*The Royal Air Force Overseas*	171
4	*Aircraft of the Royal Navies*	173
5	*Commonwealth Air Forces*	177
6	*The United States Air Forces (U.S.A.F., U.S. Army, U.S. Navy and U.S. Marines)*	178
7	*Western Alliance*	181
8	*Markings behind the Iron Curtain*	183
9	*The Korean War*	190

and Markings 1907-1954

COLOUR PLATES

	Page
British Aircraft Colouring Schemes 1916-18	33
Colour Schemes of Four Nations 1917-18	34
National Markings, British and Allied Aircraft, 1914-18	51
Colours between the Wars	52
Royal Air Force Squadron Markings 1924-37	85
Camouflage Schemes 1939-41	86
R.A.F. Colours 1940-42	103
The Mid-War Years	104
The Wellington in Profile	121
Wartime Profiles	122

	Page
Enemy Colours in the Early War Years	139
Individual Insignia of the U.S. Twentieth Air Force	140
Colours in the Air Offensive by Day over Europe 1943-45	157
Wartime Markings in Four Air Forces 1944	158
Standard Marking Scheme used by Fighter Squadrons of the R.A.F. and R.Aux.A.F.	185-188
Post-War Colours and Markings (1)	175
Post-War Colours and Markings (2)	176
Official Colour Shades (M.A.P.)	233

SKETCH AND DRAWING PAGES

Squadron Markings illustrated 1917-18	42
French and Belgium Aircraft Markings 1914-18	50
Miscellaneous Aircraft Markings of the Allies 1914-18	56
Aircraft Insignia of Germany and the German Allies 1914-18	59
R.A.F. Aircraft Markings 1920-39	78
Spanish Civil War, Abyssinian War and Miscellaneous Markings	87
Royal Air Force Identity Markings	102

Ministry of Aircraft Production Camouflage Schemes	132
Allied Aircraft Markings 1939-46	133
United States Air Forces 1939-47	147
United States Eighth Army Air Force Formation Markings	148
American Air Forces	150
Germany and the German Satellites	152
National Insignia of the Commonwealth, N.A.T.O. Countries and Communist Countries	184
National Insignia of the World	189

APPENDICES

1	*Presentation Aircraft 1914-18 and 1939-45*	192
2	*Markings of the Military Aerostats 1907-1954*	194
3	*Serial Allocations (R.A.F./R.A.A.F.)*	197
4	*Royal Air Force Unit Code Letters 1939-1945*	200

5	*Royal Air Force Squadron and Unit Badges*	204
6	*General Sequence of U.K. Based Day Fighter Schemes*	229
7	*The Future of Aircraft Markings*	230

TABULATIONS

Sopwith 1½ Strutter—Table of Markings	20
Avro 504 Series—Representative Markings	32
French Air Service—Representative Unit Markings	49
French Aircraft Identity Markings 1914-18	49
American Expeditionary Force Squadron Markings 1918	55
German Air Service—Identification Marking System 1912-18	64

United States Aircraft Designation Markings	151
British Rigid Airship Markings 1911-1930	196
British Non-Rigid Airship Markings 1914-19	196
British Service Aircraft Serial Number Allocations 1912-1954	197
Australian Type Number Series 1920-1954	199
Royal Air Force Unit Code Letters 1939-1945	200
British Standard Doping Scheme Markings	231

Return from photographic missions in the two world wars! Above is shown an A.E.G. CIV flown in the Middle East, 1918, its splotched purple and brown camouflage partly obscuring the number C7054/17 which indicates that it was the 7054th German observation class aircraft built during 1917.

" Every picture tells a story "—indeed sometimes a complicated one! The Spitfire shown below had the white-centred roundel to avoid confusion with the Japanese ' meat ball.' The markings on this aircraft have confounded air-historians because they were never officially allotted! They are in fact the initials of the pilot, Clive R. Caldwell, whose rank of Wing Commander is indicated by the pennant. (Note: the black spot at 10 o'clock on the white disc is not a ' spot ' on the negative—it is a plug hole for a battery test-lead.)

PART 1

British Service Markings

CHAPTER ONE

Pre-War Markings

On a lonely grouse moor near Blair Atholl in Scotland, under conditions of great secrecy, one of the first military aeroplanes, the Dunne D.1 biplane, underwent test in 1907. To conceal the contour of its unique wing form the main-planes were dazzle-painted. This is the first known instance of aeroplane camouflage. So elaborate were the security arrangements, that the attendant soldiers were disguised too—by the enforced wearing of civilian clothes. These troops were from the Air Battalion, Royal Engineers, the unit responsible for all military aircraft up to May, 1912, when the Royal Flying Corps was formed. Their heterogeneous collection of aircraft bore no distinctive markings other than their manufacturers' trade marks, until early 1912 when a simple letter/numeral identification system was used. Examples are 'B3' on a Breguet biplane at Larkhill in August, 1912, and 'F3' on a Bristol biplane at the Central Flying School at this same time. As most early aircraft had only lifting and control surfaces covered with fabric, the most suitable area for placing the markings was on the rudder, as the only covered vertical area.

The Admiralty by mid-1912 had some sixteen aircraft, mostly of Short Bros. manufacture, bearing the trade mark and factory number of that firm. For the 1912 Naval Review, their aircraft were given a letter/numeral identification system using significant initial letters; thus 'H' stood for Hydro-aeroplane, 'M' for Monoplane and 'T' for Tractor-aeroplane.

In November, 1912, the newly-formed Air Committee, instituted as a permanent body under the Committee of Imperial Defence, recommended a standard marking and identification number system for all service aircraft.

Separate blocks of numbers were allotted to the Navy and the Army, with sections of the Army's block of numbers to be reserved for aircraft built at the Royal Aircraft Factory and for aeroplanes used by the Central Flying School. These serials were the only authorised markings, and they were confined to the rudder.

The Royal Aircraft Factory had in the past marked

A pre-war, standard B.E.2a, showing the clear finish and the serial number as the only authorised marking. No. 226 was Bristol built.

certain of their products on the rudder with the letters R.A.F. and underneath, the appropriate design number, e.g. R.E.1. On the introduction of the standard numbering system, Nos. 201 to 400 were allocated to this establishment and machines bearing the designations B.E.1, 2, 3 and 4 became Nos. 201 to 204 respectively.

International Insignia

The Hague Committee in reviewing the Rules of Conduct in Warfare had envisaged aerial fighting some

Markings of early 1915—Union Jacks and serial numbers. One machine bears rudder stripes, then being introduced. The aircraft are Bristol Scouts 'C' of the R.N.A.S. on the Western Front. Serials show them to be of a batch of 24, Nos. 1243-1266 ordered late in 1914.

An early example of camou-flage in 1915. Note the small Union Jack on the rudder and the absence of fuselage mark-ings. The bright finish of the engine cowling and wheel discs tends to defeat the object of camouflaging the fabric.

years before 1914, but failed to call for distinctive national markings. In August, 1914, when Nos. 2, 3, 4 and 5 Squadrons of the Royal Flying Corps joined the British Expeditionary Force in France, their aircraft carried no markings other than a serial number. B.E.2A, No. 347, was the first aircraft to touch down on 13th August, 1914. Nine days later the first engagement in the air with the enemy took place and the need for recognition markings became apparent. The issue of pamphlets showing silhou-ettes of enemy aircraft did not assist identification appre-ciably, for although the outline of the German Taube was distinctive, many aircraft of French design flown by both friend and foe were indistinguishable. As a national flag could not be flown from an aircraft as a practical proposi-tion, the R.F.C. resorted to painting a Union Jack emblem prominently on their aircraft. These were at first painted at the pilot's discretion and varied greatly in size, position and in some cases, composition.

Troops in the opening weeks of the Great War were apt to fire up at friend and foe alike. Air Chief Marshal Sir Philip Joubert de la Ferte wrote that for years after-wards he remembered the roar of musketry that greeted two of our aircraft as they flew over a column of British Infantry during August, 1914. Some identification mark-ings on the undersides of aircraft were clearly necessary. From late August, this took the form of a Union Jack in the shape of a shield, but it was far from satisfactory. A Field Headquarters Memorandum issued the following October, impressed the need for making the Union Jack emblems as large as possible, utilising the full chord of the wing. The shield form was in consequence abandoned.

Meanwhile our French allies had identified their air-craft by means of the tricolour painted in concentric circles, red outer-most. It was proving a conspicuous marking. On the other hand, our Union Jack was found to be unsuitable for identification purposes, because of the similarity at a distance of its St. George's Cross with that of the German Cross. So, by a G.H.Q. Order of 11th December, 1914, the R.F.C. in the Field, adopted the French roundel, but with the colours reversed, that is with a blue circle outer-most. This was, shortly afterwards, adopted

throughout the R.F.C. and has re-mained so today, the well-known symbol of the R.A.F. However, until well into 1915, small Union Jacks in addition to the roundels were painted on aircraft, usually on the rudder or at the wing-tips. This was to assist recognition in the event of forced landing in friendly territory—a not uncommon occurrence—should the local peasantry not appreciate the significance of the new roundel.

At first the roundels replaced Union Jacks on the rudder and the undersurface of lower mainplanes in accordance with the current instructions, but from May, 1915, vertical red, white and blue stripes of equal width were introduced to replace the rudder roundels. This was again an adoption of a French policy. The stripes took up the complete rudder width with blue leading, white in the middle and red aft. Roundels about this same time began to appear on fuselage sides and on the upper surfaces of wings, to constitute the standard six locations for inter-national insignia, that remains unaltered to this day. Up to the end of 1916, the roundels on each wing were usually placed well inboard, but from 1917 onwards the tendency was to place them well out, with the outer circle about a foot from the wing-tip. Shortly after the introduction of camouflage in 1916, it was found necessary to outline the roundel by a thin white or yellow circle, as the blue outer circle did not contrast well against the khaki-green background.

Natural Finish

Most R.F.C. and R.N.A.S. aircraft, up to mid-1916,

A brand new Short 320 seaplane in 1917 displays its constructors' nameplate. The factory number S.382 has been placed immediately below the official Admiralty number N1498.

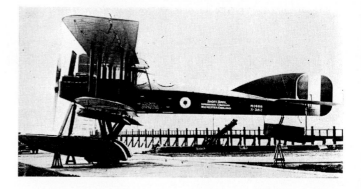

had a natural finish for all fabric and wooden parts. The fabric used was in the main unbleached Courtrai or Irish linen of the finest quality treated with proprietary dopes. Dope was employed to tighten fabric and by filling up the interstices of the material, give a continuous surface, thereby preventing penetration by air or moisture. To protect the dope from erosion by the elements, the fabric was clear-varnished. The resultant colour varied according to the varnish used and the number of coats, from a light grey to a buff. Where the rotary engines were installed a linseed oil varnish was used, as the normal clear varnish was affected by the spitting oil. This gave the aircraft a much cleaner, pale creamy yellow appearance. A widely used varnish for all aircraft, prepared to a Royal Aircraft Factory specification, produced a pale primrose finish.

Camouflaged Aircraft

From 1914 onwards various experiments were made in camouflaging aircraft, but not until late 1916 was a standard scheme generally adopted, that of painting the fuselage and upper surfaces of all operation aircraft in khaki-green. It varied in hue considerably, ranging from a dark green to a light khaki, and was seen in many intermediate shades. Undersurfaces had a natural finish. Two standard varnishes were used by units and contractors, P.C.10 which was mixed with khaki-green pigment and V.114 for undersurfaces.

This S.E.5 shows the distinctive features of a Royal Aircraft Factory built machine, the neat and characteristic official way of marking the serial number, the 'R.A.' on the rudder denoting the doping scheme and their style of handling markings.

These varnish designations were specification numbers issued by the Royal Aircraft Factory, they were suitable only for application on doped fabric or wood. For metal parts, such as engine cowlings, the contractor was allowed a free hand. Sober colours such as black or grey were most common.

Night-flying aircraft were painted dark olive-green on all surfaces, but not until August, 1918, was a standard night camouflage adopted using a modified roundel, without the white circle.

Aluminium Finish

Popularly called 'silver doping', large numbers of home-based aircraft were doped with Clarke's Britannia Dope and then covered with a preparation known as 'Silver Glaucous', which was finally clear-varnished for protection. The silver finish that it produced certainly gave the aircraft a most pleasing silvery appearance.

Serial Numbers

The service, or serial number of an aeroplane was painted either on the fin or rudder and often on the fuselage near the tail. On certain training aircraft it was also marked beneath the wings. There was no hard and fast combination. The number was usually in white against a dark background, in black against a light finish and sometimes the characters were outlined in a contrasting colour. Some machines, particularly those from the Sopwith works, had the serial number painted in black on a white rectangular background on the fuselage sides. The general methods of presentation are evident from the many illustrations in this work and the range of numbers used is tabulated in the Appendices. For some reason the number '13' was not allotted, it may be conjectured that it was a case of official superstition!

It should be emphasised that a serial number was allotted when an aircraft was ordered, as an official identification number throughout construction and subsequent service. They were first marked by the contractor. The stencils used by different firms varied considerably, some firms employed sign-writers for these markings. Again in service, after a repainting the style of marking might depend on the stencil used or the whim of an amateur sign-writer.

Constructors' Markings and Numbers

By March, 1918, fifty-seven firms were engaged in the manufacture of complete aircraft. Many of these contractors delivered their aircraft marked with a nameplate, trade mark or symbol. These markings were usually painted out in service on operational aircraft.

Aircraft firms, such as Fairey's, Short Bros. and Phœnix, marked their own identification number on the fuselage, usually adjacent to the official serial number. Their aircraft were numbered from No. 1 upwards, Fairey's and Short Bros. using a 'F' and 'S' prefix respectively. These numbers applied to all types of aeroplanes built within their own works; it did not apply to aircraft of their design built under sub-contract by other firms. Normally constructors' numbers ran consecutively in batches with official serial numbers. For example, Short Type 184 seaplanes with official serial numbers N1080 to N1099 bore Short Bros. factory numbers S314 to S333 respectively.

Handling Markings

A universal marking, instituted during the second

year of the war, was 'LIFT HERE' with an indicative arrow. Aeroplanes could be swung round manually, either by an individual or a team, depending on the size of the machine. It was important that the strain of lifting should be exerted at a strong part of the structure. For similar reasons 'TRESTLE HERE' was marked on some aircraft in order that the weight of the fuselage was borne by a structural member and not by the covering fabric.

Part Number and Inspection Markings

Main components were initially marked with part numbers and Aeronautical Inspection Department approval stamps. Due to the urgent need for aircraft it was sometimes obligatory for the A.I.D. to pass sub-standard components, that were, for example, of poor finish or non-interchangeable. These items were marked 'P-P' indicating that they were passed for the sake of production. Although such inspectors' concessions would not apply to structurally weak parts, it was hardly a marking to inspire a pilot with confidence. Fortunately it was not a common marking.

Most of these markings were painted in 1 in. stencilled characters on the fabric covering the component. A typical aileron marking is 'B.C.47881 C.C.' with B.C. standing for the manufacturer—the British and Colonial Aeroplane Co. Ltd., 47881 the firm's part number and C.C. the doping scheme.

Doping Scheme Markings

Several different doping schemes were used and covered surfaces were marked with 1 in. code letters to denote the particular scheme. These letters were often placed as a suffix to the part number of the item concerned, as shown in the preceding paragraph. Code letters used are given on page 202.

Presentation Aircraft

All the previous markings were normally the responsibility of the contractor. Up to March, 1915, all military aircraft were delivered to the Royal Aircraft Factory for acceptance, testing and checking, but from then onwards, Acceptance Parks were formed to receive aircraft from the factories. To these units fell the pleasant task of marking presentation aircraft.

These markings appeared on the fuselage but no standard size or position was adopted. Apparently the Germans did not appreciate their significance, for when the seventh presentation aircraft by Zanzibar fell into their hands bearing the inscription ZANZIBAR VII, they reported the capture of a Zanzibar Type VII biplane! The Turks, intrigued by the capture of a B.E.2C bearing the name of the town that had donated its cost, reported in an official communique the capture of a British aircraft bearing its town of manufacture! It must have confused intelligence staffs.

Several hundred aircraft were donated to the nation in the years 1914 to 1918, many by Commonwealth societies and individuals. A representative aircraft from current production was selected to bear the presentation details. (Page 192 gives a selection of these markings.)

In addition, the Army had a Regimental Savings Scheme for Aircraft. For every £2,500 put into savings by the personnel of each major unit, the War Savings Association arranged to have an aircraft marked with the name of the regiment.

Unit Markings

Individual unit markings were first introduced for B.E.2C aircraft of Corps Squadrons in April, 1916. They consisted of simple devices in black, white, red or yellow. From late 1916, squadron markings were widely adopted on the Western Front. Occasionally unit devices were changed to confuse enemy intelligence and in March, 1918, all squadron markings were forbidden in the Western Front area. An exception was made for fighter squadrons as some means of unit identification was desirable for tactical reasons in the heat of a dog-fight. At home and in the minor theatres unit markings were generally adopted from early 1917

Unit markings were painted by the unit personnel and as squadrons did not have an establishment for a painter or sign-writer, the work was usually placed in the hands of a 'handyman'. His efforts, though effective were often inconsistent.

To identify individual aircraft within a unit a large letter or numeral was usually painted conspicuously on the fuselage sides and was often repeated on the upper surface of the top wing. It was easier to see and remember than the serial number. The range of identification letters and numbers used increased as the aircraft establishment of units increased by stages throughout the war, although it did not necessarily follow that letters were allotted alphabetically or numerals consecutively.

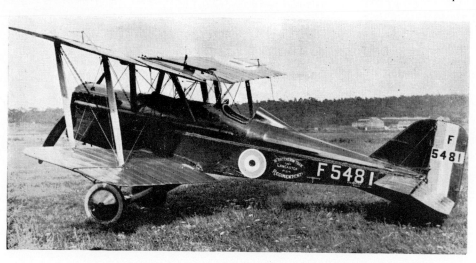

A Regimental Savings Scheme Aircraft contributed by the 16th Battalion Yorks and Lancs. Regt. The aircraft is a S.E.5A built by the Austin Motor Company.

CHAPTER TWO

The Single-Seat Fighters

Names such as Mannock, McCudden and Ball live on. They became Aces when the criterion of success was the greatest number of enemy aircraft destroyed. The units with which they flew became known as 'crack squadrons' and in them were founded traditions that held good in the Battle of Britain. Single-seat fighters were regarded as the *élite* of the flying Services and to be a fighter pilot was the ambition of all adventurous youth.

At first the R.F.C. in France concentrated on the two-seat reconnaissance types; single-seat aircraft taking the role of 'scouts', a term that long remained for fighting aircraft. Scouts were allotted to most of the squadrons at the Front and not until enemy opposition in the air became a menace, was the necessity for complete squadrons of fighting aircraft realised. In 1916 scout squadrons were formed with an initial establishment of twelve aircraft, this was later raised to eighteen, then twenty-four and finally twenty-five aircraft per scout squadron in September, 1918. Most scout squadrons had adopted unit markings by early 1917, these were simple devices and no precise instructions were issued concerning them, except to call for a periodic change or exchange of markings between units to confuse enemy intelligence. During March, 1918, No. 1 Squadron R.N.A.S. was directed to bear the same markings as No. 65 Squadron for an intelligence ruse. Instructions were given that their Camels not on patrol would be kept under cover in hangars.

Early Scouts

Most squadrons in 1914-15 had one or two Martinsyde S.1 or Bristol Type 'C' Scouts attached. The Martinsyde had a natural finish with a number (e.g. 748 or 2452) painted in 6 in. digits on the rudder above a 8½ in. × 5 in. Union Jack. Later machines, numbered 2820-2831 and 4229-4252, had normal fuselage roundels.

The markings of the first R.N.A.S. batch of Bristol Scouts may be observed in a preceding illustration. Later Scouts 'C' and 'D', used by both the R.F.C. and R.N.A.S., had the newly adopted roundel. A characteristic of these machines was the large presentation of their serial numbers in 13 in. thick, black characters, normally towards the

The natural finish of a Martinsyde S.1. Polished plywood, clear protective varnished fabric, and sheet-metal fishplates. It was unusual in later types to mark fuselage roundels over the fabric sewing.

rear of the fuselage. The last R.N.A.S. and R.F.C. batches Nos. N5390-5419 and A2376-2380 respectively, were in standard khaki-green with large white serials similarly placed. Whether in khaki-green or not, front fuselage covering of aluminium sheet was left in its natural state except for the application of lanoline. Distinction between the machines of the two services can be made by the serial tables (Appendix IV) with the exception of eight R.F.C. aircraft, Nos. 5564-5, A1769-72 and A1790-1, transferred to the R.N.A.S.

Sopwith Tabloids, in natural finish, were used in limited numbers by the R.N.A.S. A serial number (123-124, 1201-1213) was marked in black on a white rectangular patch painted on the rudder. Union Jacks were carried in various positions.

The D.H.2

In February, 1916, the first single-seat scout squadron, No. 24, reached France equipped with the D.H.2 pusher biplane scout. Its lightly doped, linseed-oil varnished fabric gave the wings and tail an almost transparent appearance. Indeed, the roundels on the top of the upper

The almost transparent fabric of the D.H.2 is obvious from this picture where the outline of the top wing roundel can be seen showing through the underside. The contrasting shades on the nacelle represent the polished finish of the nose and decking and the linseed-oil varnished fabric at the sides.

wing showed through on the undersurface and the tracery of wing spars and ribs could be easily followed. Their markings were consistent, as all were built by the designing firm, the Aircraft Manufacturing Company; features were the stencilling of part numbers in black 1 in. digits on all major components. The white of the rudder stripe, for example, bore the part number 'AMC 6514' at the top..

All wing struts were centrally marked with the firm's monogram, the letters A.M.C. superimposed, occupying a space of 2 in. × 2 in. In the firm's peculiar way, the serial number was not placed centrally across the rudder stripes, but in the manner illustrated. The ranges of numbers were 5917-6015, 7842-7941, A2533-2632, A4764-4813 and A4988-5087. Only one, No. 8725, went to the R.N.A.S. Major Lanoe G. Hawker, V.C., the Officer Commanding the first D.H.2 squadron, flew machine 5964, in which he gallantly met his end on 23rd November, 1916. Major J. B. McCudden, V.C., was allotted No. 5985 of No. 29 Squadron for his first operational flight.

A standard Sopwith-built Triplane of the batch N5420-5494.

The B.E.12

To meet an urgent need, the Royal Aircraft Factory designed an interim fighter by converting a B.E.2C into a single-seater and installing a more powerful engine. In utilising B.E.2C fuselages, quick production was facilitated. The Daimler Motor Co., as a B.E.2C contractor, produced the first two hundred machines. At first deliveries were in standard B.E.2C plain finish, with the serial numbers, 6478-6677, in 8 in. black digits on the fin and adjacent to them the B.E.2C fin part number in 1 in. stencilled digits. Machines subsequent to No. 6527 were in standard camouflage with standard national insignia and serials outlined in white; this also applied to Daimler's second batch, A4006-4055. Those built by the Standard Motor Company were finished in standard khaki-green bearing numbers 6136-6185 on the fin and the firm's trade mark on the interplane struts. B.E.12s were before the days of squadron devices but identification letters were usually carried in service. In No. 21 Squadron (Western Front) these were marked in grey on the fuselage sides, imme-

diately above the lower mainplane. Machine No. 6573 was No. 4 in this unit.

F.E.8

Another R.A.F.-designed fighter was the F.E.8 with the configuration of a D.H.2. The two prototypes, 7456-7, and the first seventy production machines, built by Vickers (No. 7595 *et seq.*) were delivered in natural finish and initially so used in service. Later machines, A4869-4987 by Darracq of Fulham, were delivered in khaki-green. The positioning of the wing roundels, rather inboard, was usual for the period, but nacelle roundels varied. F.E.8s at home bore these each side of the nacelle nose; on the Western Front, in Nos 5, 40 and 41 Squadrons, large nose identification numbers or letters were carried, and the roundel was in consequence painted further back. A German photograph of a F.E.8 ending upon their side of the lines, shows that 7624 bore its number in white at the rear of the nacelle—the F.E.8's fin could only take small markings. The unit number, a black '6', was marked each side of the nose and behind it was the roundel without any outlining against the khaki-green varnish. Most strange was the tail marking with horizontal red-white-blue stripes.

French Aircraft in British Service

Over a thousand aircraft, mostly fighters were acquired from French industry. Those for the R.F.C. were delivered direct to R.F.C. depots in France for re-marking. The French favoured an aluminium finish, a form of camouflage in the air if not on the ground, but certainly a pleasing sight. This finish was retained and ex-French machines became the only R.F.C. aircraft to sport this silverish finish at the Front. An oddity of the Nieuport Scouts, supplied in quantity, was their very narrow lower wing, which allowed only a tiny roundel. To assist recognition, the undersurface of the top wing was also marked with full-size roundels. In the absence of a fin, serial numbers were placed centrally on the rudder, across the stripes, in the style 'B'3591'. The range of numbers appropriate to these aircraft is given in Appendix IV. Lt.-Col. W. Avery Bishop, V.C., D.S.O., M.C., D.F.C., the Canadian Ace credited with 72 victories, used silver-grey Nieuport Scouts A306, A6769 and B1566 in No. 60 Squadron during the spring of 1917.

Aircraft of French design were also built in this country under licence. A famous French fighter so produced was the S.P.A.D. S.VII ordered by the Admiralty in 1916 from Mann Egerton of Norwich. Subsequently, the Admiralty expressed a preference for the Sopwith Triplane, then in production for the R.F.C., and the War Office agreed literally to a 'swop'. Spads allotted R.N.A.S. numbers from N6210 up, had R.F.C. numbers from A9100 up substituted. The firm's heading, occupying a 2-in. × 1 ft. space on the fuselage, was stencilled as follows:

MANN EGERTON & CO. LTD.
AIRCRAFT WORKS,
NORWICH
ENGLAND

Unfortunately, the black lettering did not stand out well against the khaki-green finish which was common to all these machines, including a batch, Nos. A8794-8893, built by the Air Navigation Co. of Addlestone. Both manufacturers marked the serial numbers in white on the fin. A French-built S.VII sent as a pattern was also taken over by the R.F.C. as A8965.

Martinsyde Elephant

A clumsy-looking fighter that earned the unofficial name 'Elephant', the Martinsyde G100/G102 put in much hard work as a fighter-bomber on the Western Front with No. 27 Squadron. In the Middle East, too, Elephants served in Nos. 30 and 72 Squadrons, not without some action as fighters. In one month of 1917, combat reports were submitted by the pilots of machines 7459, 7466, 7467 and 7468 of No. 30 Squadron.

Dark brown cowling and clear-varnished fabric was the factory finish of all Elephants, the picture on page 192 being typical. Later in service some were coated khaki-green, an example being A3962, which had all upper-surfaces expect the fin in khaki-green.

Type G100 (120 h.p. Beardmore) received the numbers 4735-4736 (prototypes), 7258-7307 and 7459-7508. Type G102 (160 h.p. Beardmore) were numbered A1561-1610, A3935-4004 and A6250-6299. B865 was alloted to a rebuilt machine.

Bristol Monoplane Scout

Considered unsuitable for the Western Front, the Monoplane Scout served at home and in the Middle East. The five prototypes, A5138 Type M1a and A5139-5142 Type M1b were initially in clear finish with black fin serials. Production machines, Type M1c, had a dark khaki-green finish with either black or white serials in the C4901-5025 range marked on the fin.

The D.H.5

An unusual-looking fighter by a famous designer, the D.H.5 had a negatively staggered lower wing, which gave the pilot an unobstructed downward view. It was facetiously explained as intending to confuse the enemy as to its direction travel! The A.M. Co. prototype A5172 had a trim, natural finish, but all production models had the standard P.C.10 khaki-green varnish. They appeared at a time when squadron markings were coming into vogue and they were a popular presentation aircraft. Unfortunately, they were not popular with pilots and were soon replaced.

Only by the method of presenting the serial number or, of course, by the range of numbers, could the products of the three contracting firms be identified. The Darracq

Camels of No. 4 Squadron, A.F.C. in March, 1918. Note that the Boomerang squadron device is also marked on the fuselage decking and that the individual identification letters are repeated on the top wing, offset slightly to starboard. The two Camels in the foreground were Ruston-Proctor-built.

D.H.5s, A9363-9562, were in the manner illustrated on page 192, those by A.M.C., A9163-9362, were in the firm's usual style and the British Caudron method for B331-380 is shown on page 56. An unusual refinement was a full-stop!

Sopwith Triplane

The Triplane was well known by its unorthodox lines; as related earlier it was originally ordered for the R.F.C. but was taken over by the R.N.A.S. in exchange for Spads. Apart from the prototype, N504, all production machines were delivered in the standard khaki-green. Those emerging from the Sopwith works had fin name-plate and white serial number background, but in service, the fin was often painted over a khaki-green. The first sub-contract machines had serial numbers marked 'Sopwith fashion', no doubt as a result of N5420, the first Sopwith production triplane, having been sent as a pattern to the contracting firm— Messrs. Clayton and Shuttleworth. Normal armament was a single Vickers gun, but experimental aircraft, N533-538 and N5910-5912, built by Oakley and Son, had twin Vickers. The last machine, N5912, is still in existence.

Several triplanes are worthy of note. N5451 reached the Balkan theatre and was apparently the only triplane to go East. N5458 went West; in December, 1917, it was sent to the U.S.A. for exhibition. The triplanes of 'B' Flight, No. 10 Squadron, R.N.A.S., bore names such as BLACK SHEEP, BLACK ROGER, BLACK DEATH, BLACK PRINCE and BLACK MARIA.

The Sopwith Pup

Officially the Sopwith Scout in the R.F.C. and Type 9901 in the R.N.A.S., the 'Pup' was generally known by its Sopwith 'Zoo' name. All naval Pups were Sopwith built and bore the Sopwith name-plate stencilled on the fin together with the firm's method of marking serial numbers on the fuselage. R.F.C. aircraft, built by two sub-contractors, had fin serial numbers. Whitehead's used black numbers against a painted white background and Standard's neatly outlined the characters in white. The latter contractor had the firm's trade mark on all four inter-plane struts, facing outwards. Early naval Pups numbered between 9496

and 9949 had a natural finish, but later deliveries and all R.F.C. machines were finished in drab khaki-green.

Notes on individual machines:

3691, prototype. 9937, used by 'B' Flight, R.N.A.S., Cranwell, written-off for ground instruction work December, 1917. A6150, first Whitehead-built Pup. A7301, first Standard-built Pup. A6194, marked with unit number 4 in red, forward of fuselage roundel, was captured intact by Germans. N6204 was sent to Russia as a gift from the British Government.

Sopwith Camel

The Camel was a worthy successor to the Pup and perhaps the most famous of World War I fighters. Supplied to both R.N.A.S. and R.F.C., it accounted for 1,294 enemy aircraft. First production models in April, 1917, were from a Sopwith-built R.N.A.S. order for Nos. N6330-6379, of which N6332 (a much-photographed machine), N6338 and N6344 were transferred to the R.F.C. Camel N6340 went to Farnborough for testing to destruction, the remainder passed into R.N.A.S. use.

Large orders for the R.F.C. were placed with Sopwith's and seven sub-contractors, but on completion, deliveries to either Service, for the R.N.A.S. deployed several Camel squadrons on the Western Front in support of the R.F.C. These were Nos. 1, 3, 4, 6, 8, 9 and 10 Squadrons (later to become Nos. 201, 203, 204, etc., R.A.F.). Thus apart from the first batch, no distinction by serial number could be made for Camels serving in either the R.F.C. or R.N.A.S.

However, the characteristics of Sopwith-built machines could be singled out when first in use by the finish in 'Sopwith fashion'; but later in service, they were often re-marked and in particular the clear-finished tail fin with the Sopwith name-plate was apt to be varnished over in khaki-green. The range of numbers was always a safe guide: N517-8, the two prototypes; B3751-3950, B6201-6450 and N6330-6379 were Sopwith-built; all other Camels were produced by sub-contracting firms. It is noticeable that early Camels built by Boulton & Paul and Ruston Proctor used the Sopwith method of presenting the serial number. This can be traced to N6344 of the early Sopwith batch, having been sent in turn to each of these firms as a pattern.

The whole fuselage, including the underneath, was painted khaki-green. Fuselage roundels were certainly larger than those of its contemporary, the S.E.5A, owing to the Camel's deeper fuselage. At three places on each side of the fuselage towards the rear, were LIFT HERE indications with the appropriate arrows. Khaki-green was standard for all Camels on delivery.

In training units, Camels were often painted according to the whim of an instructor. Camel C42 was all white and bore the name WHITE FEATHER. The thousandth aircraft built by Ruston

A Camel close-up showing the metal cowling and wood panelling. The wheel discs of fabric, rendered taut by doping were clear varnished on delivery, being sometimes painted in khaki-green in service. This particular machine was operated by No. 203 Squadron.

An Austin-built S.E.5A bearing the Boomerang squadron device of No. 2 Squadron, A.F.C. This machine, C9539, is of 'C' Flight which bore the unit letters U, V, W, X, Y and Z. The marks just discernible on the wing-tips are component part numbers. As 'flying shots' in that war were extremely rare, the reader can only be shown the underside of an aircraft by the photograph of one that landed like this—which was not uncommon!

Proctor, Camel E7232, had only the rudder marked normally with the usual stripes; its top wing carried an extended, brilliant orange Japanese Rising Sun; its lower wing was striped in red and white. It had no roundels.

The S.E.5 and S.E.5A

Contemporary with the Camel and no less famous, were the S.E.s; the S.E.5 and the more powerful S.E.5A with strengthened undercarriage. The S.E.5 was designed and built only by the Royal Aircraft Factory, but the S.E.5A went into quantity production, both at the R.A.F. and by several contractors.

All S.E.5s and S.E.5As were delivered in khaki-green with engine cowlings similarly painted, they were, in fact, one of the few types to be so uniformly finished. Roundel positions and their size relative to the aircraft are admirably illustrated on page 11. It will also be apparent from an illustration on page 12 that the fuselage roundels were of necessity small, to clear the fabric lacing.

One way of telling an S.E.5 from an S.E.5A was by serial number. S.E.5s were numbered A4561-4563, A4845-4868 and A8898-8947. The manner of marking the serials was indicative of a R.A.F. product, neat, white figures marked across the fin, in this manner—'A'4848'. By the same style, the R.A.F. built S.E.5As, C1051-1150 and D7001-7050, could be identified. All the above batches had the letters 'RA' stencilled in black on the white of the rudder stripe. This was painted upside-down on at least one machine! Two arrows each side pointed to lifting positions and between each set the words LIFT HERE looking very much the work of a sign-writer. On subcontracted machines each arrow bore a small stencilled LIFT HERE

S.E.s were treated to flamboyant schemes in training units, but do not appear to have rivalled the Camel in bizarre finishes. On the other hand, S.E.s were not considered suitable for night flying and apart from a short experimental period in home defence, none donned the sombre dark olive-green.

One machine used by Major Dallas, of No. 40 Squadron, is of particular interest, for it was camouflaged in the now familiar brown and green. The fin serial number, D3711, and the white of the rudder stripes was partially smeared over. The S.E.5 was a favourite mount of the Aces. Ball used S.E.5s A4850 and A8907 with radiator and spinner painted red.

Major E. Mannock, V.C., D.S.O., M.C., scored most of his seventy-three victories with No. 74 Squadron in which his favourite 'mount' was Wolseley-built S.E.5A C6468.

Major James Byford McCudden, V.C., D.S.O., M.C.,

M.M. and Croix de Guerre, scored most of his fifty-four victories on the S.E.5 whilst serving as Flight Commander of 'B' Flight, No. 56 Squadron. His first S.E.5 in this unit, Vickers-built S.E.5A B519, was taken over on 16th August, 1917, but a month later he exchanged it for a R.A.F.-built machine S.E.5 A4863. This latter machine had a large identification letter 'G'. The 'G' was repeated on the top wing, offset 4 ft. to starboard from the centre of the plane and again repeated under both port and starboard sides of the bottom wing. When McCudden returned from leave in London during October, 1917, he was most annoyed to learn that this aircraft had been smashed on landing by an inexperienced pilot. He then took over Martinsyde-built S.E.5A B35, but when another R.A.F.-built machine, S.E.5 A4891, was available with special-narrow-chord elevators, he took over the machine and passed B35 to the youngest member of his flight. Although bearing the serial A4891, the true identity of the S.E.5 was B4891. By December, 1917, the squadron was using a numeral instead of a letter for an individual marking. McCudden's A4891 had the number '6' forward of the roundel and repeated on the wings in the same positions as the previous 'G'.

McCudden believed in letting his flight pick out their leader by distinct markings. The '6' was therefore marked as large as was practicable. In addition, from January, 1918, A4891 was fitted with a large spinner painted red, which had been taken from a L.V.G. that McCudden had shot down. There was no mistaking McCudden's aircraft.

S.E.5A, 'W' of No. 56 Squadron, flown, by Captain D. Grinnell-Milne in September, 1918, bore the name SCHWEINHUND in 3 in. white letters on the khaki-green varnished plywood nose panel. The choice of this name is not without interest: Grinnell-Milne was an escaped prisoner-of-war and having been called a 'schweinhund' so often he expressed a wish to pass the appellation on to something else! The Commanding Officer, Major E. J. L.

17

Gilchrist, M.C., drew attention to this name and pointed out that unofficial markings were forbidden. Grinnell-Milne, something of a humorist, then pointed out that as the squadron were engaged in low-flying for ground strafing the name might be disconcerting to the Germans. He further proposed sketching a portrait of the Kaiser on the radiator in such a way that when the shutter was opened and closed rapidly, the Imperial moustache would wiggle and eyes blink: the idea being that this apparition of their leader might put enemy ground gunners off their aim! The C.O. was apparently not amused!

The Sopwith Dolphin

The Dolphin was designed as a high-altitude fighter, but became well known as a ground attack machine. For its time it had the unusually heavy armament of four guns —two Lewis plus two Vickers. All Dolphins were delivered in standard day camouflage with grey panelling. Sopwith's built the majority themselves, orders calling for C3777-4276, D3576-3775 and E4629-5128. At this stage of the war, 1918, Sopwith's had abandoned their earlier policy of marking the firm's name on the fin of operational types, the fin was therefore finished in khaki-green to tone with the general finish of the fabric. The forward panelled sections were varnished in blue-grey, but serialling remained in the usual Sopwith style. Sub-contracted Dolphins were numbered from C8001 by Darracq's and from D5201 by

Hooper's. No. 79 Squadron Dolphins were marked first with a white dumb-bell, then a white square aft of the fuselage roundels. For other markings see pages 42-45.

The Sopwith Snipe

The last of the Sopwith fighter types to take the field, the Snipe, went into quantity production in mid-1918. It was finished in the usual khaki-green with blue-grey panelling. From August, 1918, onwards, in accordance with new instructions regarding the identification of aircraft, serial numbers were marked both on the rudder and the fuselage.

B9962-9967 were the six prototype batch numbers marked in 'Sopwith fashion'. The first production models of the firms making Snipes are as follows: Sopwith, E7987; Boulton & Paul, E6137; C.O.W., E6537; Napier, E6787; Portholme, E8307 and Ruston Proctor, E6937.

The inconsistencies and variations in squadron markings are again emphasised. There was often little time to pay attention to detail and sometimes a machine delivered direct from the Aircraft Park would be required on patrol before the painting of unit markings could be arranged, for it is a grim fact that in single-seat fighter squadrons the wastage of aircraft, that required replacement, was 66 per cent. per month.

The Snipe remained in service for some years after the war in Nos. 1, 17, 19, 29, 32, 41, 46, 56 and 111 Squadrons and in addition some forty were converted to two-seaters.

The Vickers 'Gunbus'

The need for a two-seat fighter aircraft to escort and protect the work of reconnaissance aircraft dates from the opening months of the war, when observers in aircraft used rifle or revolver fire to ward off enemy machines. As early as 1913, Vickers had produced the prototype of a two-seat pusher biplane, first with a forward-firing Maxim and later with a Lewis gun. Known colloquially as the Gunbus and officially as the Vickers Fighter it went into service early in 1915. The first squadron to be completely equipped with these machines was No. 11 Squadron which arrived in France during July, 1915. Their Gunbuses had a natural finish with wing roundels inboard by one-sixth of the span, an 18 in. nacelle roundel and a small Union Jack on the tail as shown on page 56. The fabric was linseed-oil varnished to protect it from the oil-spitting Gnome engine—this was apparently one of this engine's lesser vices, for one Gunbus pilot experienced twenty-two forced landings in thirty flights due to engine trouble! Some early machines had all the fabric painted in a brown and green foliage camouflage, with roundels only under the bottom wing and a tail Union Jack.

A standard F.E.2B. The position of nacelle roundel and position and outlining of the serial number is typical of both F.E.2B and F.E.2D versions.

The term 'Gunbus' was applied to several Vickers two seat pusher types. Representative R.F.C. serial numbers are: Type F.B.4, 664; Type F.B.5, 648; Type F.B.5A, 2346; Type F.B.9, 5271. The Admiralty purchased the prototype and allotted it the R.N.A.S. number '32'. Under the Admiralty's peculiar nomenclature for aircraft, its Gunbuses Nos. 861-864 were known as Type 32. A case of a marking becoming a designation!

The F.E.2B and D

Gunbuses were followed in the field by the Royal Aircraft Factory-designed F.E.2B. The first F.E.2 with the pre-war marking of number only—604, had crashed in February, 1914. From this unpromising start, modified and re-engined to become the F.E.2B, the type did yeoman service in the mid-war years and in fact stayed in service until the end.

Large-scale production commenced in 1915, deliveries at first being in a natural finish with standard varnish V114. The fabric contrasted slightly in shade from the varnished wood of the nacelle decking. From late 1916 onwards, khaki-green was the normal finish. Wing roundels in standard positions occupied the full chord, nacelle roundels were comparatively small, their size being gov-

erned by the fabric lacing as may be seen in the illustration. serial numbers in black were invariably placed across the rudder stripes and usually outlined in white against the red and blue sections.

In service units, identification letters or numbers were often marked each side of the nacelle. F.E.2B units pioneered formation flying and found that some easy means of individual identification was most necessary. No. 11 Squadron, R.F.C., adopted a simple but effective system. The establishment of the two-seat fighter squadrons was eighteen aircraft, usually divided into three flights of six machines each. This squadron had the top wing of their aircraft marked centrally on the port side with an 'A', 'B' or 'C' for 'A', 'B' or 'C' flights respectively; in a corresponding position on the starboard side was a number 1 to 6 for each machine of the flight.

The F.E.2D with a Rolls Royce engine in place of the F.E.2B's Beardmore, reached service in 1917. Its general markings were identical with those of the F.E.2B. Both types did night flying. F.E.2Bs of No. 100 Squadron, I.A.F., actually bombed Germany itself from French bases and many F.E.2B/D were used by home defence squadrons.

These aircraft were painted dark olive-green all over, including the under-surfaces. The usual national insignia was retained, but it was not outlined; serial numbers in black were outlined in white. From August, 1918, the 'night roundel' was used for all night-flying aircraft.

Notes on individual machines:

F.E.2B—A822 and A5702 used by No. 100 Squadron. A5439 of 25 Squadron shot down by Richthofen. A5684 converted to anti-Zeppelin single-seater. D3776 built by Garrett of Leiston, Suffolk. F5858 crashed on delivery flight November 7th, 1918. FE2D—A6382 shot down by Richthofen to make his thirty-fourth victory. A'1 built by R.A.F. A9900 built by Ransomes, Sims and Jefferies of Ipswich.

Sopwith 1½ Strutters

Known throughout the flying services as the 1½-Strutter it was officially referred to as the Sopwith two-

Continued on page 21

SOPWITH 1½ STRUTTER.   TABULATION OF MARKINGS

Contractor	General Markings	Serial Identification Numbers		Remarks
		Single-seat	Two-seat	
SOPWITH	Natural finish. Firm's name-plate stencilled in black on tail-fin. Serial number in black on fuselage sides near tail.	9651/2/5/7, 9660/1/4, 9666-73, 9700, 9704/7, 9711/4/5/8, 9720/3/4/ 7/9, 9732/3/6/8, 9741/ 2/5/7	9376-9425, 9653/4/6/8/ 9, 9662/3/5, 9674-99 9701-5, 9707-8, 9710/2/ 3/6/9, 9721/2/5/6/8, 9730/1/4/5/7/9, 9740/ 3/4/6, 9748-50, 9892-7 A377-86, A1902-31, A2983-91 (N.B.—Marked in the style A'377)	156 to R.N.A.S. 9396 and 9420 interned in Holland. Several transferred to R.F.C. and re-numbered e.g. 5719 and 7942.
	Natural finish but with upper surfaces of wings, tail and top decking of fuselage in light khaki-green. Firm's nameplate and official serial number located as above.	Nil		49 to R.F.C. (ex-Admiralty contract). Delivered to R.F.C. Acceptance Parks for re-marking.
	Standard day khaki-green camouflage, except for tail. Fin in natural finish with Firm's name-plate.	N5088-9, N5120-79 (N5125-49 to French), N5500-37, N5550-9	N5080-7, N5090-119 (N5506 and N5515 converted to two-seat type)	150 to R.N.A.S., 45 subsequently diverted to French Air Service. Nos. N5538-49 cancelled.
WESTLAND	Standard day camouflage. Firm's trade mark adjacent serial number.	N5600-4 (Nos. marked in 4 in. characters at rear of fuselage)	A1511-60, N5605-24	25 to R.N.A.S. 50 to R.F.C.
MANN EGERTON	Standard day camouflage. Firm's name-plate stencilled on fuselage.	N5200-19	N5220-49, N5630-54 (N5235-42 to Belgium)	50 delivered to R.N.A.S. 8 diverted to Belgian Flying Corps.
FAIREY	Natural finish. Factory number stencilled adjacent to serial number.	Nil	A954-1053 (Factory Nos. F27-126)	100 to R.F.C.
VICKERS (Crayford)	Natural finish. Serial numbers on fuselage-sides, near tail.	Nil	A1054-153, A8744-93 (Marked thus: A/1054)	150 to R.F.C.
RUSTON PROCTOR	Standard day camouflage.	Nil	7762-7811, A2381-430, A8141-340, B2551-600	350 to R.F.C. A8204/88 transferred to R.N.A.S.
HOOPER	Standard day camouflage. Serial numbers in white on tail fin.	Nil	A6901-7000 (Marked thus A/6901)	100 to R.F.C. A6987 to R.N.A.S.
MORGAN	Standard day camouflage.	Nil	A5950-6149	100 to R.F.C.
WELLS	Standard day camouflage.	Nil	A5238-5337	100 to R.F.C.

NOTE.—'-' = 'to'; '/' = 'and'. E.g. N5212/32 would mean N5212 and N5232. N5212-32 would mean N5212 to N5232 consecutively.

There were many inconsistencies with 1½-Strutters of which markings are but one aspect! A'377 has a partial camouflage of 'plan-view' surfaces only. A'1924 has standard camouflage. Even the method of marking the serial numbers varied!

seater in the R.F.C. and designated Types 9400 and 9700 for the two-seat and single-seat versions respectively, used by the R.N.A.S. These machines were finished in several schemes, but late Sopwith-built deliveries to the R.N.A.S. were so characteristic of the firm, that a description of the finish of their early Camels applies equally to the late 1½-Strutters, even to the number of LIFT HERE markings.

The 1½-Strutter commenced operations on the Western Front in the summer of 1916 with No. 70 Squadron, R.F.C., which had 'A' and 'B' flights of early Vickers-built machines with Vickers gun-synchronising gear and 'C' flight of ex-R.N.A.S. machines with Scarff-Dibovsky gear. Later it was joined by Nos. 43 and 45 Squadrons, R.F.C. In the R.N.A.S. the machine was widely used by units operating from Dunkirk, bases in the Adriatic and from various ships of the Royal Navy.

They were built in single-seat and two-seat versions, by several different contractors, for both Services. Some were subsequently converted from single-seat to two-seat, several transferred R.N.A.S. to R.F.C. and vice versa and other diverted to our Allies. Only by a tabulation is it possible to identify easily, individual machines.

Notes on individual machines: 3686 prototype. A1108 shot down by Richthofen; its serial number was displayed on the wall of Richthofen's hut as a trophy. A1913 captured intact by the Germans and given German markings (pre-1918 type crosses). A6006 carried on H.M.S. *Queen Elizabeth*. N5219 and N5244 despatched to Russia. N5220 used at Flight Observers' School, Leysdown. N5223 served in No. 6 Wing, Mudros and 7998 in No. 70 Squadron.

The Bristol Fighter

The soundness of the Bristol Fighter's design can be judged from the fact that it remained in service until 1932 and thereby qualifies for recording in both Parts I and II of this book. Yet, on its first operational mission with No. 48 Squadron in April, 1917, it was deemed a failure. On that occasion, five out of six machines were lost. However, this disastrous start was retrieved in subsequent service and skilfully handled, as a famous pilot put it, 'the crew of a "Brisfit" could see off a couple of Richthofens.'

During the war period all were delivered in standard khaki-green with either grey or black engine cowlings. Wing roundels occupied the full chord and fuselage roundels were centrally placed, slightly aft of the Scarff gun mounting.

The latter roundels were small in relation to the depth of the fuselage, being of 22 in. diameter. A feature of wartime Bristol Fighters—as with the Bristol Scouts—was the large presentation of the serial number in 13 in. characters, occupying practically the whole of the fin, marked in the style—C-4800. Only one LIFT HERE marking was placed each side on the bottom edge of the fuselage below the start of the fin. In the white of the standard rudder striping, at the bottom, was stencilled in small letters the doping scheme, which was initially C.B. These markings were remarkably consistent, for an aircraft type produced in quantity, no doubt due to the British and Colonial Aeroplane Co. Ltd. (as the Bristol Aeroplane Company was then known) building the majority themselves at Brislington and Filton.

The first production batch, designated Bristol F2A, were numbered A3305-3354, the prototypes having taken up the two previous numbers, A3303-3304. Unfortunately, many of this first batch fell to the enemy and A3340 to Richthofen himself. Subsequent machines, designated F2B from a small structural alteration, were numbered A7101-7300, B1101-1350, C751-1050, C4601-4900, D7801-8100, E2151-2650 and F4271-4970, which represents orders totalling 2,550 machines. Although extensively sub-contracted, the firms concerned barely got into production by the time of the Armistice, except for the Gloucestershire Aircraft Co. Ltd. of Cheltenham (later to become Gloster Aircraft Co.) and Angus Sanderson & Co. of Newcastle-on-Tyne. It was also put into production by National Aircraft Factory No. 3 at Aintree, but only 126 of the 500 ordered were delivered and it is doubtful if any saw active service. Many F2Bs went straight into storage, to reappear years later for peacetime service in the R.A.F.

It was used during the war by Nos. 11, 20, 22, 48, 62 and 88 Squadrons and by five Long Range Spotting Flights on the Western Front; by Nos. 67 and 111 Squadrons in Palestine and No. 139 Squadron in Italy. At home some were allotted to Home Defence Squadrons.

Contractors for the Bristol F2B and their first production model are as follows: E1901, Sir W. G. Armstrong Whitworth & Co. Ltd.; C9836, Gloucestershire Aircraft Co. Ltd.; F5074, Harris and Sheldon Ltd.; D2626, Marshall and Sons; E5179, Standard Motor Co. Ltd; E2561, Angus Sanderson & Co.; D2126, National Aircraft Factory No. 3. Machines numbered F5999, F6116 and H7062 were re-built at R.A.F. Depots from salvaged parts.

CHAPTER FOUR

Corps Reconnaissance Aircraft

At 8.30 a.m. on 13th August, 1914, a B.E.2A in natural finish, bearing the number '347', landed in France, the first aircraft of the B.E.F. to arrive. With the R.F.C. units that arrived later that day, Nos. 2 and 4 Squadrons were equipped throughout with B.E.2As and B.E.2Bs, all in clear finish, with no other marking than a number on their rudders in the 201-400 range. The B.E.s were the backbone of the R.F.C. and in the subsequent versions, 2C, 2D and 2E remained so, for the first two years of the war. But, that they should have remained in service, and indeed in production after that, is something of a national tragedy, measured in the lives of many young men, sacrificed for the sake of standardisation. The B.E.s, hopelessly outclassed, fell easy prey to German fighters.

fuselage roundels, painted white on camouflaged machines and black on clear-varnished fabric.

Some units painted roundels on the tail-planes. It was pointed out to the Officer Commanding No. 7 Squadron as late as March, 1917, that this was not necessary.

The R.N.A.S. had four B.E.2As pre-war, marked with Nos. 49-52 in black 14 in. digits painted on a square white background that contrasted only slightly with the pale-yellow natural finish. Of these No. 50 was the favourite machine of the trim-bearded, almost legendary, Commander Samson, who used this aircraft in England, France, Flanders and in the Dardanelles campaign. Apart from those four machines the R.N.A.S. used only the B.E.2C of the B.E. series, ordering altogether 308 in the course of the war. Their last B.E.2C, No. 10000, was the

B.E.2Cs of No. 13 Squadron bearing the standard markings of the period, and ready to leave for France on 12th October, 1915. The contrast between the fabric and the varnished wood cockpit decking is noticeable.

Because of prolonged service, B.E.s passed through the various stages of markings; the B.E.2A/B from pre-war unmarked fabric, except for a number, to painted Union Jacks, thence to roundels under the wings and a small Union Jack on the rudder below the serial number. In the spring of 1915, rudder striping was adopted and in the absence of a fin, the number was marked across the stripes. By this time roundels were marked in the standard six positions. A typical example so marked was No. 2884, a B.E.2B, and the first machine to be made by Whitehead's of Richmond. It was named *Helena* after Mr. Whitehead's daughter.

By the time the B.E.2Cs had arrived in quantity from extensive sub-contracting, markings had stabilised and the illustration of No. 13 Squadron is typical. A few were subjected to early experiments in camouflage, but the example shown in Chapter 1 is typical of early experiments on aircraft types in general and not of B.E.2Cs in particular. Those machines remaining in service with Corps Squadrons late 1916 were given the standard khaki-green camouflage and at this time the first of the squadron devices were being displayed. The B.E.2Cs of No. 2 Squadron, for example, had an 18 in. equilateral triangle just aft of the

only British Service aircraft to correctly bear a five-figure number for with the following letter prefix system, the range of numbers was 1-9999. Although a milestone in numbering, No. 10000 was not accorded any publicity, possibly due to its late delivery from Blackburn's in July, 1917, and to its short life, for it crashed at Eastchurch, Kent, the following month.

B.E.2Cs of the R.F.C. in particular were popular presentation aircraft, a number were contributed from town councils. In each case the town's name was marked on the fuselage side, usually in 3-4 in. letters, between the two cockpits. One example, No. 1748, had LIVERPOOL marked along the whole of the fuselage.

Identification between R.F.C. and R.N.A.S. B.E.2Cs could be made by serial numbers in the appropriate ranges and although there were inter-Service transfers, practically all these were re-numbered in the appropriate range. Both Admiralty and War Office contract instructions called for the same natural finish, but whereas the Admiralty instructed that the identification number be placed on the fuselage, the War Office requested that it be marked on the fin. B.E.2Cs at home kept their natural finish in R.F.C. training units, but were given a silver glaucous finish in

R.N.A.S. Flying Schools. A few employed in Home Defence in late 1916 and early 1917 were painted dark olive green on all surfaces.

The B.E.2D was used mainly by R.F.C. training units at home and in the Middle East, its finish and markings differed in no way from B.E.2Cs in similar service.

By the time the B.E.2E came into service the khaki-green was standard. They carried the normal nationality markings with serial numbers marked on the fin in red or black and edged with white.

Notes on contractors' finish of B.E.2 series and representative batches:

British and Colonial Aeroplane Co. (Bristol)—B.E.2C—Wooden fuselage decking given clear-varnish and it contrasted slightly from the fabric. Fin serial numbers in 8 in. digits. (4070-4219).

Daimler—B.E.2C—Part numbers stencilled in 1 in. characters on side of fin and rudder and on undersurface of mainplanes, ailerons, fuselage, tailplane and elevators. (2031-2036).

Hewlett and Blondeau—B.E.2C—Firm noted for the fine appearance of its products. Early products had a smooth, shiny finish. This was probably due to lightly sandpapering the doped fabric before varnishing, a practice later forbidden by the Inspectorate of Naval Ordnance. Serial numbers in 6 in. black digits were marked on the fuselage, just aft of the roundel. (1189-1194).

Grahame White—B.E.2C—Dark varnish on fuselage decking between cockpits. Serial numbers on fuselage sides just forward of tailplane, 6 in. digits in black. (8293-8304).

Blackburn—B.E.2C—Firm's trade mark on all interplane struts, facing outwards. Firm's name-plate in 6 in. × 4 in. patch on fin. Serial numbers marked on fuselage side midway between roundel and end of fuselage. (1123-1146).

Vulcan—B.E.2E—Serial number on fin in 8 in. black characters outlined in white, presented in the manner 'A1792'. Firm's trade mark on centre of inter-plane struts, facing outward.

Altogether twenty-two different firms in Great Britain built aircraft in the B.E.2 series.

A Bristol-built B.E.2E of the batch A2733-2982, which has been repainted in service. Of interest is the roundel on the fin, which was not uncommon late 1916 to early 1917.

Close-up of a R.E.8 of No. 69 Squadron, R.F.C. (later No. 3 Squadron, A.F.C.). Note the squadron marking, a large white disc and the individual number on the fuselage decking as well as on the fuselage side.

Notes on individual machines:

B.E.2A—No. 242 towed by tender in 1915 Lord Mayor's Show. B.E.2C—Nos. 952-963 built by Vickers for R.N.A.S. and transferred to R.F.C. 2015, used by R.A.F., Farnborough, as test machine. 1763, used for 'effect of weather on performance tests'. 1675, interned in Holland. 2699, exhibited in Imperial War Museum. 4116, Immelmann's thirteenth victory. 4112 of 39 Squadron, the pilot of which shot down the German Zeppelin L32. 9951, delivered to Cranwell Naval Air Station 4th May, 1917. B.E.2D—5746 and 6240 served in No. 16 Squadron. B.E.2E—A1829, A1833 and A1835 transferred to R.N.A.S. and re-numbered 9459-9461. Nos. 6823 and A2785 served in No. 16 Squadron and 5836 in No. 34 Squadron.

The R.E.s

A machine closely following the design of the B.E.2E, the R.E.8, reached the Western Front in late 1916. Throughout the following year it was delivered in quantity, either as a replacement for corps reconnaissance squadrons re-equipping or for new squadrons taking the field. Like the B.E. series it had its roots in pre-war days. The original R.E.1 of 1913 had no markings, not even at first its allotted number—'607'—but the second machine bore the designation R.E.1 on the rudder and beneath it in small (2 in.) numbers—'608'. Not until the R.E.5 design was this series put into production, early 1914. Their only markings were their official serial numbers in 8 in. digits on the rudder, e.g. '651'. When war came, R.E.5s served with Nos. 2, 7, 12 and 16 Squadrons in France, undergoing the evolutionary stages of British aircraft national insignia.

The R.E.7 used mainly as a bomber was the next type to go into production. This aircraft had standard national markings except that the wing roundels were placed well inboard, the distance between centres being equal to half the wing span. Fuselage roundels were

marked large and occupied part of the fuselage decking to give a 34 in. diameter marking. Serial numbers were marked in 8 in. letters on the fin, examples being 2185 (C.O.W.-built), 2245 (Austin-built), 2350 (Siddeley-built) and 2236 (Vickers-built). Those remaining in service late 1916 were given the standard khaki-green.

With the R.E.8, only the two prototypes Nos. 7996-7 had a natural finish, all production models had standard camouflage. Wing roundels were usually fully outboard, almost touching the wing-tips at a tangent. Wheel discs were often painted khaki-green, this was rather unusual as with most types, they were regarded as an undersurface for the colour scheme.

Instructions were stencilled on the fuselage regarding ballast, a typical example being:

DO NOT FLY WITHOUT PASSENGER OR 150 LBS.
BALLAST IN THE GUNNER'S COMPARTMENT.
TAIL TO BE ADJUSTED TO ITS MIDDLE POSITION
BEFORE GETTING OFF GROUND.

The wording and its location varied, but it was normally in 1 in. lettering near the cockpits. Examples are illustrated.

R.E.8 squadron markings additional to those illustrated on sketch pages are:

No. 5 Squadron—White horizontal bar, 6 in. wide, just forward of roundel.
No. 7 Squadron—Two white bands, approximately 6 in. wide around rear of fuselage.
No. 12 Squadron—Marking the same as No. 10 Squadron F.K.8s.
No. 53 Squadron—A crescent behind the roundel in the manner of No. 25's D.H.4s.

Notes on contractors' finish with representative serial number range:

Austin—(A3169-3268)—Serials marked in white characters on fin in the manner A Ballast instructions
3169
stencilled in white below decking of gunner's cockpit and immediately forward of roundel.

Daimler—(A3531-3680)—Serial numbers marked on the fin in the manner A using 8 in. black characters out-
3531
lined in white.

R.A.F.—(A66-115)—Serial numbers marked across rudder stripes in 8 in. black characters in the manner A'66. 'R.A.' marked in 1 in. stencilled letters in white of rudder.

C.O.W.—(A4664-4763)—Serial numbers in white on fin marked in 6 in. characters in the manner A Firm's
4664.
trade mark on wing-struts, facing outwards.

Notes on individual machines: A3561 was rebuilt as a R.E.8A and completely re-marked. The serial number in black was written on the fin in the manner 'A3561' and instead of rudder striping, it bore a 2 ft. × 1 ft. flash. A3186 and A4173 had a small fin roundel, as per B.E.2E A2885 illustrated. A4346 of No. 63 Sqn. in the Middle East had the ballast instructions marked around by a ½ in. white line forming a rectangle; this was probably marked in service. D4960 was used in Russia, 1919 (Napier-built). F6016 'K' of No. 3 Sqn., A.F.C., bore the name MARJORIE on the fuselage in 4 in. letters; the significance of this was probably known only to the pilot! Rebuilt R.E.8s in service included B7893 (5 Sqn.), B7917 (3 Sqn. A.F.C.), F5909 (12 Sqn.), H7038 (6 Sqn.) and H7265 (3 Sqn.).

The F.K.8

The A.W. F.K.8 was one af the lesser-known types to do valuable Corps work. It was generally known as the 'Big Ack' or the 'Ack W.' The former name distinguished it from the F.K.3 or 'Little Ack', the latter term was no doubt suggested by the fact that the engine cowling had the letters 'A.W.' embossed. The F.K.8 served on the Western Front and in the minor theatres.

Early machines, such as A2683 were delivered in natural finish. Wing roundels were placed inboard by one-sixth of the span each side and did not utilise the full chord, being of 66 in. diameter, even so they did not clear the ailerons and were marked partly over them. The fuselage roundel centrally placed had a diameter of 34 in. Serial numbers were marked on the fin in 8 in. black characters in the manner—'A-2683'. The engine cowling was painted a matt black. From A2684 onwards deliveries were in standard khaki-green with the usual thin white outline for the roundels; serials were marked as before, except that they were now in white. Machines numbered from C3507 upwards were built under contract by Angus Sanderson.

Bombing Aircraft

British bombing aeroplanes were a bone of contention between the Army and the Navy. The Admiralty in building up a strategic bombing force, met with opposition from G.H.Q. of the B.E.F., who firmly believed in the tactical deployment of all available force upon the Western Front. The position was further complicated in 1917 by a Cabinet decision to create an Independent Air Force. This, however, portended the formation of a new Service—the Royal Air Force, which officially came into being on 1st April, 1918, and embraced all bombing aircraft within its administrative, if not tactical, control.

R.N.A.S. Bombers

The R.N.A.S. had strong claims for bombing aircraft and gave evidence of this early in the war. During November, 1914, three Avro 504s attacked the German Naval Zeppelin sheds at Friedrichshafen, damaging one Zeppelin and destroying a gas-works. For this operation, four 504s were despatched direct from the Avro, Manchester works, to Belfort, France. They were clear-varnished, with gloss black engine cowlings and wheel discs. The cowlings bore the firm's triangular trade mark (1914 pattern). The numbers 179, 873, 874 and 875 were marked in black 10 in. digits on their rudders; red ring markings were carried. In the operation 179 failed to take-off and 874 was shot down and exhibited in Germany.

bombers were sponsored by the Admiralty who placed the first orders. This is borne out by the serial numbers of the first batches in the R.N.A.S. range—Nos. 1455-1466 and 3115-3142.

Early deliveries were in natural finish with both rudders painted each side in equal, vertical, red-white-blue stripes. Wing roundels utilised the full chord of the massive wing, including the ailerons. Due to the overhang of the upper wing in relation to the lower, roundels were also marked on the underside of the top wing. Fuselage roundels were placed at a point halfway down the fuselage, the depth at that point conditioning their diameter.

The prototype 0/100 bore the number 1455 on the extreme end of the fuselage, but for security reasons, early production models did not bear visible serial numbers. One of these early machines, the third to leave for France, made a forced landing owing to bad weather. The pilot and observer on enquiring their whereabouts, realised, but only too late, that they were in German hands. Their machine re-marked with German crosses (early pattern) over the British roundels and rudder stripes, was exhibited throughout Germany.

The first of these machines to go on operations with No. 7 Squadron, 5th Wing, R.N.A.S., in April, 1917, were given standard day camouflage in khaki-green, their national insignia remaining as before. Later that month,

A Mann Egerton-built D.H.9 which shows well the contrast of the wood-panelled forward parts of the fuselage in battleship grey, and the rear fabric coverings in khaki-green. The firm's nameplate has been stencilled in small lettering at the rear of the fuselage. This applied to one hundred machines—D1651-1750.

A number of bombing aircraft were purchased for the R.N.A.S. from French industry, these were delivered in clear or aluminium finish. Standard British insignia was marked on delivery together with an Admiralty serial number on the nacelle. Examples are: 9155, Farman F.40; 3946, Breguet Concours; 8501, Voisin LA. The curious-looking Caudron G.IV was bought from France and was also made in this country by the British Caudron Co. British-built machines bore the Nos. 3333-3344.

The Handley Pages

Handley Page became synonymous with large bombers during the 1914-18 War, as the Oxford Concise Dictionary will show. It is perhaps, not generally realised that these

after one had been shot down in a daylight operation by a German scout, it was decided to use 0/100s only at night. The undersides were therefore varnished with the available P.C.10; this was later changed to dark olive-green. A variety of shades could be and were produced from the P.C.10.

Having proved its worth, the 0/100 with a modified fuel system, went into large-scale production as the 0/400 —this was *the* Handley Page. The overall finish was dark olive-green, with fuselage roundels of 52 in. dameter, large in itself but looking small against the massive bulk of the fuselage. Wing roundels of the same size, looking almost absurdly small were marked on the upper and lower surfaces of the top wing only. In accordance with the usual night finish, there were no rudder stripes, but an innovation

A Handley Page 0/400 makes a large roundel look small! This aircraft in standard British markings had been handed over to the U.S. Army. Note the fin flash in place of rudder stripes, and the night handling markings.

was a rudder flash, outlined in white as illustrated.

Being operational at night, squadron insignia was rarely used, but often a letter/numeral identification system was used, large characters being marked on the nose and/or on the fuselage each side of the roundel, thus 'A * 2'. The serial number, in white, was marked at the rear of the fuselage and repeated under the rudder flash as illustrated. It was the only type to have special night handling markings, giving the LIFT HERE marking an unusual prominence.

Notes on individual machines:

3135 was B3 and 3123 was D3 of 5th Wing, R.N.A.S. B9446-9451 had Sunbeam Arab engines fitted in place of the usual Rolls Royce Eagles. D5401, first built by Birmingham Carriage Co. D4561, first built by Metropolitan Wagon Co. D9681, first built by Clayton and Shuttleworth. F5349, first built from parts pre-fabricated in America. D8326, modified for use by R.A.F. Communications Wing as H.M. Air Liner *Silver Star*.

Three went on the Civil Register in 1919: F5414 as G-EAAF, F5417 as G-EAAW and F5418 as G-EAAG.

Day Bombers

Standard day-bombers 1917-18 were all of De Havilland design, the D.H.4, D.H.9, D.H.9A and, had the war continued, a D.H.10 would have carried the war into Germany. The D.H.9A remained in service until 1932.

D.H.4

The D.H.4 was the first real day-bomber, previous machines being adaptations of general purpose aircraft. In

April, 1917, the first D.H.4 squadron, No. 55, was ready for action only eight months after the appearance of the prototype, which had a natural finish and the number 3696 at the rear of its fuselage. From the illustration it would appear as if the first batch had a diversity of finishes and that some machines had a two-colour scheme. This was due to the D.H.4's construction, a departure from contemporary practice, in that the forward-half of the fuselage was plywood-covered and the rear half fabric-covered. A dark protective wood varnish and clear-varnished fabric made a striking contrast. For service in France all were painted with P.C.10 in its various khaki-green shades, but nevertheless wood and fabric sections contrasted slightly, the fabric taking a deeper shade. D.H.4s built by Westlands had a very dark khaki-green finish with an overall consistency being obtained. Late 1918 production models were finished in blue-grey panelling with khaki-green fabric; those used by the Communications Wing, Hendon, in 1919, numbered in the F2633-2732 range, were given an overall silver doping.

Notes on contractors' markings:

Aircraft Mfg. Co.—A2125-2174, diversity of finishes. A7401-8089, C4501-4540 and D8351-8430, finished in khaki-green.

Westland—B9476-9500 and D1751-1775 for R.F.C. N5960-6009 (Rolls Royce Eagles installed) and N6380-6429 (R.A.F. 3A installed) for R.N.A.S., of which 17 were transferred to R.F.C. All were finished in deep khaki-green with wheel discs and radiator in natural finish. The firm's trade mark, inscribed in a circle, appeared at the extreme rear of the fuselage side.

D.H.4s of the first production batch (A2125-2174). The aircraft in the foreground show the contrast between the plywood and fabric covered parts. Two other machines have fuselages in

* = Roundel.

Berwick—B2051-2150—All fitted with B.H.P. engines and finished in khaki-green.

Vulcan—B5451-5550—Firm's trade mark appeared centrally placed on all inter-plane struts, facing outwards. Khaki-green finish.

The following D.H.4s went on the civil register in 1919: F2964 G-EAHG, F2699 G-EAHF, F2702 G-EAJC and F2704 G-EAJD.

D.H.9

Designed to supplement and eventually replace the D.H.4 and to utilise the B.H.P. engine, the D.H.9 went into production by several contractors. Constructed on the same principle as its predecessor, the markings described for the D.H.4 apply equally to the D.H.9. Constructors' characteristics, too, follow through, for most D.H.4 builders turned over to D.H.9s. The wooden sections were normally finished in battleship grey and the fabric khaki-green. Notes on D.H.9 constructors and representative batches:

Aircraft Mfg. Co.—C6051-6121, C6123-6350. Numbers marked in usual A.M.C. fashion.

Berwick—C2151-2230.

Cubitt—D451-800. D529 and D530 had a particularly trim appearance as each of their 269 main components had been given a finish with particular care as their assembly was demonstrated to a visiting party of M.P.s at the Croydon works.

N.A.F. No. 2—D1001-1500 (not all completed).

Short Bros.—D2776-2875, fitted with Fiat engines.

Vulcan—B9331-9430. Vulcan trade mark on inter-plane struts.

Waring and Gillow—D5551-5700.

Westland—B7581-7680. Constructor's trade mark at rear of fuselage side.

N.B.—C6051-6121 were the first batch of D.H.9s to be built, yet some contractors had machines with lower serial numbers, e.g. C1151 (G. J. Weir). This is due to D.H.4 orders being changed to D.H.9.

Notes on individual machines:

C6122 airframe to Westland's to become prototype D.H.9A. D568 was used in Burma for a survey of the Irrawaddy after the war.

D1197 used for delivering commodities to Belgium after the Armistice. It bore the words 'Aircraft Transport and Travel Ltd., Belgian Service' on a white rectangular background above the roundel. Letter 'B' aft of roundel.

D1717, 'A' Flight of 98 Squadron, was attacked by fifteen enemy aircraft in the afternoon of 28th July, 1918; it force-landed and burst into flames.

D3117, converted to ambulance for Somaliland Expedition, had a large red cross on a white background and 'Z' Squadron number '6' well forward on the fuselage.

D.H.9A

The D.H.9, re-designed to take a Liberty or Rolls Royce Eagle engine, was a welcome replacement to day-bombing squadrons; although No. 110 Squadron was the only unit to become fully operational with this type by the time of the Armistice. This squadron, initially equipped with D.H.9As at the expense of His Exalted Highness the Nizam of Hyderabad, had its machines inscribed with the name HYDERABAD.

The Aircraft Mfg. Co. were too preoccupied with the projected D.H.10 to undertake development of the D.H.9A. This work was entrusted to Westland's, who were the first firm to produce this type. They achieved an overall khaki-green consistency, with radiator and top cowling in natural metal finish. Their aircraft were numbered from F951 in early 1918, F957 having a particularly trim appearance to provide photographic illustrations for the D.H.9A Handbook. Earlier D.H.9 contracts numbered from E701 were cancelled in favour of D.H.9A production, but later these contracts were reinstated as D.H.9As. Thus deliveries were not in numerical/chronological sequence from this firm. As with all their aircraft, up to mid-1919, the firm's trade mark was at the rear of the fuselage side.

Deliveries from other firms had battleship grey panelling with khaki-green fabric. These manufacturers, with their first production models were as follows: Aircraft Mfg. Co. E8407, Vulcan E9857 and Mann Egerton E9657. The last-named firm had their trade mark in the same manner as the D.H.9 illustrated, but a peculiar feature, known only in Mann Egerton-built D.H.9As and D.H.10s, was the method of marking the serial number, see page 65.

shades of khaki-green, but unusual is the fact that their upper surfaces are in natural finish. These aircraft are pictured at Hendon straight from the production line of the Aircraft Mfg. Co.

CHAPTER SIX

Training Aircraft

An example of composite French-British markings. This Caudron G.III trainer, built in France and bearing its factory markings has been handed over to the R.F.C., who have added yet another number, the first two digits of which can be seen on the rudder.

There was little difference between operational and training aircraft in the early days of the war, indeed, the only difference in some cases was their role. An example is the Maurice Farman 'Shorthorn' which was used by the B.E.F. for reconnaissance, the very same machines having previously formed the main equipment of the Central Flying School. Up until 1916, the designs of the Farman Brothers were used extensively for training. They were supplemented by other types, obsolescent or unsuitable for work at the Front. Several attempts were made to standardise with a tractor biplane trainer, the A.W. FK3 and the D.H.6 were produced in their hundreds in 1917, but the Avro 504 series was found to be so admirably suited for all stages of flying instruction, that from mid-1917 it became the standard trainer with production running into several thousands.

Trainers in the R.N.A.S.

The Central Flying School had originally been established with Naval and Military Wings, but shortly before the war, the Admiralty had removed its training establishments to Eastchurch. Thus when war came each service had its own nucleus for training and expansion went forward on entirely separate, if not divergent lines. The Admiralty took over well-established civilian schools, including the pre-war centre of British aviation—Hendon. They became Naval Air Stations and several of the school's aircraft were impressed. Such aircraft needed no further attention than the application of a R.N.A.S. number on the rudders. An impressed Henri Farman was so marked '887' and a Maurice Farman '888' Aircraft were ordered from British, French and American industry to equip the naval flying-schools. For the first two years, training machines were in natural finish, but from early 1917 the Admiralty specified Clarke's Britannia Dope with a silver glaucous cover and a final clear varnish for training aircraft. Roundels were required to be marked as large as practicable and serial numbers to appear on fuselage sides or nacelles as appropriate. The R.N.A.S. had one flying-school in France at Vendome, all its aircraft were delivered

straight from French factories, and were numbered in the special N3000-3300 range.

Unlike the R.F.C. training schools, no unit markings, or individual markings, apart from a letter or number, seemed to have been used on naval aircraft. As H.M. ships were always kept trim, H.M. Naval aircraft likewise bore no undue embellishment. Flying-boat trainers are dealt with in the chapter on Naval aircraft and float-plane trainers needed little treatment at all, for their difference was only in equipment and the fitting of dual control. They were distinguishable from operational types only by their serial number, e.g. of the twelve Short Type 827 seaplanes Nos. 8218-8229, the last four, Nos. 8226-8229 were fitted with dual control for training.

Notes on R.N.A.S. Training Aircraft Types

Avro 504B. At first used operationally, having racks for 4 × 16-lb. bombs, this aircraft went into R.N.A.S. schools during 1917. The finish was as given for No. 9827 in the following table; this applied to machines numbered 9821-9830. Another batch, bearing the Parnall firm's markings, were numbered 9861-9890.

B.E.2c. Small numbers used as trainers. The batch 9456-9475 were transferred from the R.F.C. to the R.N.A.S. They were fitted with 90 h.p. Curtiss engines and sent to R.N.A.S. schools. Finish was natural or silver glaucous.

Caudron G.III. A trainer widely used in France, it was also employed by the R.N.A.S. Nos. 3264-3288, N3050-3099 and N3240-3269 were built in France and bore markings similar to the example illustrated. Those with 'N' prefixed numbers were bought specially for the R.N.A.S. Flying School at Vendome in France. Machines numbered from 8941 were built in Britain by the British Caudron Company.

Curtiss JN3. Natural finish. Nos. 8392-8403 Canadian-built, remainder numbered from 1362 and 3345 were all built in the United States. Nos. 3345 and 3343 went to the French Government.

Curtis JN4. Natural finish or silver glaucous. Some

machines had a combination of both, the undersurface and fuselage sides being in natural finish with the other surfaces in silver glaucous.

Grahame White Type XV. Known as Type 1600 in the R.N.A.S., as that was the serial number of the prototype. Normal finish was clear-varnish for fabric and wax-polish or clear-varnish for woodwork. Serial numbers marked on tail and in some cases repeated on nacelle were as follows: 3151-3162, 3607-3616, 8305-8316 and 8752-8801.

Maurice Farman 'Longhorn'. Natural finish up to 1917 when a number remaining in service were given the silver glaucous dope. Early machines, e.g. Nos. 109, 888 and 909 had serials marked in large letters on the tail before tail striping had been adopted. From 1915 onwards R.N.A.S. Longhorns usually had serials marked on the nacelle in 8 in. digits. There were several different contractors and three different types of engine used; distinction could be made by serial number, as follows:

Serial Number	Constructor	Engine
8921-8940	Brush	70 h.p. Renault
N5000-5016	Robey	75 h.p. Rolls Royce 'Hawk'
N5030-5059	Brush	80 h.p. Renault
N5330-5349 } N5750-5759 }	*Phœnix	75 h.p. Rolls Royce 'Hawk'

Maurice Farman 'Shorthorn'. General markings as for 'Longhorn', above. Apart from a few acquired in 1914 and early 1915 only one batch was ordered for Naval schools. This was for twenty numbered N5060-5079 built by the Eastbourne Aviation Company.

Short S38. An aircraft of the box-kite type, invariably in natural finish. Nos. 1580 up built by Supermarine, Nos. 3143 onwards by Norman Thompson.

Trainers in the R.F.C.

The R.F.C. in August, 1914, was denuded of training aircraft at the Central Flying School by the transfer of aircraft to meet the needs of the Expeditionary Force. Orders were immediately placed for training aircraft with firms holding licence to build aircraft of proven French design. Later, licence was extended to several contractors for the pusher-type Henri and Maurice Farmans. These aircraft were the backbone of 1914-16 training. By 1917 a swing to a tractor-type trainer was obviously desirable as service aircraft were, in the main, of that type. The A.W. FK3 and D.H.6 were intended to meet such a need, but both were inferior in handling qualities to the Avro 504 which was generally adopted in 1917 as the standard trainer.

It is a popular misconception that flying training was carried out in Schools of Aeronautics and several published references have been made to this effect. These establishments were, in fact, for ground instruction only, to teach the theory of airmanship; true, they had a few aircraft for ground instructional purposes, but none flew.

The capacity of the Central Flying School for training pilots was limited. In 1915 squadrons of training aircraft were formed with the title of Reserve Squadrons and with an initial establishment of eighteen aircraft. Later, to economise in manpower, depot-training was instituted by banding together two or more Reserve Squadrons. The importance of this to markings is that where a numerical individual marking system was used, the range of numbers might well extend to fifty.

It was in these flying training units that some of the most fantastic finishes could be seen. They were, of course, the work of an instructor, for no pupil would dare take such a liberty in disregarding the standard finish, as laid down in regulations. The instructors who embellished their machines must have been men of some standing, a pilot who had seen active service and perhaps sported a medal ribbon. There is some evidence that Australians and Canadians were the chief offenders, and that they thoroughly enjoyed contravening the regulations with the object of horrifying some of the more staid, senior British officers. No doubt they succeeded.

Notes on R.F.C. Training Aircraft Types

Avro 504A and J. Large numbers used in 1917. Details given in table on page 32.

Typical of many Henri Farman F.22s built in this country under licence by the Aircraft Manufacturing Company, this picture shows well the solid looking aluminium-covered nacelle and the flimsy appearance of the wings and control surface.
The manner of marking the serial, 2838, over two of the three stripes reveals it as an A.M.C. product.

*Those built by Phœnix bore the representative trade mark on the nose of the nacelle.

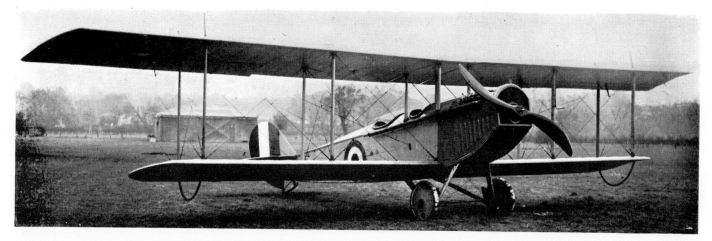

A Curtiss J.N.3 used by the R.N.A.S. In common with most Curtiss aircraft delivered to the R.N.A.S. the roundel is not in the correct proportions as specified by the Admiralty.

Armstrong Whitworth FK3. Intended as an operational machine to supplement the BE2C squadrons, the machine was widely used as a trainer. Early aircraft built by Armstong Whitworth Nos. 5328-5334 and 5504-5553 had a khaki-green finish with the serial number marked on the fin in black, being outlined thinly in white.

Large numbers were built by Hewlett and Blondeau, the usual finish for these was the normal khaki-green, except that the fuselage sides were in natural finish. A portion of the tail fin was also left clear for the serial numbers which were A1461-1510, A8091-8140 and B9501-9800.

D.H.6. A machine designed as an easily built training aircraft, that had a 'cut-off-by-the-yard' appearance General finish, apart from the prototypes Nos. A5175-5176, was in khaki-green. Several contractors built the D.H.6:

Aircraft Mfg. Co., B2601-3100 and B9031-9130. Serial numbers marked in 'A.M.C. fashion'.

Grahame White, A9563-9762, C1951-2150, C7601-7900 and D951-1000. Grahame White name-plate marked on fabric of fuselage sides toward rear. Serial numbers marked in white on the fin in the manner shown
    A
  9563

Kingsbury Aviation Co., C5126-5275.
Harland and Wolff, C5451-5750.
Morgan and Co., C6501-6700.
Savage Ltd., C6801-6900.
Ransomes, Sims and Jefferies, C7201-7600. Numbers marked in black centrally across rudder stripes in the manner C
  7201
Gloucester Aircraft Co., C9336-9485.

Grahame White Type XV. Nos. A1661-1710 used at R.F.C. schools. See also under R.N.A.S. trainers.

Henri Farman. Used by Reserve Squadrons 1915-17 in limited numbers. The machines had a natural finish with clear-varnished fabric and woodwork and a polished aluminium nacelle nose. Serial numbers were marked across the rudder stripes and in training schools it was usually marked again on each side of the nacelle nose in 6-8 in. white numbers, the prefix letter being omitted. Serials were: Aircraft Mfg. Co. built—A1712-1741 and

B1401-1481. Grahame White built—A1154-1253 and A2276-2375.

Maurice Farman S7 'Longhorn'. With a clear natural finish and having large black rudder numbers such as 426, 431 and 450, these Longhorns could be seen at the Central Flying School as early as 1912. It was put into large-scale production 1914-16 and late 1917 many Longhorns, with fabric browning with age, could still be seen in Reserve Squadrons. From 1915 onwards it was built purely for elementary flying training, without the slightest possibility of operational use. Because of this, it was one of the few types for which the factory finish did not specify national insignia. The Aircraft Mfg. Co. marked serial numbers centrally on each rudder in the manner A plain black 8 in. characters were used. Other
  6801,
markings by this firm were the factory reference number and doping scheme marked in 1 in. letters on the fin, e.g.

A.M.C.

53611

C.C.

Serial numbers were: Aircraft Mfg. Co., 2960-3000 and A4061-4160, all fitted with Renault engines, and C9311-9335 by Brush, fitted with Curtiss engines.

Maurice Farman S11 'Shorthorn'. By far the most widely used trainer in the first years of the war, the Shorthorn, too, dates back to 1912 at the Central Flying School. A natural finish was usual with no other marking than a serial number, normally marked on the rudder and sometimes repeated on the nacelle. Numbers were A324-373 and and B4651-4850 built by the Aircraft Mfg. Co. and A2176-2275 by Whitehead's of Richmond.

Trainers in the R.A.F.

When the Royal Air Force was formed on 1st April, 1918, by integrating the Royal Flying Corps and the Royal Naval Air Service, the Avro 504 series was already established as the standard training aircraft. A number of earlier types remained in service, but with the wastage rate of aircraft in training units as 20 per cent. per month, they soon disappeared. The short life-span of a representative ten training aircraft shows this to be only too true.

N5000-5009 were ten 'Longhorns' built by Robey early in 1917. N5000, after continuous use at Eastbourne, was condemned in March, 1918. N5001, N5002, N5003, N5005 and N5007 had, by January, 1918, been broken up to provide spares. N5004 was damaged beyond repair in an accident at Killingholme. N5006 was wrecked at Eastbourne late in 1917 and N5008, wrecked at the same place, never flew again. N5009, the only one of the ten to survive until the formation of the R.A.F., had its frame and fabric so deteriorated that it was struck off charge and scrapped twenty days later. The Avro 504A, J and K were predominantly the school machines of the R.A.F. in 1918.

Avro 504s

The markings of the Avro 504 series with their twelve variants by eighteen different constructors could fill a book. A trend in markings can, however, be expressed. Early deliveries for R.F.C. or R.N.A.S. were in the finish described for No. 789 in the table. From mid-1916 a clear-varnish or khaki-green finish seems to have been optional, serial numbers being marked in white on dark backgrounds and black on a light finish. Serials were in general marked on the fuselage, forward of their normal position, 7 ft. forward of the tail unit being usual for most 504As and Js. In April, 1918, due to complaints from the public about low flying, the Directorate of Training issued new instructions regarding the identification of aircraft. Serial numbers were to be marked both on the rudder and on the fuselage sides, toward the rear. In addition these numbers were to be repeated on the undersurface of the bottom wing in not less than 3 ft. characters. These were to read in opposite directions for port and starboard sides. Although Avro 504As, Js and Ks were predominantly concerned, the instruction included operational types on the training establishment.

Specimen layout of these wing undersurface markings:

	Starboard		Port		
*	F2311	↑	F2311	*	(Avro 504K)
*	F1946	↑	F1946	*	(Camel—2-seat version)
*	F9075	↑	F9075	*	(S.E.5A)

* Roundel. ↑ Fuselage and direction of travel.

The Avro 504K held by the Science Museum bears D7660 on the fuselage and E3104 under the wings! It was evidently made up from parts of at least two machines.

The Gosport School of Special Flying for Instructor training was perhaps the best-known of all training units. Details of the unit's markings and representative aircraft with, in brackets, the manufacturer, are as follows:

'A' Flight: Triangle on sides of fuselage (see illustration). This marking was white on khaki-green or black on clear-varnish. White wheel discs. Avro 504Js—A1996 (Bleriot), C609 (Humber), D41 (A. V. Roe).

While Nos. 1-4 Squadrons of the Australian Flying Corps served overseas, Nos. 5 and 6 were training squadrons at Minchinhampton and Nos. 7 and 8 at Leighterton. The boomerangs marked on the Avro 504Ks are symbolic of Australia.

'B' Flight: Wheel discs half blue and half white. Avro 504Js—B4222, C4344 and C4447 (A. V. Roe).

'C' Flight: Wheel discs of dark blue. Avro 504Js—B3101 (A. V. Roe), D6266 and D6269 (Brush).

'D' Flight: Wheel discs and propeller tips in red. Avro 504Ks—B3196, B4242 and B4266 (A. V. Roe).

'E' Flight: Wheel discs white with red centres. Avro 504Js—A9799 (Grahame White), B3158 and B4243 (A. V. Roe).

'F' Flight: Red disc on fuselage sides aft of roundel. Wheel discs black with white centres. Avro 504Js—A9810 (Saunders), C4431 and D42 (A. V. Roe).

AVRO 504 SERIES.   REPRESENTATIVE MARKINGS

Type	Serial Number Rudder	Serial Number Fuselage	General Finish	Wheel Discs	Other markings	Remarks
504	789	—	Clear-Varnish Gloss Black Cowling	Gloss Black	10 in. × 6 in. Union Jack at bottom of rudder. Wing roundels one sixth of span in board. No fuselage roundel. No rudder stripes.	A. V. Roe-built. Triangular trade mark on cowling.
504B	—	9827	As above		Standard national insignia—roundels and rudder stripes.	A. V. Roe-built. Winged triangle trade mark on cowling.
504J	—	A9788	Khaki-Green	Clear-Varnish	Two small 'Lift Here' markings both sides of fuselage.	Saunders-built.
504J	—	C4451	Clear-Varnish	Clear-Varnish	Wood panelling in clear-varnish. Standard national markings.	King George VI learnt to fly in this aircraft.
504K	F 8859	F8859	Khaki-Green	Khaki-Green	White zig-zag line down fuselage sides making four inverted Vs.	Instructor's machine.

Khaki-green or clear-varnish was optional for 1918 production 504Ks. The silhouette of an Emu, marked in a red bar is indicative of this Australian Flying School. In the background a machine bears an instructor's initials near the front cockpit—'T.A.B.'

BRITISH AIRCRAFT COLOURING SCHEMES 1916-18

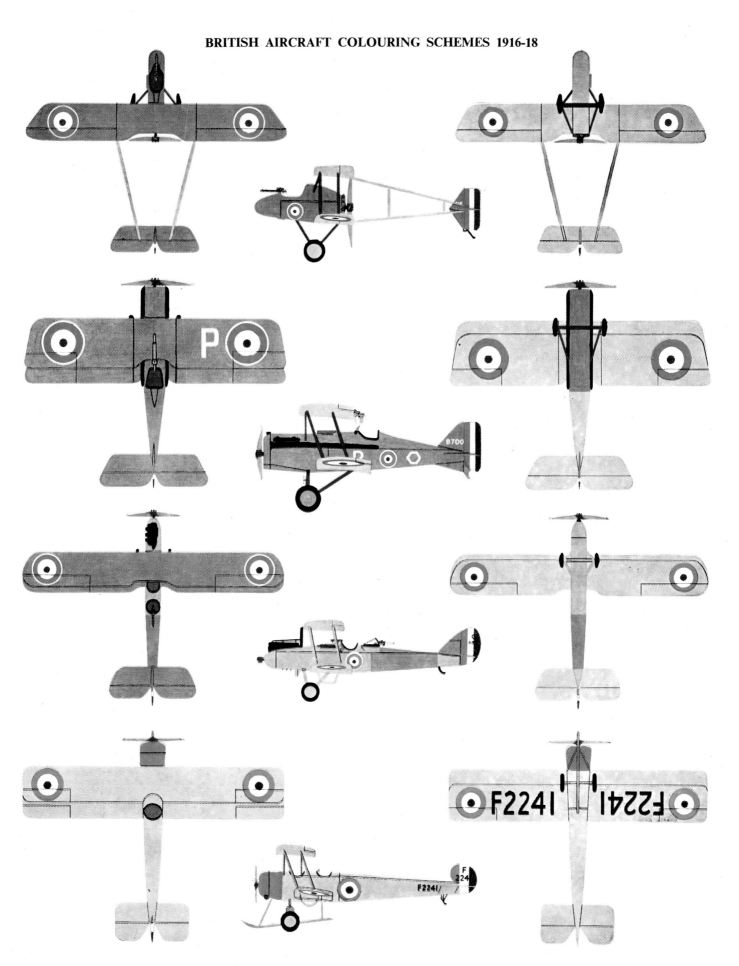

A F.E.8 shows a typical finish for a pusher biplane 1916-17 and below it are typical 1918 finishes for a S.E.5A (in No. 85 Squadron markings); a D.H.9 with the colouring distinctions for some ply-wood and fabric covered aircraft, and an Avro 504K in a training school.

COLOUR SCHEMES OF FOUR NATIONS 1917-18

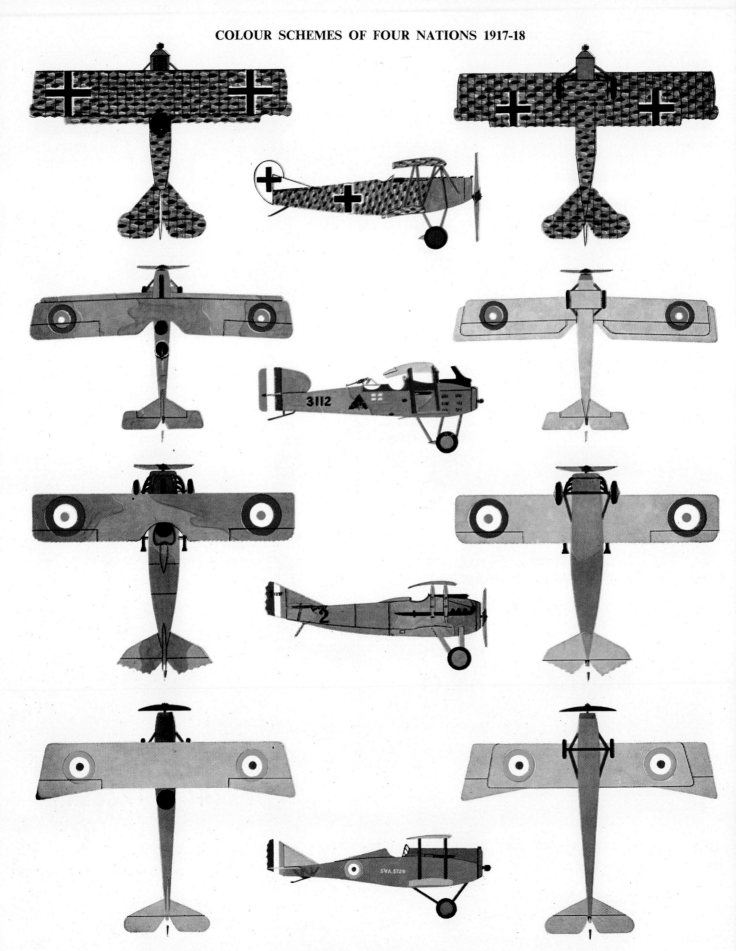

A Fokker DVII displays a typical dyed fabric used by Germany 1917-18, and below is a Breguet 14 with the markings of the 96th Squadron, American Expeditionary Force. In the same camouflage is a French Spad S.7 and at the bottom an Italian Ansaldo.

British Naval Aircraft

CHAPTER SEVEN

Introduction

'Seaplane' is a term that embraces float-planes and flying-boats. Service seaplanes were, with few exceptions, controlled by the Admiralty through the Royal Naval Air Service up until April, 1918. In spite of inter-Service rivalry, bitter at times, there had always been a certain amount of co-operation on technical matters between the R.F.C. and the R.N.A.S., but whereas the R.N.A.S. had both landplanes and seaplanes, the R.F.C. had landplanes only. Such uniformity as had been achieved in the general finish of aircraft by inter-Service liaison and then by the Ministry of Munitions becoming the production agency for both Services, concerned chiefly landplanes. Seaplanes were specifically an Admiralty concern until April, 1918. Even when the Royal Air Force was formed and standardisation the natural and, indeed, desired result, flying-boats remained a class apart. Their very construction was different, they needed special protectives to resist the corrosive effects of sea-water. Camouflage, too, is essentially related to the elements and in this respect the contrast to landplanes was fundamental.

'Ship-board aircraft' was the term used for machines designed or adapted for a take-off from a vessel, with a wheeled or skid-type undercarriage.

International Insignia

The transition of the Union Jack to roundels followed the experience of the British Expeditionary Force. Late 1914 most seaplanes operating from the French and Belgian coasts had large Union Jacks painted on the fuselage sides. By mid-1915 the roundel was generally adopted, at first a red ring only, but apparently there were exceptions.

A skipper of a trawler, incensed by German U-boat outrages, refused to rescue the crew of a stranded flying-boat with the comment, 'I ain't going to rescue no ruddy 'Uns'. When the crew protested that they were British, as

obviously the machine bore no indication, the skipper retorted, 'Then give us a sight of your flag.' Flags were not carried and what might have been an unfortunate incident was finally cleared by the production of a Royal Naval officer's cap for the skipper to inspect.

The Admiralty late in 1915, perhaps noticing the varying proportions of the insignia, defined in Orders the proportions of a roundel as 5 : 3 : 1 for the diameters of blue, white and red respectively. Roundels were to be marked as large as practicable, but proportions were not to vary. White or yellow outlining on dull finishes and the usual blue/white/red rudder striping followed normal R.F.C. practice.

Roundels occupied the usual six positions. Flying-boats hulls usually bore the roundels towards the rear, but it was not usual for roundels to be marked at all on the hulls of:

(a) Training types of flying-boats.
(b) Operational flying-boats in dazzle-painting.

General Finish

Up to the end of 1916 proprietary dopes were used for all fabric parts, with an overall clear-varnish finish, but flying-boats with their large wetted area were a different proposition.

A standard finish for the lower parts of flying-boat hulls produced a very dark brown to black shiny surface. This was obtained by first applying some three coats of varnish; with the last coat still wet, black lead was rubbed into it and when

The general rule and the exception! N2113 is a Blackburn-built Sopwith Baby in factory finish; whilst N1413 was re-marked in service from a similar original finish.
The machines illustrated were allotted to the Naval Air Station at Killingholme and operated from a sub-station on Hornsea Mere during 1918.

Markings on this Hamble Baby convert gives interesting statistical information. Details on the nameplate show it to be the 193rd aircraft built by Parnall. P.1/17 under the serial number indicates it was the 17th aircraft of its type. This firm built 130 Babies, N1190-1219 and N1960-1985 as float-planes and N1986 et seq as illustrated.

dry, it polished to a glossy finish with the wood grain of the planking, cedar or mahogany, faintly visible. It gave a pleasing appearance, but the object was, of course, to provide a good planing surface to assist take-off. However, by 1917, the man-hours involved made this process impracticable and a mixture, known as flying-boat anti-fouling composition, was applied. It produced a shiny, but not glossy, black finish. All other woodwork was given coatings, usually three, of a clear-varnish and metal fittings were black stove-enamelled.

As a general rule it may be said that a clear finish was appropriate to all naval aircraft on delivery, numbered up to 10,000, those with the 'N' prefix being delivered in khaki-green.

Camouflage

Khaki-green for upper-surfaces was generally adopted for all naval aircraft late in 1916. Camouflage was used on some seaplanes earlier by painting blotches of grey over the conspicuous pale yellow varnished fabric, but it was by no means general. Bizarre forms of dazzle-painting were used by Yarmouth Air Station from June, 1918, for the very antithesis of camouflage—to render aircraft conspicuous to assist search aircraft in the event of a forced-landing at sea. Dazzle-painting applied only to operational flying-boats, but the khaki-green finish was typical for all types of naval aircraft in the N1000-8000 range.

Special Markings

During August, 1917, instructions were issued by the Admiralty that all seaplanes would be marked on the hull or fuselage as appropriate with the maximum permissible load in pounds. The figure given was inclusive for the weight of the crew themselves, all armament, fuel and equipment.

Parts of hulls or floats were fabric or thin ply-covered and care had to be exercised not to step on these parts. Warning notes were initially stencilled by the manufacturer and maintained in service. A Curtiss H.12 hull bore this notice in 2 in. letters: DO NOT WALK ON
FINS OR CANOPY

Serial Numbers

The range of numbers used will be found in the Serial Table. Numbers were at first marked in 1 ft.–1 ft. 6 in. figures on the rudder, but when rudder striping became general, the R.N.A.S., unlike the R.F.C. in the main, made the rear of the fuselage or hull the standard position for serialling. Eight-inch figures were then usual, but there were exceptions. With the standardisation after April, 1918, both fuselage (or hull) markings and across the rudder stripes became the regulation method of presentation. As a general guide it may be said that numbers up to 1346 were marked on the rudder, from thence to 10,000 at the rear of the fuselage. By the time the two-position method was introduced, few naval aircraft other than the 'N' prefixed series were in service.

Unit Markings

Few units used formation markings, but some seaplanes attached to ships had a two-letter combination to denote the parent ship and a number for each individual aircraft aboard.

Short Seaplanes

General finish as described above but with the addition of a factory number as shown in Chapter 1, together with a name-plate. This name-plate took various forms, in size, location, and indeed in wording, as two examples will show:

SHORT BROS.	N1084 *Short Bros.*
8060 AERONAUTICAL ENGINEERS	S.318 AERONAUTICAL
S.202 ROCHESTER ENGLAND	ENGINEERS
	EAST SHEPPEY

A representative run of Short Factory numbers S.163 to S.247 corresponded respectively to R.N.A.S. Nos. 3063-3072 for Type 827 seaplanes, followed by 8031-8105 for Type 184 seaplanes. Torpedo-carrying Short seaplanes, known as the Short 320 because of a 320 h.p. engine, were built in quantity by Short Bros. and by Sunbeam, who also made the engines. Short-built 320s were numbered from 8317 and Sunbeam-built from N1360. The Short name-plate and works numbers were not, of course, applicable to the latter aircraft.

Short seaplanes were extensively sub-contracted, particularly the Type 184, for which the contractors and a representative production batch were: Brush N9060-9099,

Mann Egerton 8344-8355, Robey N2900-2949, Sage 8380-8391, Saunders 8001-8030, Westland 8356-8367 and J. S. White N2950-2999. No. 8359 identified an important machine, the only aeroplane to have participated in the greatest naval battle of all time—the Battle of Jutland. Twenty-five years after the event the Germans damaged No. 8359 in an air-raid during 1941 when it was housed in the Imperial War Museum.

Short Type 827 seaplanes 8550-8561, being Fairey built, had 'F' numbers in addition to their official serials. Of the same type, machines 3063-3065 and 3096-3098, bore respectively the markings BRITONS OVERSEAS, Nos. 1-6, being presentation aircraft.

Sopwith Seaplanes

The Sopwith two-seat seaplanes of 1914-15 illustrate well the peculiar Admiralty system of using a representative serial number as an official type number, e.g. Sopwith Type 806—Nos. 801-806, Type 807—Nos. 807-810 and Type 860—Nos. 851-860. These numbers were marked on a white rectangle that contrasted only slightly against the pale yellow fabric of the rudder. The firm's name appeared in small letters beneath the rectangle.

Sopwith single-seat types are for ever being confused. It is hoped that this matter will be finally cleared by reporting the appropriate identification numbers. Machines between 1436 and 1579 were Schneiders based on the original Sopwith seaplane that won the 1914 Schneider Cup Trophy at Monaco. Their markings were in the same manner as the two-seat machines. Nos. 3707 to 3806 were modified Schneiders, numbers being marked in the usual

fuselage position and with the familiar Sopwith name-plate appearing on the fin. Nos. 8118-8217 were the famous Sopwith Baby seaplanes, a greatly improved version of the Schneiders, but being marked in the same way as 3707-3806. All other Sopwith single-seat seaplanes, N300 and batches from N1010, were improved Babies built by Blackburn's and finished in khaki-green.

Wight Seaplanes

Early Wight pusher seaplanes bore numbers such as 128, 171, 1300; they were used in limited numbers. The Wight Type 840 tractor seaplane was produced by three firms, the parent firm, J. S. White, building machines from 831, Beardmore from No. 1400 and Portholme from No. 8281.

Fairey Seaplanes

A characteristic of Fairey seaplanes was the 'F' pre-fixed factory number that was normally marked adjacent to the serial number. By the time Fairey's produced sea-planes of their own design a khaki-green finish was general and as both serial and factory numbers were usually marked in black, they did not show up well. Fairey IIIBs were numbered from N2230 (F277) with machines from N2246 (F293) onwards being converted to IIIC. Campanias started the 'N' production series at N1000 (F16), but Campanias numbered from N1840 did not bear 'F' numbers, having been built by Barclay Curle. Large white identification letters were marked on the fuselage of some machines, just aft of the roundel, N2362 (F182), for example, was PC4, another was XL3.

The Hamble Baby was an improved Sopwith Baby

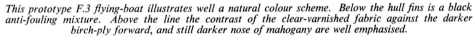

This prototype F.3 flying-boat illustrates well a natural colour scheme. Below the hull fins is a black anti-fouling mixture. Above the line the contrast of the clear-varnished fabric against the darker birch-ply forward, and still darker nose of mahogany are well emphasised.

designed by Fairey; in fact the prototype, Sopwith-built Baby 8134, was given the factory number F129 after rebuilding to Fairey's design.

French Flying Boats

The F.B.A. was the only flying-boat of French design to go into British general service (a Donnet Lévèque boat, No. 18, and two Tellier boats, N84-85, were in fact acquired). British-built F.B.A.s were numbered from N1040 by Norman Thompson and N2680 by the Gosport Aviation Company. A clear-finish was usual; Norman Thompson embellished their machines with serial numbers of some 2 ft. in height and the Gosport firm had the serial number in usual 8 in. digits but strung out in the manner: N-2 . 7 . 2 . 0. The latter firm also had its initials G.A.C. marked each side of the nose of the hull in 6 in. black letters.

American Flying-Boats

Over 200 Curtiss boats were used by the R.N.A.S./ R.A.F. after being shipped over from the U.S.A. in parts and assembled in this country; their finish was therefore similar to the British boats described below. Those numbered below 3594 were of the H.4 type and were known as 'Small Americas'; with numbers of 8650 up and in the 'N' series, all Curtiss boats were of the 'Large America' type, H.12 or H.16.

The Curtiss H.12s 8650-8699 were a distinguished batch: 8695 was instrumental in sinking the German U-boat UC72 and the crews of 8662 and 8676 shared £120 prize money for destroying the UB20. 8666 rose higher, so to speak, and shot down the Zeppelin L22. A month later, on the 14th June, 1917, 8677 destroyed the L43.

British Flying-Boats

The 'F' boats (F for Felixstowe) were the standard operational flying-boats of 1917-18. Normal forms of national insignia were carried as explained earlier, but in addition, owing to a large overhang of the upper wing, roundels were sometimes marked on the underside of the

mainplane. A few had a clear-varnished finish, but khaki-green fabric was usual. Of those in dazzle-painting, F2A N4289 was in post-box red with yellow lightning marks running diagonally across; N4295 and N4302 from the same station, Yarmouth, had a plain-varnished finish. All production 'F' boats were numbered in the N4000-4999 range; N4310-4321 and N4360-4370 were built in Malta Dockyard.

Norman Thompson flying-boats were used mainly for training; a characteristic of their machines was the large marking of the serial number in some 2 ft. digits on the side of the hull. Not until late 1918 was the firm constrained to use the regulation 8 in. characters. An anomaly was that serials were not in chronological/numerical sequence. N.T.2b flying-boats numbered from N2260 were built after those numbered from N2501. Machines of this type numbered N2760 or over were built by Supermarine.

Notes on Ship-board Types

Many Bristol Scouts, Sopwith 1½-Strutters, Pups and Camels were adapted or built for ship-board operation, but markings were little affected. A version of the Hamble Baby, known as the Convert, was built by Parnall's for deck-landing, serials were N1986-2059. Khaki-green Fairey IIIAs with wheel or skid-type undercarriages bore the serials N2850-2899 and the Fairey numbers F220-269. Specially built for use on ships, the Beardmore WBIII, officially known as the Beardmore SB3 (SB for ship-board), was made in two versions, N6100-6112 were SB3F with folding undercarriages and N6113-6129 were SB3D with a dropping chassis.

Notes on Torpedo Bombers

The Sopwith Cuckoo was the only production torpedo-bomber. Fairfield Engineering Company were given the first production order for C7901-8000, later changed to N7000-7099. Similarly, Pegler's order for fifty, D3276-3325, was changed to N6900-6949. Both firms failed to keep delivery dates and at short notice Blackburn Aircraft produced the first production models.

The original and only Sopwith-built Cuckoo bearing 'T' for torpedo-plane, pending the marking of its true serial—N74. Production Cuckoos built by Blackburn were finished in the same style as Baby N2113 shown earlier, in the N6950-6999 serial range.

Experimental and Miscellaneous Aircraft and Markings

Factory finish. An Avro 504K bearing the inscription 'No. 342 Built by the Eastbourne Aviation Co. Ltd.' R.A.F. Nos. D1601-1650 and E4324-4373 were built by the Eastbourne Company, and were numbers 201-250 and 324-373 respectively.

Experimental Aircraft

There were well over a hundred different types of experimental aircraft in the 1914-18 War. In general it could be said that their markings followed the characteristics of their designing firm, for no official instructions specifically concerned them. Their serial numbers were in batches of three or six, it being Ministry of Munitions policy to order three prototypes, or six if a development programme using different engines was envisaged. Examples of experimental batches are Sopwith Snipe B9962-9967 (6), Nieuport B.N.1 C3484-3486 (3), B.A.T. Baboon D9731-9736 (6), B.A.T. Basilisk F2906-2908 (3). As will be seen, experimental batches occurred throughout the serial range, but from 1916 onwards, naval prototypes had a special allocation in the N1-999 range and for a short time in 1918 the R.F.C. had an 'X' for experimental serials as the Serial Table in Appendix IV shows.

Ex-Enemy Aircraft

Whenever possible, each new type of enemy aircraft that fell into our hands was carefully examined by experts from the Technical Department of Aircraft Production, Ministry of Munitions. This department registered the aircraft and allotted a serial number with a 'G' for 'German' prefix. To avoid confusion with German markings—and it had been often confused—the words ENGLISH NUMBER were sometimes marked under the number. It was wrong, of course, as the writer with Scottish connections is only too pleased to point out; the markings should have read BRITISH NUMBER.

If the machine was for ground examination only or for exhibition to the public, German markings were retained, but if the machine was required to fly, the German crosses were painted out and replaced by roundels. A large white broad arrow, the War Department arrow, was often painted on the fuselage, to indicate that it was Government property and so discourage would-be souvenir hunters.

Pfalz D.III 4184/17 provides a typical example; it force-landed in the British Lines near Bonnieul on 26th February,

1918, and was taken to a R.F.C. depot. It was reported to the Ministry of Munitions who allotted the number G141, which was marked in black on its aluminium-doped fuselage in the normal serial position. An Albatros D.III (G56) and an Aviatik (G24) were flown by the Testing Squadron, Martlesham Heath, during 1917.

Two German biplanes, an Albatros and a D.F.W., built by Beardmore, were impressed in August, 1914, by the R.N.A.S. as Nos. 890 and 891 respectively.

Miscellaneous Aircraft

Apart from presentation aircraft from donations, for which an aircraft from current production was identified with the gift, some patriotic persons gave aircraft which were their own personal property. Mr. McClean,* for example, owned several machines and even had his own numbering system! Two short S.38s, with Short factory numbers, S27 and S39, were respectively Nos. 11 and 10 in the McClean series; they were both loaned to the Admiralty in 1912. When war came, Mr. McClean gave two of his later Short biplanes to the R.N.A.S., distinguishable in service by the large rudder numbers, 904 and 905. Miss Trehawke Davies who, although as passenger, was nevertheless the first woman to loop-the-loop in an aeroplane, gave her Bleriot Parasol monoplane to the R.N.A.S. to become No. 903. Early Bristol biplanes, the T.B.8, were ordered a dozen at a time, as their numbers 1216-1227 reveal. Other Bristols, of the box-kite type, taken over with flying schools, received numbers such as 948, which was impressed at Brooklands. From France came R.E.P.s and from America Burgess Gunbuses and Thomas T2s, almost forgotten types, for they proved of little use. Their only marking was an official number, e.g. 3809, on the fuselage sides and the usual roundels. All had a clear-varnished finish.

Some numbers were allotted to machines which did not in fact materialise, orders having been cancelled. For example, N5770-5794 was allotted to B.E.2C aircraft to

* The late Sir Francis McClean, A.F.C., Hon. F.R.Ae.S.

have been fitted with 150 h.p. Hispano engines, but the order placed with Robey's was later cancelled. Other aircraft actually built to an identification number, never went into service with that identity; a particular case is the eight Wight Type 840 seaplanes, allotted Nos. 8542-8549, which were built, but dismantled and issued to R.N.A.S. depots to provide spares. In modern parlance, this would have been called cannibalisation.

Contractors' Markings

Stencilled or hand-painted name-plates, trade marks and factory numbers were marked by various contractors. Some firms used coloured transfers which were usually affixed to the centre of interplane struts. Standard's, for example, put a Union Jack motif facing outwards at the centre of the outboard interplane struts of their Sopwith Pups and R.E.8s; a symbol that later became familiar on the radiators of Standard cars. Well-known in advertisements today, the Avro 'winged triangle' was painted usually in white on the cowlings and undercarriage shock-absorber fairings of Avro 504s. On early Avro machines it was a triangle only, the wings being an addition and dating from 1915.

The famous shipbuilding company of Beardmore used an additional nationality marking on their aircraft products by painting the elevators with lengthwise blue/white/red stripes in the same manner as the rudder. Apart from appearing on the few aircraft of Beardmore design, it was marked on the following aircraft built by the firm under sub-contract: B.E.2Cs 8326-8337, 8488-8500, 8606-8629, 8714-8724; Nieuport 12s 9201-9250, of which 9213-9232 were renumbered A5183-5202 (in the manner A/5183 on the usual fuselage position) on transfer to the R.F.C. from the R.N.A.S.; Sopwith Pups (Type 9901) 9901-9949, (Type 9901A) N6430-6459; Sopwith Camels N7100-7149 and Wight Type 840 seaplanes 9021-9040.

Blackburn-built aircraft bore a distinctive trade mark on the fin as illustrated, it applied to all aircraft of Blackburn design and to the following machines built under contract by the firm: B.E.2Cs 9951-10000, Sopwith Babies numbered between N1010 and N2134, Sopwith Cuckoos N6950-6999, N7150-7199 and from N7981.

Mention has already been made of the factory numbers marked visibly on Fairey and Short-built aircraft and it is clear from pictures on pages 36 and 39 that Parnall's and the E.A.C. also allotted a number of their aircraft. In addition the Phoenix Dynamo Works gave a number to their products, e.g. F.3 flying-boat N4044 built by the firm had at the extreme tail-end of the hull, this marking in white 3 in. lettering:

PHŒNIX BRADFORD
No. 201

The Sunbeam Motor Car Co., too, had their own numbering system, their own designed bomber, N515, being No. 171, the previous 170 numbers having been allotted to batches of Short 827s, Short 320s, Short Bombers and Avro 504Bs.

A firm's name-plate was a common marking on delivery, but if the aircraft went to the Western Front it was usually painted out at the Aircraft Depot, for from mid-1917 it was regarded by R.F.C. H.Q. in France as an unauthorised marking.

Rarely did aircraft bear their type-name, except at the A. and A.E.E. after April, 1918, when it became a general rule for experimental types to bear their type-names in small letters on the fuselage side. Some of the experimental Sopwith types, e.g. Snappers F7031 and F7032, had SNAPPER in 1 in. letters at the top of the fuselage side just aft of the roundel. There has been controversy over the correct spelling for the Blackburn Blackburd—an experimental torpedo-bomber of which three were built—N113-115. On N113 at the top of the fuselage side the name is clearly shown to be Blackburd, not Blackbird. Of course, it is possible that the painter couldn't spell!

Service Finish. An unofficial night camouflage on a Camel of No. 51 (Home Defence) Squadron that apparently entailed painting out or smearing over all markings!

*Presented by an Australian and flown by Australians, this Daimler-built R.E.8 of No. 3 Squadron, A.F.C.,
bears the inscription 'Presented by Mr. H. Teesdale Smith of Adelaide'.
Attention is drawn to the individual letter 'J' on the mainplane centre-section, which replaces the
markings 'B' and '4' either side of it, and which have been partly painted out.*

Australia

The only machines used in Australia were a few R.N.A.S. and R.F.C. aircraft at Point Cook for training, but on the war fronts the Australian Flying Corps mustered four squadrons. Their aircraft supplied from R.F.C./R.N.A.S. sources had standard markings, which were numbered in the normal Service serial range.

No. 1 Squadron A.F.C. (previously No. 67 Squadron, R.F.C.), served in Egypt and Palestine 1917-18, examples of their aircraft being B.E.2E 6826 (clear finish), Martinsyde Elephant A3945 (aluminium finish) and Bristol Fighter C4626 (khaki finish). No unit or individual markings were carried.

Nos. 2, 3 and 4 Squadrons (previously Nos. 68, 69 and 71 Squadrons, R.F.C.) markings have been dealt with elsewhere (see Index). In addition to these operational units, there were two A.F.C. training schools in England at Leighterton and Minchinhampton. A S.E.5A at the latter school had a large white 'A' marked immediately aft of the roundel with a superimposed white silhouette of a kangaroo, showing its 'Aussie' connections. The serial B129 was marked on the fin.

Canada

In Canada, Nos. 78-97 (Reserve) Squadrons of the R.F.C. (Canada)—later R.A.F. (Canada)—were formed as training squadrons in 1917. They were a law unto themselves in the matter of markings, with their own serialling system for the 2,291 aircraft supplied wholly by Canadian Aeroplanes Ltd., Toronto. Since 2,289 of these were Curtiss J.N.4 (CAN) or J.N.4A (CAN), a description of this aircraft is practically a description of the Force.

The 'Jennies' were in clear finish with the usual pale yellowish result from the doped and varnished Irish linen, but late deliveries had a cotton fabric processed in Quebec which gave a greyish tone. Aluminium cowlings were in natural finish or painted brown to match the dark varnish used on all the woodwork. Serial numbers were initially only on each side of the rudder in black 8 in. characters, in the manner—C254. The 'C' prefix stood for Canada and numbers were allotted consecutively.

National insignia was not marked by the contractor, nor were instructions issued concerning such markings; as a result units or individuals made their own unorthodox attempts. C827 had a small roundel on the fuselage sides and another on the underside of the fuselage; on the fin, the colours in the proportions of a roundel were marked —in the shape of a square! C705 in Texas, 1917, had rudder stripes, but marked obliquely at 60 degrees to the fuselage datum.

Rescue markings were pioneered in this Service. In order to aid spotting of aircraft that had force-landed in this spacious and sparsely populated Dominion, it became usual for wing-tips on the upper mainplane to be painted red up to one foot inboard. C1451 modified to carry a stretcher, bore a large Red Cross of Geneva on the fuselage sides, probably the first aircraft to be so marked.

At least one unit had its own mark. No. 85 Squadron adopted the St. Andrew's Cross, as shown on page 45.

South Africa

A South African Aviation Corps saw service in S.W. Africa during 1915. Standard R.N.A.S. aircraft were used, including B.E.2Cs 968-969 and Henri Farmans 3617-3628. In addition to the R.N.A.S. identity, a S.A.A.C. number was given, 3618, for example, being No. 7. Later, the S.A.A.C. merged into No. 26 (South Africa) Squadron of the R.F.C.

New Zealand

Although New Zealand had no flying units, many New Zealanders flew with the R.F.C., R.N.A.S. and R.A.F., some with great distinction.

SQUADRON MARKINGS ILLUSTRATED 1917-1918

In each case a representative machine of the squadron has been chosen and sketched. All aircraft may be taken to be in standard khaki-green finish unless otherwise stated, with all unit marking and individual letter/number in white, except where notification is given to the contrary. Serial numbers were in white when marked directly on khaki-green, black when marked on the rudder stripes, or in a rectangular white field. Where no location is given, the details refer to Western Front units.

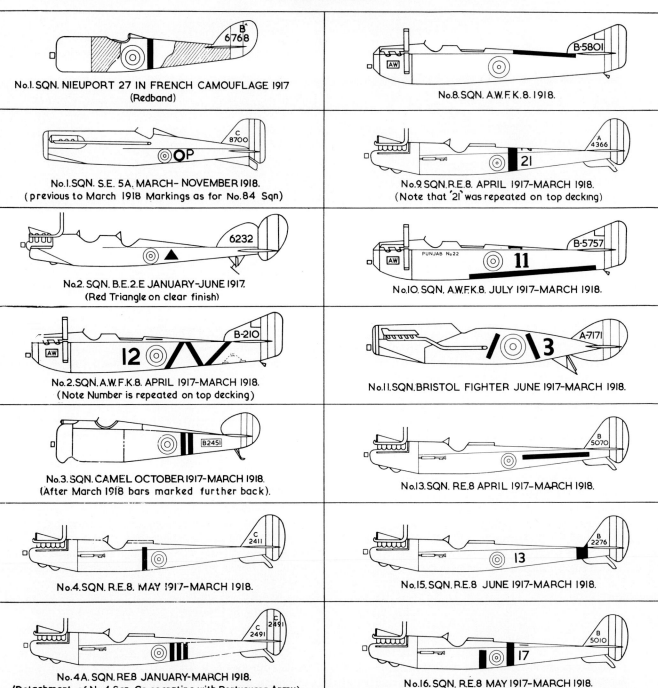

No.1. SQN. NIEUPORT 27 IN FRENCH CAMOUFLAGE 1917
(Redband)

No.8. SQN. A.W.F.K.8. 1918.

No.1. SQN. S.E. 5A. MARCH– NOVEMBER 1918.
(previous to March 1918 Markings as for No.84 Sqn)

No.9. SQN. R.E.8. APRIL 1917–MARCH 1918.
(Note that '21' was repeated on top decking)

No.2. SQN. B.E.2.E JANUARY–JUNE 1917.
(Red Triangle on clear finish)

No.10. SQN. A.W.F.K.8. JULY 1917–MARCH 1918.

No.2. SQN. A.W.F.K.8. APRIL 1917–MARCH 1918.
(Note Number is repeated on top decking)

No.11. SQN. BRISTOL FIGHTER JUNE 1917–MARCH 1918.

No.3. SQN. CAMEL OCTOBER 1917–MARCH 1918.
(After March 1918 bars marked further back).

No.13. SQN. RE.8 APRIL 1917–MARCH 1918.

No.4. SQN. R.E.8. MAY 1917–MARCH 1918.

No.15. SQN. R.E.8 JUNE 1917–MARCH 1918.

No.4A. SQN. RE.8 JANUARY–MARCH 1918.
(Detachment of No.4. Sqn. Co-operating with Portuguese Army)

No.16. SQN. R.E.8 MAY 1917–MARCH 1918.

No.6. SQN. R.E.8 APRIL 1917–MARCH 1918.

No.18. SQN. D.H.4. JUNE 1917–MARCH 1918.

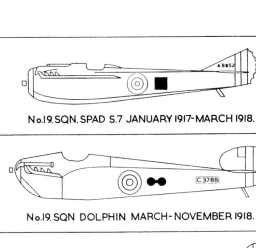

No.19.SQN. SPAD S.7 JANUARY 1917-MARCH 1918.

No.19.SQN DOLPHIN MARCH-NOVEMBER 1918.

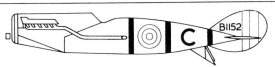

No.21.SQN. R.E.8. MARCH 1917-MARCH 1918.

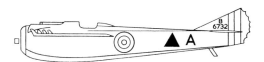

No.22.SQN. BRISTOL FIGHTER JULY 1917-MARCH 1918.
(letter repeated on centre of top wing)

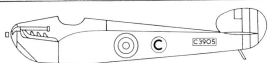

No.23.SQN. SPAD S.7. FEBRUARY 1917-MARCH 1918.

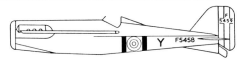

No.23.SQN. DOLPHIN MARCH-NOVEMBER 1918.
(White 'C' marked on red disc)

No.24.SQN. S.E.5A. MARCH-NOVEMBER 1918.
('Y' repeated on top starboard wing)

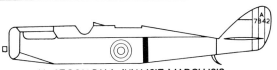

No.25.SQN. D.H.4. JULY 1917-MARCH 1918.

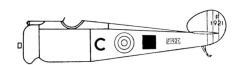

No.28.SQN. CAMEL ITALIAN FRONT 1918.

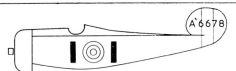

No.29.SQN. NIEUPORT 17.C.I. DECEMBER 1917-MARCH 1918.
(Aluminium finish, black markings)

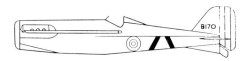

No 32.SQN. S.E.5A MARCH-NOVEMBER 1918.

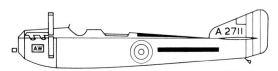

No.35.SQN. A.W.F. K.8. FEBRUARY 1917-MARCH 1918

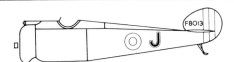

No.37.SQN. CAMEL NIGHT SCHEME HOME DEFENCE 1918.
(Serial F8013 in white. 'J' black with white outline)

No.40.SQN. NIEUPORT 17.C1 MAY-JULY 1917.
(K in red)

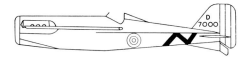

No.40.SQN. S.E.5A. MARCH-NOVEMBER 1918.

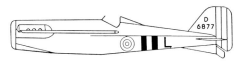

No.41.SQN. S.E.5A. MARCH-NOVEMBER 1918.

No.43.SQN. CAMEL SEPTEMBER 1917 MARCH 1918.
(Markings as above used on Camels March-Sept 1918)

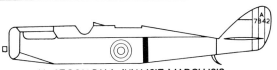

No.27.SQN. D.H.4. JULY 1917-MARCH 1918.
(Letter marked on nose & repeated under bottom wings)

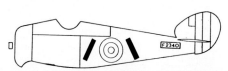

No.43.SQN. SNIPE SEPTEMBER–NOVEMBER 1918.

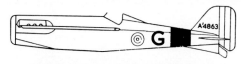

No.56.SQN. S.E.5. JULY 1917–MARCH 1918.
(McCudden's aircraft)

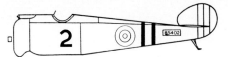

No.44.SQN. CAMEL HOME DEFENCE 1918.
(White markings)

No.56.SQN. S.E.5 A. MARCH–NOVEMBER 1918.
(G.Milne's machine, serial painted out SCHWEINHUND marked on nose)

No.45.SQN.CAMEL ITALIAN FRONT 1918.

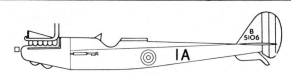

No.59.SQN. R.E.8. MARCH–NOVEMBER 1918.

No.46.SQN.PUP MAY–NOVEMBER 1917.

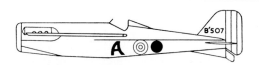

No.60.SQN. S.E.5 A. JUNE 1917–MARCH 1918.

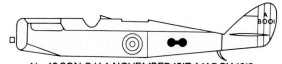

No.49.SQN. D.H.4. NOVEMBER 1917–MARCH 1918.

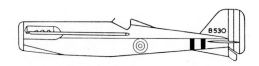

No.60.SQN. S.E.5 A. MARCH–NOVEMBER 1918

No.51.SQN. MARTINSYDE G.102 HOME DEFENCE 1917–1918.
(Clear finish, Black markings, various types of aircraft used by this unit)

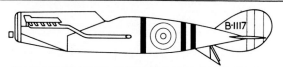

No.62.SQN. BRISTOL FIGHTER MAY 1917–MARCH 1918.
(White markings)

No.52.SQN. R.E.8. MAY 1917–MARCH 1918.

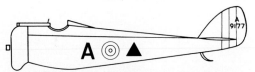

No.64.SQN. D.H.5. OCTOBER 1917–JANUARY 1918.

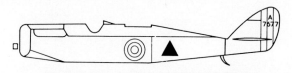

No.55.SQN. D.H.4. MARCH 1917–MARCH 1918.

No.65.SQN. CAMEL MARCH–NOVEMBER 1918.
(Prior to March 1918 a white horizontal line aft of the roundal was used)

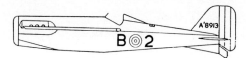

No.56.SQN. S.E.5. TEMPORARY HOME DEFENCE DUTY 1917.

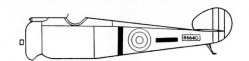

No.66.SQN. CAMEL NOVEMBER 1917–MARCH 1918.

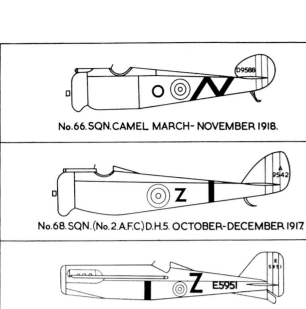

No.66.SQN.CAMEL MARCH- NOVEMBER 1918.

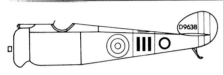

No.68.SQN.(No.2.A.F.C.)D.H.5. OCTOBER-DECEMBER 1917

No.68SQN.(No.2,A.F.C.) S.E.5A. APRIL- NOVEMBER 1918.

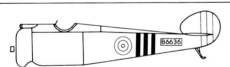

No.70.SQN CAMEL MARCH- NOVEMBER 1918

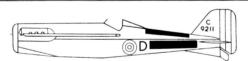

No.71.SQN.(No.4.A.F.C.)SNIPE ARMY OF OCCUPATION 1919.

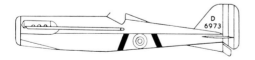

No.73.SQN.CAMEL JANUARY-MARCH 1918.
(Two bars only used from March 1918.)

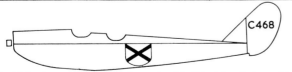

No.74.SQN. S.E.5A. 1918.
(Individual numbers or letters used & sometimes marked on nose only)

No.84.SQN. S.E.5A MARCH-NOVEMBER-1918.

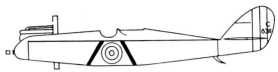

No.85.(RESERVE) SQN. CURTISS J.N.4A. (CAN) R.A.F CANADA.
(Clear finish, red cross on white shield)

No.87. SQN.DOLPHIN MARCH- NOVEMBER 1918.

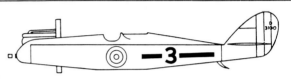

No.103. SQN. D.H.9. JANUARY-MARCH 1918.

No.139.SQN. BRISTOL FIGHTER ITALIAN FRONT 1918.

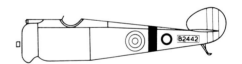

No.144. SQN. D.H.9. PALESTINE 1918.

No.201. SQN. CAMEL MARCH- NOVEMBER 1918.

No.203. SQN. CAMEL MARCH- NOVEMBER 1918.

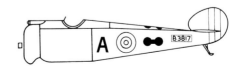

No.208. SQN. SNIPE NOVEMBER 1918.

No.209. SQN.CAMEL MARCH- NOVEMBER 1918.
(Markings in white, black serial)

No.210. SQN. CAMEL MARCH-NOVEMBER 1918.

A Bristol MIc in service with No. 72 Squadron in the Middle East. Khaki-green finish is standard, but the unit marking is elaborate by R.F.C. Western Front standards, and the painting out of the serial number on the fin is unorthodox.

Western Front

The khaki-green finish adopted in 1916 for the upper surfaces of all operational aircraft was not chosen primarily as a camouflage, but because it proved more effective than any other colour in excluding the harmful actinic rays of the sun, that caused the fabric to deteriorate. It was varnish, known as P.C.10, composed of brown ochre and aniline green pigments in a nitro-cellulose varnish. Sometimes lamp-black would be added to give a darker tone, for there was not standard shade.

Home Defence

Night and day defence were roles that required contrasting markings. For day-fighting little attempt at concealment was made, although the wily McCudden, when stationed in England, flew a Home Defence Sopwith Pup for which he had the surfaces light blue to render it less conspicuous. On the other hand, No. 61 Squadron flew chequered S.E.5As on this duty in 1918, C8711 having a red/yellow chequered fuselage without the usual roundels.

Up until 1917 various types, including school machines, flew at night in clear finish on anti-Zeppelin patrol, but that year it was deemed advisable to darken such aircraft by covering all surfaces with khaki-green. In August, 1918, a standard scheme was evolved, it entailed mixing a good proportion of lamp-black with P.C.10 to produce a very dark green. The whites of roundels were excluded by extending the red disc outwards and the blue ring inwards, using a matt finish; roundel outlining, too, was abolished.

Camels proved the most suitable type for night-landings and the 1918 policy was to equip all night-fighting squadrons, Nos. 151 and 152 (Western Front), Nos. 37, 44, 50, 61, 78, 112 and 143 (Home Defence) with this type. No. 37 Squadron Camels, which had the 'night scheme', bore large identification letters just aft of the roundel, marked in black and edged with white. These letters were the initial letter of the pilots' surnames. Camel F1385 had 'C' for 'Coote', a pilot who had served in McCudden's Flight with No. 56 Squadron. Serial numbers, e.g. F8013, were marked in small (3 in.) white characters on the fin.

Middle East

Clear skies led to a sky-blue camouflage and R.F.C.

Henri Farmans were so treated in 1916, but the roundel-blue paint used crumbled after a few weeks. In any case, it was deemed an ineffectual camouflage.

Fabric clear-varnished deteriorated in the sun and the heat absorption caused warping to wooden framework. Khaki-green finish gave protection against harmful rays, but an aluminium finish proved the least heat-absorbing. Unfortunately, it was not a good protective. A compromise therefore resulted, from late 1917 the specified finish was one coat of red-brown, khaki or khaki-green varnish with a top-coat of aluminium varnish. V.114 was still used for undersurfaces. Some Bristol Fighters, e.g. A7200 of No. 67 (Australian) Squadron, delivered in khaki-green, were given an aluminium coating to the uppersurfaces, except for the fin with its white-painted serial number. If one was not aware of the sequence of coatings, it would appear as if the fin only had been camouflaged!

The 1916 campaign in Mesopotamia proved particularly gruelling to the clear-varnished B.E.s and Martinsydes engaged, their fabric was, in fact, bleached by the sun.

Mediterranean Areas

The R.N.A.S. in the Dardanelles Campaign, 1915-16, were divorced from the trend in Europe; Union Jacks were still carried as national markings, being marked on the rudder above or below the serial number. They were intended to indicate nationality in the event of forced-landing, the need of larger markings not arising due to little enemy opposition in the air. All were in clear finish; an example being Henri Farman 1518 at Cape Helles, 1915.

At Italian naval stations, such as Otranto, standard finishes were used except for Italian aircraft supplied to the R.N.A.S., e.g. F.B.A. flying-boats N1075-1078. Gibraltar saw little action, but three clear-varnished aircraft are known to have served there—Caudron G.IIIs 3286 and 3288, together with Wight Type 840 Seaplane 1406. Seaplane carriers like the *Ben-my-Chree* operated aged and worn seaplanes such as Schneiders Nos. 1560-1561 and Short 830s, Nos. 820-821.

Africa

Clear finish, although unsuitable, was used in the early African campaigns. In East Africa, 1915-16, an attempt at bush camouflage was made by daubing brown and green paint on the nacelle and planes of a Voisin, but it was the work of individual pilots and not an official policy.

French Service Markings

The French sometimes marked roundels on the rudders but rarely on the fuselage sides. This Nieuport 12 was handed over to the British, as its R.N.A.S. number 3163 reveals. That it still bears French type roundels can be gauged by comparing them with those on the R.F.C. monoplane opposite and noting the reverse order of the shades of colour in the roundels.

National Insignia

As early as July, 1912, the French Army recommended a roundel as a method of presenting the Tricolour on their aircraft. This roundel, with blue innermost and red outermost, was later copied by the British but with the colours reversed. It was marked on the usual wing positions, but in the case of Caudron, Farman and Nieuport biplanes, with an over-hanging top-mainplane, it was also marked on the undersurface of this wing.

Unlike British practice, the French did not apply a roundel to the fuselage sides, although at least one escadrille of Nieuport Scouts had vertical red/white/blue stripes on the fuselage sides in lieu. Rudder striping was the same as the British. In general, the shade of red was brighter and the blue lighter than the British, the relative standards being the colours of the Union Jack compared to the colours of the Tricolour. The proportions were specified as of 40 cm., 70 cm. and 1 m. diameter for the blue, white and red zones respectively.

General Finish

Up to 1916, clear finish was used for most French aircraft, Bleriot XI, Caudron GIII and GIV, Maurice and Henri Farman types. During 1916, a number of Henri Farmans were painted pale blue and that year a grey or silver-grey overall finish became general for Nieuport and S.P.A.D. aircraft. By 1917 a green and light brown to buff camouflage became service colouring. Undersurfaces on camouflaged machines were in clear or grey finish, except in night camouflage, which was an overall blue-black. Night finish applied to Voisin, Letord, Breguet and A.R. aircraft with night-flying escadrilles. On these machines only the rudder striping was indicative of nationality.

Factory and Service Markings

Each aircraft firm allotted their aircraft a serial number that served also as a service number. To identify the number with a particular firm, prefix letters as tabulated were used. Loading data was usually given beneath this number, e.g. the 156th Salmson 2A2, bore the marking:

S.A.L.   2A2   30 cm. lettering specified
No.   156 ⎱
PC   200 ⎬ 8 cm. figures specified
PU   310 ⎰

'PC' stood for *poids combustible* (fuel load), 'PU' for *Poids utile* (useful load). Figures of weight were in kilograms.

The French equivalent of LIFT HERE—*Lever Ici*—was sometimes marked on the fuselage, but it was not standard practice. Functional titles such as PHOTO appeared on photographic reconnaissance machines as illustrated.

Unit Markings

The French Escadrille with an establishment of about ten aircraft corresponded to the British Squadron. Each escadrille was known by a number that remained constant and by a prefix that varied according to its equipment, thus MF44 would become V44 when Voisins replaced its Maurice Farmans.

Most escadrille had their own insignia, usually confined to nacelle or fuselage sides, but the horse-shoe emblem of MF44 was also marked on the uppersurface, port and starboard sides of the tailplane.

Probably the best-known escadrille were those of the Cigognes Group with the stork emblems illustrated. They were the élite of the French Flying Corps. Another famous unit was the Escadrille Lafayette, originally known as the Escadrille American. The German Government protested about this name to a then neutral America and in consequence it became a number—N124 (N for Nieuport). This in French opinion lacked 'zing' and it was called Escadrille des Voluntaires and yet changed again finally to Escadrille Lafayette. Whatever the name, their adopted insignia, the profile of a Red Indian Chief's head, left little doubt as to the American character of the unit.

Individual Markings

French 'Aces' received much publicity and were acclaimed as national heroes; distinctive individual markings were their prerogative. Rene Fonck, the French 'Ace of Aces' with seventy-five victories had a silver Spad VIII marked as shown on page 50. The Cigognes leader, Commandant Brocard had the SPA 3 stork on his Spad with a 6 in. red/white/blue riband line around the fuselage. By the cockpit a small four-leafed clover was marked in green. Georges Guynemer (fifty-four victories) had a silver-grey Spad VIII with a similar riband; his machine was renowned by the name he gave it VIEUX CHARLES, marked in 6 in. characters beneath the cockpit decking. Adjudant Dorme of N3 was a pilot older than the average, his silver Nieuport bore the name by which he was known with affection throughout France—Pere Dorme. Charles Nungesser (forty-five victories) had a camouflaged Nieuport 17 (N880) with a 1 ft. high letter 'N' in white at the rear of the fuselage, but on his Hanriot HD.1 he carried the macabre motif illustrated. Adjudant Belin had the white outlines of three sitting ducks in echelon on the fuselage sides of his Nieuport 27 (N1368), but Belin with several victories was himself no sitting target.

British Aircraft Types in French Service

Several thousand Sopwith 1½ strutters were built in France and received clear, aluminium or camouflaged finishes. Identity markings on the rudder were SOP 1A2 and SOP 1B2 for two-seat reconnaissance and bombing types respectively.

Of actual British-built aircraft, Short bombers and Sopwith 1½ strutters as listed in Chapter III were supplied to France, also several pattern aircraft for French evaluation; known examples being, Bristol Scout No. 1247, Camel B3891 and two examples of the British-built Caudron GIV Nos. 3335-6.

Naval Aircraft

A grey finish was usual for naval aircraft from 1917 onwards where previously a clear finish had been general for Borel, Nieuport and Hanriot floatplanes together with F.B.A., Donnet and Tellier flying-boats. Late in the war an anchor was added to the roundels of naval aircraft in the manner that remains unchanged to this day. Large black numbers, similar to pennant numbers on ships were marked on a square white background positioned on fuselage sides or forward on hulls. These had a prefix for each base, 'D' for Dunkirk, 'H' for Le Havre, etc. Examples are D23, D28 and D35 on Hanriot floatplanes and D9 on F.B.A. flying-boat No. 325B. F.B.A. flying-boats known to have been based on Le Havre were H4, H47 and H48.

Typical French naval aircraft markings, with a constructor's number on the nose of the hull, in this case No. 332, and a large identification panel denoting the aircraft's base. This F.B.A. flying-boat unfortunately fell into enemy hands and ended up in German markings!

A Hanriot D.3 C2 in typical French camouflage of green and light brown with clear undersurfaces. Its function of general reconnaissance is indicated by the word PHOTO by the gunner's cockpit. Many enthusiasts have been led astray by tail markings on French photographs because black does not contrast against red; in this case the initial letter ' H ' of the tail marking is 'lost' by this limitation in photography.

REPRESENTATIVE UNIT MARKINGS OF THE FRENCH AIR SERVICE 1914-1918

Escadrille	Description of Insignia	Escadrille	Description of Insignia
SOP 13	In a circle, the number 13	SPA 85	A jester with a grenade
AR 20	A lion rampant (The Belgian Lion)	SPA 86	A five-point star and a wing
AR 21	A snail, winged and horned	N 87	Black or white cat with arched back
AR 22	The number 22 with the digits entwined	N 90	Crowing rooster
SOP 24	A pelican	SPA 91	Eagle hovering with a skull in its claws
F 24	An owl perching on a bomb	SPA 94	Skeleton carrying a scythe representing the 'Grim Reaper'
C 27	Mosquito spying with binoculars		
SPA 28	A Falcon	SPA 97	Five-sectioned pennant
SOP 28	A Mammoth	VB 101	A five-pointed white star
SPA 31	A knight, plumed and armoured	SPA 102	The morning sun
SAL 33	A red battle-axe	VB 109	A bat in human form
SPA 37	A vulture, hovering	SOP 111	} A swan within a circle or an elliptical surround
N 38	A thistle	BR 111	
SPA 42	A winged shield	VB 114	Silhouette of an owl
BR 44	A boar in a hexagonal surround	VB 116	Chinese dragon
SPA 48	The head of a cock	BR 119	Black spade with aircraft individual number marked on it in white
AR 50	A humming bird		
C 56	A beetle with wings outspread	BR 120	Cross of Lorraine marked in a triangle
SPA 57	A white bird in flight	BR 123	A hovering eagle
AF 58	A crowing rooster	BR 127	A winged elephant
MR 59	A goose in flight	N 152	Crocodile with gaping jaws
SOP 61	A knight in armour, mounted	SPA 161	A sphinx
SPA 62	A gamecock	AR 201	Riband knotted with a roundel
N 65	Dragon (in various forms), usually black	BR 202	Demon carrying a bomb
SOP 66	} A bird motif, Egyptian pattern with wings outspread	AR 203	A pierrot
BR 66		AR 205	Fairy riding on a bomb
AR 70	A blue bird in flight	C 220	Duck holding an umbrella
C 74	A windmill, Dutch style	SOP 221	Face of a fat girl
SPA 78	A black panther about to spring	SOP 222	Shapes as per C 11 (see sketch)
SPA 83	A fire-breathing dragon	F 465	A bat flying
N84	Foxhead, with winking eye	VB 482	A shrike

FRENCH AIRCRAFT IDENTITY MARKINGS 1914-1918

Code	Design	Marking and Position	Code	Design	Marking and Position
AR	Section Technique d'Aviation	Marking on rudder: AR/Type number/serial number written one under the other.	Ha	Hanriot	As per illustration opposite.
			LET	Letord	Rudder marking with PC/PU figures. Fuselage marking of LET and serial number.
BL	Bleriot	Rudder marking with number in the manner—BL 543.			
BRE	Breguet	Type No., e.g. BRE 17c2/serial number/PC and PU values, marked on rudder stripes, one under the other.	MF	Maurice Farman	MF and number marked on plain inboard side of twin-ruddered machines. MF number repeated on nacelle.
CAU	Caudron	Firm's name, address and serial number marked on the plain inboard side of rudders. Serial number with 'C' prefix repeated on nacelle.	MS	Morane Saulnier	Rudder marking, MS No./Type No./PC-PU values.
			N	Nieuport	N and number marked on rudder stripes.
			PS	Paul Smidt	PS number only on rudder stripes in the manner PS 22.
D	Donnet	'D' and number marked on nose of flying-boat hulls.	S	S.P.A.D.	Full details on rudder stripes including type of engine fitted.
F	Farman	Large 'F' in sign-writers' style followed by a number marked on rudder stripes.	SAL	Salmson	SAL and type number in large characters on rudder stripes.
			T	Tellier	'T' and number marked on nose of flying-boat hulls.
FBA	Franco-British Aviation	'FBA No. 00' marked on nose of flying-boat hulls.	V	Voisin	'V' number at top of rudder stripes.

(Other codes in limited use were: A, Antionette; BO, Borel; D, Deperdussin; D.N.P., Duperon, Niepce and Fetterer; G, Goupy; M, Morane; SA, Savary; SO, Sommer and T, Train.

FRENCH AND BELGIAN AIRCRAFT MARKINGS

ESCADRILLE SPA26

INSIGNIA OF 'LES CIGOGNES'

FUSELAGE OF SPAD S VIII S445
used by Rene Fonck

ESCADRILLE SPA3

ESCADRILLE SPAIO3

ESCADRILLE SPA73

V.15 II
RED   BLUE
TYPICAL VOISIN
RUDDER MARKING

A PRESENTATION MARKING

AN ESCADRILLE MARKING
SOP226

A PILOT'S INDIVIDUAL MARKING
ON A VOISIN NACELLE

ESCADRILLE SPA8I MARKING

WHEEL MARKING OF A FRENCH SPAD
S.7 serving in Russia

ESCADRILLE SPA6 MARKING

ESCADRILLE MARKINGS

SPA265

SOPI29

CII

BRII7

LAFAYETTE

HALL-MARK OF AN ACE
Riband and Stork

NACELLE MARKING
Of a Belgian Flying Corps Farman F.40

UNIT MARKING
On a Belgian Flying Corps Hanriot H.DI

50

NATIONAL MARKINGS, BRITISH AND ALLIED AIRCRAFT, 1914-18

British markings are shown for the following finishes: Clear varnish (left), khaki-green (middle) and for night-flying aircraft from August, 1918 (right).

Left to right: Belgium, 1915-18. France from 1914, but the roundels were marked on the wings only and not until 1940 did they appear on the fuselage sides of French aircraft. Portugal, 1916-18.

Left to right: Italy, 1915-18; the order of the colours was sometimes reversed. American Expeditionary Force, 1917-18, and U.S. Navy from May 1917; positioning was as for France.

China (left) and Japan (right) each used the rudder solely for serial-marking. The middle markings are of the U.S. Army in Mexico, 1916-17 and the U.S. Navy of the same period.

Imperial Russia, 1915-17. Left to right: Fuselage and wing insignia with roundel alternative, optional rudder or fin roundel and rudder marking exclusive to the Russian Navy.

Here are shown the national markings used by Britain and her Allies in the Great War of 1914-18. Unless otherwise stated they show the insignia that appeared in the six standard positions i.e., one each side of the fuselage, on the port and starboard side of the uppersurface of the top wing and on the port and starboard sides of the lowersurface of the bottom wing. The rudder markings, shown as rectangles, have the hinges represented to indicate the leading edge of the rudder.

COLOURS BETWEEN THE WARS

British aircraft—home and abroad. A Bristol Bulldog IIA displays the pre-1937 silver finish of the R.A.F. in the markings of No. 17 Squadron and below, a Hawker Fury bears the finish of the Yugoslav Air Force.

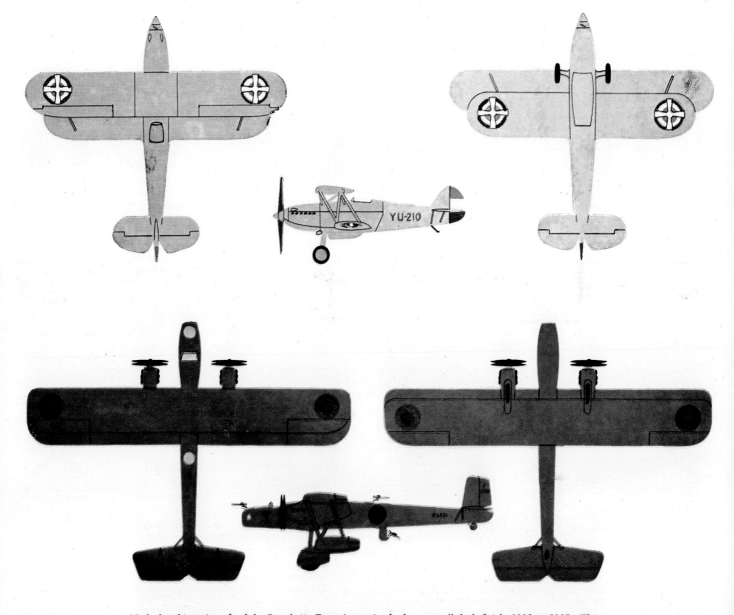

Night bombing aircraft of the Royal Air Force in service had an overall drab finish. 1925 to 1937. This applied to Hyderabads, Hinaidis, Virginias, Heyfords and Hendons. The representative aircraft illustrated is Heyford I K3491 of No. 99 Squadron.

This Nieuport 83, ex-N10591 in French service, is shown bearing an American Expeditionary number as its most conspicuous marking. This was typical of the 1,109 A.E.F. aircraft of 17 different types which were held at the Issouden schools alone, late in 1918. The '3' in front of the number indicates that this aircraft belonged to Air Instruction Center No. 3.

The United States Army

America's No. 1 aeroplane in official service was a Wright Type 'A' biplane procured in 1908. From then until entry into the European War a total of 532 aircraft were ordered by the Army from 14 different manufacturers. All were in clear finish with a consecutive serial number allotted by the Aviation Section of the U.S. Signal Corps. Serials were conspicuously displayed in black; on No. 35 a Curtiss 'N' it appeared on the rudder, but on No. 28 a Burgess 'H' it was well forward on the fuselage.

As a result of the Mexican Border incidents of 1916 a national distinguishing mark became necessary for the small supporting detachment of U.S. aircraft. The star in a circumscribed white circle adopted, varied from the example illustrated to a size as large as the rudder would allow. It was essentially a local marking and not until late 1917 did distinctive national markings become general at home, based on A.E.F. practice, using the A.E.F. roundel on the wing positions. They were placed inboard by one-sixth to as much as one-third of the span, but were always as large as practicable, often touching both leading and trailing edges. Rudder striping followed U.S. Navy practice described later and the fuselage sides were left clear for serialling.

From 1917 it was usual to mark serials in black 12 in. to 18 in. digits in the centre on each side of the fuselage, although on some machines it appeared only in small digits at the top of the white rudder stripe, yet again, on other machines it appeared in both positions. A prefix was sometimes used, 'S.C.' for Signal Corps which gave way later to 'A.S.' for Air Service. War brought a prodigious increase in production and thus to the range of numbers. Only 55 aircraft were serviceable upon the declaration of war, yet, twenty months later, 14,000 aircraft had been accepted and orders for over 60,000 more cancelled. As this indicates, 5 digit serial numbers were in the majority.

The experimental centre, Wright Field, allotted an additional number, headed by the letter 'P', marked on the white of the rudder striping. For specimen aircraft shipped over from Europe, this was often the only identity

number, an example being P33 a Spad VII.

A standard finish using a cotton fabric employed nitrate dope with two coats of clear varnish giving a pale yellow to buff finish, or, in the case of combat aircraft, concerning mainly D.H.4s, an acetate doped linen with a clear varnish or enamel, produced a greyish finish. Camouflage was not general within the States, but a preparation, Valspar Olive Drab, was applied in some units to all upper surfaces, other units excluded fuselage sides.

Unit symbols were rarely displayed and serials were usually sufficiently large to obviate the necessity of individual identity markings within units. Other markings, strange to British practice were evident, the C.O.'s machine at Lonefield Airfield, Curtiss J.N.4D SC34018 had 'COMMANDING OFFICER' in 10 in. letters along the fuselage sides.

Apart from the D.H.4s of which 4,587 were produced in 1917, America built mainly training aircraft, the majority being of Curtiss design including some 3,500 J.N.4Ds, nearly a thousand J.N.4H and over a thousand J.N.6D. The only other trainer built in quantity was the Standard SJ-1, 1,600 being produced.

The United States Navy

In 1911 the U.S. Navy formed an aviation section. When war was declared, April 1917, there were 135 aircraft on strength. No official national insignia had been used, nor indeed had it been necessary, but on some seaplanes an anchor symbol had been marked on the rudder, to signify naval property rather than national identity.

On the 21st April, 1917, the Secretary of the Navy promulgated a standard insignia to be marked forthwith on all naval aircraft. Full details were issued to units and contractors, the illustration on page 51 is drawn to this specification. Colour shades were those of the United States flag. This insignia was marked in the wing positions only with the outside diameter equal to the chord of the wings, placed well inboard with a half-span measure between centres. Rudder striping followed British and French practice, but with colours in the reverse order. An exception was some Nieuport 28s which had white as the leading colour, followed by blue and red finally.

Fuselage and hull sides were left clear for serial numbers.

Naval seriation was completely separate from the Army, although the methods and variations in positioning the number were the same. An 'A' for 'Airplane' prefix denoted the naval series, but it was sometimes omitted. Plans for a strength of 1,700 aircraft were made in 19117 and subsequently increased, but the range did not exceed A4,000 by the end of the war.

Pre-war a clear finish was general, but from mid-1917 a standard finish of overall navy-green pigment varnish or enamel was specified, a proprietary varnish, Valspar Low Visibility Grey, being also used. With this finish serial numbers on the fuselage or hull were in large white characters.

In 1918, the Navy came to use the A.E.F. roundel in place of the star insignia; this was the invariable rule for all American aircraft in the European Theatre. Strangely, the work of the U.S. Navy around our British shores and the French and Irish coasts in 1918 is little known. Flying-boats engaged had a navy-grey finish, A.E.F. roundels both in the wing positions and on the sides of the hull. Serial numbers appeared in small characters only in the white rudder stripe, in their usual place on the hull side was a large individual marking in white, indicative of the station and the flying-boats individual number on the station, e.g. K-11 was a Curtiss H.16 No. 11 machine at Killingholme, Lincs., similarly LV-11 was a Curtiss HS.1 No. 11 of L'aber Varch, France.

United States Marine Corps

Marine Corps aircraft were finished as for general naval aircraft, a typical machine mid-1918, a Thomas Morse SV-4C scout had a navy-grey overall finish, wing insignia of the star-type placed well inboard and the serial A3243 marked only in the white rudder stripe. A Marine Day Bombing Wing in France used American-built D.H.4s with A.E.F. roundels and navy-grey finish. The Marine character of the machines was revealed by a special insignia designed by their Commandant, Major A. A. Cunningham, which was marked toward the rear of the fuselage sides.

American Expeditionary Force

General Pershing landed at Liverpool with his staff on 8th June, 1917, *en route* to France to organise an American Expeditionary Force. For the Air Service a vast training organisation was set up mainly in France, but extending to Britain and Italy. Up to November, 1918, 4,791 aircraft were procured from France, 261 from Britain and 19 from Italy. Additionally, 1,216 aircraft were shipped from the U.S.A., all but three being D.H.4s.

Mistaken ideas have been held concerning the nationality markings on American aircraft in Europe. British daily papers in 1917 showed pictures of American aircraft with the star insignia, but gave no indication that it was a marking exclusive to the U.S. Navy and Marine Corps at home. To complicate matters, the Germans reported that United States aircraft bore the American flag, no doubt mistaking the unit insignia of the 1st Squadron for a national insignia. The A.E.F. marking was in fact yet another variation of the Allied roundel (see page 51) marked in the same positions as on French aircraft, with rudder striping having the colours in the reverse order to other Allied aircraft.

A large black A.E.F. number was marked on aircraft in training units, the machines being in their original finish and previous serial numbers were not obliterated. French roundels too, were often retained on the training aircraft supplied, the A.E.F. number only showing it to be American property.

Aircraft in combat units did not bear A.E.F. numbers marked, but invariably A.E.F. roundels were used. Original finish, camouflage and markings, whether French or British were usually retained. Unit insignia was evidence of *esprit de corps* that official instructions did not discourage and considerable care was exercised both in the choice and execution of the markings. As a general rule, unit markings appeared on the panels enclosing the engine on D.H.4s and on the fuselage sides of other machines. An individual aircraft-in-unit number was normally placed aft of the unit insignia and great care was also given to this digit. These numbers were often marked in isometric projection, with a white 'face' on camouflaged machines, 'depth' being shown in grey. White or black outlining was not uncommon.

The A.E.F. accounted for a total of 776 enemy aircraft for a loss of 289 themselves. Greatest of the American 'Aces' was Captain Edward (Eddie) Rickenbacker who scored 26 victories. He flew a silver-grey Nieuport 28, individual number '5' and later as leader of the famous 94th Squadron he used a Spad XIII with the number '1'. The 94th, most famous of the American pursuit squadrons became well-known as the 'Hat-in-the-Ring' Squadron, from their unit insignia appropriate to the first all-American fighter squadron at the front, symbolising Uncle Sam's hat being thrown into the ring—the Western Front.

A Spad XIII in the markings of the 22nd Pursuit Squadron, A.E.F.

A.E.F. Squadrons and Squadron Markings Western Front—November 1918

Squadron	Date to Front	Equipment and Insignia
1st	8 Apr. 18	Initially equipped with A.R.2s and Spad XIIIs, Salmson 2A2s were used from July, 1918, with 'Old Glory' (the American Flag) painted on the fuselage sides.
8th	14 Aug. 18	An American Eagle holding an American Liberty Bell on D.H.4s (Obs.).
9th	26 Aug. 18	Night-flying Breguet 14 and A.R.2 bombers with an appropriate insignia of searchlights forming the Roman numeral—IX.
11th	5 Sep. 18	D.H.4 day-bombers marked on the side of the nose with an 18 in. white circle and inset, the cartoon character 'Mr. Jiggs' carrying a bomb.
13th	28 Jun. 18	Macabre figure of the Grim Reaper with a bloody scythe (Spad XIIIs).
17th	15 Jul. 18	Ex-R.A.F. Camels used until November, 1918, when exchanged for Spad XIIIs. The Great Snow Owl was then adopted as the unit insignia.
20th	5 Sep. 18	Day bomber D.H.4s for which a circular three-leg motif was adopted.
22nd	22 Aug. 18	Spad XIIIs in French camouflage marked with stars and comets.
24th	14 Aug. 18	Salmson 2A2s with a small black fuselage marking showing the American Eagle pouncing on a daschund running away with tail between legs.
25th	22 Oct. 18	Masked executioner insignia. Nominal unit with 4 ex-R.A.F., S.E.5As on charge, November, 1918.
27th	28 May 18	Initial equipment of Nieuport 28s exchanged for Spad XIIIs. American Eagle insignia.
28th	22 Aug. 18	Spad XIIIs with fuselage insignia of an American Indian's head bearing a single feather.
41st	29 Oct. 18	The emblem of a Camel marked in a 'V' on Spad XIIIs was symbolic of the unit's initial equipment of Sopwith Camels and of the Vth Pursuit Corps.
49th	14 Aug. 18	A snarling wolf's head marked on Spad XIIIs.
50th	14 Aug. 18	D.H.4s (Obs.) bearing a Dutch woman mascot copied from a popular advertisement.
85th	25 Oct. 18	Winged Cupid sitting on the Globe marked on the nose of D.H.4s (Obs.).
88th	24 May 18	Salmson 2A2s with 'bucking bronco' badge. A few Sopwith 1A2s were used initially.
90th	11 Jun. 18	Two dice in red and white marked on Salmson 2A2s which replaced earlier Sopwith 1B2s.
91st	7 May 18	Insignia as per sketch for mixed equipment of Spads, Salmsons and D.H.4s.
93rd	14 Aug. 18	American Indian's head with two feathers in forelock on Spad XIIIs.
94th	9 Apr. 18	The famous 'hat-in-the-ring' marked on Spad XIIIs after initial Nieuport 28s.
95th	4 May 18	A 'kicking mule' motif marked first on Nieuport 28s then on Spad XIIIs.
96th	29 May 18	24 Breguet 14s were on strength bearing the 'Red Devil' insignia illustrated.
99th	12 Jun. 18	Silhouette of American bison on Salmson 2A2s replacing Sopwith 1B2s.
100th	26 Oct. 18	A devil riding a bomb was the characteristic marking on these D.H.4s.
103rd	18 Feb. 18	Formed from the famous Lafayette Escadrille. (See index). Nieuport 28s and Spad XIIIs.
104th	7 Aug. 18	Salmson 2A2s bearing a winged sphinx insignia marked on the fuselage.
135th	28 Jun. 18	D.H.4 (Obs.) with the Statue of Liberty against a blood-red rising sun.
138th	28 Oct. 18	A 'billy goat' charging through a 'V' (denoting Vth Group) marked on Spad VIIs.
139th	12 Jun. 18	The figure of Mercury used on Spad XIIIs until disbandment in Dec. 18.
141st	18 Oct. 18	Bengal Tiger playing with a German helmet and an Iron Cross (Spad XIIIs).
147th	28 May 18	A ratting terrier on the fuselage sides firstly on Nieuport 28s then Spad XIIIs.
148th	20 July 18	Ex-R.A.F. S.E.5As used until a few days before the Armistice when the unit re-equipped with Spad XIIIs. Marking was the 'Head of Liberty'.
155th	9 Nov. 18	Night-bomber unit with an upward pointing arrow. (D.H.4s and F.E.2Bs).
163rd	27 Oct. 18	Day-bombing D.H.4s with a 'winking cat on a bomb' marking.
166th	20 Sep. 18	A complicated insignia, that varied from one D.H.4 to another, consisting mainly of the American flag twisted into wings over a map of Germany.
168th	30 Sep. 18	A winged skull marked on the side of the nose of D.H.4s (Obs.).
185th	5 Oct. 18	Spad XIIIs and Sopwith Camels for night-flying with a bat emblem.
186th	25 Oct. 18	Salmson 2A2s used, but there are no indications of a unit emblem.
213th	14 Aug. 18	Another variation of an American Indian's head used for the Spad XIIIs.
258th	10 Sep. 18	A lion in various postures was the emblem of this Salmson 2A2 unit.
278th	29 Oct. 18	D.H.4s used for corps observation. No markings known.
354th	21 Oct. 18	A witch on a broom with a propeller embellished these observation D.H.4s.
638th	28 Oct. 18	A black cat for luck in a 'V' denoting Vth Pursuit Group (Spad VIIIs).

MISCELLANEOUS AIRCRAFT MARKINGS OF THE ALLIES 1914-18

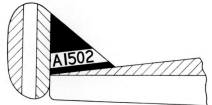

TAIL OF A.W.F.K.3 BUILT BY HEWLETT AND BLONDEAU
(Khaki green fin and fuselage decking, clear sides)

RUDDER OF VICKERS F.B.5A. 1915
(Black markings, standard Union Jack colours)

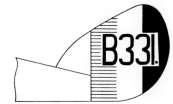

RUDDER OF D.H.5. BUILT BY BRITISH CAUDRON CO.
(Standard R.F.C. striping)

MACABRE INSIGNIA ON A HANRIOT SCOUT
(Used by Lt Nungesser of the French Flying Corps)

MARKINGS ON NIEPORT 28
(Used by Capt Rickenbacker of 94th Sqn. A.E.F.)

INSIGNIA OF 8th SQN. A.E.F.
(Black eagle and bell marked on A.E.F. roundel)

INSIGNIA OF 9th AERO SQN. A.E.F
(Study in black and grey with yellow beams)

INSIGNIA OF U.S. MARINE CORPS SERVING IN FRANCE, 1918.
(Black wings and anchor, standard A.E.F. roundel)

INSIGNIA OF 91st AERO SQN. A.E.F.
(Black knight, red devil)

INSIGNIA OF 95th SQN. A.E.F.
(Brown mule, blue background, yellow surround)

INSIGNIA OF 96th SQN. A.E.F.
(Red devil, silver bomb, black background)

INSIGNIA OF 25th SQN. A.E.F.
(Black executioner)

BLACKBURN TRADE MARK
(Normally marked on fins in black on light finish, white on dark finish)

AVRO TRADE MARK
(Marked on cowling of A.V. Roe built aircraft)

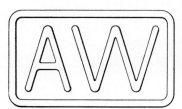

A.W. TRADE MARK
(Embossed on engine cowling)

Aircraft of the Allies

Italian S.I.A.7B with plywood covered fuselage finished in clear varnish, uppersurfaces of planes in silver-grey, undersurfaces and fin in clear varnish. In this particular aircraft, the green of the national marking occurs in the centre of the roundel and at the trailing edge of the rudder.

Belgium

Belgium had a small but efficient pre-war Flying Corps with 24 Henri Farman biplanes built by Bollekens of Antwerp forming the main equipment. In 1914, most of their country was over-run by the Germans and their Flying Corps was re-formed into a number of flights and equipped by the French. Nieuport, Spad and Hanriot Scouts were supplied, the last-named giving rise to a misconception that the Hanriot was Belgian-designed. The Belgians, intensely nationalistic, marked their machines in their national colours using the accepted roundel form.

General finish for the Corps was grey-green fuselages with silver-grey wings; fighter flights however were allowed considerable latitude. The 9th adopted a white thistle emblem and had their machines painted each in a different colour, but after the R.F.C. had chased an all-yellow Hanriot thinking it to be a German, cowlings only were coloured. This scheme also applied to Sopwith Camels used towards the end of the war. Willy Coppens, a Belgian 'Ace' serving in this unit, was dissatisfied with the camouflage of his Hanriot HD.1 No. 6. He remarked that it reminded him of a varnished toy snake and gave instructions for it to be painted all-blue, except for the national and unit marking. Later, Hanriots HD.1 Nos. 17 and 45 were used by this famous Belgian.

British aircraft also were supplied and included 36 R.E.8s fitted with 150 h.p. Hispano engines and of many Camels supplied, the following are known by number:

A Nieuport-Macchi of the Italian Navy cleverly marked as a 'sea monster'. The serial number, M13041 has in consequence been transferred from the nose of the hull to the tailfin. The white tapes around the wing struts are typical of all Nieuports, French or Italian, landplanes or seaplanes.

B5710-1, B5745, B5747-8 and B7235-7. To protect Colonial interests, Short 827 seaplanes Nos. 3093-3095 were shipped to the Belgian Congo.

Only one Salmson 2A2 bore Belgian markings and that unofficially. It was a French machine found abandoned in a field by a Belgian officer who 'adopted' it. All went well until after the Armistice when equipment was all being handed back; this officer was in possession of an aircraft not officially on charge and awkward questions might be asked. The officer solved his problem by repainting it with French roundels, flying it to a French airfield and just walking away—quickly!

Italy

It is perhaps not generally known that Italy was the first country to use the aeroplane in war. A detachment of several aeroplanes was used in 1912 near Tripoli following the declaration of war with Turkey the previous year. By 1913 Italy had several squadrons organised, their machines were in clear finish with unit and identification markings placed conspicuously in black upon fuselage sides, e.g. a Bleriot XI monoplane had this marking:

IVa SQUADRIGLIA
Bi 23

When Italy joined in the Great War, May, 1915, roundels and rudder striping in national colours were adopted but as notified on page 51 the colours were in no set order. Camouflage was not general, a clear or silver finish being usual with squadriglia markings replaced by unit emblems. Identification markings consisted of manufacturers initials followed by a serial number similar to the French system but being marked in a central position on fuselage or nacelle sides. Ca was the well-known abbreviation for Caproni, Ma—Macchi, P—Pomilio, SP—Savoia-Pomilio, S.I.A.—Societa Italiano Aviazione, S.V.A. for Ansaldo aircraft needs some explanation, 'S' and 'V' represented the designers Savoia and Verduzio, 'A' was for the manufacturers, Ansaldo.

The Italian 'Ace', Major Francesco Barracca (36 victories) flew S.V.A. 6758 and Scaroni, the country's second 'Ace', flew an Italian-built Hanriot HD.1.

A few aircraft were exchanged with Britain, for example Sopwith Babies Nos. 8214-5 were sent as pattern aircraft for Italian production of this type. Six Caproni Ca42s, giant triplane bombers, were used by the R.N.A.S. as numbers N526-531.

The R.A.F. in Italy had almost complete mastery of the air, they accounted for 386 enemy aeroplanes and 27 balloons for a loss of 47 aeroplanes and 3 balloons. R.A.F. units serving in Italy, 1918, were Squadrons Nos. 28, 45 and 66 (Camels), Nos. 34 and 42 (R.E.8s) and No. 139 (Bristol Fighters).

Portugal

Portuguese aircraft were not used operationally, but several Portuguese officers trained and flew with the French. No. 4A Sqn. R.A.F. co-operated with the Portuguese Army in France, early 1918.

Roumania

As with most European countries, Roumania was influenced by French aviation, purchasing French aircraft before the war and placing orders for more when war came. A general belief was that the Roumanian national marking was identical to the French, it certainly was similar, but in fact a pale yellow replaced the white portion of the French roundel, thereby making an insignia of Roumanian national colours—red, blue and yellow.

Some R.N.A.S. aeroplanes from Mudros were handed over to the Roumanians, these were Nieuport 17 No. 3978,

The Italians marked 'wound' stripes for each bullet hole received! Note the roundel under the hull of the flying boat. A wise precaution, as this Italian-built aircraft is a copy of an Austrian Lohner!

Nieuport 12s Nos. 8524, 8525 and 8731, Henri Farmans Nos. 3004, 3007 and 3008.

Russia

The Russian Government in 1912 puchased a few Nieuport Monoplanes for their Army and Curtiss flying-boats for their Navy, at the same time permission was sought to manufacture certain French types under licence. By 1914, 329 aircraft had been built, but war increased little the tempo of production, for up to the 1917 Revolution only 963 aircraft were reported to have been built. This total included 70 Sikorsky bombers, some with four engines, the most successful machines of indigenous design.

National markings took the various forms illustrated on page 51. One Sikorsky bomber had two roundels on the same side of each tail fin, one above the other. A grey overall finish was usual for all Russian aircraft and serials if allotted were not always visible, although a F.B.A. flying-boat bore the marking at the nose of the hull:

Nikolavyevich
578

Serbia

A few aircraft were used by the Serbs in French markings, red, white and blue being also Serbian national colours. After the pathetic retreat of 1915, the personnel of the French Escadrille MF99 returned to France, leaving their Maurice Farmans at Scutari for the Serbs; later they were supplemented from France with Spad VIIs and Breguet 14s.

Russian aircraft photographs of any period are rare. The marking on the outboard side of the rudder on this Maurice Farman seaplane shows it to belong to the Imperial Russian Navy.
This service also used F.B.A. and Curtiss flying-boats, with Russian type roundels marked forward on the sides of their hulls.

AIRCRAFT INSIGNIA OF GERMANY AND THE GERMAN ALLIES
1914-1918

GERMANY 1914-17

GERMANY 1918

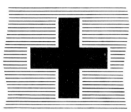

Variations of the examples illustrated used in all standard positions

TURKEY

1914

All positions

1915-18

BULGARIA
1914-18

GREEN BAND ALONG TRALING EDGE

Top wing only

Fuselage sides
and bottom wing

AUSTRIA 1914-18

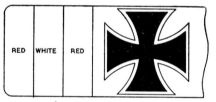

RED   WHITE   RED

Top Wing (Upper and under surface) of
Flying Boats

Fuselage sides
and bottom wing

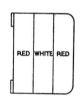

RED WHITE RED

RED

WHITE

RED

Rudder alternatives

A

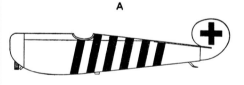

E

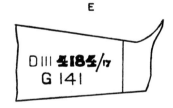

DIII 4184/17
G 141

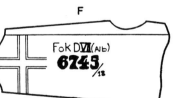

FoK DVII (Alb)
6745/18

C

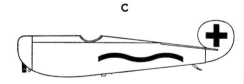

B

D

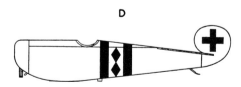

 FIGS. A-D   FOUR FOKKER TRIPLANES OF THE RICHTHOFEN CIRCUS WERE MARKED AS SHOWN EARLY IN 1918.
FUSELAGE AND WINGS WERE PAINTED SCARLET, RUDDER WHITE WITH BLACK CROSS, THE FUSELAGE
MARKINGS WERE IN WHITE.

FIG. E   A COMPOSITE MARKING, DIII 4184/17 STENCILLED ON BY THE GERMAN MANUFACTURER AND G141
ADDED BY BRITISH AFTER CAPTURE.

FIG. F   A TYPICAL FOKKER SERIAL MARKING, SHOWN HERE FOR A FOKKER DVII BUILT UNDER SUB-CONTRACT.

CHAPTER FOURTEEN

Germany and the German Allies

These Albatros D.Vs of a German Jagdstaffel show many inconsistencies in their tail markings. D.2042/17 nearest the camera has a clear varnished rudder and grey painted fuselage, but the machine next to it has a rudder covered with dyed 'lozenge pattern' fabric and a fuselage with the top half splashed with purple and brown paint as a form of camouflage.

National Insignia

Known colloquially as the Iron Cross, the Cross Patée was used as the national marking of German aircraft from the opening weeks of the war until March 20th, 1918, when instructions were issued that it was to be replaced by the Greek Cross, or *Balkankreuze*, by April 15th, 1918. Unlike the Allies who used a different marking on the rudder to wings and fuselages the Germans had the same marking in all the normal positions with the cross at the tail occupying both fin and rudder.

On early machines in natural finish a black cross on its own was sufficiently conspicuous, but with the introduction of printed fabrics and camouflage, white edging or a white square field was used to give contrast. The proportions of the cross itself and the edging varied as illustrations show.

General Finish

Early machines had a pale cream factory finish which in service often deteriorated to a greyish-white. This applied to early pre-1916 Aviatik, Albatros and D.F.W. biplanes, and Fokker monoplanes. In 1916 some fabrics in their natural off-white colour were printed with a close pattern of black dots giving an overall grey shade at a distance. That same year a true camouflage was introduced by spray-painting blotches of green purple and brown over upper-surfaces, as shown on page 8, this applied particularly to observation aircraft types. The round-sectioned fuselages of Albatros and Pfalz types precluded the possibility of having a well-defined upper- and undersurface line to the fuselage. A merging line of uppersurface brown, green and purple into a grey or blue-grey undersurface occurred about a foot below the fuselage datum line on these types. During 1918, many aircraft had a weather-proofed plywood finish to save weight and paint.

Printed fabrics were introduced in 1917 with a four- to six-colour scheme in a mosaic pattern of lozenges, hexagons or irregular shapes. Colours were yellow, green, pink, brown, blue and black for 'D' class aircraft with an 'elongated hexagon' style pattern, each unit measuring approximately $2\frac{1}{2} \times 5$ in. overall. 'G' class aircraft fabric was patterned with regular hexagons, 18 in. across the flats, in sage green, reddish mauve, bluish mauve, black, blue and grey.

Large bombing aircraft often had a dual scheme, for the printed fabrics were of poor quality and not considered

The Austrians painted a somewhat distorted Cross Patée on the nose of their flying-boat hulls. This Lohner boat, so marked, fell into Italian hands.
Without a knowledge of the serial Rol: DVII 3910/18, it is apparent that this photograph could not have been taken before 1918, because of the Balkankreuze *(Greek cross) that came into effect that year.*

No better example exists of hexagon patterned dyed fabric than on this A.E.G. G. IV captured and photographed by the British and numbered G. 105 in the register of captured enemy aircraft. The hexagons were regular and measured 18 in. across the flats.

suitable for the lifting surfaces. Thus e.g., Friedrichshafen GIII 326/17 had a fuselage covering of fabric printed with hexagons, but a natural off-white fabric on the wings, hand-painted with hexagons to match. An example of the infinite care the Germans took with their camouflage.

It is impossible to generalise, but a trend with certain types can be expressed. A.E.G. machines, particularly the CIV, were given a sprayed camouflage and the firm's trade mark invariably appeared on the rudder as shown on page 8. Albatros CIII biplanes had a square white field for national markings, later DV and DVa scouts had a dark varnish on the plywood covered fuselage with wings and tail unit in mosaic pattern fabric. Fokker EI, II, III and IV monoplanes had a clear finish and Fokker DVII and DVIII scouts, usually a mosaic pattern fabric throughout; one known exception, a clear white finished Fokker DVII, marked with 'Fok. DVII F5125/18' along the bottom edge of the fuselage side, was a machine flown by a pilot destined to become head of the *Luftwaffe*—Reichmarshal Göring. Hannoveraner biplanes had the mosaic patterned fabric for all surfaces including over the plywood skin of the fuselage. Pfalz DIII scouts with ply-covered fuselages were often painted silver over-all except for the aluminium engine cowling which was given various colours. L.F.G. Roland machines had a finish of purple, brown and green camouflaged uppersurfaces, with an undersurface light grey.

Components such as cowlings, struts and fittings were painted at the manufacturer's discretion, grey being usual. Instructions were, however, issued to firms concerning colour-coding control and piping systems. Petrol pipes were always white with small arrows at 2 ft. intervals indicating the direction of flow. Other pipes were in blue and control cables and runners in grey.

Identification and Data Markings

The Air Service identity numbering system is explained later, but in addition to this number a works number plate bearing the date of manufacture appeared on major components. Usually it was marked on a label, some $4 \times 2\frac{1}{2}$ in., affixed to the fuselage side and the uppersurface of mainplanes.

Data markings were not general, but it was the practice of the Friedrichshafen and Pfalz works to mark in black a few figures relating to loads. Standard Pfalz DIII fuselage markings (1 in. lettering) were:

Leergewicht	725 kg.
Nutzlast	180 kg.
Zulassiges Gesamtgewicht	905 kg.
Haupthenizatank	

The weights were in kilograms and referred respectively to weight empty, useful load and permissible total weight.

Unit and Individual Markings

A vivid contrast from the sober and strictly functional markings of German aircraft was adopted by the *Jagdstaffeln*. These fighting units, capable of rapid re-deployment along the Front, were formed following the success achieved by Oswald Boelcke, commanding the hand-picked pilots of *Jagdstaffel 2* using Albatros DI scouts. When the famous Manfred von Richthofen took over *Jagdstaffel 11* in

These two seaplanes of the Imperial German Navy show well the variations in markings. One is in clear finish and the other in sea-grey camouflage, yet it is the clear-varnished machine that has a white background for the national markings. No. 900 has a cross on the fuselage, but not No. 580. Both are Sablatnig built; 580 being Type SF2 and 900 Type SF4.

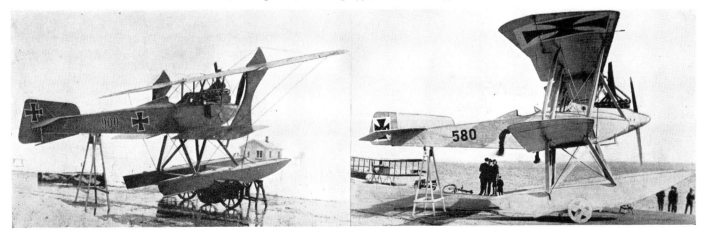

A Gotha WD13 seaplane (the WD12 modified for Turkish use) in the national markings of Turkey which were first red with a white border, but later black replaced the red to avoid confusion with the red of British and French roundels.

January, 1917, he was of sufficient standing to ignore convention and introduce bizarre schemes that were later adopted by all *Jagdstaffeln*, hence the apt term—'circuses'.

Bright scarlet, surely the most conspicuous of colours, was chosen by Richthofen for his unit's Albatros DIIIs and later Fokker Dr.I triplanes. Each individual machine had some distinguishing stripe or device in a contrasting colour, except for Richthofen himself who used a completely all-red machine.

Initially it came as a surprise to us, their enemy, the Germans previously so careful in the matter of concealment, were now flaunting the very antithesis of camouflage before the R.F.C. Major Bishop, the Canadian Ace with 72 victories had this to say—"The scarlet machines of Baron von Richthofen's crack squadron, sometimes called the "circus," heralded the new order of things. Later, nothing was too gaudy for them. There were machines with green planes and yellow noses; silver planes with gold noses; khaki-coloured bodies with greenish-grey planes; red bodies with green wings; light blue bodies and red wings; every combination the Teutonic brain could conjure up. One of the most fantastic we ever met had a scarlet body, a brown tail, reddish-brown planes, the enemy markings being white crosses on a bright green background.'

Nevertheless, there was some order in this seeming chaos, a 'Jagdstaffeln characteristic' it could be termed: No. 1 had red noses and wings; No. 2 yellow fuselage undersurface; No. 3, black and white checks on the fuselage; No. 4, snake insignia of various colours and distortions! No. 6 had black and white striping and No. 10 were mainly yellow in colour.

Richthofen became known as the Red Knight because of his all-red aircraft; Jacob Weiss of his unit broke tradition after his leader had been finally shot down, by using an all white Fokker Dr.I Triplane 545/17 (Weiss is German for white!). Otto von Keudell who engaged in several combats with Major McCudden and eventually became his victim, had an Albatross DV with red wings and fuselage, green tail and a 'K' for Keudell marked in white upon the fuselage sides. Identification letters or individual numbers were unusual, but a pilot's monogram on scout aircraft was not uncommon.

Naval Aircraft

German naval aircraft normally had a clear or grey finish, and the mosaic patterned fabrics were rarely used. A characteristic of naval machines was the large number marked on the fuselage sides. In some cases this number replaced the national marking on the fuselage side, but often it was just forward

Aircraft of the Aces! The Fokker Triplane Dr.I 404/17 used by Hauptmann Ritter von Tutschek who scored 27 victories. A similar machine, Dr.I 144/17, fell into British hands, it had a green paint wash over the fuselage and upper surfaces and was cerulean blue underneath.

*Nieuports in false colours! A Type 17 (right) and Type 12 (left) captured by the Germans and re-marked.
It is noticeable that the Germans followed French practice with Nieuports by placing national markings
under the top wing. The three sets of binding tape spaced out along the struts are a hall-mark of
Nieuports under any guise.*

or aft of this cross. The numbers, allotted consecutively and reaching about 2,400 by the Armistice, were invariably in black, in about 18 in. characters. There were no prefix letters, this number sufficed for service, unit and individual marking all in one. Examples are 679 Gotha W.D.11, 747 Albatross W.4 and 1521 Friedrichshafen FF49c.

The Austro-Hungarian Empire

At the outbreak of the First World War, Austro-Hungaria mustered some sixty monoplanes and fifty biplanes, mostly of German design. During hostilities German industry supplied types in quantity, Fokker EI and DII, Albatros DII and DIII scouts and A.E.G. CIV biplanes.

By 1917 Austria was making her own aircraft, in particular the Aviatik DI (Berg Scout). Camouflage in the *Luftfahrttappen* followed French lines, but serialling was on an original system of a two-number combination marked in about 1 ft. characters on fuselage sides, e.g. a Fokker DIII was 04.44, where 04 denoted type and 44 the serial number of that type. Type allocations were as follows: 01-09, licence built German aircraft; 10-19 Lohner; 20-29, Phönix; 30-39, O.A.W.; 40-49, Lloyd; 50-59, Oeffag; 60-69, Ufag; 70-79, Fischamend; 80-89, W.K.F.; 90-99, M.A.G. Serialling on naval flying-boats consisted a prefix letter and individual number: A, single seat flying-boats; G, Phönix or Pola boats; KG, multi-engined boats; K, all other classes of boats; L, Lohner boats; S, school or training machines and R, reconnaissance types. German nationality markings were used and in addition on naval craft the Austrian colours of red, white and red were marked as shown on page 59. Sometimes this scheme was extended to the tail unit, and it was not unknown to have the rear of the fuselage banded in these colours.

Bulgaria

Some Russian volunteer officers and an Englishman, Snowden Hedley, flew for Bulgaria in the Balkan war, causing not a little embarrassment when Bulgaria threw in her lot with Germany. Aircraft were supplied from Germany complete with the Imperial German insignia to which Bulgaria added a green line along the wing to show some individuality. Green was chosen from Bulgarian national colours.

Turkey

Turkey had used French R.E.P. and Nieuport monoplanes together with a few German machines in the Balkan wars of 1912-13, but profited little from the experience gained. During the Great War only a few Turkish flying units functioned, equipped wholly from German sources.

The Turks used their flag as a basis for aircraft national markings, but for a period changed the colour from red to black to avoid confusion with British or French markings, using a plain square with a white border. In the top of the border was marked the Turkish Flying Corps number, an A.E.G. CIV e.g. was serialled AK62. General finish of the corps machines was plain varnish.

Aircraft of the Aces! Leutnant Fritz Friedrichs, who scored 21 combat victories, is shown here seated in his silver-finished Pfalz DIII.

THE GERMAN AIR SERVICE IDENTIFICATION NUMBERING SYSTEM 1912-1918

All German military aircraft bore an Air Service number marked by the constructor. It was made up of several parts, each one having particular significance as is shown below:

Example: Fok D VII (Alb) 6745/.18

'*Fok*' stood for the designing firm—Fokker. Representative letters were allotted to firms as shown in Table A. These letters were marked either in capitals or small letters.

'*D*' was the German Army class of aircraft, in this instance a single-seat fighter. Code letters and the classes of aircraft are defined in Table B.

'*VII*' indicated that this aircraft was the seventh design in the 'D' class by the designing firm. This classification was not exclusive to Fokker for some other manufacturers reached their seventh design in the single-seat fighter class. '(*Alb*)' showed that the machine was built under sub-contract by the Albatros Works. This marking was only appropriate to aircraft built under licence and was shown bracketed. The letters used were again as per Table A.

'**6475**' was the Air Service serial number allotted from No. 1 upwards for each class separately per year. The quantities built, given in Column 4 of Table B are therefore indicative of the range of numbers allotted in each class. 'CL' was grouped with 'C' for numbering.

'**18**' stood for the year of allotment, i.e. 1918.

TABLE A.—German Aircraft Manufacturers 1914-1918

Marking	Name of Firm				
AEG	Allgemeine-Elektrizitats-Gesellschaft.	GERM	Germania Flugzeugwerke G.m.b.H.	OT	Ottowerke G.m.b.H. (Munich).
AGO	Ago Flugzeugwerke G.m.b.H	GO	Gothaer Waggonfabrik A.G.	PFAL	Pfalz-Flugzeugwerke G.m.b.H.
ALB	Albatros Gesellschaft m.b.H.	HALB	Halberstadter Flugzeugwerke G.m.b.H.	RAT	Joseph Rathgeber Waggon-fabrik.
AV	Automobil und Aviatik A.G.	HANSA	Hanseatische Flugzeugwerke A.G.	RIN	Albert Rinne Flugzeugwerke.
BFW	Bayerische Flugzeugwerke A.G.	HN	Hannoversche Waggonfabrik A.G.	ROL	Luftfahrzeuggesellschaft m.b.H. (Roland Holz und Metallearbeitung G.m.b.H.)
BAYRU	Bayerische Rumplerwerke G.m.b.H.	JUNK	Junker Flugzeugwerke, Dessau.	RU	Rumpler Werke G.m.b.H.
DAIM	Daimler Motoren Gesellschaft	KON	Kondor Flugzeugwerke, G.m.b.H.	SAB	Sablatnig Flugzeugbau G.m.b.H.
DFW	Deutsche Flugzeugwerke G.m.b.H.	LI	Linke-Hoffman Werke A.G.	SCHUL	Schutte-Lanz Luftschiffbau.
EUL	Eulerwerke (Frankfurt).	LVG	Luft-Verkehrs-Gesellschaft m.b.H.	SSW	Siemens-Schuckert Werke G.m.b.H.
FDH	Flugzeugbau Friedrichshafen	MARK	Markische Flugzeugwerke.	STAAK	Societes Zeppelin.
FOK	Schweriner (Fokker Flugz-eugwerke) Industrie Werke.	MER	Merkur Flugzeugbau G.m.b.H.	TORP	Luft-Torpedo G.m.b.H. (Berlin).

TABLE B.—German Air Service Classification System

Class Code	Allotment Year(s) of	Class of Aircraft	Number Built Approx.
A	1911-1915	Mostly of the 'Taube' monoplane type	550
B	1911-1918	Biplanes for reconnaissance or training of 100 h.p. or under.	6,000
C	1915-1918	General Purpose aeroplanes of 100 h.p. and over	} 34,000
CL	1917-1918	Aircraft specially designed for close support to troops.	
D	1916-1918	Single-seat fighting aeroplanes.	12,000
Dr.	1917	'Dreidekker' armed single-seat triplanes	350
E	1915-1916, 1918	'Eindekker' armed single-seat monoplanes.	1,000
F	—	Allotted for Civil Aircraft, but was not used.	—
G	1915-1918	'Grossflugzeug' (Big aeroplane). Mostly twin-engined.	2,000
J	1917-1918	Armoured close support aeroplanes.	800
L	1918	Passenger-carrying aeroplanes.	10
N	1916-1918	Night-bombing aeroplanes.	200
R	1915-1918	'Riesenflugzeug' (Giant aeroplane). Multi-engined.	64
W	1914-1918	Aeroplanes converted to float-planes.	10

TABLE C.—Representative German Air Service Identification Markings

Aircraft Type	Markings	Position on Aircraft			
A.E.G. G III	G.212/15	Occupying all of fin	Halberstadt CLIV	Halb C.L. IV (Rol) 9440/18	Mid-fuselage
Albatros CIII	C.1388/16	Top edge of fin	L.V.G. B III	L.V.G. BIII 3250/18	Fuselage side by cock-pit decking
Albatros DVa	D.5390/17	Bottom of fin			
D.F.W. CV	Cv 9036/18	Rear of fuselage	L.V.G. C V	L.V.G. CV 9740/17	Very large on fuselage side
D.F.W. RII	RII 15/16	Rear of fuselage			
Fokker E.IV	Fok. EIV 189/16	} Bottom edge mid-fuselage	L.V.G. C VI	L.V.G. CVI 7221/18	Mid-fuselage
Fokker D VII	Fok D VII 461/18				

PART 2

CHAPTER ONE

British Service Aircraft Markings

Post-war production to wartime designs. During 1919-1920 a number of deliveries were made from wartime contracts. General finish was khaki-brown fabric with blue-grey panelling. The unusual way of marking the serial number was peculiar to Mann Egerton built D.H.10As F8421-8495.

Reorganisation and Standardisation

During the post-war years a complete reorganisation of the Royal Air Force was carried out. About a quarter of a million personnel were demobilised and the vast total of 22,647 aeroplanes and 103 airships was run-down into a newly planned, compact Air Force.

Reorganisation was followed by a period of standardisation that had visible effects in the matter of markings. Markings could be classified into three distinct groups. Firstly, there were those required by International Convention, indicating national identity. Secondly, those markings decreed by the Air Ministry concerning the general finish identity numbers and specification designations. Thirdly, manufacturers markings; although it was no longer easy to ascertain the maker from a particular style of marking, for in this new era of standardisation, markings were literally to regulation size and style. The foregoing groups applied to aircraft on delivery; fourthly were those markings applied in service such as unit insignia and in a few cases, individual markings.

National Markings

The familiar roundel remained unchanged except for the standardisation of its proportions, and with a bright general finish replacing the drab camouflage; outlining, to give contrast, was no longer necessary. There were no basic changes until August, 1930, then, in order to avoid confusion in identity with French Air Force machines, the order of the colours on the rudder was reversed. Red now came next to the rudder post with blue at the trailing edge and white in between as before; the proportions of the three divisions remaining equal. This change was effected in the Force by October, 1930.

The next change reflected the progress in the performance of aircraft. Faster machines needed smoother control surfaces; the practice of marking stripes on the

rudder was therefore abandoned altogether in 1934. The following year roundel sizes on the wings were regulated to ensure that they did not overlap on to control surfaces.

General Finish

With the cessation of hostilities standard khaki-green varnish was no longer necessary as a camouflage and its issue was suspended, but the need for a protective varnish was in no way affected. For service in the United Kingdom, a clear varnish or aluminium dope was permitted for all types from early 1919 onward, but for aircraft overseas, or liable for shipment abroad, new khaki or brown pigmented dopes were introduced.

The Bristol Fighter originally in khaki-green now has an aluminium doping. The roundel has been re-marked much larger than on wartime Bristol Fighters.

By 1922, the post-war role of the R.A.F. could more clearly be envisaged; that of a Force with its strength mainly employed on policing duties in sub-tropical climes. It was therefore logical that in the general trend towards standardisation, the choice of a standard finish throughout the R.A.F. should rest with specification V84, an aluminium dope already in use in some overseas areas because of its heat-resisting properties. Thus until 1936, an overall aluminium finish was standard, varying from a bright silver to a silvery-grey, depending on factors of time, the number of coatings and the condition of the fabric.

Identification Markings

The authority for allotting serial numbers was the Deputy Director of Aeronautical Inspection. As a result of his review of the serialling system in 1921, a new series came into effect, whereby original serials of ground instructional airframes were cancelled and replaced by a new number suffixed by 'M'. This series started at 1M and is still progressing.

A new trend became evident in 1928 when serials with the 'J' prefix, started at No. 1 in 1918, reached 9999. Instead of continuing into the 'K' series with No. 1, serials had to contain five characters in a letter/numeral combination, thus K1000 was the first serial in the 'K' range. The Naval series, in the same way after reaching N9999 followed on at S1000. 'S' signified 'seacraft' and applied to those aircraft designed for flying over water with the appropriate equipment, flares, dinghies, etc.; but this distinction was abandoned in 1930, thereafter all aircraft coming into the one 'K' series.

Positioning of the serials in black 8 in. characters on each side of the fuselage and rudder is obvious from the many illustrations, but the marking of serials on the underside of the wings is not quite so straightforward. Up to the spring of 1927, only training aircraft, mostly Avro 504Ks and 504Ns, had serials marked under the wings. During 1927 it became general, 30 in. characters being specified and to be clear of the roundels by at least 1 ft. They were marked in black on aluminium doped aircraft reading in opposite directions for port and starboard sides as shown on page 33.

Serials greatly assist in the identification of aircraft of this period shown in photographs. Lest the reader be somewhat indignant that his ability to recognise aircraft types is being questioned, the writer would point out that in the Hawker variants: Hart, Hind, Hardy, Hartebeest, Audax and Demon there was a marked similarity. To tax the reader further, the Hart alone was produced in several versions, known officially as Hart (S.E.B.D.), Hart (T), Hart (Special), Hart (Communication), Hart (Intermediate) and Hart (India). With reference to the Hart (T) trainer alone, K4755, K4940 and K5786 were built respectively by Hawker Aircraft, Armstrong Whitworth and Vickers. It is doubtful if even the most expert could extract this information except by a knowledge of the serials. Here is a marking that is the key to a wealth of detail.

A serial number is also the only means of tracing a particular aircraft. K7414 was the number of a Hawker Audax built by A. V. Roe in 1936. In 1937 this machine served in No. 114 Squadron, but the following year it was reported on the strength of Station Flight, R.A.F. Duxford. During the early war years it was 'logged' by spotters at both Nos. 1 and 11 Flying Training Schools. The next tracing is in 1943—in South Africa! Thus by its individual number can its history be traced.

One irregularity in serials of this period should be mentioned. Aircraft Depots in the Middle East 1923 to 1936 issued an 'R' for 'Rebuilt' which was marked immediately after the prefix letter of the serial. For example, when Fairey IIIF Mk IVB K1715 was rebuilt as a Gordon in December, 1934, it became KR1715.

Miscellaneous Markings

The Aeronautical Inspection Directorate was responsible for many of the miscellaneous markings stencilled or stamped on aircraft. Familiar is the W/T marking necessitated by the general introduction of metal airframes and fitted wireless telegraphy apparatus. To prevent the risk of fire by one part of an aircraft acquiring a charge of electricity and 'sparking over' to another part, and to increase the efficiency of wireless communications, each component is bonded so that it is in good electrical contact with the whole. Before acceptance an aircraft is rigidly checked for bonding and if satisfactory the W/T marking is stencilled on. It appears on the sides of fins and rudders and usually on the underside of mainplanes and ailerons, tailplanes and elevators. Originally it stood for wireless telegraphy but it has become an anachronism in these days of radio telephony.

Each single part of an aircraft is inspected at every stage of its manufacture by a representative of the Aeronautical Inspection Directorate. When each part is completed it is stamped wherever practicable on approval with a metal or a rubber stamp. Major components and assemblies such as the planes will bear an inspector's stamp mark. A typical marking would be 'A.I.D. P567 11.5.34', relating to a particular government inspector and the date of inspection. Many contracting firms also have inspection staffs,

Squadron markings. A Hawker Woodcock (J7971) with the black zig-zag markings used by No. 17 Squadron throughout its successive equipment of Snipes, Woodcocks, Siskins, Bulldogs and Gladiators.

approved by the A.I.D.; in these cases prefix letters on the stamp denote a particular firm and a number the individual inspector. To give a typical example, stamp marking *P. R. Co. 8* related to Pye Radio Company (now Pye Ltd.) Inspector No. 8.

Manufacturers' part numbers appeared on major assemblies in 1 in. stencilled characters. In the case of fabric covered parts the doping scheme was given as a suffix to the number, e.g. C.E.3 would signify Cellon Scheme 'E' three coats, necessary information to ensure that any repair to the fabric was finished in the same scheme.

Manufacturers' Markings

Conspicuous trade marks were not allowed in this period and factory numbers were visible only on **Fairey** aircraft, Short Bros. having given this practice up shortly after the war.

With a standard finish specified, manufacturers had no option in the style of markings, but their interpretation of the official instructions did show slight variations, particularly in regard to the serial number positioned on the fuselage. De Havilland, Bristol and Armstrong Whitworth had a hyphen, e.g., K-4226 (Queen Bee), K-3951 (Bulldog). Westland and Avro aircraft usually had full stops in the manner K.2320. (Wapiti).

Unit Markings

The Air Ministry in 1924 reviewed the policy of unit identification markings on aircraft but no set policy resulted. Meanwhile some squadrons had already adopted an insignia which was provisionally permitted, provided the Air Officer Commanding the Area approved and the marking in no way obscured nationality markings. Direction was however forthcoming in 1924 concerning a standard colour scheme for each flight within a squadron, to be marked on wheel discs. Normally a squadron consisted of three flights, 'A', 'B' and 'C', but in the early post-war years several squadrons functioned on a two-flight basis, i.e. 'A' and 'B' flights only. Red was specified for 'A' flights,

yellow for 'B' flights and green for 'C' flights. Later this same colour coding was used on the fins of flight leaders' aircraft and the practice of painting the wheel discs lapsed.

Lack of central direction in the matter of squadron markings led to some units taking the initiative; forcing A.O.C.'s in 1926 to state a policy to prevent irregularities. Fighting Area went in for bright colours. Inland Area with army co-operation and miscellaneous units used only the numeral of their unit designation. Coastal Area units used various schemes and the Wessex Bombing Area, being apparently operationally conscious, were considering a new overall finish with the object of concealment rather than embellishment.

Squadron badges were permitted on the fins of aircraft. Often this was in the form of a silhouette but elaborate coloured devices were not uncommon. The manner of presentation was no doubt largely dependent upon the ability of the aircrafthand detailed to paint the marking.

Squadron and Unit Badges were not officially recognised by the Chester Herald of the Royal College of Heralds until 1936 when Crown Approval was obtained for some of the devices and mottoes which units had adopted, to be officially recorded. At the same time a standard surrounding frame was approved. Since then, many badges have been, and still are being, approved for formations and units of the Royal Air Force.

Individual letters or numerals were used in some units, but no standard method was promulgated.

Factory marking. The hallmark of Fairey aircraft of prewar days, its factory number adjacent the official serial number. N9678 is a Flycatcher.

67

A typical line-up of the late 'twenties. Armstrong Whitworth Siskin IIIAs with the crosses of No. 29 (Fighter) Squadron. Note that the top front portion of the fuselage is dark green to avoid glare and that below this, faintly visible, is an individual identity marking, J-8664 being B1 of 'B' Flight. In the background are Siskins of No. 43 (Fighter) Squadron.

Retention of Wartime Stocks

From the large stocks of aircraft available after the war, the Sopwith Snipe, showing a marked improvement in performance over the Camel, and having proved itself in combat, was chosen as the standard service fighter. In the new overall silver finish, Snipes were the first to bear the new squadron insignia in 1924, an example being machine E6544 with the zig-zag marking of No. 17 Squadron. A few S.E.5As, Martinsyde Buzzards, and Nieuport Nighthawks were retained in use, but not in squadron service. Only in the early post-war years did single-seat fighters serve in the Middle East or India. Known examples used overseas, in silver finish but with no unit or individual markings except serials, were Snipes: E6617 (Coventry Ordnance Works built); E6939, E6943, F2444 (Napier built); E7565, E7771 (Ruston Proctor built) and E8384 (Portholme built). Nighthawks: JR6925 and JR6926.

Post-War Designs

The markings of post-war fighters that went into squadron service are given below by types. Unless otherwise stated all were in silver overall finish with black serial numbers and squadron markings as shown on page 85. Representative serial numbers appropriate to the squadrons mentioned are given in brackets.

Gloster Grebe and Gamecock

The first of a famous line of fighters, the prototype Grebe, J6969, made it debut at the 1923 Hendon Air Pageant bearing the display number '14' just forward of the fuselage roundels. One hundred and thirty Grebes were built, the first production batch, J7283-7294 all going to No. 25 Squadron. Other squadrons using this fighter were No. 19 (J7417), No. 29 (J7381), No. 32 (J7399) and No. 56 (J7408). No. 29 was one of the first squadrons to extend unit markings to the uppersurface of the top-wing, having the marking XXX in the centre of this wing, occupying some 10 ft.

Grebe J7283 was modified to become the Gamecock prototype. Gamecocks served in Nos. 3, 23, 32 and 43 Squadrons. Two of No. 23's machines were serialled

J7914 and J8406 and being of 'A' Flight had red wheel discs. Readers who have that memorable book 'Reach for the Sky' may recall that Douglas Bader flew in this unit. The black and white checks of No. 43 Squadron were marked forward of the fuselage roundel, along the full length of the top wing and along the fuselage decking, typical examples being J7904, J7905 and J8421.

Hawker Woodcock

The first Hawker fighter, the Woodcock, was used only by Nos. 3 (J7725) and 17 (J7971) Squadrons and the Home Communication Flight. Serialling was in small batches from J6987 the prototype, to J8313 the last production model.

Armstrong Whitworth Siskin

A peculiarity of the Siskin was the large size of the top wing relative to the bottom wing, necessitating the marking of wing roundels on the *underside* of the top wing instead of the lower one.

The Mk IIIA and IIIB were the versions of the Siskin to go into squadron use, production models being numbered from J6998. Several batches were built under subcontract, J8887-8894 by Blackburn, J8937-8966 by Gloster and J9897-9909 by Bristol. Service use was by Squadrons Nos. 1 (J9909), 17, 19, 29 (J8056), 32 (J8864), 41 (J7761), 43 (J8644), 54, 56 and 111 (J8960).

No. 29 Squadron's marking differed slightly from that on their previous Gamecocks, the XXX marking being now marked on both port *and* starboard sides of the wing, and *not* in the centre. The choice of XXX as a marking may be taken as showing a good squadron spirit—being a general brewer's mark for 'Extra Strong'! No. 41 squadron marked their aircraft serials in white to contrast more with their red stripe which extended the length of the fuselage.

Bristol Bulldog

Bulldogs went into service in 1929, remaining in production until 1935 and bridging the serial range from 'J' to 'K', with J9480 the Mk. II prototype and the Mk. IIA

68

production models running in batches from J9567 to K3513. Non-standard IIAs were K2476 fitted with Hartshorn ailerons, K2188 converted to a trainer, K2206 and K2227 with cowled engines. (The Mk. I was not used by the R.A.F.)

Service was in the following squadrons: No. 3 (J9568-9579 were the initial equipment at Upavon, 1929), No. 17 (J9580-9590 initial equipment, 1929), No. 19 (K2155-2166 initial equipment at Duxford, 1931), No. 23 (K1678), No. 29 (K1081), No. 32 (K1606), No. 41 (K2184), No. 54 (K2145), No. 56 (K2225), No. 111 (K2209). It was usual for the fuselage decking to be painted black or khaki-green.

A two-seat trainer version, the Mk. II(T.M.), was serialled K3170-3186, K3923-3953 and K4566-4575. At Cranwell these Bulldogs each had an individual number marked just aft of the roundel, K3925 being '3'.

Gloster Gauntlet

The Gauntlet I first went into production to equip and provide backing for only one squadron, following the successful trials of J9125, the prototype. These aircraft, K4081-4104, came off production from the first day of 1935 and by May, No. 19 Squadron at Duxford had a full establishment of Gauntlets. In this unit flight leaders had their tail fins marked in the appropriate flight colours with a small white dolphin in the middle. It will be remembered that this squadron flew Sopwith Dolphins in the 1914-1918 War, hence the adoption of this device as a squadron badge.

Gauntlet IIs following the Mk. I in production were numbered K5264-5367 and K7792-7891; they were distributed to the following squadrons at the locations given: No. 17 Kenley (K5348), No. 19 Duxford (K5284), No. 32 Biggin Hill (K5294-5301 initial equipment), No. 46 Kenley later moving to Digby (K7794), No. 54 Hornchurch (K5312), No. 56 North Weald (K5291), No. 65 Hornchurch (K5331), No. 66 Duxford (K5313), No. 73 Debden, No. 74 Hornchurch (K7834), No. 79 Biggin Hill (K7869), No. 111 Northolt (K5309), No. 151 North Weald (K7831), No. 213 Church Fenton (K7805).

Gauntlets were used for meteorological work, K7801 being on the strength of Met. Flight, Duxford, 1936. A few were shipped out East; K7852 being at Heliopolis in 1941 and not until February, 1944, was the Gauntlet finally declared obsolete.

Gloster Gladiator

The Gladiator rightly qualifies for an appearance in two Parts of this book. It was in the summer of 1936, when a silver finish was still general, that Nos. 3 and 72 Squadrons received their Gladiators. When war came it was a camouflaged Gladiator of No. 603 Squadron that shot down the first German aircraft over this country and as late as March, 1945, K8043 was still flying.

Early production Gladiators were numbered K6129-6150 and K7892-8077, but only 185 of the 208 were delivered to the R.A.F., the remainder being sold to foreign governments. Squadrons to use the Gladiator were Nos. 3, 17, 19, 33, 54, 56, 65, 72, 73, 79, 80, 87, 247, 263 and in four auxiliary squadrons.

Hawker Fury

Three squadrons used the Fury, the first being No. 43 Squadron at Tangmere in 1931, which took over the first twelve machines of the initial production batch, K1926-1946. Later K1927 was withdrawn and attached to No. 22 Squadron at Martlesham Heath for airscrew trials, its squadron markings having to be painted out. No. 43's markings were as shown in the colour chart towards the end of this book, with a similar dicing along the top wing. The squadron commander had a black and white chequered tail fin, and flight commanders had fins in the appropriate flight colours.

The production of a second batch, K2035-2082, provided the equipment for Nos. 1 and 25 Squadrons. No. 1 Squadron's aircraft bore markings as shown in the chart, but in this unit the squadron commander had the appropriate rank pennant marked as large as the fin of his Fury K2048 would allow. His machine had silver wheel discs, flight commanders having appropriately coloured wheels and fins. Later machines in this unit were marked with identification letters on their engine cowlings, 'A' Flight aircraft being 'A' K2902, 'B' K2042, 'C' K2063 and 'D' K2039.

No. 25 Squadron first took delivery of machines K2052-2062 painting them with their black line markings. To maintain the three squadrons using this type, several small additional batches were produced numbered from K2874, K2899, K3730 and K5663. Perhaps the most famous of Furies were K2039, K2041, K2881 and K5673 of the Aerobatic Flight, No. 1 Squadron. Their performance at pre-war Hendon Air Displays has perhaps never been surpassed. Invited to demonstrate abroad, they were some of the few aircraft bearing R.A.F. markings to fly in foreign countries.

The Fury II with a more powerful Kestrel engine

(Mk. VI in place of a Mk. II) replaced in squadron service the earlier Furies. No. 25 Squadron taking the first eighteen of the Hawker built batch K7263-7285. All other Fury IIs, numbered from K8218, were built under sub-contract by General Aircraft, of which, 43 became instructional airframes, e.g., K8304 as 1706M.

Hawker Demon

It is strange that the two-seat fighter, having proved itself in the 1914-1918 war, should have been allowed to lapse. For, although the Bristol Fighter had been retained in service up until 1932, it was as an army co-operation aircraft that it had been used in the post-war years.

The Demon, appearing in 1933 as the first post-war two-seat fighter, served first in No. 23 Squadron which became a composite unit with two flights of its original Bulldogs and one flight of Demons from a pre-production batch numbered K1951-1955. Squadron markings however were practically identical, and bearing No. 23's colourful red and blue, it was at first difficult to realise that there were two different types

of aircraft when the Demons and Bulldogs were flying in the one formation. Later, when the unit became a full Demon squadron individual identification letters were used, examples being 'H' K2848, 'J' K2847, 'M' K2845 and 'O' K2846. Other units and representative aircraft were: No. 29 Sqn. (K5729), No. 41 Sqn. (K3764-3779 initial equipment), No. 64 Sqn. (K4509, K4511, K4517, etc.), No. 65 Sqn. (K3780-3788 initial equipment), No. 601 (K4500, K4504, K4513, etc.), No. 604 (K4498, K4499, K4501, etc.).

Demons produced after September, 1939, were all built by Boulton Paul and could be distinguished by their serials of K5683 onwards.

After their flying days, Demons were still of use as ground trainers for gunners. These bore the instructional airframe number series, examples with previous identities are as follows: 1003M (K2855), 1005M (K3802), 1030M (K5718), 1038M (K4538), 1109M (K2853), 1147M (K8187), 1234M (K8215), 1235M (K5728), 1655M (K3979), 1760M (K4505), 2352M (K8181), 2395M (K2842).

J9574, the eighth production Bristol Bulldog IIA, is shown here serving with No. 3 (Fighter) Squadron whose aircraft carried a green band along the fuselage side. The fuselage decking of green was usual with Bulldogs to reduce glare for the pilot.

R.A.F. General Purpose 1919-1936

The D.H.9A and Bristol F2B

To equip the post-war Force, aircraft for policing duties overseas were most needed. For this purpose hundreds of D.H.9As and Bristol F2Bs (usually known as Bristol Fighters) built to wartime contracts were retained in service, being used respectively in light bomber and army co-operation squadrons. Not only were additional stocks kept in store, but both types, with several improvements incorporated, were produced in small quantities for some years after the war. These later aircraft could be distinguished by their serials of J6586 and over.

By 1923, most D.H.9As were in the now standard silver finish, unit or individual insignia being the variable markings. Stationed in Iraq were the D.H.9A Squadrons Nos. 8, 30, 55 and 84. The leader of No. 8 using machine E954 had a large winged figure eight marked aft of the fuselage roundel. No. 30's aircraft had 30 marked on their nose. In No. 84 various insignia were used, including a swastika on the fin of H3633. Outstanding in Iraq during 1929 was D.H.9A J8177, painted blood-red overall; it was personal to the A.O.C., Sir Robert Brooke-Popham.

Out in India Nos. 27 and 60 Squadrons flew D.H.9As, No. 27 using individual identification letters 'A' to 'M' marked in white on an 18 in. × 14 in. black rectangle just aft of the fuselage roundels, 'A' being E9687. No. 60 were 'N' to 'Z', 'R' being E8758, 'S' E951 and 'T' E878 being replaced in November, 1929, by J7109 when E878 crashed on landing at Risalpur. At home, Nos. 39 and 100 Squadrons each had eighteen D.H.9As at Grantham in 1925, No. 39's aircraft having a number forward of the fuselage roundel, '6' was J7061 and '7' E960. No. 207 Squadron had a flight identification system marked on their fins, J7041 as 'C' Flight leader had 'C1', the rest of the this flight 'C2' to 'C6'.

With the silver finish, the large serials on wartime Bristol Fighters gave way to standard positioning. As a general rule it could be said that early machines with 'A' or 'B' prefixed serials disappeared in the war, but a few of the 'C' series survived, the Under Secretary of State for Air himself chancing his neck in C766 of No. 6 Squadron as late as 1928. Other Bristols in the E, F and H series were available in their hundreds. Rarely does an aircraft marking appear in Hansard, but shortly after the war a question was raised in the House of Commons about a Bristol Fighter reported missing October, 1918, quoted by number—E2256.

The Bristols were marked by units in various ways, No. 208 Squadron in the Middle East had playing card symbols marked in a white circle on the fin. FR4588 and JR6767

were red hearts, JR6785 a red diamond, JR6788 a black club and F4950 had the white circle only. No. 5 Squadron in India had a black 5 marked as large as the fin would allow, with an individual letter in front of the fuselage roundel.

Bristol Fighters worthy of note are D7864 the first to be fitted with Handley Page automatic slots, J8430 used by the Duke of Windsor when he was Prince of Wales and J8458—the last built.

Armstrong Whitworth Atlas

The Atlas, standard army co-operation type of the early 'thirties was a welcome replacement for the ageing Bristol F2Bs at home in Nos. 2, 4, 13, 16 and 26 (AC) Squadrons, the University Air Squadrons and at training schools. Several batches were produced numbered from J8777, one batch actually bridging the J to K prefix change-over, with J9951-9999 being followed on with K1000-1037. Later batches and overseas service are revealed by K1188, K1474 and K1505 at No. 4 F.T.S. in Egypt, 1932. That several were rebuilt in the Middle East is indicated by the serials on some of No. 208 Squadron's aircraft, JR9958, JR9975 and KR1572. Of the later batches, K1172-1197 and K1454-1506 were built as trainers and K1507-1602 and K2514-2566 as army co-operation aircraft.

Westland Wapiti

The Wapiti as a D.H.9A replacement owed much to its predecessor, for the prototype was built from J8495, the last D.H.9A and the first production Wapitis, J9078-9102 utilised many D.H.9A components. Factory finish for these and subsequent machines can be described as standard; except that the fuselage roundel was centred directly on the gunner's cockpit making an admirable aiming point of the poor chap. Fortunately for his peace of mind these were days of peace. The length of the fuselage decking was painted black to reduce glare. Serials were originally in Westland style, e.g., 'J.9380', but this was not always followed for re-marking in service.

As a general purpose aircraft it fulfilled many roles in different units and bore their varied markings. The same white lettering on black rectangles of No. 27 Squadron's D.H.9As appeared on the nose of their Wapitis, A, B and C being respectively K1299, K1284 and K1283. When standard frames for unit motifs were introduced, the unit badge, an elephant, was marked in a frame on the fin. This was symbolic of the unit's equipment twenty years earlier—Martinsyde Elephants. Fuselage serials in this unit were annotated according to the role of the aircraft, army co-operation or light bomber, machine 'J' being K-1300^{AC} and 'R' K-2257^B. No. 60 Squadron carried on their letter system, aircraft 'Z' of 'C' Flight being J9733. No. 30 Squadron after experiencing difficulty in locating aircraft force-landed in the desert, marked their wing tips red up to 5 ft. inboard and their tail planes similarly up to 2 ft. inboard. Wing roundels were marked over this portion. J9412 was a typical example. The C.O. of No. 55 Squadron had 55 on the nose of his aircraft (K1395), with the rest of the squadron marked A3 K1391, C2 J9632, etc.

At home several squadrons of the Auxiliary Air Force used the Wapiti, No. 605 Squadron A.A.F. placed their unit crest forward of the fuselage serial position and further forward the number—605.

Westland Wallace

The factory finish of the Wapiti applied also to the Wallace with the addition of fabric panel fasteners to facilitate servicing. Serials were in small batches between K3562 and K5082 for the Mk. I and from K6012 for the Mk. II with its 'glasshouse like' cockpit cover. Wallaces served in several R.A.F. units and A.A.F. squadrons. Machines K3564 and K4018 had the marking 501 in 14 in. figures between the fuselage roundel and serial number, denoting No. 501 Squadron A.A.F. Several ended their days as instructional airframes, 1813M being ex-K3907 and 2537M ex-K8701.

Fairey Fawn and Fox

Markings on Fairey types were standard except for the factory number appearing adjacent to, but smaller than, the serial number on the fuselage.

The Fawn originally intended as a D.H.9A replacement equipped three squadrons in the mid 'twenties. Fawns of No. 12(B) Squadron, e.g. J7212 (F513) had the number 12 marked in a small circle on the fin. In No. 100(B) Squadron an individual number was placed aft of the roundel, J7771 (F786) being '4'. No. 11 used Fawns.

With the Fox high-speed light bomber a new Fairey style became evident, that of having the length of the fuselage decking in an anti-glare black. Fuselage roundels were some 4 ft. aft of the gunner's cockpit. The prototype built as a private venture did not bear service markings

Fairey Tails. The reason for the adoption of a fox-head badge in No. 12 (B) Squadron is evident when J7943 reveals the aircraft as a Fairey Fox. No. 6 (B) Sqn. had a 'gunner's stripe' on the fin with the squadron crest in its centre.

Demons and Hinds looked almost alike, but whereas Demons were fighters and qualified for the bright colours of fighter squadrons, Hinds as light bombers could bear only their unit number, in this case No. 40 Squadron. Hawker Harts (India) of No. 39 Squadron in India shortly before the war. Note the unit badge on the fin in a grenade frame, denoting the unit's role as a bomber squadron. The badge itself is a bomb with wings.

and production for the R.A.F. was to equip No. 12 Squadron only, examples being J7941 (F847) and J9028 (F955).

Fairey IIIF and Gordon

Factory finish for both these types was as for the Fox. Fairey IIIFs are a complicated series, produced both as naval (N and S serials) and general purpose (J and K) aircraft, but there were interchanges of duties. Basically Gordons were IIIFs with radial engines and many IIIFs were converted subsequently to Gordons with no resultant change in markings. Fortunately a definite ruling can be given to this aspect; K1729-1748 and K2603 upwards were built as Gordons, all with numbers other than those were converted IIIFs.

Production IIIFs numbered from J9053 served during the early 'thirties with these day bomber squadrons: No. 8 (at Aden), No. 14 (Amman), Nos. 35 and 207 (Bircham Newton), No. 45 (Helwan) and No. 47 (Khartoum). These same units were re-issued with Gordons. No. 47, who marked 47 on their machines as large as the nose would allow, received their first Gordon, K2630, in October, 1932. No. 207 Squadron had the unit number marked in 1 ft. figures, just forward of the fuselage roundel. Flight numbers the same size appeared on the fin, in the same way as the unit's old D.H.9As, 'B2' of 'B' Flight being K1167 (F1311).

Hawker Hart, Hardy, Hind and Audax

So uniformly finished on delivery were the Hart and Hart variants, that their general description is epitomised in the word standard. Except for No. 605 Squadron A.A.F., who took it upon themselves to have a green fuselage decking, finish was silver overall.

Hart light bombers were built by several firms: J9933-9947, K2424-2475, Hawkers; K2967-3030, K3808-3854, Vickers; K3031-3054, K3855-3872, K3875-3904, K4437-4495 Armstrong Whitworth. In addition Hawker-built K2083-2132, K3921-3922 and K8627-8631 were produced specially for units in India. Hind light bombers were made in three batches numbered from K4636, K5368 and K6613. Audax to re-equip army co-operation squadrons were built in several batches from K1995, complicated by certain machines from K3128 and K4365 being converted to Hart

(Specials); in addition K4838-4862 and K5561-5585 were equipped for service in India only. The Hardy was used by three squadrons in succession, No. 30, No. 6 and No. 237, each using the same equipment, handed from one to the other, from the forty-seven production models built by Gloster's; K4050-4070, K4306-4321 and K5914-5923.

Squadron markings usually took the form of unit designation numbers marked on the fuselage side by the rear gunner's cockpit, with unit crests marked on the fin. No. 12 had the number in thick 15 in. figures on its Harts with the unit's fox-head badge, recalling earlier equipment, marked on the fin. Later this unit had Hinds, e.g. K5395, similarly marked. Some other squadrons marked in this manner with a representative aircraft indicated were: No. 18, 12 in. figures (Hart K2431); No. 21, 12 in. figures (Hind K5373); No. 57, 22 in. figures in appropriate flight colours for flight leaders' aircraft, remainder black (Hart K2448); No. 98, 12 in. figures (Hind K5368), No. 142, 12 in. figures (K3901 the first aircraft delivered to the unit); No. 603 A.A.F., 10 in. figures (Hart K3859). No. 15 Squadron differed by using Roman numerals in the same position, thus XV appeared on its Harts (K3903) and later its Hinds (K5463). On the Audax of No. 16 Squadron (K3701) a 4 in. thick black band was painted around the fuselage, just forward of the roundel. Subsequently many Harts, Hinds and Audax were converted to trainers.

Hawker Hector

Of the Hart variants, this could be most easily identified by the shape of its nose to accommodate the Dagger engine. Serialling, too, was straightforward, the prototype, K3719, was a modified Audax and all production was by Westland's only—K8090-8167 and K9687-9786. First deliveries were to No. 4 Squadron (K8091-8099) in February, 1937, and later to Nos. 2, 26, 53 and 59 Squadrons. No. 2's machines had a black 18 in. equilateral triangle over the serial position, with the number marked across it, figures being outlined where necessary. In 1937 Hectors of Nos. 4 and 13 (AC) Squadrons were painted with distemper to assist recognition by ground troops during manoeuvres. K8120 of No. 4 Squadron was painted light green and bore the Army's II Divisional Sign on the fin.

CHAPTER FOUR

Bomber and Transport Aircraft in the R.A.F. 1919-1936

The Pennant on this Vickers Vernon of No. 70 (B.T.) Squadron indicates that it is employed on Royal Mail Service. This picture gives an idea of the enormous fuselage roundel on Vernons and seemingly the serial number has been enlarged to match.

The D.H.10 and Vickers Vimy

At the time of the Armistice a squadron of heavy bombers, Handley Page V/1500s, were forming up at Bircham Newton with the object of raiding Berlin. Had the war continued, raids on Germany from Britain would have become repetitive operations. The Armistice produced an anti-climax, production was geared and deliveries of some bombers continued to complete contracts. The R.A.F., able to take its pick for post-war use, ruled out the Handley Pages as uneconomical, the D.H.10 and Vimy being retained.

D.H.10s with a finish as shown on page 65 were used by No. 120 Squadron at Hawkinge for a mail service to Cologne for the British Army of Occupation. September, 1921, the R.A.F. standardised on the Liberty-engined D.H.10 using them in No. 216 Squadron in the Middle East, E7847 and E7854 (built by Siddeley Deasy Car Co.) being examples. In 1923 all were withdrawn from service.

The Vimy will be ever remembered as the first aircraft to fly the Atlantic non-stop in that memorable flight by Alcock and Brown, June, 1919. This particular Vimy was not a service aircraft and being before the time of civil registration, it carried no markings. It had a clear finish.

B9952-9954, the Vimy prototypes, were followed by

production batches in the F, H and J serial ranges. Early deliveries were in khaki-brown and blue-grey, but late production and those used overseas were in silver overall. No. 70 Squadron in Iraq marked fuselage serials in the normal position, but in large black characters in isometric projection; F3184 and H654 were so marked. Not until March, 1933, were Vimys finally withdrawn from service, H657 at No. 4 F.T.S. Egypt being one of the last in use.

Bomber Transports—Vickers Vernon, Victoria and Valentia

Bomber transports of the years 1923-1936 were all Vickers aircraft in an overall silver finish. The Vernon used by Nos. 45 and 70 Squadrons was first to enter service. No. 45 marked a camel motif on the nose of their aircraft, recalling their wartime service as a Sopwith Camel squadron and symbolic of their post-war stations in the Middle East. No. 70 kept an unmarked silver finish, except for national and serial markings, e.g., J6872.

Victorias replacing the Vernons were used by Nos. 70 and 216 Squadrons and the Indian Command Bomber Transport Flight. Several versions went into service with different engines; Mk. IV (Lion V), Mk. V (Lion XIA), Mk. VI (Pegasus II L3), then came the Valentia, an improved Victoria with a strut-braced undercarriage. There has been much controversy over the identities of these types. J8231 was reported by enthusiasts as a Victoria V, Victoria VI and a Valentia. In truth all were right! This machine was converted Mk. V to Mk. VI in February, 1935, and to a Valentia the following December. In fact, all Victorias surviving 1935-1936 were converted to Valentias, but machines numbered K3599 and above were built initially as Valentias.

Night Bomber. A Heyford 1A of No. 10 (B) Squadron bears the squadron crest on the nose and the individual letter D in yellow in two positions. The serial number, K4032, is 'lost' in the dark finish and its presentation in white, under the wings, is 'lost' in shadow.

Identification signs in units were usually by 2 ft. black letters marked each side of the nose and repeated on the fuselage sides some 10 ft. aft of the roundel centre. In No. 216 Squadron, J9760 and J9764 were 'A' and 'E' respectively.

Day Bombers—Boulton Paul Sidestrand and Overstrand

Well-known as these two aircraft are, they formed the successive equipment of one squadron only—No. 101. The prototype Sidestrand appearing in 1926 had a silver finish with the fuselage decking in khaki-green only as far back as the rear gunner's cockpit, but on production models this ran the full length of the fuselage decking and was extended over the nose and along the bottom of the fuselage; thus only the fuselage sides were left in silver. Later, black replaced the khaki-green. The squadron number was placed as illustrated with an individual letter (12 in.) forward on the nose, both in appropriate flight colours, e.g. J9176 of 'B' Flight had 100 and F in yellow.

The same identification system remained in 1935 for the Overstrands. They differed by having the fuselage decking only in a light green, with an 18 in. letter on the nose, just aft of the turret. Four Overstrands, including J9186, the prototype, were built from Sidestrand airframes; additionally production Overstrands were numbered K4546-4565 and K8173-8177.

Torpedo-Bombers—Hawker Horsley and Vickers Vildebeest

The Horsley, standard torpedo-bomber of the 'twenties, was finished in the usual silver, but its ungainly engine cowling, painted black, did not give it the sleek appearance characteristic of later Hawker biplanes. J7511 the prototype was followed by several production batches. No. 100 Squadron had the unit number marked forward of the fuselage roundel with an individual number aft, J8607 being 100·12 (port side, figure height = roundel diameter). No. 36 Squadron used only an individual letter aft of this roundel, S1443 was 'M' and S1604 'P'. Horsleys were also used by Nos. 33 and 504 Squadrons. Machine J8611 can be linked with later days, being used as a Merlin engine test-bed.

Vildebeests in overall silver finish replaced the Horsleys. No. 100 Squadron discontinued marking the unit number but retained the individual number system. No. 36 followed this example, K2923 being 13. Marks could be identified by number. Mk. I, S1707-1715 and K2810 upwards; Mk. II, K2916 upwards; Mk. III, K4156 upwards and Mk. IV, K6369 upwards.

The Heavy Bombers—Vickers Virginia, Handley Page Hyderabad, Hinaidi, Heyford and Fairey Hendon

During 1923 a new finish, Nivo, an overall dull green was instituted for night bomber aircraft. The night-roundel was re-introduced for all positions and rudder striping was discontinued. Serials remained in black at their normal positions, but on the underside of the lower plane, the numbers were in white, 4 ft. high, 4 in. thick strokes. This finish applied to Virginias, Hyderabads and Hinaidis; it also applied to Heyfords and Hendons with the difference that from the 1936 Air Exercises, these serials were marked in black. Exceptions to this finish were prototypes such as J6994 the first Hyderabad.

Most squadrons used a letter identification system, Hyderabad J8813 having a large, white thick E by the front gunner's cockpit. Hyderabad serials were confined to the 'J' range, but Hinaidis had both 'J' and 'K' serials as three of No. 99 Squadron's aircraft will show—J9303, K1069 and K1925. Virginias were built in quantity, a total of 179 in fact, in several batches as the strength of No. 58 (B) Squadron in 1936 will show: J7132, J7422, J7427, J7438, J7566, J7718, K2324, K2334, K2336, K2666, K2674, K2676.

The Heyford, best-known of all the pre-war bombers, was produced initially for No. 99 Squadron, K3490 being its first Heyford, arriving on 7th November, 1933. Other Mk. Is numbered consecutively followed. These aircraft were marked with an identification letter in dull red on the nose, repeated on the fuselage sides, just aft of the roundel, 'C' Flight machines 'T', 'V', 'W' and 'X' being K3491, K3495, K3497 and K3499 respectively. K4021 upwards were Mk. IA bombers built for No. 10 Squadron; this unit had a similar system, K4034 being 'C'. Later came the Mk. II of which K4863-4875 were allotted to No. 7 Squadron. By the time the Mk. III was in production, i.e. machines numbered upwards of K5180, the Heyford was selected for Nos. 9, 97, 102, 149 and 166 Squadrons. Marks I, IA and II were withdrawn before the war, but the Mk. III served in yellow training colours 1939-1940.

The Hendon, first of the monoplane bombers and last to be finished in the dark green, was used only by No. 38 Squadron. Apart from K1695, the prototype, only 14 (K5085-5098) were built.

Sidestrands had fuselages finished in dark green and silver. The unit number '101' and individual letter 'G' were in standard 'B' flight colours—yellow. The outrig on the rudder bears a small marking, 'W/T', to signify that it is in good electrical contact with the fuselage!

CHAPTER FIVE

Training and Communications Aircraft 1919-1939

crest appeared on the fin and 14 (1 ft. black figures), the individual number, was placed centrally on the fin. During the War, G-ADLF was 'conscripted' as 2891M for ground instruction.

Training Equipment

There were so many trainers provisioned during the war available for post-war training that even ten years after the Armistice, Avro 504Ks such as 'H3069' at Leuchars were still being roughly handled by pupil-pilots. By 1925 steps to provide new trainers resulted in two orders of one hundred each, for Avro 504Ns (J8496-8595 and J8676-8775), with later orders following until K2423 the very last of the famous 504 series was delivered. By then, another Avro, the Tutor, had emerged to become the standard trainer of the early 'thirties—but on 22nd February, 1932, K2567 entered service, the first of thousands of Tiger Moths. The Avro monopoly of service training aircraft was breaking!

Trainers received the standard silver/aluminium finish until 1935 when a distinctive orange-yellow overall finish was introduced. Some trainers were not completely in this finish, for example, engine cowlings were sometimes left in their shining metal finish. Roundels and other markings were in no way affected. The yellow finish did not apply to all training type aircraft, nor was it exclusive to this class of aircraft. It was specified for all aircraft on the establishment of training units liable to be used by inexperienced pilots. The object was to warn others, and as to the choice of colour—yellow in the International Colour Code is 'Fever. Keep Well Away'.

Service flying schools gave complete flying training to enable trainees to enter squadron service. Thus many service types of aircraft were held. Batches of Hawker Harts starting with K3146-3158 were built specifically as trainers and many later machines, built as light bombers, were eventually converted for training. With the creation of a Volunteer Reserve and the general expansion of the R.A.F. in 1935, many Elementary and Reserve Flying Training Schools were opened to which hundreds of Harts, Hinds and Audaxs' were allotted. General finish from 1937 was yellow overall except for engine cowlings and the metal panel at the rear of the fuselage in polished duralumin finish (example Audax K5208 of No. 11 F.T.S.).

Civil aircraft, for once, enter our survey, for some service personnel received initial training at civil flying schools under Government contract. A typical machine was Blackburn B2 in silver finish at Hanworth, bearing the registration G-ADLF on the fuselage sides. The school

The R.A.F. College, Cranwell

Cadets with permanent commissions received their flying instruction at Cranwell which had the largest airfield in the United Kingdom. The College was divided into three squadrons 'A', 'B' and 'C' and in the early days their aircraft were identified by a squadron letter/individual number system, e.g. Avro 504K still in wartime khaki-green had 4 marked in a 9 in. letter 'C' on the engine cowling (white on black cowling). F4751, one of the eighteen Bristol Fighters on strength in 1924 had B4 in 9 in. black letters on the side of the nose of the machine, which had a clear finish. When the silver finish became general, Cranwell fitted into the normal system of identification numbers forward of the roundel.

Central Flying School, Upavon

Formed in 1912 the C.F.S. became the school for instructors and as such it had a variety of equipment besides basic training types. A display team from this school using D.H. Genet Moths J8816-8821 were the first to pioneer formation flying—upside down! Tutors K3238-3242 also formed an aerobatic flight and later Tutors K3362-3365 were used with the upper-surfaces of both wings painted with a brilliant orange Japanese Rising Sun. There were no roundels on the top wing. This was for the benefit of spectators, facilitating observation as to whether or not the machines were flying upside-down. No identification characters, apart from the usual serial numbers were marked on these aircraft. It was, however, noticeable that the C.F.S. advocated anti-glare precautions and painted the fuselage decking of their Tutors and Moths a dark green.

Flying Training Schools

Backbone of flying training in the 'twenties and early 'thirties were the five Flying Training Schools. No. 1 at Netheravon using Avro 504Ns and Atlases before disbandment in 1930. Later No. 1 was re-formed at Leuchars for Fleet Air Arm training. No. 2 at Digby, having moved there from Duxford in June, 1924; D.H.9As, Bristol Fighters, Vimys, Avro 504 K/Ns, Siskins and IIIFs were used before the influx of the Hart trainers. No. 3 at Grantham (formerly named Spitalgate) had a variety of successive equipment, and No. 4 in Egypt, at Abu Sueir, used Avros, D.H.9As, Bristol Fighters, Vimys, Atlases and Audaxs', with an odd IIIF (J9140) for navigational training. No. 5 had a variety of types at Sealand, e.g. Snipe

An Oxford University Air Squadron Tutor bearing its appropriate crest. The fuselage band is, of course, the University colour of dark blue. The diagonal line across the fuselage is shadow and should not be mistaken for a marking.

E6837, Siskin III J7177, Atlases J9436, K1501 and K2523, Tutors K3409 and K3441, Harts (T) K4894, 4921 and K4925. In these schools it was usual for an individual character to be marked adjacent the roundels on the fuselage, e.g. Avro 504K J9263 was 'M' of 3 F.T.S. and Tiger Moth K2575 was '3' of 3 F.T.S.

With the expansion in the mid-'thirties came the opening of more schools; No. 6 Netheravon, No. 7 Peterborough, No. 8 Montrose, No. 9 Thornaby, No. 10 Ternhill and No. 11 Wittering. Then came the opening of Elementary and Reserve Flying Training Schools using chiefly Tiger Moths, Hart and Hart variants and by 1938 Magisters. As the illustrations show, training was also carried out in Auxiliary Air Force Squadrons and University Air Squadrons.

The School of Army Co-operation had undoubtedly the most revolutionary equipment, by using in 1934-1939 the Cierva C.30A autogiro, built under licence by A. V. Roe and appropriately named by the R.A.F.—Rota (K4230-4239). Finish was silver overall, but a wingless aircraft set a problem in national markings. A 24 in. roundel was marked on the top of the fuselage, just behind the rear cockpit and immediately below it were similar roundels on the fuselage sides. Serials were marked in the fuselage position only in the Avro manner—K.4296 (which, incidentally, was the number of a float-plane version of the Rota).

Communications Aircraft

Using a variety of equipment marked with the unit insignia of two chevrons on their fins, including Fairey IIIF J9061 for the personal use of the Duke of Windsor, then Prince of Wales; No. 24 was the only squadron with a communications role. There were, however, several flights overseas with this function; the Palestine Communication Flight in 1936 had two Gordons, J9798 and K2707. At home certain aircraft for this duty were held by station flights. In 1933, for example, sixteen Gipsy Moths

were allotted to certain stations. Markings were standard.

Some Harts were built specially for communications duties, K3873-4 being the first. A Dragon Rapide K5070 in silver finish was ordered in 1934 specially for the use of the Air Council Members.

Ground Training

Many airframes after useful flying service continued to serve as ground trainers under a new identity in the 'M' series; representative examples are:—Atlas 641M (ex-K1514), Gipsy Moth 709M (ex-K1849), Avro 504N 780M (ex-K2372), Rota 1142M (ex-K4237), Avro 504N 1251M (ex-K2402), Tutor 1699M (ex-K4830), Fury 1721M (ex-K8284) and Prefect 4039M (ex-K5067).

Notes on Identification of Training Types

D.H.53: light monoplane trainer, known serials J7268-7273 and J7324-7327. Hawker Tomtit: limited production service in No. 3 F.T.S., J9782 was No. 9 of that School. Moths: batch numbered from J8815 were Genet Moths; a batch from J9103 were Cirrus Moths and batches from J9922, K1103, K1200 and K1825, Gipsy Moths; K2567 and above Tiger Moths. Tutors: K1230-1240 and K1787-1796 had Mongoose IIIc uncowled engines, K1797 and batches from K2496 had cowled Lynx IV engines, K8172 was the last built. Hinds: 124 converted to trainers from 'K' serialled batches. L7174 onwards were built as trainers. Magisters: production from L5912 in yellow overall with polished metal cowlings.

A Cambridge University Air Squadron Tutor in the air bearing its appropriate crest. By the nature of the marking on the fin, it is evident that this is the C.O.'s machine. Some C.U.A.S. Tutors had a fuselage band similar to the O.U.A.S. aircraft, but in light blue with a red stripe.

R.A.F. AIRCRAFT MARKINGS 1920–1939

BADGES OF RANK MARKED ON AIRCRAFT FLOWN REGULARLY BY OFFICERS OF AIR RANK OR BY SENIOR OFFICERS

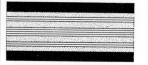

MARSHAL OF THE
ROYAL AIR FORCE

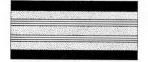

AIR CHIEF MARSHAL

AIR MARSHAL

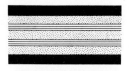

AIR VICE-MARSHAL

AIR COMMODORE

GROUP CAPTAIN

WING COMMANDER

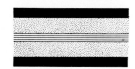

SQUADRON LEADER

 AIR FORCE BLUE

 ROYAL BLUE

 RED

MISCELLANEOUS MARKINGS 1920–1939

TYPICAL BONDING MARKINGS
(Approx. 6 ins. square or 3 ins. dia. circles)

RED CROSS FIRST AID
STOWAGE PANEL
(4 ins. Cross x 1 in. thick arms)

D.T.D. FUEL SPECIFICATION
224 in RED 230 in BLUE
(1 inch digits marked
adjacent fuel orifice)

REPRESENTATIVE UNIT BADGES

No. 19 Sqn. (Gauntlets)
4 inch high on centre of fin

No. 207 Sqn. (Gordons)
6 ins. long above unit
identification letter/numeral

No. 10 Sqn (Heyfords)
18 inch high on
nose of aircraft

No. 23 Sqn.
(Bulldogs and Demons)
6 inch high fin marking

UNIT SYMBOL FRAMES–OPERATIONAL AIRCRAFT 1936–1939

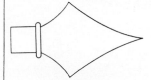

(Spearhead)
All Fighter Squadrons

(Grenade)
Bomber and Torpedo–Bomber Units

(Six Point Star)
General Reconnaissance
and Army Co-operation
Aircraft

British Naval and Coastal Aircraft

This line-up of Fairey Fly-catchers of No. 405 Fleet Fighter Flight shows well the meticulous attention the Fleet Air Arm gave to the marking of their aircraft.

The distinction between Naval and Coastal aircraft was that the former were chiefly ship-borne and came under the Admiralty for operational control, whereas coastal aircraft, including flying-boats of general reconnaissance squadrons, came under the Air Ministry both administratively and operationally. The Admiralty sought continually throughout this period to wrest full control of naval aviation from the Air Ministry, and in 1937 they succeeded.

NAVAL AIRCRAFT

Naval Aircraft Markings

The finish for all naval aircraft was silver overall. Generally the markings described on pages 65-67 apply with one major difference dating from the late 'twenties. Naval aircraft had a thick stripe or panel on the fuselage as illustrated. This was sometimes in colour, but often in black. On this, either in black or white to contrast, were tactical recognition numbers allotted within a 1-999 range. The manner of presentation was apparently not fully documented for there were many variations.

On some aircraft this panel replaced fuselage roundels, but particularly on foreign service such as the China Station, roundels were retained, recognition numbers and bands being either forward or aft of this. Serial numbers were normally marked in the standard manner on rudders and on the fuselage sides except for Ospreys and Nimrods in certain units, but serials did not appear on the under-surface of the lower planes. Recognition numbers were often repeated in this position in black without the coloured panel background. This was often pointless as bomb-racks when fitted, partially obscured this number. In some torpedo-bomber squadrons the marking was repeated yet again on the top wing. To analyse Baffin K3553:—

Fuselage side (Port)	←–/61/ * (yellow band)	
Top Wing, Upper Surface	*61 ↑	61*
Bottom Wing, Lower Surface	*61 ↑	19*

Where ↑ = direction of travel, * = roundel.
Number was in 24 in. figures.

Fleet flights were re-organised into squadrons April, 1933, and the allocation of numbers was revised but the system remained. Twelve numbers were allotted to each squadron, e.g. No. 811 Squadron made up of six aircraft each from Nos. 465 and 466 Torpedo Bomber Flights on H.M.S. *Furious* were Nos. 601-612. These numbers remained irrespective of replacement aircraft, thus when the unit re-equipped, 609 was first a Baffin (S1570) then a Swordfish (K8840).

By 1939 there had been a change-over to a new three-code system. Carrier aircraft had a three symbol combination; as, for example, W4F on Shark K8518 denoting the particular carrier, unit, and individual identity within the unit. Aircraft on ships other than carriers had a single number/single letter combination and land-based machines bore no indication of their unit, only an individual letter.

Unit and Individual Markings

Machines other than fighters had purely functional markings with a chequered tail-fin denoting a formation leader as the only embellishment. Fighters on the other hand had various schemes which on Nimrod S1630 extended to three rows of dicing along the top wing and fuselage decking. Ships' crests were sometimes marked in the centre of the fin; or, in the case of No. 801 Fleet Fighter Squadron, a squadron marking was adopted.

Fleet Equipment

Times and equipment change. In 1918 nearly all 2-3 seat float planes were of Short design, but within a few years Fairey's had taken the lead and could proudly boast that five out of every six Fleet aircraft were of their design. The remainder were chiefly Blackburn types. As previously mentioned, Fairey aircraft bore visible factory numbers adjacent to official serials, but the practice had to stop for security reasons in 1937, when consecutive factory numbering would have compromised a new system of serialling, whereby certain blocks of numbers were omitted. Blackburn's as early as 1920 had to give up marking their conspicuous trade mark, Cuckoo N8011 of No. 210 Squadron in silver finish being the last known example to bear this marking. The Cuckoo can be mentioned as the machine to bear the most uncomplimentary marking ever to be borne on an operational type of aircraft. On its heavily, perhaps excessively loaded, Mk. II version with a Wolseley Viper engine, these words were painted in red along the fuselage side:

DANGER: WHEN CARRYING A TORPEDO MACHINE MUST NOT BE DIVED FOR ATTACK UNLESS TANKS ARE HALF FULL.

A warning that did not instil confidence in the aircraft!

A Fairey IIIF in Fleet markings. The naval identification band is marked in a blue band and the tail chequered in blue and white denotes a formation leader. This aircraft ended up in different markings, for it was sold, together with IIIFs S1377, S1786 and S1817 to the Greek Navy.

Target Aircraft—The Queen Bee

This era saw the introduction of pilotless aircraft into service with the Queen Bee (basically a wireless-controlled Tiger Moth) becoming standard gunnery practice aircraft for the Fleet. Queen Bees at inland establishments had the ends of the top wings painted blood-red up to 4 ft. inboard. General finish was silver with the serial marking on the fuselage and under the wings in typical 'D.H. fashion'—K-3598. Service identification markings were usually placed aft of the roundel in characters as large as the fuselage side would allow, K-5112 was **LA** and K5110 of 3 A.A.C.U. Malta was **28**. Some later machines were painted red overall.

Notes on Fleet Aircraft by Types

Blackburn: Fuselage serials marked in the manner—N.9832. Blackburn I S.1049/46/, Darts N.9808/63/ and N.9817/73/. Ripons had black engine cowlings, an example in service being S.1265 with /75/ in a yellow band immediately aft of fuselage roundel. Baffins, many of which were converted Ripons, were given dark-green fuselage deckings. K4071-80 built as Baffins for No. 810 Squadron. Last production

model, K4778 to No. 812 Squadron. Service example S.1656/612/. Shark: Fuselage decking dark green. Prototype K4295. First production K4349-64 for No. 820 Squadron. Production Mk. II K4880 upwards, production Mk. III K8891 onwards. Service examples K5619/682/ and K8466/659/. Instructional airframes: 990M (ex-K4357), 1752M (ex-L2374) and 1867M (ex-K8906).

Fairey: Flycatcher N163-5 (F406-8) Prototypes. Production from N9616 (F435). S1418 last production model. Service examples N9982/5/ and N9983/7/. IIID: N9451-9499 (F345-393) first production batch. Service examples: N9777 (F641) of M.A.E.E. Felixstowe numbered **3** for 1924 King's Cup Air Race entry, S1102-5 (F840-3) used in first Service Cape Flight, 1926. IIIF: Production (interim version) from S1140 (F881), Mk. I S1147 up, Mk. II S1208 up, Mk. III S1303 up and Mk. IV K1158 up. So complicated were the structural differences in IIIFs that a designation was usually marked by the serial, e.g. S1340 (F1080) was followed by IIIF Mk. IIIM in 2 in. lettering. 'M' stood for 'All metal except wood ribs in fin and rudder'. Other suffixes were 'C' (Composite), 'C & M' (Metal except wings and tail unit), 'A/M' (All metal) and 'B' (strengthened for catapulting) applicable to all numbered between S1474 and S1864. In addition to this marking on the fuselage, all main components were stencilled in 1 in.-2 in. letters with one of the following: 'C' for composite, 'WP' for wooden parts or 'MP' for metal parts. All IIIFs had black fuselage deckings.

The Hawker Ospreys and Nimrods of No. 800 Fleet Fighter Squadron show many variations in markings. The three leading Ospreys 123 (K5756), 124 (K5753) and 125 (K5744) have red markings, with the formation leader identified by red and white checks on the fin and tailplane. Flight leaders have this portion in a particular colour.

Seal: basically radial-engined IIIF. Production from K3477 (F1843). Service example K3535/813/. Seafox: shipboard seaplanes, prototypes K4304-5, production batches from K8569 and L4519. Service use K8574-5 H.M.S. *Neptune*, K8581-2 H.M.S. *Ajax*, etc. Swordfish: pre-war examples K5660-2 (F2142-4) prototypes. Production from K5926. Decking was not normally painted, although it was a regulation in at least one squadron that fuselage decking would be black. Service examples K6009/912/ chequered fin, K8375/610/ later K8376 was /610/, L9717 /A4S/.

Hawker: Nimrod, Mk. I numbered S1577 up, Mk. II from K2909. Osprey Mk. I numbered S1677 and K2774 up, Mk. III S1699 and K3615 up, Mk. IV K5742 up. Not all served with the Fleet—K3616-9 were allotted to No. 24 Squadron.

Two very early types in this period are the Parnall Panther with post-war production by Bristol's of N7400-7549 following the wartime Parnall-built prototypes N91-96 and the Westland Walrus N9500-9535 following the design of the equally ugly Armstrong Whitworth Tadpole J6585.

COASTAL AIRCRAFT

Flying-Boats—General Markings

During the early post-war years there remained a few F5 flying-boats in their various wartime finishes, but for new aircraft an aluminium doped finish was specified for the superstructure and a high polish for hulls, the woodwork taking on an almost reddish-brown gloss. Hull roundels were thinly outlined in white. Later for metal hulls a white enamel was used until 1931 when it was changed to grey marine, cellulose enamel. The conditions set out on pages 65-67 apply with hulls being treated as fuselages for marking purposes, but with the observation that on hulls the roundel was set well back as illustrated. Southampton flying-boats of the Far East Flight, 1927, were in gleaming white with one to four black bands marked around the hull for individual identification. At moorings, it was found that barnacles attached themselves only to this *striped* portion—a point *against* aircraft markings!

Notes on Flying-Boat Markings by Type

Saro: Cloud, prototype K2681 and production K2894-8, K3722-9 and K4300-2. Used at Calshot for training. London, roundels marked on underside of top wing instead of lower wing. K3560 prototype, K5908 first production. No. 201 Squadron marked individual letters as large as fin would allow, 'R' being K5909.

Short: Rangoon, serials S1433-5, K2134 and K2809. Singapore: N179 prototype, several production batches ending at K8859. Mk. III examples K3592 '2' of 210 Squadron, K4578 of 203 Squadron marked with '4' (2 ft.) under pilot's cabin. K6914 'C' of No. 209 Squadron.

Supermarine: Seagull (all marks) highly polished hulls. Known serials N9605 and N9642-4. Southampton: wing roundels inboard by one sixth of span. Mk. II S-1299 had a red 'A' outlined in in white on the nose. In No. 210 Squadron serial numbers less prefix letters were repeated in 2 ft. black figures forward on the fuselage side, under pilot's cockpit, examples (S)1464 and (K)2965. Scapa: S1648 prototype,

K4191-4200 and K7304-6 production, used by No. 202 Squadron. Stranraer: K3973 prototype, production from K7287. Used first by No. 228 Squadron. K7301 served both in Nos. 209 and 240 Squadrons. Walrus: Prototype K4797. Production K5772-5783, K8338-8345, L2169-2336, etc. When allotted to Catapult Flights, numbers such as '053' marked forward on hull side in 2 ft. black figures.

General Reconnaissance Aircraft—The Anson

After extensive trials with prototype K4771, the Anson was chosen as the standard land-based general reconnaissance aircraft with an initial order for 174. Numbered from K6152 they had a standard silver finish, but additionally serials in 40-in. characters were marked on the upper surface of the wings as well as the usual presentation underneath. These numbers were marked in opposite directions, i.e. where * = the roundels and ↑ is direction of travel, it was: *K6159 ↑ 6ⓈI9Ж*. This applied to all early deliveries, K6152 to Martlesham Heath, K6153-62 to No. 48 Squadron, K6163 to Central Flying School, etc. It was noticeable that these machines bore no individual letters or numbers. With the serial marked in eight positions on the one machine, it was hardly necessary! This marking lapsed in later deliveries numbered from K8703 (K8703-6 to 11 F.T.S. July, 1937, K8707-10 to 6 F.T.S., August, 1937, etc.). These machines came in for the new trainer marking schemes explained in following chapters. By 1938, when L7903 *et seq.* were delivered, standard camouflage was the factory finish.

A pale marine blue was general for most flying-boats of the 'thirties, with the hull roundel marked well aft. This Blackburn Iris S1263 bears the crest of No. 209 (GR) Squadron as did also S1264 and K4011.
Markings for the Blackburn Perth were the same as for the Iris shown; the Iris VI being in fact redesignated Perth in August, 1933.

Shadow-shading. Typical of 1938 this Wellesley of No. 35 (B) Squadron bears the unit number in red thinly outlined in black with the individual letter 'G' in white to render it conspicuous for formation flying. The undersurface black is shown to be along the fuselage side directly in line with the trailing edge of the wings.

A New Era in British Service Markings

As the war clouds gathered in Europe so the R.A.F. was expanded in an attempt to meet the threat of war. At the same time the Force became operationally conscious and so bright finishes gave way to camouflage. It was not an immediate change. Camouflage in brown and green was introduced early in 1937 as the standard finish by contractors for front line operational aircraft coming off production. Early in 1938 it was extended to all front line aircraft and following the Munich crisis in September, 1938, to all aircraft on operational stations. This last change, coming at a time of crisis was performed hurriedly by station personnel —and in some cases with originality!

A marking indicative of a threat happily never realised, was a patch of gas detector paint, for which diamond-shaped stencils were provided for its application. After 1940 it was, in general, discontinued.

Camouflage

Camouflage essentially relates an object to its surroundings, achieving concealment by blending colour, tone and patterns into a background. Camouflage colours are by no means invariably dull colours, for light shades of blue give concealment against a bright sunlit sky and even the colours of the rainbow would merge into the sky at the times of the *Aurora Borealis*. For most conditions, however, certainly for Western Europe, summer and winter, browns and green were undoubtedly the best functional camouflage colours

Two standard schemes for uppersurfaces known as Schemes 'A' and 'B' were evolved in dark green and dark brown, one the mirrored image of the other. To illustrate this method the reader is invited to place a mirror at the wingtip of the Blenheim on page 86 and incline the mirror until he can see two Blenheims, one in the book and the other in the mirror. On comparison the two patterns will become obvious. Scheme 'A' applied to aircraft with even serials and 'B' to those with odd numbers, e.g. in 207 Squadron, Battles K9186, K9188 and K9190 had Scheme 'A' and K9185, K9187 and K9189, Scheme 'B'.

Undersurfaces remained temporarily in silver on fighters and army co-operation aircraft until mid-1938 when it was replaced by sky-grey. Following this came a general major change for fighters, the whole of the port undersurface was painted black and the opposite starboard side sky-blue or sky-grey, with the division taking place down the centre-line of the fuselage. All bombers on the other hand had an all-black undersurface except for white serial numbers as explained below.

Definition of Surfaces

To define the surfaces: Uppersurface applied to the plan view of the aircraft and included the sides of the fuselage, fin and rudder; it also applied to the top surface of lower wings in the case of biplanes and to the top of floats in the case of seaplanes. Undersurface applied to the underside, including undercarriage or float struts as applicable and to all interplane struts in the case of biplanes. Where

K5698 before and after Munich! No. 23 Squadron gave up their bright colours shown in Chapter 2 for just a crest on the fin in 1936. During the Munich Crisis in 1938, a 'panic camouflage', was given to their aircraft and later the code letters MS were allotted to the unit.
(Continued at bottom of next page).

Target towing aircraft were in a class apart for markings, having 3 ft. wide black diagonal stripes, spaced 6 ft. apart on an all-yellow background. Roundels are noticeably absent and where necessary serials were in white to contrast. This particular Wallace K4344 was built from Wapiti airframe K2313.

two contrasting surfaces met, a merging line was recommended, but alternatively an undulating line was acceptable.

National Insignia

When bright finishes changed to camouflage, the bright red and blue of roundels went to dull red and blue, but the white portion, left with the only possibility of going 'dirty white' remained—white. As the roundel did not contrast well against green, brown or black it was outlined with a circle of yellow, equal in thickness to the other colours. This was by far the most conspicuous colour and it defeated the object of the camouflage. Functionally, if not intentionally, our national marking was a yellow ring!

On all camouflaged surfaces, the yellow outlined roundel applied with the exception of the early silver undersurfaces where outlining was not necessary. When fighters changed to their half black undersurface finish, roundels were not marked, as this was in itself more conspicuous than roundels for recognition purposes.

By March, 1939, a modification of the roundel itself was promulgated for uppersurface (including fuselage sides) positions. The conspicuous yellow and white were replaced by the red/blue night roundel, but the old standard roundel was retained for marking on the undersurfaces of general reconnaissance aircraft. Application was to all operational aircraft initially, being extended to all aircraft a fortnight before war was declared. Although it was the official intention at this time to dispense with the yellow outline, some units did in fact use it for this new night roundel.

Serial Numbers

There are two aspects to serialling, the range of numbers and their positioning on the aircraft. With large

aircraft orders resulting from expansion, the ranges of numbers went from K to L, to be followed in quick succession by N, P and R. (M, O and Q were not used so as to avoid confusion with letters physically similar). For security reasons, after L7272 (a Vega Gull II used by the British Attaché in Buenos Aires) a new feature of serialling became evident; that of omitting blocks of numbers to conceal their true run. To give a typical example, an order for 150 Fairey Battles covered 214 numbers as follows:

P2155-2204 = 50 aircraft
P2233-2278 = 46 ,,
P2300-2336 = 37 ,,
P2353-2369 = 17 ,,

Total: 150 ,,

Serials continued to be marked in black on fuselage sides and rudders in general, though fighters in particular rarely had the serial repeated on the rudder. Thirty inches became the standard size for presentation of the serial under the wings which applied to aircraft in general, with the exception of fighters after the new 'half and half finish' was introduced. When marked on light surfaces it was in black, but when marked against the black undersides of bombers, it was conspicuously in white.

Unit Markings

Security as well as concealment became necessary with the onset of war. On the other hand a unit marking, though revealing to enemy intelligence, is consistent with maintaining *esprit de corps* within a unit. An official compromise allowed three standard frames for unit badges to be marked (see page 78). They were permitted on both sides of the fins

(Continued from bottom of opposite page).
The serial number of the aircraft was painted out, hence '98' for K5698 chalked(!) on the rudder. Later they were given standard fighter scheme undersurfaces of port side black, and starboard side light grey; the only two-seat biplane fighter to be so marked.

of single-engined aircraft and on the fuselage sides, near the pilot's position, for twin-engined aircraft, with the exception of Blenheims in a fighter role. This marking applied to squadron aircraft from early 1936, even before the introduction of camouflage, with the stipulation that it was not to be large, to facilitate its obliteration in time of emergency. Initially in camouflage, bomber squadrons marked up their unit designation number (e.g. '98' for No. 98 Squadron) on their fuselage sides, in pursuance of earlier traditions, but following the Munich crisis a code letter system was introduced, which came into effect for all squadrons from March, 1939. Three letters were used on each aircraft, two together denoting the particular squadron and the third, a space apart, usually separated by the roundel, gave individual identity within the unit. For individual identity any letter of the alphabet was permissible, but for two-letter combination squadron codes, 'C' and 'I' were not used.

Here follows a complete list of all squadrons in service, April, 1939, with their appropriate code letters given in brackets. Where known, a representative aircraft is quoted for each squadron by type, serial number and individual letter: Nos. 1 (NA) Hurricane L1694 'F', 2 (KO) Lysander L4705 'X', 3 (OP) Hurricane L1720 'D', 4 (FY) Lysander L4752 'V', 5 (QN), 6 (XE), 7 (LT), 8 (YO), 9 (KA) Wellington L4276 'M', 10 (PB) Whitley L7189 'L', 11 (OY), 12 (QE), 13 (AN), 14 (BF) Wellesley L2654 'F', 15 (EF), 16 (KJ) Lysander L4805 'B', 17 (UV) Gauntlet K5348 'B', 18 (GU) Blenheim L1177 'K', 19 (WZ) Spitfire K9795 'B', 20 (PM), 21 (JP) Blenheim L1479 'L', 22 (VR), 23 (MS), 24 (ZK), 25 (RX) Blenheim K7058 'K', 26 (HL), 27 (MY), 28 (US), 29 (YB) Blenheim L1503 'E', 30 (DP), 31 (ZA), 32 (KT) Hurricane L1813 'K', 33 (TN), 34 (LB), 35 (WT), 36 (VU), 37 (FJ) Harrow K7031 'O', 38 (NH) Wellington L4354 'U', 39 (SF), 40 (OX) Battle K9508 'S', 41 (PN), 42 (QD), 43 (NQ) Hurricane L1744 'A', 44 (JW), 45 (DD), 46 (RJ), 47 (EW), 48 (ZW), 49 (XU) Hampden L4045 'Q', 50 (QX), 51 (UT), 52 (MB) Battle K7606 'N', 53 (TE) Blenheim L4887 'G', 54 (DL) Spitfire K9901 'D', 55 (GM), 56 (LR) Hurricane L1983 'N', 57 (EQ), 58 (BW) Whitley K8920 'L', 59 (PJ), 60 (AD), 61 (LS) Hampden L4114 'P', 62 (JO), 63 (NE), 64 (XQ), 65 (FZ) Spitfire K9906 'O', 66 (RB) Spitfire K9805 'R', 70 (DU), 72 (SD), 73 (HV), 74 (JH) Spitfire K9948 'H', 75 (FO) Harrow K6992 'X', 76 (NM), 77 (ZL), 78 (YY), 79 (AL) Hurricane L1889 'E', 80 (GK), 82 (OZ) Blenheim L6684 'L', 83 (QQ) Hampden L4094 'K', 84 (UR), 85 (NO) Hurricane L1833 'J', 87 (PD), 88 (HY) Battle K9674 'F', 90 (TW) Blenheim K7175 'B', 97 (MR), 98 (OE), 99 (VF), 100 (RA) Vildebeest K6384 'T', 101 (LU), 102 (TQ), 103 (GV), 104 (PO), 105 (MT), 106 (XS) 107 (BZ), 108 (MF), 110 (AY) Blenheim N6198 'B', 111 (TM) Hurricane L1621 'D', 113 (BT), 114 (FD) Blenheim N6155 'F', 115 (BK), 139 (SY), 142 (KB) Battle K9321 'M', 144 (NV) Hampden L4141 'P', 148 (BS), 149 (LY) Wellington L4253 'P', 150 (DG) Battle K9483 'O', 151 (GG) Hurricane L1724 'M', 166 (GB), 185 (ZM), 201 (VQ), 202 (JU), 203 (PP), 204 (RF) London K5911 'G', 205 (ZM), 206 (WD), 207 (NJ), 208 (GA) Lysander L4711 'B', 209 (FK), 210 (VG), 211 (LJ), 213 (AK) Hurricane L1790 'F', 214 (UX) Wellington L4249 'L', 215 (BH) Harrow K6938 'K', 216 (VT), 217 (YQ) Anson K8745 'Q', 218 (SV), 220 (HU), 223 (QR), 224 (PW), 226 (KP), 228 (TO), 230 (FV), 233 (EY), 240 (SH), 269 (KL), 500 (SQ), 501 (ZH) Hurricane L1866 'B', 502 (KG), 504 (AW), 600 (MV), 601 (YW), 602 (ZT), 603 (RL), 604 (WQ), 605 (HE), 607 (LW), 608 (PG), 609 (PL), 610 (JE), 611 (GZ), 612 (DJ), 614 (YX), 615 (RR) Gauntlet K7854 'A', 616 (QJ). On 3rd September, 1939, all code letters were changed.

Training Aircraft

A yellow finish remained standard for trainers, but from 1938 uppersurfaces were camouflaged in the usual brown and green, but it extended only to half-way down the fuselage sides. This meant a sharp contrasting line along the sides, rather nullifying the effect of the camouflage from an angle of depression from whence the enemy was most likely to pounce! A simple coding used by No. 1 A.A.C.U. was a flight letter/individual number combination, e.g. Queen Bee Z3 was No. 3 of 'Z' Flight.

Transport Aircraft

From 1938 communications aircraft were given the same finish as trainers with certain exceptions in silver overall. No definite policy seems to have been accorded to our new bomber-transport of the period—the Bristol Bombay built by Short and Harland of Belfast. The first production models which commenced delivery in March, 1939, numbered from L5808 were in pre-1937 silver finish and not until mid-1939, on machines L5819 *et seq*, were Bombays delivered in camouflage.

No. 1. Sqn. (Fury)

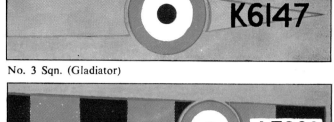

No. 3 Sqn. (Gladiator)

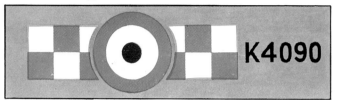

No. 19 Sqn. (Gauntlet)

No. 23 Sqn. (Gamecock)

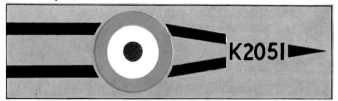

No. 25 Sqn. (Fury)

No. 32 Sqn. (Bulldog)

No. 41 Sqn.

At the top, squadron markings are shown as they appeared on a particular aircraft and below are the symbolic markings of R.A.F. fighter squadrons that were adapted to the various types of fighter aircraft.

No. 43 Sqn.

No. 46 Sqn.

No. 54 Sqn.

No. 56 Sqn

No. 64 Sqn.

No. 65 Sqn.

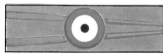

No. 66 Sqn.

No. 72 Sqn.

No. 74 Sqn.

No. 79 Sqn.

No. 87 Sqn.

No. 111 Sqn.

No. 151 Sqn.

No. 213 Sqn.

No. 600 Sqn.

No. 601 Sqn.

No. 604 Sqn.

Squadron markings were often repeated on the uppersurface of the top wing in this biplane fighter era. These wing markings are of Nos. 1, 19, 23 and 32 Squadrons as may be ascertained by comparing them with the fuselage-side markings above.

CAMOUFLAGE SCHEMES 1939-41

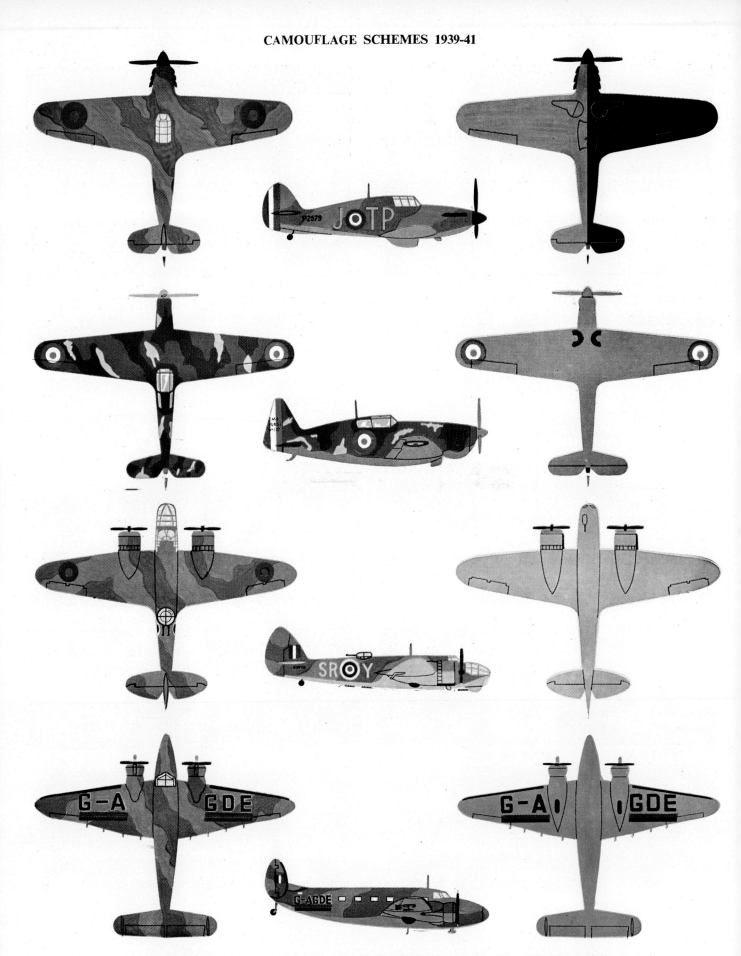

Top to bottom: A Hurricane of the Advanced Air Striking Force in France, 1940; a Morane Saulnier 406C1 of the French Air Force during the same period; a Blenheim IV in standard R.A.F. day bomber markings of 1940-41 and a Lockheed Lodestar of B.O.A.C. in the recommended camouflage for civil aircraft.

MISCELLANEOUS MARKINGS – SERVICE AIRCRAFT OF THE 'THIRTIES

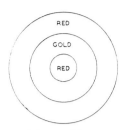

Wing positions

Rudder

SPANISH GOVERNMENT AIRCRAFT

SPANISH CIVIL WAR 1936-39

Condor Legion
Fuselage Roundel
of Me 109 s

Fuselage side

Rudder

NATIONALIST AIRCRAFT

Silhouette Insignia
of 'Patrulla de Toros'

Condor Legion He 51
unit insignia

Imperial Ethiopian
Air Force Roundel

Condor Legion
Me 109 unit insignia

Condor Legion
He III unit insignia

'Fasces' wing & rudder positions from 1936

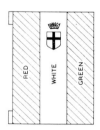

THE ABYSSINIAN
WAR

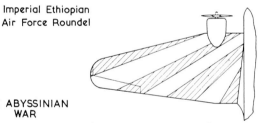

'Forced Landing Stripes' Italian
Bombers in East Africa.
(Orange Red on Colonial White finish)

Insignia of
'La Disperata'
Squadriglia

U.S NAVY

N3N-3   1759

U.S. NAVY

Typical Tail
Group U.S. Navy

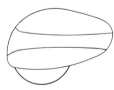

Wheel Spat Heyfords
No. 10 Sqn. R.A.F.
(Flight Colours on Nivo)

BRITISH
AIRCRAFT

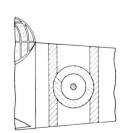

Fuselage Bands Ansons
R.A.A.F. (various colours)

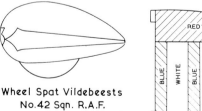

Wheel Spat Vildebeests
No. 42 Sqn. R.A.F.
(Flight Colours on Silver)

U.S. COAST GUARD

Rudder

The establishment of Commonwealth Air Forces could be said to have originated from a decision of the British Government during 1919, to present each of the Commonwealth countries with one hundred aircraft from the´ vast post-war surplus. This gesture known as the 'Imperial Gift' was gratefully acknowledged by Canada, Australia and South Africa. India accepted the aircraft but found little use for them; New Zealand declined the aircraft at first, but later changed her attitude and accepted when it was too late to receive the full quota.

Apart from South Africa, national markings followed R.A.F. practice and the general finish too was based on British service aircraft, but in the matter of identifying their aircraft, each Dominion had their own serialling systems.

In the early days, the R.C.A.F. with duties which included surveying and forestry patrols, had mostly civil bush flying types of aircraft. The Force was rather more 'station conscious' than 'unit conscious', the individual letters and later numbers served both for unit, station and individual identification.

Events in Europe led in 1937 to Canada placing an order in Great Britain for twenty-five front-line fighters—Hurricanes. These were the first camouflaged aircraft to enter the R.C.A.F. They were in standard British shadow-shading having been diverted from R.A.F. contract as numbers L1759-63, L1878-88, L1890, L2121-3 and L2144. On reaching Canada they were re-numbered in the R.C.A.F. series, *circa* 309-333.

Training aircraft of the R.C.A.F. showed a considerable latitude in markings as may be gauged by comparing the photograph at left and that at top of the opposite page. Since national markings followed R.A.F. practice, Fleet Type 7 No. 206 with rudder stripes is evidently of an earlier period than the Fleet Type 16B. Silver or yellow was the general finish for these aircraft. On No. 206 the inverted 'V' behind the serial is merely protective greasing over zip-fasteners.

Canada

Canada's Imperial Gift aircraft (12 D.H.4, 12 D.H.9A, 58 Avro 504K, 11 S.E. 5A, 3 F3, 2 Curtiss H.16 and 1 Snipe) were in their wartime finishes, but gradually this gave way to a general all-silver finish except for some trainers marked in yellow overall. For identification markings Canada adopted a peculiar system based on civil registration. In 1922, civil registrations G-CYAA to G-CYZZ were allotted for service aircraft which displayed the last two letters only, as large as fuselage or hull sides would allow. It was placed towards the rear of the fuselage (or hull), aft of the roundel, although it sometimes replaced a roundel on the fuselage or wing positions. There was no set rule. Examples of machines in service were: AT—Avro 504K, UT—D.H. Puss Moth, ZL—Vickers Vedette and ZZ—Vickers Vista, the last of this series.

Thereafter followed a numerical series with allocations in blocks according to roles: 1-300 Trainers (e.g. No. 13 Avro 504K, 117 D.H. Gipsy Moth, 184 Avro Tutor), 301-400 Fighters (e.g. 303 Siskin), 401-600 General Purpose (e.g. 508 Wapiti), 601-700 Transports (e.g. 621 Fairchild 51), 701-800 Bombers (e.g. 740 Douglas Digby), 801-1,000 Flying-Boats (e.g. 803 Vedette and 903 Vancouver). Numbers were marked large on the sides of training aircraft, but on other machines, position and size was as for R.A.F. aircraft. From the inception of the numerical series, roundels on the usual positions were invariably marked. However, on the top wing of Siskin R.C.A.F. No. 23, the outside diameter of the starboard roundel was 1 ft. greater than that of the port side roundel!

Australia

Australia received 128 gift aircraft of which S.E.5As were delivered in khaki-green, Avro 504Ks some in clear and others in khaki-green finish, D.H.9s in khaki-green with blue-grey panelling and D.H.9As in silver finish. Many were kept in store and not used until Nos. 1 and 3 Squadrons formed at Point Cook in 1925 with S.E.5As, D.H.9s and Avro 504Ks. The S.E.5As were re-covered and aluminium doped, given standard British national markings of the period and were marked with R.A.A.F. serials, one each side of the rear of the fuselage, an example being A2-36. New equipment was also purchased from Britain and finished rigidly in British service fashion, except for the serialling range.

The original gift machines had been numbered from No. 1 for each different type of aircraft. This number was preceded by a type number for each different type and the whole prefixed by an 'A' for Australia. Thus D.H.9As as Australian Type 1 were numbered A1-1, A1-2, A1-3, etc. S.E.5As were Type A2 and therefore numbered A2-1, A2-2, A2-3, etc. Up to A10, type numbers were re-allotted as earlier types passed out of service, but from A11 onwards there has been consecutive allotment. A13 was an exception in the series as that type number was alloted not to an aeroplane, but to the Link Trainer.

Presentation of the serial was usually in 8 in. characters on the fuselage sides, sometimes also appearing on the rudder. There are always exceptions; at Point Cook, Wapiti A5-23 was marked only with the number 23, but in 2 ft. figures just aft of the roundel.

Ansons were the most modern equipment in R.A.F. service, 1938, the first to arrive A4-1 to A4-12 being ex-R.A.F. K6212-23. These were in standard R.A.F. aluminium finish with the Australian numbers replacing the R.A.F. serials on fuselage sides and rudders.

Individual letters or numbers were rarely marked except for the repetition of the last part of the serial number in large letters on the nose or fuselage side. Instead coloured bands positioned as shown on page 87 were often used. On some Tiger Moths these bands were 18 in. wide, marked some 2 ft. aft of the fuselage roundel, being broken to allow the serial (e.g. A17-26) to be clearly displayed.

South Africa

In addition to the British Government's gift of one hundred aircraft delivered in 1920, an additional machine was inscribed and presented by the City of Birmingham. These aircraft had R.A.F. wartime finishes, original serials deleted and 10 in. South African Air Force numbers painted over, either in black or white to contrast respectively against clear of khaki-green finish. Numbers were allotted in blocks according to type: 100+ D.H.9, 200+ D.H.4, 300+ S.E.5A and 400+ Avro 504K. Later aircraft, ordered chiefly from Britain had standard R.A.F. finish but with British roundels replaced by South Africa's own colours. Basically, this meant red being replaced by orange.

Serials continued to be somewhat larger than on the fuselages of R.A.F. machines. Prefix letters were not used, except in one particular case to denote the type of engine fitted to Wapiti's numbered from 601; J615 for example having the 'J' for a Jaguar engine and P610 having the 'P' for Panther.

From 1938 many ex-R.A.F. machines were bought for a nominal sum, including Hinds K5379, K5400, K5505, K5541, K6623, etc. By the time war came, South Africa had eight modern aircraft, six Hurricanes, one Battle (L5374) and a Blenheim. These machines were in standard R.A.F. shadow-shading: the Hurricanes numbered in the S.A.A.F. 301-400 range were ex-L1708, L1710, amongst others.

New Zealand

The few service aircraft in New Zealand, in 1925, had various finishes. Avro 504Ks were in clear finish with black cowlings, D.H.4s were in khaki-green and of three Bristol Fighters in use, two were in silver and one in khaki-green.

For identification, constructors' numbers were marked in small figures on the rudder and sometimes additionally on the fuselage sides, examples being Bristol F2Bs 6857 and 7120 and D.H.9 5636. With new equipment later acquired, general finish and markings followed British practice. Serials were allotted in blocks of three-digit numbers without regard for numeral/chronological sequence and were prefixed with the self-evident letters—NZ. Examples are Grebes NZ501-503, Vildebeests NZ101-112 and Avro 504Ks numbered from NZ201.

Camouflage was not used pre-war in the Dominion, but in 1939, Wellingtons in Vickers factory being prepared for delivery in standard shadow-shading, bore serials such as NZ304, as part of a New Zealand order for thirty. With war in Europe following, New Zealand graciously handed them over to the R.A.F. to equip No. 75 (New Zealand) Squadron of Bomber Command.

India

An Indian Air Force formed in 1933 under R.A.F. supervision had strict R.A.F. markings and only by a knowledge of the serial numbers of the aircraft handed over, was it possible to distinguish those aircraft on charge to the Indian Government. Examples are Wapiti IIA K1403, Hart (India) K2116 and Victoria VI J8231.

Rhodesia

During 1936, six ex-R.A.F. Harts (K2986, K3025, K3028, K3877, K3888 and K3889), some still in R.A.F. squadron markings, arrived at Salisbury for re-numbering SR-1 to SR-6 as the initial equipment of the Southern Rhodesian Air Force. Equipment that followed included a Dragon Rapide which bore the number SR8 in 30 in. digits just aft of the cabin door.

Malaya

The Straits Settlements Volunteer Air Force formed in March, 1936, used a special version of the Audax, the Audax (Singapore). Aircraft were marked forward of the fuselage roundels with a 30 in. individual number, K3720 was '1', K5143 and K7312 were '3' and '4' respectively.

Typical of Royal New Zealand Air Force aircraft is this Vickers Vildebeest, the first of a batch of twelve, in standard R.A.F. markings with only the serial number indicative of its Service by the self-evident letters —NZ.

Boeing F4B-4 biplanes of the U.S. Marines showing the unit, mission and individual markings. Often in Navy and Marine units the middle mission symbol was marked on a coloured band that went around the fuselage. This photograph was taken in the late 'thirties when the Marines still used the vertical rudder stripes.

Markings of United States service aircraft in this period may be classified into four groups according to the administrative control of the various formations. Foremost in strength was the U.S. Army Air Corps (later U.S. Army Air Force) and of equal status came naval aviation under the Navy Bureau of Aeronautics. Also under this Bureau, but with its own Commandant, came the aircraft of the U.S. Marine Corps. Finally there was the Aviation Division of the U.S. Coast Guard under the Treasury Department but which in time of war was placed under the operational control of the U.S. Navy. It was the policy to mark the aircraft with their administering authority; the words: U.S. NAVY, U.S. MARINES and U.S. COAST GUARD appearing as appropriate, at the rear of the fuselage in 8-10 in. lettering. The U.S. Army on the other hand, had their marking from 1927 onwards under the wings in the

manner: * U.S. ↑ ARMY * (where* = national insignia and ↑ = fuselage and direction of travel).

A common national markings was of course desirable and the well-known star insignia was adopted throughout the U.S. Services from June 1st, 1921. Consistent with previous practice, it was applied to the wings of aeroplanes only being normally about one-sixth of the span inboard. No national marking appeared on fuselage sides and rudder markings varied according to the period and the service.

U.S. Army

Vertical rudder stripes in the Allies colours of red, white and blue became an anachronism in post-war years as America pursued her isolationist policy. They were replaced on Army aircraft in 1926 by seven horizontal red stripes adapted from 'Old Glory', the American Flag.

General finish of Army aircraft varied from khaki and khaki-green to silver overall with special schemes in certain pursuit squadrons. A series of experiments in camouflage were carried out, but only a few heavy bombers had a drab finish.

By an Army Reorganisation Act of June, 1920, the Signal Corps lost control of army aviation which now became a separate branch of the Army. This was reflected in serialling; the prefix letters S.C. for Signal Corps giving way to A.S. for Air Service. Another change to serialling came the following year. Hitherto, since the inception of army aviation in 1909, serialling had been in the one numerical series, but from July 1st, 1921, it was broken down into a separate series for each Fiscal Year. Thus A-S 23-1236 in 14 in. characters on the fuselage side of Engineering Division XCO-6 biplane, would indicate that it was the 1,236th aircraft procured in the Fiscal Year 1923. (N.B. The American Fiscal Year is from July 1st to June 30th). If an aircraft was later modified and expenditure from the Fiscal Year appropriation was involved, a new serial number was allotted.

From 1924 the serialling prefix was A.C. for Air Corps. A Consolidated Courier may be quoted as a typical example, bearing in 3 in. lettering this inscription at the rear of its silver-finished fuselage:

U.S. ARMY
CONSOLIDATED—X017
AC 28-229

Unit insignia was usual in squadron service, the U.S. Army having officially recognised a number of motifs in 1919 based on A.E.F. squadrons. Typical examples are: 162nd Squadron—silhouette of the U.S.A. and 174th Squadron—an alley cat silhouetted against the moon. These markings were placed centrally on the fuselage and the fin was used for unit and/or individual identity marking.

The vast subject of aircraft nomenclature is not within the scope of this work, but since Army aircraft carried type designations, usually marked on the rudder at first, the system qualifies for explanation. It consisted of three main parts, firstly the manufacturer, then an initial or initials denoting the class of aircraft and separated by a hyphen, the number of different types acquired within that class. E.g. Curtiss

PW-8 would denote the eighth type of Pursuit plane with a water-cooled engine to enter Army service. These designations could be conditioned by four prefix letters, 'X', 'Y' and 'Z' for Experimental, Service Trials and Obsolete respectively, and, later, 'R' for Restricted Use. An alphabetical suffix was applied for modifications of the basic type thus the fourth modification of the Boeing PW-9 would be PW-9D.

It was a simple but effective system, with the object of giving a brief and accurate description of the aircraft type.

Class designations were divided into nineteen basic classes as follows: A—Ambulance, AO—Artillery Observation, CO—Corps Observation, DB—Day Bombardment, GA—Ground Attack, IL—Infantry Liaison, M—Messenger, NBL and NBS—Night Bombardment (Long or Short Distance), NO—Night Observation; PA, PG, PN and PW—Pursuit, air-cooled, ground attack, night and water-cooled respectively; R—Racer, T—Transport; TA and TW—Trainer, air-cooled and water-cooled respectively; TP—Two-place Pursuit.

The above system lasted only until 1924 when the basis of the present-day system was instituted.

U.S. Navy and U.S. Marines

The Navy and Marines, too, gave up the old rudder striping, but rather than take on a new feature like the Army, they left their rudders clear. Blue was the general finish for fuselages and silver for lifting surfaces, although it was by no means exclusive, for primary trainers were chrome-yellow overall.

In squadron service a three-unit system of identification was used, marked centrally on the fuselage side, an example being 5-F-6. The first number denoted the unit designation; the middle letter, the role of mission as it was known in America and the final figure related to the individual number of the machine within its squadron. Thus 5-F-6 meant machine No. 6 of Combat Squadron Five. Nine mission letters were in use, namely: B—Bombing, F—Fighting or Combat, J—Utility or General Purpose, N—Training, O—Observation, P—Patrol, S—Scouting, |T—Torpedo-Bombing and X—Experimental. Marine squadrons could be identified by the mission letter appearing in a coloured disc.

A symbol was sometimes used instead of an 'O' for observation to avoid confusion with 'O' for Zero.

In some cases, particularly at training stations, the base was indicated by two significant letters, thus 4SD-F-10 would refer to the 4th Combat Squadron at San Diego. Base symbols used were: CS—Coco Solo, DT—Detroit, GL—Great Lakes, HH—Hsin Ho, HR—Hampden Roads, LB—Long Beach, LT—Lakehurst, MA—Managua, MS—Minneapolis, OD—Oakland, PA—Pensacola, PH—Pearl Harbour, PP—Port-au-Prince, QO—Quantico, RB—Rockaway Beach, SD—San Diego, SM—Squantum, SP—Sand Point and SY—Sumay.

Like the Army, unit insignia was marked on the fuselage side, typical was the motif of Combat Squadron 6 in the U.S. Navy, whose Grumman F3F-1 biplanes bore a silhouette of Felix the Cat carrying a grenade. Serials usually marked on the fin and the rudder was allotted by the Bureau of Aeronautics. Presentation was not large, being in 3 in. black or blue digits. An 'A' prefix was used for the serial range up until the late 'thirties.

United States Coast Guard

An aviation division of the U.S. Coast Guard was established in 1926 with three Loening OL-5 amphibians and two Vought UO-4 seaplanes, starting the numbering system as Nos. 1 to 5 respectively. This simple consecutive numbering continued, being marked on the aircraft under the words U.S. COAST GUARD at the rear of the hull or fuselage.

General finish was either in an aircraft manufacturer's scheme, or in naval silver finish. National insignia was not displayed on the wings, instead on the underside of the wings (lower wings in the case of biplanes), marked as large as practicable, were the initials: U.S.C.G.

Above: Typical of the U.S. Army aircraft of the 'thirties is this biplane with the United States red-centred star insignia in the wing positions and the thirteen alternate red and white stripes on the rudder with a broad vertical blue stripe next to the rudder post. On the fuselage side, a unit emblem appeared in place of a national emblem.

At side: Navy fashion. A three-seat Great Lakes TG-2 torpedo-bomber in factory finish ready for delivery to the U.S. Navy. The fuselage decking is painted grey to reduce glare. As a safety measure, propeller blades were tipped with four-inch bands of red, yellow and blue, in that order from the tip.

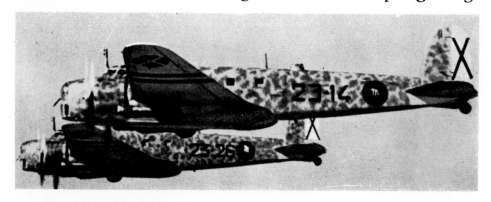

Fiat B.R.20 bombers of the Italian Legion in Spain. The camouflage is of splotched green upon terra-cotta and it will be noticed that it extends completely round the engine cowlings. No national marking appears on the fuselage side except the unit number 23 followed by the individual number. The 'M' was for 'Mussolini Squadriglia'.

Campaigns and Minor Wars

The inter-war years were years of uneasy peace. During that era, several campaigns were fought, now almost forgotten, eclipsed by the two major wars. For some, the fighting of the First World War did not end in 1918. British units, including R.A.F. detachments, fought on in both North and South Russia until late 1919, in an attempt to crush Bolshevism. R.A.F. aircraft participated, D.H.9s, D.H.9As, R.E.8s and Snipes in their wartime finishes. A particularly lively action was an attack upon some vessels fitted out as Bolshevist gun-boats on Lake Onega. They were completely routed by six R.A.F. seaplanes. The individual identity of these aircraft is not known, but the following served in North Russia at that time: Fairey IIICs N9235-7 (F312-4), N9241 (F318) and Short 184s (Robey-built) N9280-3.

The value of an Air Force for policing duties was convincingly demonstrated in 1920. For years the Mad Mullah of Somaliland had menaced the peace of East Africa and yet he and his followers were utterly routed by 'Z' Force, a formation consisting of eleven D.H.9s (e.g. H5561 Alliance-built) and D3117 a D.H.9 converted for ambulance work. These aircraft were in wartime finishes and when not flying their wings were covered with grass and reeds—not as a camouflage, but to protect the wings from the sun's rays.

Punitive expeditions were frequent on the North-West Frontier of India; typical was the Waziristan Operations in 1930 when some 10,000 tribesmen advanced upon Peshawar in spite of repeated warnings to stay in the hills. Finally bombing action by No. 20 Squadron to disperse the tribesmen was the only and effective means of preventing a massacre. The aircraft used were Bristol Fighters in standard silver-overall. A suitable finish because of its relatively low heat-resisting properties

and acceptable where there is no opposition in the air.

Both France and Spain had colonial troubles resulting in punitive expeditions, the Riff Rising in 1923 was, in fact, often referred to as the Moroccan War. Some fifty aircraft of the Spanish Air Force were involved, chiefly ex-French Breguet 14s, ex-British Martinsyde F.4s and Bristol Fighters in Spanish National markings. Camouflage was not taken seriously as the Riffs had no aircraft.

America, too, had her troubles and on several occasions during this era United States Marine Corps aircraft were sent to Nicaragua. It is perhaps with some surprise, knowing America's isolationist policy, to 'log' Boeing FB-1 A6887 of the 3rd Brigade, U.S.M.C., at Hsin Ho during the 1927 'China Troubles', when a Communist inspired Cantonese Army threatened the interests of several nations.

The Abyssinian War

Italy waged a very one-sided war in 1936 against an almost primitively equipped Abyssinia. Some 500 Italian aircraft in co-operation with the Italian Army were engaged. Against this, the Ethiopian Air Force could muster only a few aircraft, unsuited for modern warfare. There were five antiquated Potez biplanes, an ex-Swissair Fokker FXVIII, a D.H. Puss Moth for the personal use of the Emperor and, ironically, a Breda presented by the Italian Government. The finish of the Italian aircraft reflected this negligible opposition by a general 'Colonial White' with bars of orange-red marked fan-wise over the upper surface of the main-planes to assist search aircraft to spot machines force-landed—the very antithesis of camouflage.

Caproni Ca 101 three-engined bombers did in some cases have the fin and plan-view surfaces in mid-green, but only to reduce glare for the upper-gunner—not that much opposition was likely. Only the rudder in equal vertical

A Dornier Do 17 of the German Condor Legion in Nationalist aircraft markings. The undersurface insignia was a white cross upon a black circle, whereas on the upper-surface of the wings a plain white cross contrasted sufficiently against the grey-green segment camouflage.

The Italians used two distinct types of camouflage in the Spanish Civil War, as shown on these S.M.79s and as illustrated opposite. These aircraft are of a Squadriglia that operated against the Abyssinians. White wingtips were a feature of both the Italian and German Legion aircraft.

stripes of green, white and red (green leading), gave official notification of national identity. Count Ciano, Mussolini's son-in-law commanded *La Disperata* Squadron whose Caproni Ca 101 bombers bore the skull and cross-bone marking illustrated on page 87 in a mid-fuselage position. Aft of this in 30 in. figures was an individual number (Count Ciano's was No. 1) and at the rear of the fuselage was the aircraft's service number with the usual 'MM' prefix.

Sino-Japanese War

Apart from the national markings of the two major contestants, the Japanese sponsored Nanking Government's aircraft, bore, in addition to Japanese national markings, five horizontal rudder stripes of equal width, coloured from the top: red yellow, blue, white and black.

The Spanish Civil War

The complexities of the Spanish Civil War were reflected in the markings of the aircraft that flew over that ravaged country, 1936-39. The opposing forces were, the insurgents—a fascist nationalistic party, against the Republican Government. When war came, part of the Spanish Air Force went over to the rebels. At that time service aircraft in Spain were finished in silver with national markings in the colours of Aragon, red, gold and purple. These colours were applied in roundel form on the usual wing positions and as horizontal stripes on the rudder (see page 87). An indication of national identity was not normally given on the fuselage sides. The Nationalists, claiming the colours of Aragon as suitable to their cause, marked the Spanish Air Force roundel upon the fuselage sides of their aircraft. To contrast with Government aircraft in other positions, a cross, in black or white to stand out, was marked in the usual wing positions. The rudders of Nationalist aircraft were invariably painted white with a large black cross as shown in the photographs.

Both sides in this civil war received help from outside. France with strong anti-Fascist feelings allowed numbers of Loire 46 and Bleriot-Spad 510 fighters together with Potez 54 bombers to reach Spanish Government Forces. Russia, too, supplied aircraft in quantity, in fact the Italians claimed the 'confirmed' destruction of no less than 209 Rata fighters. This may well have been an optimistic figure, but it does nevertheless imply that large numbers of Russian aircraft were used. The Italian Legion in Spain claimed the destruction of 222 Curtiss fighters at a time when American policy was based on the Monroe Doctrine; they were in fact Russian fighters.

During July, 1936, a number of German Air Force personnel left Berlin for Spain as 'tourists'. These were the men of the Condor Legion whose aircraft were already crated for shipping. Their first operation was the transportation in Junkers Ju 52/3m transports and Heinkel He 59 seaplanes of several hundred Moroccan troops across the Mediterranean to Spain. Then came field units, three fighter squadrons, equipped at first with Heinkel He 51s and later with Messerschmitt Me 109s of several versions. Heinkel He 111 bomber units were supplemented later by Dornier Do 17 bombers and Junkers Ju 88 bombers and Ju 87 dive-bombers. Standard identity markings for the Condor Legion were as illustrated.

NOTES ON REPRESENTATIVE SPANISH CIVIL WAR AIRCRAFT MARKINGS BY TYPE

Government Aircraft: Hawker Fury—silver finish with standard Spanish Air Force markings. Serial in black 6 in. figures in the centre of the gold portion of the rudder: Nos. 4-1, 4-2, 4-3, etc. 1-16 Rata—camouflaged in two shades of green. Roundels or stripes of red-gold-red on wings. Rudder in horizontal stripes as per page 87. White identification number marked over rudder striping in approximately 12 in.-20 in. figures. Government registration number at rear of fuselage, e.g. GA-057. Other serial examples are: Nieuport 52, 6-27; Loire 46, 3-14; Potez 54, K12-14.

Condor Legion: Junkers Ju 52/3m—segment camouflage (see Chapter 14 Pt. III) a typical identity being 22*91 (* = roundel). Heinkel He 51—segment camouflage, machine 6*78 completed over 300 sorties. Insignia of the one unit using these aircraft was Mickey Mouse. Heinkel He 59—sea-grey overall without identity numbers, but instead a symbol marked aft of the roundel. Heinkel He 111—segment camouflage on uppersurfaces with light blue undersurfaces, the division taking place along a line leading from the trailing edge of the mainplanes to the leading edge of the tailplanes. A unit operating these aircraft symbolised the Condor Legion by the insignia on its fin, a Condor with a bomb in its claws. Individual identities in this unit were 25*88, 25*92, etc.

Italian Legion: At first Fiat Cr 32 fighters operated in a clear finish, but a brown and green dappled camouflage was later introduced. Bombers had two distinct finishes and examples of both are illustrated.

PART 3

CHAPTER ONE

Here indeed this Blenheim IV shows the effect of camouflage. It will be seen that the roundels are not placed at the wing tips, but inboard by one-sixth of the span and that they are marked as large as practicable without over-lapping on to the ailerons.

Variations in Markings

Very confused ideas exist concerning the markings of R.A.F. aircraft during the war years and a perusal of books and magazines of that period helps little in assessing chronological sequence, for it so often happened that photographs were held up by the censor weeks, months, and even years, before release for publication.

There are several variable factors to consider, for although the nature of markings, camouflage patterns and shades were regulated jointly by Air Ministry and Ministry of Aircraft Production branches, some flexibility was essential to meet operational requirements at short notice. A general rule can be expressed and a particular example or exception quoted, but in so vast a subject all cannot be covered or be even known. Variations in the production of paints and dopes, units experimenting with their own concoctions, a shade substituted for a regulation shade temporarily out of stock, all provide exceptions to the rule.

Time is an important conditioning factor; major changes are often promulgated as taking effect from a certain date or within a set period. The markings of an individual aircraft may change several times, e.g. Spitfire Vb EP130 served in Nos. 19, 118, 130, 132, 501 and 504 Squadrons, necessitating six changes in squadron code letters during the war period. Therefore the reader who would query the markings quoted for a particular aircraft in this book or any other is asked first to consider the conditioning factor—time.

Camouflage

Aircraft camouflage was not an arbitrary application of drab colours, but a series of studied styles and shades considered appropriate for various classes of aircraft. Directives on camouflage and the size and style of markings were issued by the Directorate of Technical Development, which in 1940 was transferred from the Air Ministry, with the Production and Research Directorates, to form the Ministry of Aircraft Production. From this new Ministry six standard camouflage patterns were promulgated during 1941 as follows:

Pattern No. 1.	Single-engined monoplanes.
Pattern No. 2.	Twin-engined monoplanes not exceeding 70 ft. wing span (e.g. a Blenheim had a 56 ft. 4 in. span).
Pattern No. 3.	Twin-engined monoplanes exceeding 70 ft. wing span (e.g. a Wellington had a 86 ft. 6 in. span).
Pattern No. 4.	Four-engined aircraft.
Pattern No. 5.	Single-engined biplanes.
Pattern No. 6.	Twin-engined biplanes.

These patterns are illustrated on page 132. They acted as a guide for literally chalking up the aircraft surfaces for the spray painters. Exact reproduction was not necessarily followed, nor was it essential. Shadow-shading according to odd or even serial numbers no longer applied. The six patterns could be in any of the following schemes:

1. Temperate Land Scheme	Dark Green/Dark Earth.
2. Temperate Sea Scheme	Dark Slate Grey/Extra Dark Sea Grey.
3. Middle East Scheme	Dark Earth/Middle Stone.
4. Command Schemes	Various Shades.
5. P.R.U. Schemes	Various shades of Overall Blue.

Production aircraft in this country were mostly to Schemes 1 or 2, other schemes being the result of re-marking in service. There were several major exceptions as will be explained in the following chapters.

National Markings

National insignia underwent several changes. At the declaration of war the night roundel Type B was official for fuselage sides, changing back to standard Type A by December, 1939, but complaints from R.A.F. Commands reporting identification difficulties led to a compromise; standard roundels with yellow outlining for fuselage sides, night roundels of red and blue only for uppersurfaces of wings, but roundels on the undersurfaces to be marked only at the discretion of the Command concerned. During 1940 fin striping was introduced, taking various forms suggesting that no instructions were then issued regarding its application, except to state the order of colours as red leading, white in the centre and blue aft with the proviso that these stripes were to be of equal width. However, by December that year fin flashes were standardised as 27 in. high by 24 in. wide. National markings varied little from then on until June, 1942, when a complete revision took place. Dimensions, application and colours are illustrated on page 102.

Operational aircraft, excluding fighters, rarely carried national markings on the undersurface of the wings. This has been questioned as contravening the Hague Convention, which required that national identity should be clearly represented. No set positions, however, were specified under the Convention and a roundel on the fuselage side was considered to meet its provisions, since, in any case, the frontal area of an aeroplane is too limited for national markings to be displayed—and that was the view an attacking fighter or dive-bomber would present.

British aircraft did, in fact, infringe International law in an innocuous way, for the clause in the Convention that states an aircraft shall bear the insignia of only one nation is unequivocal. Occasionally it happened that in the transfer of aircraft from the United States to the R.A.F., the U.S. insignia was left in certain positions whereas British roundels appeared in other positions. At least one machine had American and British insignia side-by-side! This was not, however, a serious matter as the aircraft did not fly so marked on operations, but only for transit.

Serial Numbers

From the outbreak of war, serials were painted out from the undersurfaces of all operational aircraft and with new aircraft of this class coming into service, serials were marked only in the fuselage positions. In general they were marked in black except where a black finish neces-sitated a contrasting colour, when red was usual.

Serialling entered a new phase in 1940 when Z9999 was reached. The policy of using a five-unit combination was then continued by having two prefix letters to a three-digit number range of 100-999. Twenty prefix letters were used in an alphabetical allotment, these being: A, B, D, E, F, G, H, J, K, L, M, N, P, R, S, T, V, W, X and Z. Thus the system progressed: AA100-AA999, AB100-AB999, AD100-AD999, etc., until AZ999 was reached, when BA100-BA999, BB100-BB999, BD100-BD999, etc., followed. Several exceptions, however, should be noted. 'C' additional to the letters quoted was used once only for a series—NC100-NC999. 'G' was used only as a second prefix letter (i.e. there was no series GA, GB, GD, etc., but it was used in the combinations AG, BG, DG, etc.). 'NZ' was not used to avoid confusion with aircraft of the Royal New Zealand Air Force. 'Z' as a prefix letter has not yet been used, the present allocations reaching about XP. The continuation of the series after XA, in the same manner, is hypothetical.

The omission of blocks of numbers to conceal quantities produced continued throughout the war with the exception of aircraft acquired from America, which were numbered consecutively in the series.

Unit Code Markings

On the 3rd September, 1939, in accordance with a pre-planned mobilisation instruction, all squadron code letters were changed to confuse enemy intelligence, but the system remained and was, in fact, extended to include all flying units under operational commands. The letters 'C' and 'I' previously omitted were brought into the system *circa* 1941 and at the same time numerals (1 to 9) were brought in for use in combination with a letter. This gave well over a thousand possible combinations, though it does not necessarily follow that all were allocated. During the war there was no general re-allocation of numbers, but from time to time unit codes were changed or exchanged, as part of operational cover plans.

This Lockheed Hudson III, shows well the camouflage effects of the temporate land scheme. The letter 'A' was for individual identity within the squadron; the VX was the unit code letters, in this case No. 206 Squadron and the serial number T9444 being its official R.A.F. registration.

The unofficial markings on this Wellington T2508 in the Middle East are something of an enigma. It is understood that each symbol relates to a member of the crew, a haggis suggests a Scotsman, but a cheese and a winged lemon seems to suggest something uncomplimentary!

Unofficial Markings

Aircrew wishing to emulate the sniper who notches his rifle-butt made some visual record of their victories, usually a swastika on the cockpit side to denote the destruction of an enemy aircraft, or the silhouette of a bomb for each operation by a bomber. In some units of Coastal Command, symbols represented E-boats, destroyers, merchant ships, etc. These markings and individual insignia were not officially permitted, but they became 'accepted'.

Prototype and Experimental Aircraft

Early in the war prototype aircraft were usually in a plain polished finish produced by the designing firm to ensure the least possible surface drag in flight evaluation tests, but since they presented both a conspicuous and attractive target, standard camouflage in trainer scheme was specified (see Chapter 5). This was conditioned from early 1941 by a yellow letter 'P' for 'Prototype', marked within a 1 in. thick yellow circle, of diameter equal to that of the fuselage roundel, placed either forward or aft of this roundel, as practicable.

An 18 in. wide band around the rear of the fuselage was the distinguished mark of a day fighter from December, 1940. Its colour was officially described as 'Sky' and indeed in this photograph it almost blends with the sky. This Spitfire XII tail shows many of the smaller markings, specification and part numbers and the usual W/T marking.

Two or more prototypes were ordered for each new basic design to permit concurrent development of various aspects and to provide for loss by accident. Invariably the serials allotted were spaced out to give the impression of a production batch, although this was belied by the 'P' marking. Four experimental Horsas that were ordered are typical of this serial spacing: DK346, DK349, DK353 and DK358. Not all 'P' marked aircraft, however, had spaced serials, as the prototype classification often applied to production aircraft modified to a new standard.

Standard types of aircraft with experimental installations of a secret nature had their serial numbers suffixed with a 'G' for 'Guard' e.g. Wellington II Z8570/G with an experimental jet engine unit in the tail. This marking did in some cases also apply to certain prototypes as in the case of DG558/G the first Welkin. Aircraft used by the Royal Aircraft Establishment for testing various apparatus had no identification markings other than a serial number, Blenheim IV N6241 e.g. served at this establishment for general experimental work until an accident necessitated its replacement by R3602.

Years before the war, experimental military aircraft not built to an Air Ministry tender, being, in fact, private ventures, were allotted a provisional registration by the Directorate of Civil Aviation, since they did not qualify for a certificate of airworthiness as a civil aircraft. They were neither civil nor military aircraft and therefore outside the scope of this book, but during the war such aircraft were camouflaged and bore roundels. Trainer camouflage scheme was usual for these machines, with or without a prototype marking. Their provisional registrations marked on the fuselage sides consisted of a number with a prefix of a single letter that denoted the designing firm. Letters were allotted as follows: A—Armstrong Whitworth, B—Blackburn, E—De Havilland, F—Fairey, G—Gloster, H—Handley-Page, I—Hawker, J—Parnall, K—A. V. Roe, L—Saunders Roe, M—Short Bros., N—Supermarine, O—Vickers, P—Westland, R—Bristol, T—General Aircraft, U—Miles, W—Weir, X—Percival, Y—Cunliffe Owen and Z—Taylorcraft.

Day Fighters: Take-off by Hurricanes of No. 257 Squadron. Unusual for 1941 are the A2 type roundels on a grey instead of duck-egg blue undersurface, but no doubt a camouflage best suited to the weather. The leading machine is flown by Squadron Leader R. R. Stanford Tuck, D.S.O., D.F.C., and what appears to be a line under the cockpit cover is 26 swastikas, one for each of his victories.

The Fighting Role

The primary task of Fighter Command was to defend Great Britain against air attack, but during the opening months of the war several of its squadrons were deployed on convoy protection duties. It was further weakened by losses during 1940 in Norway and France, yet it emerged the victor, but severely strained from the Battle of Britain. Gradually an offensive force was built up and exploited as the main force of the *Luftwaffe* departed for the Russian Front. Fighter sweeps deliberately baited the Germans into combat and in a similar way night-fighting roles became more in the nature of intruder roles. Fighter-bomber units nurtured by the Command expanded and like biological reproduction were shed off to form new forces as our strength grew sufficient to attempt an invasion of the continent and the 2nd Tactical Air Force was formed. At this time, 15 November, 1943, Fighter Command became known as Air Defence Great Britain under the Allied Expeditionary Air Forces Command. The significance of this to markings is that our fighter aircraft thereby qualified for the conspicuous 'Invasion Stripes' of June-July, 1944. When A.D.G.B. was formed, Germany was not considered able to launch a major air offensive against this country, but the 'Little Blitz' of 1944 kept our fighters alerted and the cruel V1 weapon was an unexpected challenge that kept the Command busy almost to the final collapse of Germany. It also resulted in the paint being stripped from a number of fighters in order to exact maximum speed.

General Finish—Day Fighter

The uppersurface finish of fighters was a straightforward matter; from 1937 it was shadow-shading in dark brown and dark green until 1941 when the dark brown was changed to ocean grey using M.A.P. Pattern No. 1. This was a turning point of the war in the air. As our fighting role changed from the defensive to the offensive by fighter sweeps across the sea, so was it necessary to compromise between 'over-land' and 'over-sea' camouflage shades. Few realised the significance of this change of colouring, but it epitomised Britain's will and means to fight back.

Undersurfaces were subject to several changes. The half black, half grey finish of early 1939 remained the general rule until June, 1940. No roundels were marked on this surface. Then, standard roundels were introduced with a completely light blue undersurface. This was not altogether suitable for British skies in general, rather too optimistic one could say! It was, nevertheless, ideally suited for those fateful days of 1940 when the Battle of Britain was fought in the clear skies of a glorious English summer. During this time, a new undersurface shade was specified.

This new undersurface shade, duck-egg blue, is a somewhat controversial shade to describe by the very fact that it was also called duck-egg green and sometimes described as grey-green with yellowish tinge. The official responsible for its classification, not to be caught out on a subject capable of so many interpretations, designated it 'Sky Type S'. Its shade did in fact vary and, incidentally the background to Vernon Ward's well-known bird picture 'Night Patrol' shows Sky Type S in all its variations.

For all operational fighters and those from production, Sky Type S was the standard undersurface finish, but, paradoxically, fighters delivered from maintenance or storage units had the port side marked black. From June, 1940, onwards roundels on the underside became the invariable rule, outlined where necessary on the black port wing. All other markings were subject to the general rules given in Chapter 1 except for special fighter distinguishing markings.

In December, 1940, all day fighters were given an 18 in. fuselage band in Sky Type S, marked forward of the fin, together with the spinner marked in the same nondescript shade, to contrast with German fighters who usually had brightly coloured spinners. A new marking from September, 1941, was a 6 in. yellow stripe along the leading edge of the wing as shown on page 103.

Night Fighters: Hurricane IIs of No. 253 Squadron in an early night fighter black finish, that permitted a roundel on the undersurfaces. All lettering was in dull red: the unit code obscured by the wing of Z3971 was SW. The four aircraft nearest the camera were presented by Hyderabad which accounts for the names marked on the nose.

General Finish—Night Fighter and Intruder Aircraft

Before the war several fighter squadrons had a day and night role, for that reason there was no distinction in finish between day fighters and night fighters. However, the introduction of much specialised night flying and fighting equipment had, by the end of 1940, made completely separate roles for units necessary. An official night-fighting camouflage of overall black came into effect from December, 1940. A preparation, RDM2, was used which gave a velvety non-reflecting surface. Serials and codes were marked in dull red.

Fuselage roundels on early night fighters with an improvised dark finish were replaced later by standard roundels, Types A1 or A2. Uppersurface roundels were invariably of the B Type and roundels on the undersurface, of any type, were marked only at the discretion of Fighter Command.

By October, 1942, when the range of night fighters had appreciably increased and their role had advanced to the offensive, by roaming across the sea to German-occupied territory, a new finish was brought in taking into account night, dusk and dawn, land and sea camouflage. This it had not been considered prudent to introduce earlier, as night-fighter pilots had been forbidden to fly over enemy-held territory, to avoid any possibility of secret detection equipment falling into the enemy's hands.

This new scheme was at first in dark green and sea grey medium using the appropriate M.A.P. pattern for the division of colours, with undersurfaces a plain sea grey medium. At the beginning of 1943 however, this was changed to an overall sea grey. Roundels used were as follows: Uppersurface—Type B, undersurface—Type C or nil at discretion of Fighter Command, fuselage sides—Type C1. Code letters were in dull red and serials in black.

Intruder aircraft had been in night fighter schemes until the Autumn of 1942 when a day fighter scheme with black undersurfaces was tried, to be replaced the following winter by dark green and sea grey medium uppersurfaces with black underneath as before. No roundels were marked on the undersurfaces, codes and serials were in dull red.

Fighters in Northern France, 1939-1940

During the opening weeks of the Second World War, the R.A.F. units forming British Air Forces, France, were deployed in accordance with pre-war plans. The Force was divided into two elements and fighter squadrons were allotted to both. The Air Component with reconnaissance and Army co-operation duties had four fighter squadrons on its strength with the following equipment and coding: Nos. 85 Hurricane (VY), 87 Hurricane (LK), 607 Gladiator (AF) and 615 Gladiator (KW). The Advanced Air Striking Force of medium bombers, mainly Battles, had two fighter squadrons, Nos. 1 Hurricane (JX) and 73 Hurricane (TP).

It will be remembered that in 1934 the R.A.F. had abandoned rudder striping in national colours, but this practice had remained in force in the French Air Force. To the French pilot identification of friend or foe in air battle had been a simple conception. If an aircraft had rudder stripes it was French, if it had not, then it was German! Now came a new possibility—it might be British! The best position to attack a fighter was by following on its tail—and the tail was the very part which worried the French. 'He who hesitates is lost' is a proverb even more imperative to a fighter pilot than a dithering pedestrian. There must be no question of doubt or momentary wavering and the French therefore represented that the tail markings of all Allied fighters should be striped. This resulted in R.A.F. squadrons in France re-introducing rudder stripes at the expense of slightly lowered aerodynamic efficiency from late in 1939. The stripes were in post-1930 order, i.e. with red leading and in the opposite order to French fighters.

Rudder striping was exclusive to fighter aircraft in France which included the squadrons mentioned and in May and June, 1940, also those squadrons flung hastily into the Battle of France in a vain attempt to stem the German tide. If the rudder stripes were not marked on the Hurricanes of No. 501 Squadron (SD) before leaving England, there was little time to do it on arrival, for within an hour of landing on French soil the squadron was in combat with a formation of forty He 111s. Three other reinforcing squadrons of Hurricanes were based in France before the final collapse, those being Nos. 3 (QO), 79 (NV) and 504 (HX). During this critical period some units had their code letters painted out in order that German intelligence could not easily assess the extent of our reinforcements and the consequent depletion to our defensive strength at home.

Standard shadow-shading was the general finish throughout this campaign and the undersurfaces of our fighters were in the pre-war, black port-side and grey starboard side, with roundels introduced early in 1940 on this surface.

Fighters in Norway—April to June 1940

In the spring of 1940 came the unsuccessful Scandinavian venture when small British Forces were placed athwart the Germans moving inexorably towards the complete annexation of Norway. Eighteen Gladiators of No. 263 Squadron in early biplane camouflage, with fuselage sides in an undersurface grey, bearing the unit code 'HE' were first used operating from a frozen lake. They still remain there as rotting hulks, witness to the futility of matching a handful of aircraft against the might of the *Luftwaffe*. The Hurricanes of No. 46 Squadron (PO) were also landed in Norway and upon the decision to evacuate being taken, they were flown on to the aircraft carrier *Glorious*—only to be lost the following day when this famous old carrier was sunk by the *Scharnhorst* and *Gneisenau*.

Fighters in the Battle of Britain

The Battle of Britain was perhaps the most important battle in the history of our nation, for on its result hinged the fate of this very land. Had our defences relaxed, German bombers by incessant attacks upon our ports, factories and bases could have destroyed our power to fight if not our will to fight. As it was, the 'few',* the pilots of the squadrons listed, withstood the onslaught of the Luftwaffe, destroying 1,733 enemy aircraft for a loss of 915. The German attack commenced in force on the 12th August, 1940. On that fateful day the R.A.F. fighter squadrons available, and their

deployment, are listed in Appendix IV, together with the squadron code borne by the aircraft of each squadron engaged.

During the battle, five Hurricane squadrons joined the fray, these were No. 1 (Canadian) Squadron, later No. 401 (R.C.A.F.) Squadron, which arrived in this country during June, 1940, and was allotted YO for its aircraft. The other four squadrons were flown by the gallant survivors of the air forces of Poland and Czechoslovakia, their squadron numbers and codes were as follows: No. 302 (Polish) WX, No. 303 (Polish) RF, No. 310 (Czech) NN and No. 312 (Czech) DU. These units were permitted a national emblem on the fuselage side provided it did not take up more than one square foot and thereby, perhaps, compromise the camouflage.

Air/Sea Rescue

At the time of the Battle of Britain several Lysanders were attached to Fighter Command for air/sea rescue work, such as searching, dropping dinghies or directing launches; later Walrus flying-boats were attached to effect 'pick-ups'. In September, 1941, they were incorporated into four squadrons with unit codes as follows: Nos. 275 (PV), 276 (AQ), 277 (BA) and 278 (MY), using Spitfire IIC, Defiant II, Hudson III and later Warwick I aircraft. During 1942 a new squadron, No. 281 (FA), was added with Defiant II aircraft as initial equipment. Those of basic fighter type had day fighter finish including the fuselage band. Other landplanes had temperate land scheme and flying-boats temperate sea scheme. A white finish applied to the air/sea rescue aircraft of Nos. 279 and 280 Squadrons, which, being used for long range work, came under Coastal Command. All air/sea rescue aircraft had sky undersurfaces, with type 'A' or 'C' (according to the period) roundels under the wings.

FIGHTER AIRCRAFT TYPES—MARKING IDENTITY NOTES

Gladiator: Last of the biplane fighters. Prototype K5200 and production Mk. I from K6129 in 1936 all finished in silver. Many later camouflaged and used in operational units, e.g. K7946 HE.R of 263 Squadron and

* "Never in the field of human conflict was so much owed by so many to so few."—Winston S. Churchill, 20 August, 1940.

K7976 KW.A of 615 Squadron. Mk. II numbered from N2265, mostly delivered to F.A.A. or R.A.F. in Middle East. Mk. II (Met.) conversions from Mk. II for meteorological work, e.g. N2307. All types withdrawn August, 1945.

Hurricane I: Front-line fighter 1938-41. Prototype (silver) K5083. First production (shadow-shading) L1547-

A night fighter in its element. This Hurricane is in early and unorthodox night fighter camouflage. The B-type roundel without a white portion is rather compromised by the gleaming white in the fin flash. Unofficial is the unit marking, a hexagon first used on the squadron's S.E.5As in 1917, revealing the code letters VY as No. 85 Squadron.

2146. First service unit, No. 111 Squadron, Northolt, with L1548-64, later coded TM, e.g. L1564 was TM.P. Development aircraft; L1877 metal-covered wings, L1893 desert equipment, L1980 first V.P. airscrew, L2048 (Polish markings) export version. Second batch (300) numbered from N2318. All Hurricanes subsequent to N2422 (with the exception of twenty-five with V-serials) had metal-covered wings. P2535 first Gloster-built batch of which P2682 *et seq.* had airscrews. P3265 *et seq.* Hawker-built, P5170 *et seq.* Canadian-built, R4074 *et seq.* Gloster-built. V-serialled aircraft were coming off Hawker production lines at time of Battle of Britain, service examples—V6558 257 Squadron, V7238 601 Squadron, V7572 85 Squadron. AS990 last Mk. I built.

Hurricane II: Used extensively in fighter sweeps 1941-3. Many shipped abroad. IIA (8 × .303 in. guns), IIB (12 × .303 in. guns), IIC (4 × 20 mm. cannon). Production from Z2308 (Hawker) and BG674 (Gloster). Alternate armament fitting in batches, e.g. from a representative 100, Z2912-3011: Z2912-27 IIB, Z2928-31 IIA, Z2932-58 blank numbers, Z2959-82 IIA, Z2983-99 IIB, Z3000-11 blank numbers. Subsequent batches BN, HL, HV, HW, LB, LD, LE, LF, KW, KX, KZ, NF and PZ serials. PZ865 last built.

Spitfire I. II and V: Standard fighters, home defence 1938-40, fighter sweeps 1941-42, limited overseas shipments from 1941. Prototype (Cream enamel later camouflaged) K5054. Mk. I: First production (shadow-shading) K9787-L1096. First service use in No. 19 Squadron, Duxford, from September, 1938, later code WZ issued. Service examples: K9847 64 Squadron (March '40), K9918 65 Squadron (March '39), L1000 610 Squadron (October '39). K9834 renumbered N17 for World Speed Record attempt; project abandoned. No. 19 Squadron aircraft, twenty-two in all, had special fitting of Rotol airscrews in 1939-40, machines N3030, N3097, N3104, N3122, N3160, N3171-4, N3183, etc. Mk. II: P-serialled aircraft also the first built completely under sub-contract. P9553-67 finished in Turkish markings September, '39, but reverted back to R.A.F. Many aircraft in P batches were 'named aircraft' see page 193. Mk. V: R-serialled and subsequent W, X, AA, AB, etc., batches. AR212 first Westland-built Spitfire.

Spitfire IX to XXI: Used by ADGB squadrons as follows: Nos. 1, 33, 41, 64, 74, 80, 118, 126, 127, 130, 131, 165, 229, 234, 274, 303, 345, 350, 402 (R.C.A.F.), 501, 504, 610, 611 and 616. No simple rule for mark number identification by serial can be advised except for: Mk. X, 16 only, MD191-199 and SR395-400; Mk. XXI, 120 production models, LA187-236, LA249-284 and LA299-332.

Defiant: Limited use as day fighter 1940, night-fighter duties 1941-1942, air/sea rescue work 1942-1943. Prototypes (silver), K8310 and K8620. Production (shadow-shading) Mk. I L6950-7036 followed by batches numbered from N1535, N3306, T3911, V1106 and AA281. First action over Dunkirk as day fighter with No. 264 Squadron, L7038 PS.U, L7076 PS.V, etc. Many conversions for night fighting, e.g. N3407 VA.Q. Nos. N1550-1 and AA363 *et seq.* were Mk. II.

A black port wing and light starboard wing was a usual fighter undersurface marking at the beginning of the war. It was used for some years by non-operational fighters and also for Whirlwinds to provide an additional identification marking for this rather German-looking fighter. It may be noticed that the roundel on the port side is smaller than the starboard roundel to take in account the yellow outline.

Spitfire V EP166 of No. 111 Squadron in the fighter markings from 1942 after this introduction of 'C' type roundels and dark green and ocean grey camouflage. The name by the cockpit refers to its presentation by the peoples of San Paulo, Brazil, not to the pilot, who, incidentally, was Squadron Leader P. R. Wickham, D.F.C.

Mosquito: Mks. II, XII and XXX used in quantity 1942-45 for night fighting by Nos. 25 (ZK), 96 (ZJ), 125 (VA), 151 (DZ), 219 (FK), 307 (EW) 456 R.A.A.F. (RX) Squadrons and with an intruder role by Nos. 418 R.C.A.F. (TH) and 605 (UP) squadrons. (Unit codes given in brackets). No straightforward method of identity by serial markings can be advised owing to conversions both on production lines and in service, e.g. Nos. HJ240-250 produced in Mk. II version were converted to Mk. XVII.

Havoc: Night fighter and intruder purchased from U.S.A. and by conversion of Boston from the same source. Main use 1941-43. Individual letter marked on nose and not on fuselage side. Nos. AH431-529 delivered as Havoc II. Serial number did not assist type identification, e.g. Mk. Is BT461 (night fighter), BT462 (intruder), BT463-4 (night fighters), BT465 (long aerial mine fitting), etc. Service examples: BB900 YP.G and BJ492 YP.J Mk. I intruder versions with No. 23 Squadron; BJ472 VY.R Mk. II trainer in night fighter finish with No. 85 Squadron.

Beaufighter: Mk. I and II night fighter versions used 1940-44. Development aircraft, R2052-62. First type to be produced in standard night fighter RDM2 finish. Early deliveries to No. 29 Squadron, e.g. R2138 RO.L; the C.O., Sqn. Ldr. later Wing Comdr. Guy Gibson, V.C., flew R2050. Fighter versions may be classified as follows: Between R2063 and R2269 Mk. IF Bristol (Filton) built. R2270 *et seq.* Mk. IIF, ditto. T4623-47 Mk. IF Fairey built. V8131 *et seq.* Mk. IIF Bristol (Filton) built. Numbers between X7540 and X7879 (excluding X7542-3) Bristol (Weston) built. The Mk. VIF numbered in batches from V8386 served in units both at home and overseas.

Blenheim IF and IVF: Many conversions from day bomber aircraft, 1475 conversion sets being produced. Day fighters had standard blue band. Some used for night fighting, e.g. L1375 RO.J and L6637 RO.S of No. 29 Squadron.

Whirlwind: Limited operational use as day fighter and fighter bomber by Nos. 137 (SF) and 263 (HE) Squadrons. Prototypes, L6844-5. Production of 114 aircraft numbered between P6966 and P7122. P6922 had trials with No. 25 Squadron, otherwise first sixteen delivered to No. 263 Squadron.

Airacobra: Used as day fighter operationally only by No. 601 Squadron 1941. Unit insignia, a winged sword (see page 76) was marked in the white of the fin flash—thus contravening regulations. Aircraft serving in this squadron were: AH578 UF.E, AH579 UF.J, AH580 UF.L, etc. AH629 became 2796M. Nos. AH570-739, AP264-384, BW100-183 and BX135-434 were ordered from U.S.A., but 212 were diverted to Russia in standard British day fighter finish, but with Red Stars in place of roundels, 179 went to the U.S.A.A.F. and fifty-four were lost at sea. Those used in No. 601 Squadron R.A.F. had the unit code UF marked in only 2 ft. letters just forward of the fuselage roundels and the individual letter in the same size immediately in front of the cockpit door (starboard side).

A new shape in standard fighter finish, the Meteor I flew its first sortie on 27th July, 1944. EE227 illustrated, is one of the twenty Meteor FIs built (EE210-229) and is here shown in No. 616 Squadron's coding—the first R.A.F. Squadron to operate a jet fighter.

ROYAL AIR FORCE IDENTITY MARKINGS 1915-1954
ROUNDEL TYPES

A. (i and ii)

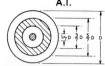
A.I.

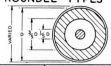
A2. (i and ii)

B.

B.I.

	ORDER OF COLOURS FROM CENTRE	PERIOD OF USE	APPLICABILITY REMARKS
A(i)	RED, WHITE, BLUE, (BRIGHT.)	1915—1942	Used on clear, silver or light coloured surfaces
A(ii)	RED, WHITE, BLUE, (MATT.)	1937—1942	Used on camouflaged surfaces for a limited period 1939-1940 or generally as alternative to A(i) above.
A.I.	RED, WHITE, BLUE, YELLOW, (MATT.)	1937—1942	Generally for all camouflaged surfaces, 1937 to March 1939. Generally for fuselage sides June 1940 June 1942.
A2(i)	RED, WHITE, BLUE, YELLOW, (MATT.)	1940—1942	Alternative on certain aircraft to Type A1 (no set thickness for yellow outline).
A2(ii)	RED, WHITE, BLUE, WHITE, (BRIGHT.)	1915—1937	General for drab surfaces 1915-1923. Limited use on wooden hulls and certain prototypes in special schemes 1923-1937.
B.	RED, BLUE, (MATT.)	1923—1947	All positions, night bombers only 1923-1937. Thereafter, apart from short period in 1939, it was exclusive to upper-surfaces.
B.I.	RED, BLUE, YELLOW, (MATT.)	MAR.-DEC.1939	Limited use on certain aircraft.
C.	RED, WHITE, BLUE, (DULL.)	1942—1947	General use on light surfaces. Excluded from all upper-surface positions 1942 to early 1945.
C.I.	RED, WHITE, BLUE, YELLOW, (DULL.)	1942—1947	General use on drab surfaces, excluding upper-surfaces 1942-1944, including upper-surfaces from 1945-1947.
D(i)	RED, WHITE, BLUE, (DULL.)	1947	All surfaces introduced for production aircraft in June 1947 and extended to service aircraft when re-painting was necessary.
D(ii)	RED, WHITE, BLUE, (BRIGHT.)	1948 TO DATE	All positions.

C

CI

'C' TYPE ROUNDEL DIAMETERS

SIZE	R	W	B	Y
SMALL	6"	8"	16"	18"
MEDIUM	12"	16"	32"	36"
LARGE	18"	24"	48"	54"

Applicability: As per fin flash
TABLE FOR 1942-47
R - RED W-WHITE
B - BLUE Y-YELLOW

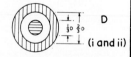
D (i and ii)

FIN FLASHES 1940-1954
NON—STANDARDISED FIN FLASHES JUNE—DEC 1940
No set dimensions given, equal division of red, white and blue specified. Variations as per illustrations.

STANDARD FIN FLASH DECEMBER 1940-JUNE 1942 24"WIDE X 27"HIGH
Equal division of colours with red leading. Positioned on both sides of fins, normally just above level of tailplane. Re-introduced 1947

STANDARD FIN FLASH JULY 1942-1947
DIMENSIONS AS PER TABLE BELOW
Positioned on both sides of fins immediately above level of tailplane, red leading.

TYPE	OVERALL DIMENSIONS	WIDTH OF COLOUR BANDS			APPLICABILITY
		RED	WHITE	BLUE	
SMALL	24" HIGH X 18"WIDE	8"	2"	8"	Single engined aircraft excluding fighters.
MEDIUM	24" HIGH X 24"WIDE	11"	2"	11"	Twin engined aircraft and all fighters
LARGE	24" HIGH X 36"WIDE	17"	2"	17"	All four engined aircraft and Avro Manchesters.

PROTOTYPE MARKING IN YELLOW
Outside diameter = Outside diameter of Roundel. Where roundel = 4', height of 'P' = 2' 9" in 4"strokes. YELLOW ring is 2"thick.

SERIAL MARKING DIMENSIONS

SERIAL TABLE

NO	POSITION	DIMENSIONS	APPLICATION OF COLOUR
1.	REAR OF FUSELAGE BOTH SIDES	A= 8" B= 29" C= 5" D= 1" E= 1"	All R.A.F. Aircraft. General rule: Night flying aircraft-dull red, Coastal aircraft-grey, all others black.
2.	REAR OF FUSELAGE BOTH SIDES	A= 4" B= 15½" C= 2½ D= ¾" E= ⅝"	All F.A.A. aircraft in black, words ROYAL NAVY in 4 inch lettering printed above.
3.	UNDERSURFACE OF EACH WING IN OPPO-SITE DIRECTIONS AS ILLUSTRATED ON PAGE 103.	A= ½ wing chord at ⅙ of span inboard, B.C.D. and 'E' in prop-ortion to No.1.	R.A.F. Training and Communication aircraft in black.

102

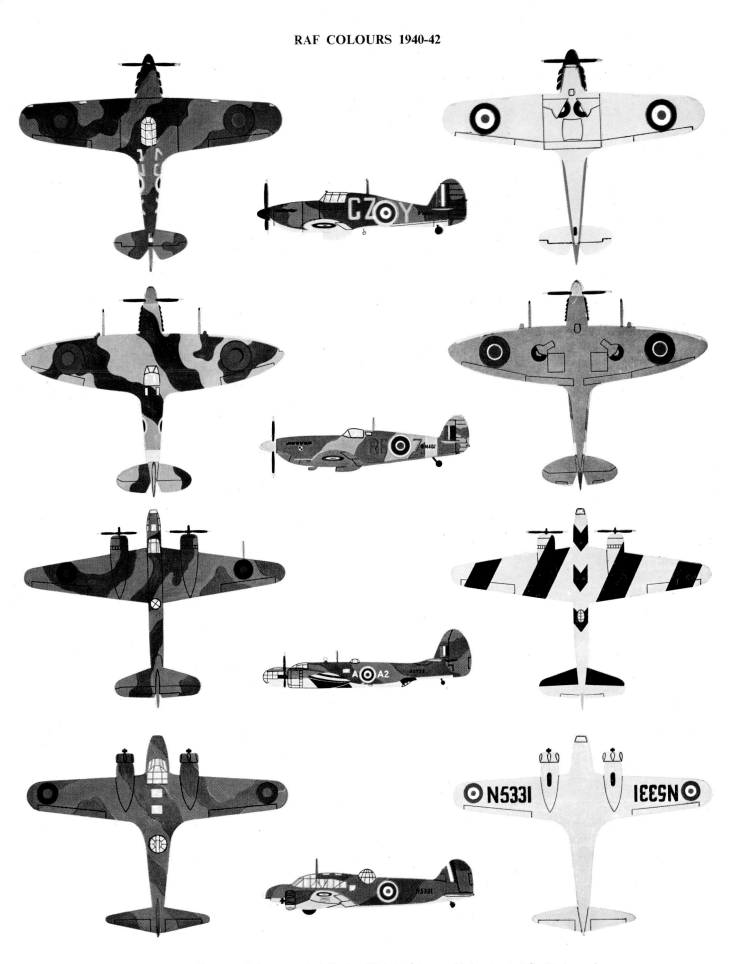

At the top a Hurricane I shows a typical Battle of Britain fighter and below it a Spitfire V shows the changes in fighter colours and markings in 1942. With black and yellow undersurfaces the Maryland displays target-towing colours and Anson N5331 is in 1940 trainer finish.

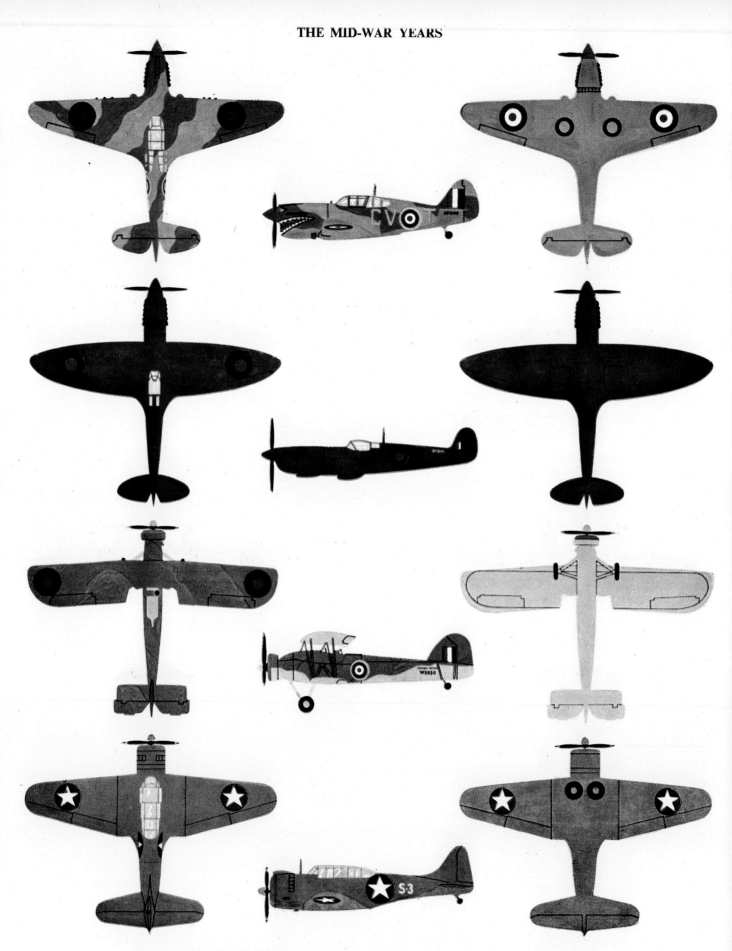

Top to bottom: A Kittyhawk in the markings of No. 3 Squadron R.A.A.F. displays tropical land scheme camouflage followed by a Spitfire in deep P.R. blue. Next a Swordfish is shown in F.A.A. temperate sea scheme and finally a Dauntless appears in U.S.N. markings, August-October 1942.

R.A.F. Bomber Command

This Blenheim of No. 139 Squadron devoid of fin flash and with a straggling division between the upper and lower surfaces, provides a contrast to later Blenheims illustrated.

Organisation and Role

Bomber Command was the largest of the R.A.F. Commands. When war came it was organised into six groups: No. 1 Group with ten squadrons of obsolescent Battles went to form the Advanced Striking Force in France, No. 2 Group had Blenheim IVs based on East Anglian aerodromes; No. 3 Group in the same district was the backbone of the force with Wellington I and IA aircraft; No. 4 Group in Yorkshire had Whitley III and IV bombers, slow and cumbersome, even unsuited for their early duties of pamphlet-dropping; No. 5 Group on Lincolnshire airfields had Hampdens and No. 6 Group, originally a training group, became later a Royal Canadian Air Force Group. Nos. 91, 92 and 93 Groups were formed for training personnel for the Command.

As well as expansion of existing groups, new techniques led to the formation of No. 8 (Path Finder Force) Group and No. 100 (Special Duties) Group. No. 1 Group was re-formed in England after losing 229 of its aircraft in the Battle of France, 1940.

In general, No. 2 Group operated by day and all other operational groups by night. Upon this fundamental difference Bomber Command can be divided in two parts for markings—Day Bombers and Night Bombers with the consequent difference in undersurface shades.

General Finish—Day Bombers

The regulations given in Chapter 1 included day bombers, but undersurfaces were, as always throughout the war, the variable factor. Until December, 1939, day bomber undersurfaces were jet-black in common with all aircraft of the Command, but from then onwards Sky Type S was specified for this role. Roundels were marked on the underside of the wings only during 1940 and were then omitted altogether on this position, until after the war.

General Finish—Night Bombers

At the beginning of the war the undersides of bombers were jet black, the white serial numbers previously marked there having been painted over in the first few days of September, 1939. Early losses of Wellingtons had shown that heavy bombers were best confined to night operations and a change in markings by extending the undersurface black partly up the fuselage sides gave indication of a lesson learned. In December, 1940, it was further extended to three-quarters up the fuselage sides and inclusive of fins and rudders; thus assisting concealment from the oblique rays of enemy searchlights. The black was a velvety non-reflecting preparation known as RDM2. Over this were marked the fuselage roundels normally Type A1 with unit code letters and serials in grey, until the general change-over to C Type roundels when code letters and serials were presented in dull red.

Special Finish

Passing from the general to the particular, there is an

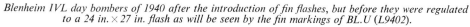

Blenheim IVL day bombers of 1940 after the introduction of fin flashes, but before they were regulated to a 24 in. × 27 in. flash as will be seen by the fin markings of BL.U (L9402).

An early production Halifax with black undersurfaces extending only to the levels of the main and tail planes. It bears the early type roundels with grey code letters, the serial is hidden by the tail-plane. The fin flash, it may be noted, is marked on both sides of each fin.

interesting exception in markings from the R.A.F.'s unsuccessful attempt to use the American Boeing B-17C (Fortress) as a high-altitude day bomber. Twenty of these machines, AN518-537, were delivered in clear finish, at first incorrectly numbered AM518-537. They were delivered to No. 90 Squadron in dark brown and green to M.A.P. Pattern No. 4, with azure blue undersurfaces, fins and rudders.

During August, 1941, the camouflage changed to temperate sea scheme, being more suited for their long unescorted daylight raids over the sea to Brest, Oslo and Kiel. However, the following September operations ceased, AN523, AN525 and AN533 had been lost on operations, AN535 was so badly damaged that it had to be scrapped, AN522 had been lost earlier in a flying accident and during August, AN534 was burnt out on the ground. Apparently night operations were then contemplated, for AN537 in October, 1941, was observed to have black undersurfaces that extended well up the fuselage sides; white letters 'WP.D' showed it to be still with No. 90 Squadron. Night operations were never put into effect, for the remaining Fortresses were dispersed. AN527 and AN530 re-finished in 'Coastal White' (see Chapter 4) went to No. 220 Squadron, AN524 became 3355M and AN526 became a familiar landmark at St. Athan as 4449M. AN532 ended up in India with U.S.A.A.F. markings. So the R.A.F. gave up the idea of high altitude day bombing. There was no need to pursue the matter for the Americans soon arrived in force and took over this side of the business, while the R.A.F. concentrated on night bombing.

Bombers in France 1939-1940

The Advanced Air Striking Force in France consisted of ten squadrons, numbered and coded as follows: Nos. 12(PH), 15(LS), 40(BL), 88(RH), 103(PM), 105(GB), 142(WT), 150(JN), 218(HA) and 226(MQ) equipped in the main with Battles which, it has been expressed, were as fitted for fighting as hackneys for winning the Derby!

They were finished in standard shadow-shading, black undersurfaces, with pre-war white serial numbers, washed over in a dark paint. Squadron codes were in some cases painted over but individual letters were left in their conspicuous grey to assist in recognition for formation flying.

One of the most dramatic episodes of the war came during this period. As the Germans poured into Belgium over the Maas bridges that they had seized by airborne troops, a desperate attempt to destroy the bridges was made by the R.A.F. So hazardous was this task known to be that volunteers were requested from the squadron chosen for the operation—No. 12. Every aircrew member of the unit responded and five crews were chosen. Five Battles set out and not one returned, the bridge was damaged but not destroyed. The men concerned, flying their obsolescent machines, to bomb low for accuracy in this heavily defended region must have known their fate—yet they went as volunteers. Modellers, choosing to make a Fairey Battle would surely wish it to record this gallant episode by those five Battles, L5227 PH.J, L5241 PH.G, L5439 PH.N, P2204 PH.K and P2322 PH.F. Flying Officer D. E. Garland, dragged from P2204 by the Germans, the only survivor from his Battle, was awarded the V.C. which also went posthumously to his navigator, Sergeant T. Gray. The other member of the crew was L.A.C. L.R. Reynolds.

Day Bomber Types—Marking Identity Notes

Battle: Limited operational use 1939-40 as related. Training duties 1940 until July, 1944, when all were withdrawn. Prototype (silver) K4303. First production (shadow-shading) K7558-7712. First service in No. 63 Squadron 1937 using K7559-70. Early service examples: K7578-84 No. 105 Squadron, K9200 No. 207 Squadron, K9404 No. 52 Squadron. L4935 *et seq.* built by Austin's, of which last 200 (L5598-5797) were finished in target-towing markings except for four (L5623-6) in Turkish Air Force markings for export. P6616 *et seq.* produced as trainers with yellow undersurfaces.

Blenheim: Mk. I prototype and first production shadow-shading from January, 1937, numbered from K7033 with white serials under their black wings in Bristol fashion —K-7113. (N.B. 1937-38 all bombers had black undersides. Late 1939 units with a day role were re-marked with light grey and later 'sky' undersurfaces). First deliveries to No. 114 Squadron (K7037-46) then No. 90 Squadron (K7047-56). Up to L1546 all Bristol-built. Batches from L6594 built by A. V. Roe and from L8362 by Rootes Securities Ltd. Mk. IV batches L4823 to 4934 and between L9170 and 9482 built as Mk. I and brought up to Mk. IV standard. All numbered from N3522 and above built as Mk. IV. Service examples: L9258 XD.E and N6223 XD.G of No. 139 Squadron. R3843, F of No. 18 Squadron, was the aircraft that dropped the artificial legs to Wing-Cmdr. Bader, the legless pilot, when he was captured by the Germans. (See also Fighter and Coastal Commands.)

Boston: Day bomber 1941-44. Individual letter marked on nose and not by fuselage roundel. Because of large engine nacelle, roundel on fuselage was marked well aft. Most Boston I and II bombers (AE, AW, AX, BD and BT serials) converted to Havocs with consequent night finish, see Chapter 2. Mk. III with W, Z and AL serials served in Nos. 88, 107 and 226 Squadrons. Service example: Z2286 OM.P flown by Sqn. Ldr. D. J. Evans in raid on Phillips Works, Eindhoven, 6th December, 1942. W8392 and AL738 were also in that unit. Mk. IIIA numbered from BZ196 Mk. IV from BZ400 and Mk. V from BZ580.

Ventura: Day bomber 1942-43 in three No. 2 Group Sqns., an example in each squadron being AE763 YH.B of No. 21 Squadron, AJ223 SB.M of No. 464 (R.A.A.F.) Squadron and AJ216 EG.O of No. 487 (R.N.Z.A.F.) Squadron. Mk. I AE658 up, Mk. II AE846 up, subsequent marks mostly delivered to other Commands.

Mitchell: Day bomber 1942-45 used by Nos. 98 and 180 Squadrons. Mk. I FK161-183 only. Mk. II batches numbered between FL164 and HD345. Mk. III Nos. HD346 and above. Service example: FW122 VO.R of 98 Squadron, an ill-fated machine that blew up over France wrecking two other aircraft in its formation.

Mosquito: Day bomber 1942-43 by Nos. 105 (GB) and 139 (XD) Squadrons, e.g. DZ464 XD.C a Mk. IV bomber. Later these two squadrons were transferred to Pathfinder Force with consequent change to night bomber markings.

Night Bomber Types—Marking Identity Notes

Hampden: Prototype (silver) K4240. Production in shadow-shading from L4032 produced for Bomber Command, but apart from a few early daring raids by day, they were used mainly for mine laying, both in Bomber and Coastal Commands. First service unit: No. 49 Squadron, August, 1938, with L4036 and L4039-47. Hampdens numbered between P5298 and P5436, AJ988-999 and AN100-167 built in Canada. P2062 *et seq.* built by English Electric Co. Sgt. J. Hannah won his V.C. on P1355 of 83 Sqn. and Flt.-Lt. R. A. B. Learoyd his V.C. on P4403 of 49 Sqn.

Hereford: Originally intended for Bomber Command and L6031, N9076-7, N9095 and N9102 did serve with No. 35 Squadron, but did not go on operations.

Whitley: Standard heavy bomber of the early war years. O.T.U. service 1940-43. Many diverted to Coastal Command. One O.T.U. did use Whitleys in trainer yellow but this was an exception to the general rule and was only for the short period of three months. Mk. I K7183 up, Mk. II K7217 up, Mk. III K8936 up, Mk. IV K9016 up and Mk. V N1345 up. Service examples: K9019 XE.K, P4938 UO-CA and Z9224 MA.P.

Wellington: The 'Wimpey' needs little introduction, it was the R.A.F.'s standard bomber 1939-42 and even in 1943 the following squadrons were still using 'Wimpeys': Nos. 115, 166, 196, 199, 300, 301 and 305; Nos. 420, 424, 425, 426, 427, 428, 429 and 431 (R.C.A.F.) and No. 466 (R.A.A.F.). Prototype (silver) K4049. Production Mk. I (shadow-shading) from L4212. Many production batches of various marks. Service examples: L4371 NH.Q of No. 38 Squadron. L7842 of 311 Squadron missing 6.2.41. R1006 CR.H, R1245 of 304 Squadron, X3350 BB.U, Z1675 BB.R, BK153 LB.B, DV824 LB.Q and LN171 TN.U presentation aircraft GOLD COAST II.

Stirling: First of the four-engined bombers to enter service in Spring 1941. Prototypes L7600 and L7605. Production Mk. I from N3635. Mk. III BK648-9 and upward of

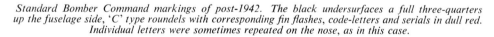

Standard Bomber Command markings of post-1942. The black undersurfaces a full three-quarters up the fuselage side, 'C' type roundels with corresponding fin flashes, code-letters and serials in dull red. Individual letters were sometimes repeated on the nose, as in this case.

This marking implies that Goering was made to eat his words! The aircraft, Lancaster B1 R5868 PO.S of No. 467 (R.A.A.F.) Squadron (ex-OL.Q of No. 83 Squadron), bears indication of 98 operations and of three decorations won by members of its crew. R5868 went on to score its century. In fact, it survived the war after 129 operations. Another famous veteran was Lancaster EE136 named 'Spirit of Russia' that in 1945 was 'rested' at No. 1659 H.C.U. as aircraft RV.G.

BK686, Mk. IV PK225-237 and conversions from EH-serialled machines, also all numbered above PW255, Mk. V numbered between PJ878 and PK186. Service examples: N3642 MG.E, N6040 LS.C, R9197 YZ.U, W7453 (of 'W' serialled Austin Motors-built batch) OJ.O, BK600 BU.Q, EF445/G BU.K.

Manchester: Limited operational use as a bomber. Numbered from L7246 and R5768. Service examples: L7389 (QR.J (No. 61 Squadron) and L7427 OL.Q (83 Squadron). Four camouflage patterns, roundels and fin flashes this aircraft was treated as a four-engined machine.

Lancaster: Manchester L7527 converted to become BT308 was the prototype of this most famous of all heavy night bombers. Many batches in several marks produced by six manufacturers in eight different factories. Those numbered FM100-229 and KB700-999 were Canadian built. Service examples: No. 7 Squadron PB966 MG.H Mk. III, No. 12 Squadron DV244 PH.E Mk. I, No. 35 Squadron ND620 TL.C Mk. III, No. 75 (R.N.Z.A.F.) Squadron ME754 AA.A Mk. III, No. 617 Squadron ED817 AJ-C

tested special mines for breaching the Mohne and Eder Dams; it was a Mk. I special. ED932 AJ.G Mk. I flew on this most famous of all raids—it was one of the Dam-busters! No. 1653 H.C.U. LL907 H.4Q Mk. I. H.M. King George VI and H.M. Queen Elizabeth (now the Queen Mother) visited an early Lancaster production line at Yeadon on 26th March, 1942, and named Lancaster Is R5489 and R5548, GEORGE and ELIZABETH respectively. The former went to No. 44 Squadron and the latter to No. 97 Squadron.

Halifax: Jointly with the Lancaster the Halifax bombed Germany; it started operations as early as March, 1941, and continued in operational service until the end of the war. Prototypes L7244-5, Production from L9485. First deliveries L9486 TL.B to No. 35 Squadron. L9608 had HALIFAX in 1 ft. lettering on the fuselage, having been officially christened by Lady Halifax. The Mk. Is numbered up to L9608 were used by Nos. 10, 35 and 76 Squadrons only. Mk. II L9609 *et seq.* R9538 went to English Electric Co. as pattern for their Mk. IIs commencing at V9976. R9539-40 went to the London Passenger Transport Board's factory as pattern airframes for their Mk. IIs commencing at BB189. Many subsequent batches in bomber Marks III, V, VI and VII. Examples Mk. III MZ954 KW.R of No. 425 (R.C.A.F.) Squadron, Mk. V DK139 ZL.P of No. 427 (R.C.A.F.) Squadron and Mk. VI MZ431 Z5.J of No. 462 (R.A.A.F.) Squadron.

Two squadrons of Bomber Command with a difference in markings were Nos. 346 'Guyenne' (coded H7) and No. 347 'Tunisie' (coded as shown) of the Free French Air Force, for the colours of the roundels and flashes on their Halifaxes were in the reverse order, to accord with French national markings. Normal 'B' type roundels were applied to the upper surface. The red diamond was No. 347 Squadron's insignia in No. 4 Group which used tail markings 1944-45. Unit individual letters were usually marked on the fin.

Coastal Command

Battleship grey and sea green were camouflage colours applied to some flying-boats at the beginning of the war. Here a Stranraer of No. 240 Squadron is shown in this finish. It may be noted that no roundels appear under the wings and that the unit code is marked forward on the hull.

The Work of Coastal Command

Maritime reconnaissance and convoy protection were the major roles of the Command. It played a very important part in the life and death struggle against the U-boat menace in the prolonged Battle of the Atlantic. For much of the war, the Command had to make do with inadequate and obsolescent equipment. From its 1939 'striking force' of two squadrons of 82 m.p.h. Vildebeests, a formidable force of rocket-firing Beaufighters and Mosquitos was gradually built up. In this Command was centralised long-range photographic reconnaissance, both for its own requirements and those of other Commands. Long range air/sea rescue and weather reporting were just two other of its many miscellaneous tasks.

At certain critical periods, some units of Bomber Command were switched over to this Command with consequent necessity for a change in markings. A variety of types were used, both land and sea based, requiring different camouflage schemes—and their tasks were ceaseless, day and night. Markings therefore had sometimes to be altered according to changing situations and their authorisation, officially under the C.-in-C. Coastal Command, was delegated to operational commanders to exercise as they deemed necessary.

General Reconnaissance

General reconnaissance landplanes of which Ansons were firstly and Hudsons generally typical, were finished in temperate land scheme with light grey undersurfaces. Ansons until early 1939 were usually in silver, but Hudsons, delivered early 1939 from the U.S.A., had been given British shadow-shading in America as part of the contract. Initially deliveries were with black undersurfaces, as for bombers, but this was changed to grey after the first few.

Flying-boats at the beginning of the war, mostly obsolescent biplane types, were hastily camouflaged in battleship grey and sea-green shades without a set pattern. Others, including most of the modern Sunderlands, had an unsuited

land scheme of green and brown, with grey undersurfaces. By 1941 all flying-boats were conforming to the temperate sea scheme of dark slate grey and extra dark sea grey. Whatever this official nomenclature implied, there is no getting away from the fact that these shades were basically green and grey. Sky Type S or sky grey was applied to the undersurfaces and the uppersurface sea scheme extended down the hull sides to the waterline.

National markings, though not following general R.A.F. practice for the first two years of war, were fairly consistent throughout both land and sea based general reconnaissance types. They were the only operational class to use A or A2 type roundels on the uppersurface of the wings. A type roundels were marked on the undersurfaces only in the early stages of the war. At the fuselage sides A or, more usually, A1 type roundels were placed and fin striping followed general practice.

By mid-1942 markings had undergone a complete revision. Undersurfaces now included the whole of the fuselage sides, fins and rudders, leaving uppersurface camouflage in temperate sea scheme applying only to strict plan view. C1 type roundels now were standard for fuselage sides, B type appeared on the uppersurfaces to conform with the rest of the R.A.F. and no roundels were marked on the undersurfaces. This was general for most of the anti-submarine aircraft in the Command.

For reporting an individual aircraft, Coastal Command used their own particular designation system and not the aircraft's serial number. This consisted of the aircraft's individual letter and the squadron number, thus the Stranraer illustrated would be L/240 in official reports and this method is used in the official histories.

'Strike' Aircraft

Most operational aircraft in 'Coastal' were required to strike to a greater or lesser degree, but the term 'strike' was applied to those aircraft kept in hand for attacks on specific targets, enemy merchant shipping or warships, as

apart from those aircraft used in regular patrolling, with bombs or depth-charges to use as the occasion arose. The basic difference in markings was that strike aircraft conformed to day bomber markings as far as the definitions of surfaces went, but that it changed from temperate land to temperate sea scheme in 1942.

Mosquitos with the Command were rather a class apart for markings, being for a time in 1942 and early 1943 in standard fighter scheme for their 'strike' role. From 1943 onwards they were marked as for day bombers but with a temporate sea scheme.

Photographic Reconnaissance

Coastal Command developed the high-flying long-range photographic reconnaissance aircraft, following Flying Officer Longbottom's early experiments with an unarmed, blue-coloured Spitfire. This type of aircraft required a new conception in markings. Because clear weather was essential to successful reconnaissance, blue was the obvious camouflage colour; not an ordinary sky blue, but the deep blue of the sub-stratosphere. Since it flew at greater heights than other aircraft, this was the overall finish. Camouflage when on the ground was not so essential for, wherever possible, P.R. aircraft were housed in hangars in order to keep in the best possible condition their highly polished surfaces, designed to give maximum performance.

Shades of blue, and varying shades at that, were applied to the Spitfires and later Mosquitos, the two main P.R. types. Other markings varied considerably. Although the P.R. Unit at Benson expanded and developed into Nos. 540-544 Squadrons, unit code letters were rarely marked on these aircraft and in some cases serials were half-size in white, placed as shown on page 104.

Meteorological Work

Early in the war Nos. 403-5 Flights with Blenheim I and IV aircraft in day bomber finish operated over the North Sea and Atlantic on 'Met' duty. Later Hudsons and Venturas took over this work and by the end of the war, Halifaxes and Fortresses, with their greater range, were able to make calibrations over a wide area. No. 517 may be taken as a typical long-range meteorological squadron, its Halifax (Met) Vs coded X9 (e.g. LL469 X9.W) were finished in white, except for the strict plan view in temperate sea scheme. When, however, some Halifax B VIIs were diverted for this use, standard Bomber Command finish was retained for a short time in No. 519 Squadron, examples being HX344 Z9.D and MZ390 Z9.K.

For high-altitude 'met', ex-H.F. aircraft came in, but in this role code letters *were* appropriate, e.g. in No. 519 Squadron, Z9.W, Z9.V, Z9.T and Z9.U was marked on Spitfire H.F. VIIs EN297, EN506, MD141 and MD160 respectively. An Oxford NM353 in this unit's marking as Z9.P finished as for a communications aircraft, added yet more colour to this unit.

Generally, aircraft for meteorological work were converted from aircraft designed for other roles.

Notes on Flying-Boat Markings

All flying-boat markings, irrespective of aircraft datum line, flying or beached positions, were marked parallel to the water-line. Pre-war biplane type flying-boats had been practically discarded by the time the new 'coastal whites' came in; these types were, with dates of withdrawal from service: Cloud (June, 1940), Scapa (July, 1941), Stranraer and London (November, 1942). The Lerwick was a more modern monoplane type, but it proved unsuccessful and only 21 (L7248-68) were built. It was used mainly by No. 209 Squadron (Code WQ). L7253 entered No. 240 Squadron the month war was declared, L7267 served in 4 O.T.U. (Code TA) during 1941, and L7254 became 3300M at the Marine Training School, Wig Bay. The Sunderland, the best known of R.A.F. flying-boats, was used by Nos. 10 (R.A.A.F.), 119, 201, 228, 246, 330, 422 and 423 (R.C.A.F.) and 461 (R.A.A.F.) Squadrons of Coastal Command during the Battle of the Atlantic. Pre-war prototype K4774 and early production Mk. I from L2158 were in silver. Early camouflage extended down to the waterline, but later Sunderlands were finished as shown on page 122, sometimes with sky, sky-grey or light blue undersurfaces, but more often completely all-white except for plan-view surfaces. Batches from T9083 were built by Blackburn and VB889 a G.R.5 was the last built. P9605 of No. 10 (R.A.A.F.) Squadron was the first R.A.A.F. aircraft to go on operations. Sunderlands remained in service until 1958. Catalinas were delivered from America at first (1940) in temperate land scheme with A1 type roundels at the nose of the hull, an understandable mistake for the American manufacturer to make, as that was where the U.S. Navy put their national marking. In service it was re-positioned aft of the gun blister. Unit code and individual letters were placed in various positions in 4 ft. lettering, but whereas Sunderlands had light slate-grey letters, dull red was specified for Catalinas. Apart from that the finish from 1942 was as shown for the Sunderland. Catalinas in 1943 were used by Nos. 190, 202 and 210 Squadrons and No. 1477 Flight

A Whitley VII in gleaming 'Coastal White' with grey undersurfaces. 146 aircraft of this type were built, supplemented by conversions from Whitley V bombers, with consequent re-marking.

in Coastal Command. It was also much used overseas, e.g. Nos. 209, 244 and 321 Squadrons in the Middle East, Nos. 259 and 262 Squadrons based in East Africa and several squadrons in the Far East. W, Z and AH machines were Mk. Is, AM serialled, Mk. IIs, FP100-324 Mk. IB, FP525-536 Mk. III, JX200-269 and 570-585 IIIA, JX270-437 and 586-662 IIIB. VA701-736 were a Canadian Vickers-built Mk. IIA batch with VA standing for Vickers aircraft; it was extremely rare that prefix letters had any significance beyond an alphabetical allocation, this was one of those rare exceptions.

Notes on General Reconnaissance Landplane Markings

The transition from land to sea schemes has already been explained. In the new finish of sea scheme applied only to strict plan view, with all other surfaces white; code and serial letters usually appeared in grey. This applied to most Fortress, Halifax, Liberator, Ventura, Warwick, Wellington and Whitley aircraft in this role. It also applied to some Hudsons but others had sky instead of white and a few, for special duties, black undersurfaces. Hudsons of No. 53 Squadron based on Rhode Island, later in Trinidad and also in British and Dutch Guiana, were white on *all* surfaces. Service examples: T9360 Hudson I of 269 Squadron in 1940, FK766 Hudson IIIA in the same squadron three years later. Hudson V AM703 of 223 Squadron burnt out at Gibraltar in February, 1942. Ventura Vs were mostly delivered to the Middle East and JS953, JT872 and JT879 served there with No. 17 (S.A.A.F.)

Squadron. FK213 Z9.G and JK109 CG.F are examples of Fortress IIA and III Marks respectively.

Notes on 'Strike' Aircraft Markings.

Mosquitos and Beaufighters were the strike aircraft adopted for this Command and used in quantity. Hudsons and Hampdens, the latter as a torpedo bomber, were also used as strike aircraft and the Beaufort was built specially for the Command. Deliveries of the Beaufort in 1939 numbered from L4441. Some of the first deliveries, L4446-7 and L4499-51 replacing the ancient Vildebeests of No. 22 Squadron. Several batches were subsequently produced until being replaced by Beaufighters. For both these types undersurfaces were in sky with code letters in dull red and serials in black. Beauforts marked for night operations had black undersurfaces, with both codes and serials in dull red. Beaufighters on the other hand almost invariably had the day finish for various marks in fighting, fighter-bomber and torpedo-bomber roles. Hampdens, converted for torpedo-bombing, were one of the types with which 'Coastal' had to make do. The Hampden T.B.s of No. 455 (R.A.A.F.) Squadron made an epic flight to a Russian base, to give cover for the Russian Convoys. Coded UB these machines were L4038, P1245, P1287, P2126, P5315, P5325, X2976, X3022, X3131, AD743, AD908, AE194, AE231, AE307 and AE310. One was shot down in mistake by a Russian fighter, but the Russians had to exercise more care later, for the Hampdens were left in Russia and were, no doubt, re-marked with red stars.

The reader should not imagine that service aircraft were kept as immaculate as their original factory finish. Coastal Command aircraft, particularly flying-boats, were more exposed to the elements than aircraft in other Commands. This Sunderland shows the effect of sea and weather upon its finish.

Training and communications aircraft displayed large black serial numbers on their yellow under-surfaces, like this Tiger Moth depicted. A hyphen between the letter and the number was not general, but pecualiar to De Havilland aircraft. Note that the roundels and figures do not overlap the ailerons.

Flying Training Command formed on 27th May 1940, by an amalgamation of Reserve and Training Commands. It then had 3,189 aircraft of fifty-six different types; more aircraft and a greater variety than any other Command. However, flying training was to a large extent standardised on six types of aircraft, but training was by no means confined to flying training. Many different types of aircraft, with essentially varying markings, were used.

Elementary and Advanced Trainers of Flying Training Command

Yellow remained the distinctive colour for trainers, but camouflage of the uppersurfaces was prudent for training aircraft at bases within striking distance of the *Luftwaffe*. Until December, 1940, the camouflage came only half-way down the fuselage, but during that month it was extended to the bottom of the fuselage sides. Under-surfaces remained in trainer yellow with, in conspicuous black lettering, the serial number marked as illustrated.

The size of the letters varied according to the aircraft type; the rule being that the height of the letters and figures would be half the chord (width) of the wing. In the case of an aircraft with tapering wings, official instructions decreed that the figure height would be equal to half the chord of the wing at a point one-thrid of the span from the centre-line of the fuselage. An easier way of expressing this is half the width of the wing at one-sixth of the wing-span from the wing-tip. All other dimensions, width of each letter, spaces, etc., would be proportional to the dimensions given for serials on page 102. Modellers can apply this simple formula for markings, provided they work off reliable drawings. Serials were marked in black on yellow surfaces.

Roundels were in the main standard to the period, 'A' type on undersurfaces, 'A1' for fuselage sides and 'B' for uppersurfaces, until mid-1942 when 'C' and 'C1' replaced respectively the 'A' and 'A1' types.

Unit codes were not used by flying training schools, each school having its own identification system; usually letters or numbers in sky, black or white, but sometimes in various colours. At the Beam Approach School, Watchford, for example, Oxfords were marked A to Z then AA, AB, AC, etc., Ansons at this school were A, B, C, etc., and Harvards BA, BB, BC, etc. Those aircraft fitted for beam approach were marked on the fuselage sides with a yellow triangle as a warning to other aircraft to give way.

Training type aircraft were not exclusive to training schools, particularly in the first two years of the war before the Operational Training Units were functioning. Advanced trainers were often attached to operational units, e.g. in December, 1939, Oxford N1190 replaced a Hind in No. 600 Squadron as a more appropriate trainer to a squadron using Blenheims; similarly Nos. 85 and 87 Squadrons with Hurricanes had respectively Master Is N7577 and N7578. In all such cases these aircraft were in trainer finish, but carried on the fuselage side, the code letters of the operational unit to which they were attached.

These Harvard Is show the early trainer camouflage before its extension in December, 1940 to cover the fuselage sides, one having the camouflage 'lifted' to provide a background for the serial number. Only P5899 in the background had the A1 type roundel, then coming into use. One aircraft has not yet acquired a fin flash—in general this is typical of 1940. The gas detector paint diamond may be noticed.

Operational Training

This was a feature of training for which Britain was best suited, for not only was there an operational atmosphere but the Operational Training Units were part of the operational command for which their personnel were being trained. Indeed, at times they *were* operational. In the first and most famous "1,000 Bomber Raid" of 30th May, 1942, no less than 367 of the 1,046 bombers operating were from O.T.U.s. Thus aircraft in these units were marked appropriate to their operational role. Perhaps only at one point could a marking difference be pointed out. Operational squadrons rarely had a strength of more than twenty-six aircraft for which our alphabet would suffice for individual lettering. At an O.T.U. up to seventy aircraft might be on charge. In No. 111 O.T.U. using the unit code X3, Liberators were X3.A, X3.B, X3.C, etc., Oxfords X3.AA, X3.AB, X3.AC, etc., Martinets X3.BA, X3.BB, X3.BC, etc., Wellingtons X3.CA, X3.CB, X3.CC, etc. In some other O.T.U.s up to four different unit code letters were allotted.

Technical Training

Technical Training Command, too, needed aircraft, particularly for wireless training, a task in which Proctors, Ansons and Dominies were chiefly used. Finish was in standard trainer style, with instead of individual identification letters on the fuselage side, a three-digit number, e.g. the Proctors and Dominies of No. 1 Radio School were numbered from 101 upwards, No. 2 from 201 upwards. All Radio Schools did not have aircraft and therefore the system was not progressive, No. 10 Radio School, for example, had its Ansons numbered from 501.

Hundreds of airframes were needed in schools for the training of ground crews. To this Command came many 'clapped-out' aircraft to be taken on under a new identity —an 'M' number. Such aircraft—if they could now be called that—were not to be flown. Representative examples, with in brackets their previous identities, are: 1632M (Spitfire I K9913), 2073M (Avro Avian IVM, ex-G-ABKB on the civil register impressed direct for ground training), 2788M (Mohawk AR670), 2831M (Hereford L6082), 3090M (Falcon glider un-registered), 3289M (Blenheim V DJ707), 3524M (Typhoon IB R7701), 3802M (Mosquito II DD612), 4181M (Kittyhawk IA ET573), 4603M (Sunderland II W3983), 4889M (Catalina I W8410), 5224M (Lancaster III JB138) and 5415M (Hurricane IIC LF398).

These airframes were sometimes handed over to Air Cadet units, e.g. Short Scion ex-G-ADDV on the civil register became X9456 in R.A.F. service and was eventually passed on to No. 1171 Air Training Corps Squadron as 2726M.

Notes on Flying Training Aircraft Types

Tiger Moth: Standard elementary trainer (see also Part II, Chapter 5) Nos. L6920-49 together with many impressed Tiger Moths were known as Mk. I. Main production batches with serial prefixes: N, R, T, DE, DF, EM, NL, NM and PG were Mk. II. DX prefixed were Australian built. BB prefixed, impressed in U.K. DG prefixed, impressed in India. PG746 was the last built.

Magister: Elementary trainer. Pre-war production batches numbered from L5912, L8051, N3773 and N5389 delivered in an overall yellow. Deliveries subsequent to P2374 were in trainer camouflage. All aircraft classified as Magisters with serials later than V1102 may be taken to be impressed Miles Hawk Trainers, e.g. BB661-667.

Master: Advanced trainer. Production from N7408 but unfortunately this aircraft crashed at Hucknall before acceptance. Service deliveries in camouflage, some of the earliest being N7416-26 to No. 5 F.T.S. Sealand in September, 1939. Mk. Is were numbered up to N9017. Mk. IIIs were numbered between W8437 and W8994. N7422 and N7447 converted Mk. Is, W8995 *et seq.* and all other Masters were Mk. II.

Harvard: Advanced trainer. Mk. Is N7000-7199 and P5783-5982 only. Mk. II, etc., in batches from AH185.

Anson: Many used for advanced flying training, communications, operational and radio training. Many from British production batches were shipped abroad for Empire Air Training Scheme, particularly the W-serialled batch, e.g. the first sixteen of this batch W1505-20 were shipped to Canada in August, 1940.

Oxford: Intermediate and advanced trainer. Pre-war deliveries from L4534. Early production by Airspeed's in alternate batches of intermediate and advanced trainers, e.g. of fifty Oxfords numbered between L9635 and L9703 with the usual 'black-out blocks', L9635-50 and L9692-703 were intermediate trainers and L9651-60 and L9680-91 advanced trainers. Extensive sub-contracting, e.g. between V3865 and V4283 were Standard-built and between P1005 and P1139, BM671 and BM877, EB978 and ED300, HM603 and HN212, LW727 and LX152 were Percival-built. RR383 was the last one built.

A Typhoon Ib still in its late wartime fighter finish shows evidence of its retirement from flying by its M-suffixed serial number, denoting that it is used for ground instruction only. This machine ZX.W of No. 55 O.T.U. originally bore the serial number MN266.

Shown in 1940 army co-operation finish when it was still an operational aircraft, the Lysander had varied markings. Similar to R2007 but with roundels under the wings it performed air/sea rescue duties. With the Cross of Lorraine inboard of these roundels it served in a Free French unit. Painted all black it landed in Occupied Territory on secret missions, and in an overall olive green with large black numbers from 3101 it bore the insignia of our last Ally to enter the war—Turkey.

The Composition of Tactical Air Forces

A tactical air force is new in name only, the R.F.C. of 1912-18 had essentially a tactical role as an integral part of the Army. The creation of the R.A.F. as a separate service altered in no way the need for aircraft to support land forces. Certainly the nature of the support has changed, air support has developed from a scouting role to organised surveillance and haphazard strafing to carefully co-ordinated strikes. Airborne forces have made possible not only the quick transit of supporting troops, but the establishment of bridge-heads behind the enemy lines.

It is obviously desirable that supporting aircraft be based within striking distance and that their identity may be easily ascertained by ground troops. A variety of aircraft types, too, are needed for the various roles. When the Allied Expeditionary Air Forces paved the way for the Normandy landings in June, 1944, the R.A.F. element consisted of an Airborne Group of transport planes, glider tugs and gliders, No. 2 Group from Bomber Command of day bombers, a Reconnaissance Wing with Mustangs and

Spitfires, sixty-one squadrons of Spitfire, Typhoon and Mustang fighters and fighter-bombers as well as a Naval wing of Seafires and miscellaneous units. To all these aircraft, to the Ninth United States Air Force and part of Air Defence Great Britain, the well-known A.E.A.F. Stripes were applicable from 4th June, 1944. In the same way that all vehicles had white stars for identification, so did the aircraft of the A.E.A.F. have the distinctive marking illustrated. This was a marking that faded out, being deliberately painted out from the uppersurfaces of many aircraft based in France, in order not to compromise camouflage. On some aircraft, Mitchells in particular, it was retained until early 1945.

Reconnaissance and Observation

The Lysander was the well-known army co-operation aircraft pre-war and in the early war years. Some in France 1939-40 had black and grey undersurfaces similar to fighters, but from late 1940 a sky undersurface was usual. Temperate land scheme was general for uppersurfaces except for special versions, used at night for landing or collecting agents in enemy-occupied territory, which were an overall black.

The Lysander was replaced in an Army Co-op. role by the Tomahawk in standard fighter markings 1941-43, e.g. AH878 was KH.G This in turn was replaced by the Mustang, but owing to this aircraft's similarity to the

It will be seen that gliders were treated the same as aeroplanes for upper-surface markings. In this case these Hotspur II training gliders have a temperate land scheme camouflage of dark green and dark earth with black stripes on a yellow undersurface.

Messerschmitt Me109, yellow bands, 1 ft. in width, were marked chord-wise around the wings a little inboard of the roundels. To place it exactly, the outer edge of the band was in line with the outer edge of the wing-flap. Otherwise the general finish was as for day fighters. Mustangs were used also as low altitude fighters and for strafing. Those numbered between AG345 and AP263 were Mk. Is, FR890-939 were the only Mk. IIs. Numbers between FB100 and KH640, excluding FR409-10, were Mk. IIIs. FR409-10 and KH641 upwards were Mk. IV. Apart from direct delivery to R.A.F. a few Mustangs, e.g. HK944 were handed over to the R.A.F. from the Twelfth U.S. Army Air Force.

The Hurricane IID, later replaced by late marks of Spitfires, Typhoons and later Tempests, were the main fighter-bomber types, to which standard day fighter finish was applicable. Service examples are: Spitfire LF.9, NH209 JX.V of No. 1 Squadron and later Spitfire F.21 LA308 JX.O of the same unit; Typhoon IBs, EK326 US.A, JP915 US.B and MN182 US.C of No. 56 Squadron which later used Tempest Vs EJ552 US.A, SN137 US.B and JN864 US.C. The yellow leading-edge strip that distinguished fighters was not usually marked after the A.E.A.F. stripes were applied.

Aircraft of the Airborne Force

For early parachute dropping training, Whitleys in night bomber scheme were used. Later these were replaced by Dakotas in olive drab or khaki and neutral grey undersurfaces. Most Dakotas of Nos. 48, 233, 271, 512 and 575 Squadrons of the A.E.A.F. were painted black underneath for night operations. Other paratrooping and glider-towing aircraft such as the Albemarles of Nos. 295, 296, 297 and 570 Squadrons, Stirlings of Nos. 190, 196, 299 and 620 Squadrons, Halifaxes of Nos. 298 and 644 Squadrons, were in night bomber finish. Theoretically many of these aircraft should have had black and yellow undersurfaces as towing aircraft, but this was operationally impracticable because it was too conspicuous. However, all the aircraft

Black stripes three feet wide, six feet apart, marked oblique to the fuselage datum were specified for training gliders and Horsa DP747 shown is so marked. For operations, black undersurfaces, marked as for bombers was usual.

of the squadrons so far mentioned in this paragraph had the conspicuous A.E.A.F. stripes from just before D-Day. Red code letters and serials were applicable.

In the same way, operational gliders to which oblique black stripes should have been applied on a yellow undersurface, were by mid-1944 mostly all with black undersurfaces. These were the Horsas, Hamilcars and Hadrians, for which 'standard night bomber finish' describes their general appearance. Unit code letters were not applied to these aircraft but for operations often a marshalling number was white-washed or chalked on the nose or fuselage sides. Less official and often unprintable were the markings chalked on the gliders by the troops they were to lift. However crude these markings were, especially in connection with the name Hitler, they left in little doubt the exuberance of the British spirit.

Gliders were accounted for in the same way as powered aircraft. Their serials, placed at the rear of the fuselage, usually in red on black sides, were their only individual identity numbers. Representative serials are: Horsas, DP305, LG736, RX774 and RZ105; Hamilcars, RR994 and R7427; Hadrians, KK643 and KK888 (ex-43-41748 U.S.A.A.F.).

Glider tugs and gliders used in training schools were marked as for target towing aircraft. Tugs included Whitleys, Masters, Martinets and also some ancient biplanes, e.g. Hector K8142. Although Hotspurs were produced in quantity for glider training, gliders of assorted types were impressed for this duty, e.g. HM510 Slingsby Tutor, HM511 Scott Primary, HM538 Prufling Secondary, HM586 Kassel Sailplane and HM587 Grunau Baby. Over 3,000 Hotspurs were produced numbered from BT479, mostly of the Mk. II version excepting BV134-140, BV146-151 and BV190-199 the only Mk. Is. None of these gliders were used operationally and therefore their black and yellow undersurfaces remained throughout their service. As school aircraft, they were often identified by large individual letters or numbers, e.g. BT722 was 44 and HH374 was 20 of No. 5 G.T.S. At least one glider qualified for special guard as the serial MP486/G on the G.A.L. 48B Twin Hotspur signified.

In general, temperate land scheme applied to gliders and tugs in training schools with target-towing undersides, although exceptions with plain yellow are on record. Roundels appropriate to the period were marked in all the usual positions. An exception with glider prototypes was that the uppersurface of the wings was marked in yellow up to 8 ft. inboard.

Air Observations Posts

The Auster is now, if not then, exclusively the air observation post aircraft. To these aircraft a particular finish applied, that of temperate land scheme on both upper and lower surfaces, with 'B' type roundels in all the four wing positions. The fuselage roundel was of 'A1' or 'C1' type according to period. As Austers were required in Army Co-operation Command in 1942 more quickly than they could be produced, many Taylorcraft models were impressed and brought up to army co-op. standard, these could be identified by their serials ES956-960, HH982-988, HL532-536 and HM501. Another measure to provide a spotting aircraft with a low stalling speed was the fitting

of some forty Tiger Moths with No. 19 Wireless Sets and work was in hand for their A.O.P. camouflage when the Austers started coming off production lines. Auster Is were numbered from LB263 and delivered to A.O.P. squadrons, e.g. LB320, LB323-4 went to No. 654 Squadron in August-September, 1942. Mk. IIs were MZ105 and 110 only. Mk. IIIs were numbered between MT368 and MT453, MZ100 and MZ255 (excluding MZ105 and MZ110), NJ747 and NK132, NX484 and NX545; Mk. IVs between MS934 and MT355 plus MT454; Mk. Vs MT356 to MT 367 between NJ609 and NJ746 and RT458 *et seq.*

An A.O.P. finish was not exclusive to Austers, but exclusive to this class of aircraft in A.O.P. squadrons. No. 651 (A.O.P.) Squadron in particular had a variety of aircraft before Auster production got into swing, examples being ES959 (ex-G-AFWM and HH987 (ex-G-AFTZ) impressed Auster Plus C models, BT440 a Piper Cub Coupe (ex-G-AFSZ), BZ100 a Vigilant from British Direct Purchase in America and HL429 another Vigilant, this time from Lease/Lend, ex-U.S.A.A.F. serial 40-264.

Target Towing and Anti-Aircraft Training

Target towing was a task carried out both by Flying Training and Army Co-operation Commands. The latter Command, formed in December, 1940, was disbanded upon the formation of the 2nd Tactical Air Force in 1943, whereupon most of its units were transferred elsewhere.

Black diagonal stripes, 3 ft. wide, 6 ft. apart, marked on the undersurfaces (see page 103) signified a tug aircraft irrespective of whether it towed a drogue or a glider. Such aircraft with Flying Training Command usually had serials marked on this black and yellow undersurface. The black stripes were either broken to allow the black figures to contrast against the yellow or were marked over the black stripes, with the strokes of the figures alternating in black or yellow where necessary to contrast. 'A1' or 'C1' type roundels, according to the period, were marked on the wing undersurface, parts of the yellow outline to the roundel merging into the yellow of this surface. Altogether a most unsatisfactory marking— viewed aesthetically. The uppersurface finish was invariably in temperate land scheme and from the Autumn of 1942 a Sky Type 'S' fighter band was marked on target-towing aircraft.

Several types of aircraft were adopted for target-towing in the early war years, but three types in particular stand out. The pre-war Henleys finished in silver and re-marked in service (Prototypes K5115 and K7554. Production L3243-3442) were the standby for gunnery training. In 1942 the Martinet went into production, 1797 being delivered in standard T.T. finish. Production batches were numbered from EM410, HN861, JW273, MS499, NR293, PW947 and RG885. Towards the end of the war a high-speed tug, the Monitor, was put into production for R.A.F. and F.A.A. use, but of the 100 ordered only twenty-three, NF900 and NP404-425 were built. The 18 in. fighter band was appropriate to these aircraft from production. In service individual letters or numbers were marked usually in grey or 'sky', examples in No. 1 A.A.C.U. were Henley L3380 was F1.D and Martinet EM583 BI.A.

The A.A.C.U.s (Anti-aircraft Co-operation Units) used a variety of aircraft not only for target-towing but to give training to the anti-aircraft defences, gun, detector and searchlight crews. Aircraft used in this role had standard temperate land scheme, with either sky or black undersurfaces depending on day or night practises. The black was not extended up the fuselage sides as on bombers. Roundels were marked on the undersurface, 'A' type on sky and 'A1' type on black until July, 1942, when they changed respectively to 'C' and 'C1' types. Unit identification letters were in red and serials on the fuselage sides in black. From 1942, unit coding was allotted to A.A.C.U.s, No. 1 being A1, B1, C1, etc., for A, B and C Flights, with No. 2 A.A.C.U. using A2, B2, C2, etc. Many impressed civilian aircraft were allotted to these units in the early war years, in 1940 No. 6 A.A.C.U., e.g. had D.H. 84 Dragons, X9399 ex-G-ACPX, AX863 ex-G-ACKB and BS816 ex-G-ACBW; D.H. 85 Leopard Moths, X9383 ex-G-ADCO, X9384 ex-G-ACSH, AW123 ex-G-ACPF and AW156 ex-G-AFZG. Their bright and varied civil schemes were replaced by standard shadow-shading.

Pilotless target aircraft also had a temperate land scheme applied with standard uppersurface markings and sky undersurfaces without roundels. An individual number was usually marked on the fuselage side. Serial numbers such as LF836-867 on Queen Bees indicate that this type of pilotless aircraft remained in production until well into the war. The Martinet III renamed Queen Martinet was an automatic controlled target, of which over a hundred were built towards the end of the war, numbered from RH122.

Transport, Communications and Miscellaneous Aircraft

CHAPTER SEVEN

Communications Aircraft

Standard markings for communications aircraft pre-war, even after the introduction of camouflage, was silver for fabric covered aircraft and a clear protective varnish to the bare metal of metal-covered aircraft. Aircraft delivered for communications work in silver included Vega Gulls P1749-54, Envoys P5625-9, Mentors L4392-436 and Proctors from P5998. From 1939 standard trainer finish applied to all U.K. based communications aircraft including the December, 1940, changes. Details are as given in Chapter 5. Batches of Proctors, Dominies, Ansons were built and various Lockheed models, Arguses and Reliants were supplied under Lease/Lend specifically for communications work. In addition many aircraft were impressed, to quote but a few: X9395 ex-G-ACIV D.H.84, X9317 ex-G-AFOF D.H. Flamingo of No. 24 (Communications) Squadron, BV984 ex-NC24731 of the U.S. Register a Piper Cub used by the Air Transport Auxiliary, AX871 ex-G-ADBM an Avro 504N of the Special Duty Flight, Christchurch, and X9294 ex-G-ACKR a D.H. Leopard Moth used by No. 1 Camouflage Unit.

Ambulance Aircraft

Standard finish for ambulance aircraft was temperate land scheme with white undersurfaces bearing A or C type roundels. A Red Cross of Geneva was marked in a white circle equal in size to that of the roundel. This finish applied to a few Dominies, an Anson (NK994) replaced later by an impressed Percival Q6 and perhaps a few other aircraft in the U.K. Two Oxfords P8832 and P8833 presented by the Girl Guides Association were specially fitted as ambulances in 1940. In addition to the usual markings these aircraft bore red crosses outboard of the undersurface roundels and serials were marked inboard.

The large numbers of Dakotas used in casualty evacuation work from the continent in the June 1944-July 1945 period did not carry red crosses, since they were not entitled under the Geneva Convention, being used on their outward journey for the carriage of warlike stores.

On ambulance aircraft the Red Cross of Geneva was marked as shown. In this particular case, the ambulance is of a Royal Australian Air Force unit in the Middle East. It has a tropical land scheme finish with white undersurfaces.

Transport Aircraft

In the early war years the Harrow was adapted for transport duties and often participated in squadron moves. One hundred were built, K6933-6970 Mk. Is and K6971-7032 Mk. IIs. After serving as bombers pre-war in Nos. 37, 75, 114, 214 and 215 Squadrons, they formed the equipment of No. 271 Squadron as transports until 1945. Two actually picked up casualties in the September, 1944, Arnhem operations. Examples in No. 271 Squadron were K6987 BJ.P and K7011 BJ.P.

Ferry Command was formed 20th July, 1941, to deliver Lease/Lend aircraft to the European Theatre whilst No. 216 Group R.A.F. ferried aircraft along the South Atlantic route to the Middle and Far East. Single engined aircraft could not make the ocean crossings by air and were there-

Most famous of the transport Liberators was AL504 Commando, often used by Mr. Churchill. Several other Liberators of this batch saw world-wide service such as AL578 illustrated. Long-range transports were mostly in a white finish by the end of the war, and the marking of roundels under the wings seemed to have been optional. Serials were marked under the wings on Transport Command aircraft from July, 1945.

fore shipped to West Africa, assembled and flown in stages across Africa. Aircraft were finished to Ministry of Aircraft Production requirements in the American factories or modification centres. As a general, but by no means invariable, rule it was temperate land scheme for Ferry Command deliveries, tropical land scheme camouflage for No. 216 Group deliveries, with naval aircraft types either in an American scheme or M.A.P. temperate sea scheme. Several transports are worthy of mention: EW999 a silver Skymaster delivered to No. 24 Squadron, November, 1944, for the use of Mr. Churchill, ex-U.S.A.A.F. 43-17126. Altogether twenty-five of these aircraft were used by Transport Command being numbered KL977-86 and KL988-99.

ideal aircraft for calibrating azimuth for our early warning radar stations and No. 1448 Special Flight formed for this purpose developed into No. 529 Squadron. Cieva C.30A machines such as AP507 (ex-G-ACWP) and V1186 were used, being ex-civil aircraft. Two C.30As, HM580-1 were actually built up from spares. All autogyros were given temperate land scheme camouflage and usually sky undersurfaces, although in the case of these wingless craft undersurfaces meant the bottom of the fuselage and undercarriage struts together with the underside of the tail plane. Owing to the rotors making these machines rather top-heavy it was important that they did not receive gusts of wind side-on when grounded. For this reason the words PARK

The Stirling is associated with Bomber Command and one is apt to think of it only in dark green, dark brown and black. Here in 1945 is a Mk. V Stirling used for transporting repatriated prisoners-of-war, in Transport Command matt silver.

A Dakota IV, KK209 used by Air Chief Marshal Sir Arthur Coningham was specially finished by Cellon Ltd., in high gloss sky blue, just after the war ended.

On 25th March, 1943, Transport Command was formed in which Ferry Command became a Group. More transport squadrons were formed of which the Dakota formed the mainstay. Hundreds were delivered to the R.A.F. in temperate land scheme and sky undersurfaces to M.A.P. specification, but many served in R.A.F. markings with an American olive drab and neutral grey camouflage. Many of the roomier bomber types, Venturas, Stirlings and Halifaxes for example, were used by the Command. They usually retained their varied camouflage, but by the end of 1944 for long distance runs by Warwick and Halifax transports, a temperate sea scheme with azure blue undersurfaces was not uncommon.

In late 1945 a new coding system for signals was introduced within Transport Command consisting of four letters. The first letter was always 'O' denoting the Transport Command series, the second letter indicated the aircraft type, e.g. A-Anson, D-Dakota or Y-York, and the third and fourth letters related respectively to the unit and individual aircraft. These four letters, e.g. ODHY, were sometimes marked on the fuselage side with either the complete code or the last two letters repeated on the nose of the aircraft.

Autogyros

Early in the war autogyros were recognised as being

TAIL TO WIND were usually stencilled on their large fins. AP510 and C.30A had type C1 roundels, one each side of the fuselage, but instead of a corresponding fin flash the whole rudder was marked in red, white and blue vertical stripes; the central white stripe being 2 in. thick, with the red and blue occupying the rest of the rudder. DR654 in standard camouflage and yellow undersurfaces was coded KX.L.

German Aircraft in British Service

Captured enemy aircraft required to be flown in British service were allotted serial numbers from the current series. In the matter of general finish they came into two categories, those required for performance evaluation and those for demonstration as an aid to recognition. The former were finished in trainer scheme with, of course, British roundels, but the serial allotted was not displayed on the yellow undersurface of the wings, as with normal trainer finish. The demonstration class were left in their German camouflage, but with German identity markings obliterated and British national markings substituted. The first enemy aircraft to be shot down in this country, Heinkel He 111H Werke No. 6353 of the German 'Lion Wing', was repaired and flown by the A.F.D.U., Duxford, in 1941—as AW177. A Junkers Ju 88A-4 that became HM509 was M2+M of a Luftwaffe unit until it landed one November night in 1941 at Chivenor—in mistake! Other examples are: DG200 Me109E, EE205 Ju 88A-4, NN644 Me 109F, TF209 Me410A-3, VD364 Me108 and VF241 Me163.

The R.A.F. in Middle East and Mediterranean Areas CHAPTER EIGHT

Fighters in Crete, Cyprus and during part-1942 in the Western Desert, had wing undersurfaces painted as shown above. This is a similar marking to U.K. based fighters in 1939. The division of colours, which were black and azure blue, did not take place along the centre of the fuselage.

General Markings

The standard finish in the Middle East for R.A.F. aircraft from 1941 was tropical land scheme of dark earth and middle stone with azure blue undersurfaces. Up until the end of 1940 aircraft from the United Kingdom were delivered to all overseas areas in temperate land scheme and were re-marked as necessary. However, by 1941, all planned deliveries to the Middle East from Lease/Lend allocations in America and British maintenance and storage units were in the tropical scheme.

Dark earth and middle stone were admirably suited to the desert terrain of North Africa, but a temperate scheme was more appropriate to Greece, to where some Desert Air Force aircraft were diverted and in Italy to where this Force advanced. Replacement aircraft to our forces in Italy were generally in temperate schemes. At the Eastern end, in Iraq, Palestine, Persia, etc., a tropical scheme was suited and used, but at the other end, Gibraltar, which came under Coastal Command, a sea scheme applied to aircraft there, with wither sky or azure undersurfaces. Other markings followed R.A.F. practice in general:

roundels were not marked on the undersurfaces of bombers, but they were on fighters. The sky fighter band and spinner was not an accepted marking in these areas, but many fighters were delivered to this theatre with these markings on. Squadron code letters, originally allotted by the Air Ministry, were re-allotted or changed by the local Command from late 1939 onwards. These letters were marked in dull red, azure blue, yellow, or white. In fact, the colours of the general issue paints and dopes. Serial numbers, usually in black on temperate land scheme, were sometimes in white. The range of numbers was, of course, allotted by the M.A.P. when the aircraft were ordered and marked on during manufacture, but two small ranges of numbers related to the Middle East. Between AX669 and AX723, HK839 and HK999, numbers were reserved for Headquarters Middle East Air Force to allocate as necessary. Several interesting aircraft came on strength this way, 'escapees' from French African territories and from Yugoslavia, also many civilian aircraft were bought or impressed, e.g. Lockheed 14 (C/N 1496) NC17398 on the American Civil Register became AX692. A few enemy aircraft types were re-marked with British roundels and registered in this series, examples being HK848 a Savoia S.79 and HK959 a Ju 88 used in Cyprus.

Desert Air Force

When Italy came into the war on the side of Germany in 1940, a woefully small R.A.F. Command protected the Suez Canal and our other vital interest, the oilfields farther eastward. To reassure a worried Egypt smarting under Italian threats and susceptible to propaganda, the R.A.F. put practically every available aircraft in the air for flights over Cairo on 22nd May, 1940. One Egyptian was heard to remark that they must surely be Italian—because there were more than three! By describing the markings of the aircraft in these formations, is to describe the colours of the Desert Air Force as the North African campaign opened. There were twenty-one Gladiators from each of three squadrons, Nos. 33, 80 and 112; some were still in silver finish. To provide backing for these squadrons, and it was quickly needed, Gladiators numbered N5750-5787 were at Aboukir and others N5788-5834 were at Heliopolis. Seventy-two Blenheims had been mustered from Nos. 11, 30, 45, 55, 113 and 211 Squadrons, many were still in shadow-shading and black undersurfaces, but attempts were made to give some of them azure blue undersurfaces.

The American-built Tomahawk and Kittyhawk became the mainstay of our fighter force. A typical Kittyhawk squadron in late 1942 was No. 3 (R.A.A.F.) with aircraft in tropical land scheme and red code letters, CV.V being Kittyhawk ET953. The serial being marked in red just aft of the roundel with the individual letter 'V' marked over it. Under Lease/Lend Requisition No. 322 dated 9th April, 1941, 1,500 Kittyhawks were ordered, giving the longest run of consecutive numbers in R.A.F. serialling— ET100 to EV699. Most of these went to the Middle East. Some fighter squadrons disregarded the regulations concerning squadron markings and displayed unit motifs.

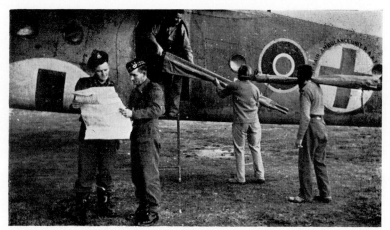

Bostons and Marylands came to supplement the day bombers, they had a plain azure blue undersurface. In contrast, four squadrons of Wellingtons, Nos. 37, 38, 70 and 148 Squadrons used for night bombing had black undersurfaces and sides.

At the end of the war, after the Desert Air Force had fought its way up from the toe of Italy, the following finishes applied to their aircraft types:—

Day Fighter finish: Spitfire VIII, Nos. 92 and 145 Squadrons. Spitfire IX, Nos. 43, 72, 87, 93, 111, 185, 208, 225, 241, 417 (R.C.A.F.) and 601. Nos. 1, 2, 3, 4, 7 and 40 Squadrons (S.A.A.F.) Mustang III and IV, Nos. 112 and 260 Squadrons (R.A.F.), No. 3 Squadron, (R.A.A.F.) and No. 5 (S.A.A.F.) Kittyhawk IV, Nos. 250 and 450 (R.A.A.F.) Squadrons and No. 11 Squadron S.A.A.F.

Night Fighter finish: Mosquito XIX, No. 600.

Photographic Reconnaissance finish (cerulean blue): Spitfire XI, No. 683 Squadron.

A.O.P. finish (temperate scheme): Auster (various marks), Nos. 651, 654, 655 and 663 (Polish) A.O.P.

Day Bomber finish: Marauder III, Nos. 12, 21, 24 and 30 Squadrons S.A.A.F. Bostons IV and V, Nos. 13, 18, 55 and 114 Squadrons. Baltimore V, Nos. 500 and 454 (R.A.A.F.) Squadrons and No. 15 Squadron S.A.A.F.

North Africa

Aircraft supporting Operation Torch, our landings

in North Africa jointly with United States units, were initially in temperate land scheme, which although rather unsuited, was a deliberate measure to mislead enemy intelligence. Gibraltar was the staging post for most of the aircraft concerned in this operation. Within a short distance of the runway, on the Spanish side, a German agent painstakingly recorded all movements and reported his observations to Germany. It was something we could do little about—except to mislead the gentleman.

Later a North African Tactical, Strategic and Coastal Air Force was built up by integrating R.A.F. and U.S.A.A.F. formations under a Mediterranean Air Command of which the Desert Air Force was but a part.

Malta

For their heroic part in the defence of Malta, the Gladiators called 'Faith', 'Hope' and 'Charity' have won immortal fame. When Malta was first attacked, a few Swordfish target tugs and a Queen Bee were the only serviceable aircraft. Crated at Kalafrana were four Sea Gladiators as spares for aircraft carriers. These four biplane fighters, N5519, N5520, N5524 and N5531, were erected and in June, 1940, they represented the sole fighter protection for Malta. One crashed but the remainder bore charmed lives for some time. By July, 1940, a few Hurricanes had arrived to supplement them. Gradually, both a defensive and a striking force was built up on Malta.

The Gladiators nevertheless deserve more than a passing mention. They were in a light grey finish with wing uppersurfaces and fuselage decking in grey and green camouflage. This extended a quarter-way down the fuselage sides. Roundels were: fuselage sides—A1 type, uppersurface of wings—B type, undersurface of wings—A type. Fins had red, white and blue striping, each stripe 5 in. wide, placed centrally and extending to the full height of the fin. 'Faith', N5519, had a black (2 ft.) letter 'R' just aft of the roundel.

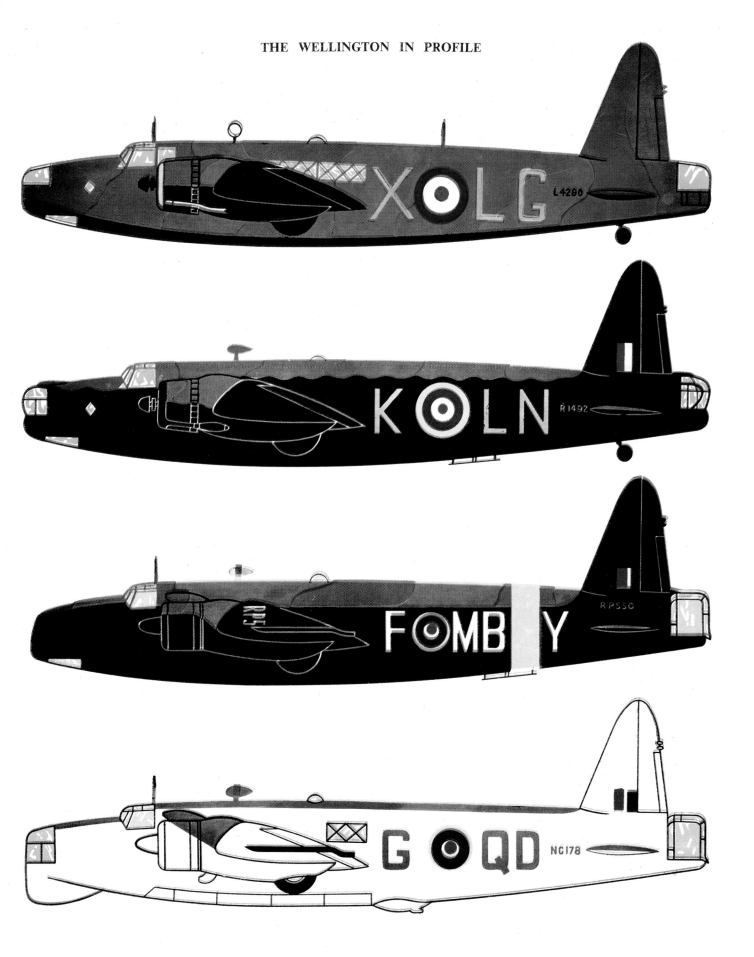

Changing times meant changing colours. Reading from the top, L4280 is a Wellington 1 of No. 108 Squadron as it appeared at Christmas, 1939. R1492, a 1c, belonged to No. 99 Squadron at Waterbeach during 1941; it was lost during an attack on Keil. RP550, a T.10, was a post-war trainer seen at Hullavington in 1947. Lastly, NC178 shows the finish of Wellington G.R.14s serving in Coastal Command during the latter half of the war.

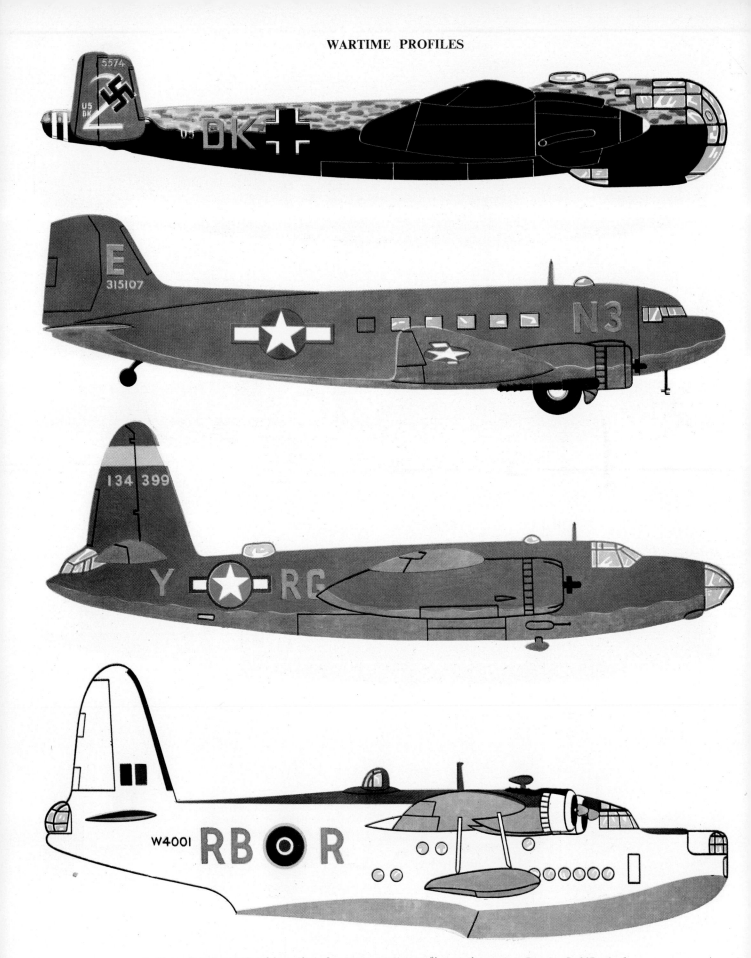

Camouflaged yet colourful are these four representative profiles; at the top is a Dornier Do217m-1 of II/K.G.2 depicted during the 'Little Blitz' of 1944. Next, in camouflage typical of some U.S.A.A.F. aircraft in the Middle East is a C-47A-80-DL as it appeared in October, 1945. In olive drab and grey is a B-26 (Marauder) of the 386th Bombardment Group based on Great Dunmow, Essex during 1944. At the bottom, the Sunderland is shown in service with No. 10 (R.A.A.F.) Squadron in 1943.

The R.A.F. in the Far East

A R.A.A.F. squadron shown at Singapore shortly before the collapse. They are using R.A.F. Buffaloes of the W8131-8250 and AN168-217 batches that were practically all delivered to the Far East direct from America, in standard U.K. day fighter scheme of 1940-41.

Campaigns in the Far East can be divided into two phases, the fateful fall of Malaya and Singapore and the campaign of re-occupation by means of invasion through Burma backed by forces built up in India, with the Japanese surrender coming as an anticlimax. In the first phase R.A.A.F. and R.N.Z.A.F. Squadrons were engaged and in the second the I.A.F. played an important part. Under Air Command, South East Asia, R.A.F. and U.S.A.A.F. formations were integrated and the scope of the Command extended to A.H.Q.s East Africa and Aden, involving even Venturas of the S.A.A.F. Canada was represented by the Catalinas of No. 413 Squadron coded QL.

Singapore and Malaya 1941-1942

Geographically tropic, a temperate land scheme of brown and green was most suited to Singapore and Malaya and it was applied to the silver finished ancient Vildebeests of Nos. 36 and 100 Squadrons that had been promised to India for £60 apiece, but held because no replacements were forthcoming. Blenheims of Nos. 34, 60 and 62 Squadrons functioned in standard day bomber finish, whilst No. 27 Squadron Blenheims had a night fighter finish. Buffaloes delivered direct from America in standard U.K. fighter finish were used by Squadrons Nos. 243 R.A.F., 488 R.N.Z.A.F. and 21 and 453 R.A.A.F.

Operational Aircraft—India and Burma 1942-1945

The most striking change was in national markings. Following the example of the Americans obliterating the red centre from their insignia, so all R.A.F. operational aircraft, stationed or operating east of 60° E. were instructed to use the new South East Asia Command roundel. Basically it was a Type 'B' roundel with a dark blue outer circle and azure inner disc. Similarly fin flashes were changed to those two colours only, with the lighter blue leading. There has been a mistaken idea that the colours were white and blue, like the R.A.F. roundel. This was not so.

Fighters and ground attack aircraft in Burma 1944-45 had identification markings peculiar to the R.A.F. in general, but consistent throughout the Burma fronts, to assist recognition. They also applied to aircraft supporting Task Force 136. A grey and green camouflage was usual, with S.E.A.C. roundels of only 18 in. diameter in all positions with a corresponding 24 in. × 27 in. light and dark blue fin flash. Eighteen-inch wide white bands were marked chordwise around the mainplanes, just inboard of the ailerons, and repeated centrally around each tailplane in a similar way. Finally another white 18 in. band went around the rudder and fin just above the flash. Unit code letters in thick strokes, but only 18 in. high, with individual letters were marked fore and aft of the roundel in the familiar way. A Spitfire squadron using code 'AF' did not mark their white bands over controll surfaces, i.e. it excluded the rudder and elevators. No. 30 Squadron using Thunderbolts on the other hand had their white bands completely encircling. In the white band just above the fin flash their aircraft had a small green palm-tree painted—the unit badge. In this unit using code 'RS', machine 'B' was KJ140. An additional identification feature of Thunderbolts was their white painted rim, 9 in. wide, engine cowling. To correspond, Spitfires and Hurricanes had white spinners. Other fighters, such as those in the Command but far away on the Cocos Islands, did not have these complicated identification bands but the camouflage, small S.E.A.C. roundel and codes applied. A Service example was Spitfire VIII MT567 coded HM.B.

This Liberator has a green and dark grey uppersurface and light blue undersurface. Few units, other than fighters, had code letters marked, rudder markings giving unit identity. The S.E.A.C. roundels and flashes should be noted. This Liberator is of the KH100-420 batch.

Supply dropping played a very important part in thick jungle and swamp infested areas of Burma. Dakotas, helped by a few Hudsons did the transport donkey work—almost literally when one realises that mules had often to be transported by air! They were of the Third Tactical Air Force of which the Dakota element comprised of Nos. 31, 62, 117 and 194 Squadrons of the R.A.F. and the 9th, 10th and 12th Combat Cargo Squadrons of the U.S.A.A.F. Most of the R.A.F. Dakotas were in American olive drab or khaki with blue or light grey undersurfaces, bearing R.A.F. serials in the following range: Mk. I, FD768-818; Mk. III FD819-967, FL503-652, FZ548-698, KG310-809; Mk. IV, KJ801-KK220, KN201-701 (about one hundred of the last batch were, indeed some still are, R.C.A.F.). No code letters were used by these S.E.A.C. Dakotas, instead the R.A.F. used the three figures of the serial number as an identity number, repeated in yellow above the fin flash, similar to the American serialling position.

Bombers in dull green uppersurfaces were giving way to bare-metal finishes in late 1944. Photographic reconnaissance and night fighter aircraft were in their usual appropriate blue or black camouflaging. Many Waco wings. Many Tiger Moths from British contracts were supplied and in addition many were impressed from Indian schools and private owners; forty-five impressed Tiger Moths were numbered between DG483 and DG548, others were DP260-6, DP464, HK413-5 and MA951. Havards in an all-yellow finish were supplied in their hundreds for advanced training, e.g. FS593 of No. 1 Indian Wing. Cornells in yellow too, were supplied to supplement the Tiger Moths as primary trainers. Most Cornells of the FZ198-427 batch were shipped to India; these however usually had S.E.A.C. roundels. Arguses and Expeditors abounded in communications finish, but from 1943 they were usually bearing S.E.A.C. roundels as their duties often took them into operational areas. Defiants and Vengeances were to be seen with the usual target-towing markings. At No. 22 A.A.C.U. of the I.A.F. some of the drogues were a brilliant red which may have prompted the marking on the nose of one of their Defiants—'Sister Anna will carry the Banner'.

Individual Aircraft Examples in S.E.A.C.

To the enthusiast, India must have been something of

The tables turned! Here are the first Spitfires to arrive at Hong Kong after the Japanese surrender, having been ferried there from the Cocos Islands by H.M.S. Smiter. Note the S.E.A.C. roundels and codes on a standard U.K. based day fighter finish. In the foreground RN133 bears a squadron leader's pennant.

Hadrian gliders were supplied in olive drab colouring and U.S.A.A.F. serials with their newly allotted R.A.F. Lease/Lend serials roughly marked on. Examples: FR639 ex-341843, FR778 ex-342140, KK861 ex-340704 and KK888 ex-341748. This was the theatre in which the Vengeance proved a successful dive-bomber; finish was as for S.E.A.C. fighters. Most of these aircraft were shipped direct to India, identification markings being: Mk. I, AN838-AP137 and FP686; Mk. II, AF745-944, AN538-837 and HB300-550; Mk. III, FB918-FD117 and Mk. IV, FD118-417. Not all went to the Far East, some were renumbered in the A27 series of the R.A.A.F. and Vengeance II HB517 was a target-tug, RP.O of No. 288 Squadron in Britain.

Non-operational Aircraft—India and Burma 1942-1945

India is a vast country, a sub-continent is perhaps a better description. Although Calcutta and bases in Eastern India were within striking distance of the Japanese, westward and to the north were bases far out of reach. At operational training units, aircraft were in operational finish, but at flying training units often camouflage did not even apply. At Jodhpur Flying School in 1943, Tiger Moths were in an all-yellow finish, mostly with 'C' type roundels in all positions including the upper surface of the a spotter's paradise. Here listed, are a few of the interesting aircraft in this theatre, with their appropriate identity marking: K7138 Blenheim I of the first production batch still flying in November, 1943; T1775 Leopard Moth used by H.Q., Delhi Comm. Flt.; V4733 Tiger Moth ex-VT-ALF; AW143 B.A. Eagle of unknown origin; BS731 Mohawk of No. 155 Squadron; DR424 Harlow PJC-5; HX792 Dragonfly ex-VT-AIE on loan from H.E.H. The Nizam of Hyderabad; HX796 Moth Minor ex-VT-AMB; LE737 Hurricane II of No. 227 Group Comm. Flt.; LR227 Hornet Moth ex-VT-AKE; LR230 D.C.3.; LV769 and MA923 Piper Club Cruisers ex-VT-AKT and VT-AKV respectively. MA944 Whitney Straight ex-VT-AKF. (N.B. VT-AAA to VT-ZZZ was the civil registration allotment to British India.)

The theatre saw a great transition from 1942 when only eight Mohawks comprised the fighter defence of N.W. India (Mohawks BB975, BJ439, BJ545, BS734, etc., were shipped to India) and No. 31 Squadron using impressed airliners such as D.C.3 MA929 was the only transport Squadron. By mid-1945 there were over a hundred operation squadrons under Air Command, South-East Asia. Then came the Japanese surrender and hundreds of aircraft marked ready for war went straight to the scrap-heap.

Aircraft of the British Fleet

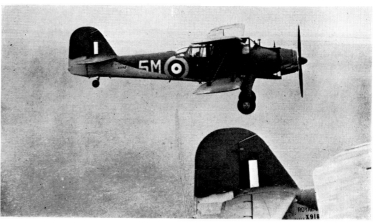

Affectionately known as the 'Applecore' the Albacore had a distinctive curving line, dividing the upper and lower surface colourings in standard F.A.A. camouflage. This aircraft shown bore the letters C5M in dull red on a shore establishment changing to 5M when its unit was commissioned to a carrier.

General Finish

The Royal Navy unlike the Royal Air Force did not impose a scheme of camouflage on all its operational aircraft before the war, although by 1938 a silver finish was giving way to a pale grey. From the outbreak of war most naval aircraft in European waters were given a temperate land scheme and a few ship-board types had various disruptive patterns in green and battleship grey. In the majority of cases it did not extend more than halfway down the fuselage sides, leaving the rest of the aircraft in pale grey. Many indeed, had a straight dividing line along the middle of the fuselage side, between the upper and lower surface shades, tending to defeat the very object of camouflage. This was later appreciated and instructions were given for contrasting colours to merge or to meet in an irregular line. Standardisation followed in 1940 and by 1941 a temperate sea scheme of dark slate grey (the official term for a grey-green) and extra dark sea grey with Sky Type 'S' undersurfaces was general for the Fleet Air Arm.

National markings at the beginning of the war showed many irregularities, the rapid introduction of camouflage causing confusion as to the manner of presenting the roundel. Types 'A', 'A1', 'A2' or 'B' being used and varying not only from unit to unit, but from aircraft to aircraft within the same unit. By December, 1940, it was evident that rigid instructions had been issued and from then onwards the types of roundels used, their positioning and their corresponding fin flashes, were in line with R.A.F. practice.

It is not difficult to hazard a guess at the reasons for the differences between marking of R.A.F. and F.A.A. aircraft up to 1940 and their standardisation subsequently. Inter-service rivalry between the Air Ministry and the Admiralty over the control of the F.A.A. was common knowledge; a perusal of Hansard will show this. Shortly before the war the Admiralty had at last wrested control of naval aviation from the Air Ministry. The latter, however, was still the production, research and inspection agency for all service aircraft, a position the Admiralty had to accept as inevitable. With a new-found independence aircraft markings amongst other things were done Navy-fashion. In May, 1940, the Ministry of Aircraft Production was formed and became the authority for the supply of service aircraft, acting as a co-ordinating body in this matter to both Admiralty and Air Ministry. Directives were issued on the nature, colour and positioning of all national and serial identity markings. Concessions were freely granted, but the effect of the standardisation was such that the reader can be referred to R.A.F. national markings for all F.A.A. aircraft in the Western Hemisphere and informed that where temperate sea or land schemes applied, the same patterns as shown on page 132 formed their basis.

The Fleet had of course a free hand in operational markings, but this too followed R.A.F. lines. Fleet fighters had the usual fighter band in Sky Type 'S' and spinner in the same shade from December, 1940. Roundels were invariably marked on the undersides of fighters, whereas almost all other operational types did not bear undersurface roundels. Training, communications and target-towing aircraft were finished as for the R.A.F., except that a temperate sea scheme often applied in place of a land scheme.

The Martlet (renamed Wildcat March, 1944) was a standard fleet fighter. Pre-Lease/Lend deliveries had R.A.F. size roundels positioned as shown. Of the 100 Mk II's, AJ 100-153 had azure undersurfaces for shipment to Bombay and the rest, AM954-999, had sky undersurfaces for operation in temperate waters. Unusual is the incorrectly proportioned fuselage roundel.

Identification Markings

Naval aircraft were numbered within the general service aircraft range, but to meet an Admiralty request, presumably as a security aid, the numbers were presented at the rear of the fuselage in 4 in. figures, i.e. half R.A.F. size. During 1940, the words ROYAL NAVY in 4 in. lettering were placed centrally above the number. On Sea Gladiators and Fulmars the Admiralty specified it should appear 8 in. above the serial and 4 in. above on all other types except the Avenger, where the serial position on the fin fillet allowed only a 1 in. space. These markings were in black but those F.A.A. aircraft in midnight blue finish 1944-46 had them in white.

Such distinction was perhaps necessary where R.A.F. and F.A.A. aircraft were jointly maintained or stored (not until 1945 did the F.A.A. have its own aircraft storage units) to assist stores accounting where two services were concerned. All airframe accounting was of course by serial number and it did not follow that the Navy used only naval type aircraft; many communications and training types were common to both services and a number of R.A.F. aircraft were handed over to the F.A.A. To quote a few typical examples where the words ROYAL NAVY would be the only indication of Admiralty property— Master N7775 one of six used by the F.A.A., Airacobra AH574 used for evaluation tests, Marylands AR720, AR736 and AR740 used and marked for target-towing, and Bostons BL227 and BD121-2 for special duties.

A new series was commenced for airframes used only in ground instruction, corresponding to the R.A.F. 'M' series. An 'A' for Admiralty denoted the series, early examples in 1941 being Buffaloes A37 and A38 previously AS417 and AS429 respectively.

The marking of factory numbers on Fairey-built aircraft had ceased shortly before the war, but it was again permitted concessional to the figures being not more than 1 in. in height. This was rather a revealing marking from the security point of view for it was liable to compromise the use of 'blackout-blocks' in the serialling system. For example, Albacores BF618 as F5704 and BF631 as F5705

in a consecutive factory number series reveals that the intervening numbers BF619-630 were not used.

Unit markings were in dull red up to 1943 when a more conspicuous yellow or white was used. This code letter system was different from R.A.F. practice. As a general rule ship-board aircraft bore only a single letter, carrier-based aircraft a figure and a letter and aircraft on shore establishment a letter/figure/letter. In the three letter system, the first letter related to the station, the figure to the role of the aircraft and the last letter to the individual aircraft; but it was not always consistent. The letters were often bunched together, either forward or aft of the roundel; alternatively, they were marked each side of the roundel. Rarely, if ever, did figure height exceed roundel diameter. An oddity was the letter 'O' which, to avoid confusion with the figure '0' had a '/' marked across it.

Special Finishes and Markings

Swordfish squadrons such as Nos. 833 and 836 (F.A.A.) serving under the operational control of Coastal Command donned a 'Coastal-white' finish in 1942 with uppersurfaces of the planes and fuselage decking only in temperate sea scheme. A few experiments in dazzle-painting were carried out on Skuas, but the idea was dropped. The communications type aircraft became the new conception of the admiral's barge. One Expediter in 1945 had a high gloss navy blue finish with sky undersurfaces. An Admiral's flag was painted on the nose and, strangely, all the roundels were reduced to half normal size. The serial and R.N. marking was in gold leaf paint!

There was often a mass of miscellaneous stencilled instructions on naval aircraft—TRESTLE HERE and SLING HERE indications, locating points marked for locking folding wings and a host of different small markings with a purely technical and local significance.

Markings in Eastern Waters

Many carriers despatched to the Pacific and Indian Ocean went via the United States to pick up aircraft allotted under Lease/Lend. These were mostly in U.S. Navy deep blue finish with azure blue undersurfaces. The Pacific Area F.A.A. roundels were invariably used as shown on page 133. Units operating with the United States Fleet had the wing roundels American fashion, i.e. port upper and starboard lower only, but in the Indian Ocean they were marked in conventional R.A.F./F.A.A. positions. Carriers operating along the South East Asian coasts had their aircraft marked with white identification stripes in the same manner as aircraft in Burma (see previous chapter). For the Middle East temperate schemes were prevalent, but undersurfaces were often azure blue.

Notes of Fleet Aircraft Markings

Notes are given by type name in alphabetical order and some typical service examples are included. Standard refers to temperate sea scheme and sky undersurfaces.

Albacore: Prototypes in pre-war silver L7074-5 (F3274-5). Production from L7076, early models had 1939 finish with straight line dividing upper and lower surface shades. 1940 onwards as illustrated. Black undersurface given to those on night operations, example BF600 NH.P1 of No. 415 (R.C.A.F.) Squadron. **Avenger**: Standard or U.S. Navy finish. FN795 bore the code CZY aft of the roundel. See also illustration. **Barracuda**: Standard finish, prototype P1767 (F4468), production of Mk. I (1942) from P9642. Representative serials from batches built are: Mk. II BV980 (Blackburn-built), DN642 (Westland-built), DP880, DR256, DT884, LS535, MD717 and MX536; Mk. III, ME107, PM973 and RJ943. **Bermuda**: Standard finish, FF419-868 ex-U.S. Army, FF869-999 ex-U.S. Navy order. A few marked for target towing. **Chesapeake**: Standard finish except that serials AL908-957 were marked 8 in. R.A.F. size. AL910 served in No. 728 Squadron, Arbroath. **Corsair**: Early deliveries standard scheme, some later deliveries to Far East in U.S. blue/grey. Mk. I JT100-194, Mk. II JT195-704, Mk. III JS469-888 and JT963-972, Mk. IV KD161 upwards. **Dauntless**: JT997-9 and JS923-8 only. **Expeditor II**: Naval communications batches numbered FR879-883, FT980-996, HD752-776 and KN100-149. **Firefly I**: Standard, numbered between Z1826 and Z2126, DT926 and DV150, MB378 and MB758. Many subsequent conversions. **Fulmar**: Standard, production Mk. I from N1854 (F3707), Mk. II from N4017. N4147 was K9P. **Hellcat**: FN serials in standard finish, most of JV, JW, JX, JZ, KD and KE series had U.S. Navy high gloss blue-grey finish except for night fighter batches, e.g. JX947-959 and KE215-9 in an overall midnight blue finish. Up to JV221 were Mk. I, JV222 and above, Mk. II. **Helldiver**: Standard JW100-125 only. **Martlet**: renamed

Wildcat. Initial deliveries finished in bottle-green. **Reliant**: Naval communications finish, e.g. FB550 and FK815. **Roc**: Early finishes as for Skua. Many irregularities in markings as with L3066-8 of No. 800 Squadron. **Seafire**: Many early conversions from Spitfire Vb airframes with consequent change in identity markings, examples—Spitfire Vb/Seafire Ib—AB902/NX889, AD517/NX884, BL586/PA115, BM314/NX950 and EN867/NX962. Mk. IIc from MA970, Mk. III LR, MB, NF and various serial ranges. Standard finish general for all marks. MB281, a IIc was 8AM at Malta, 1943. **Sea Gladiator**: See also Chapter 8. R.A.F. Gladiators N2265-2302 fitted for deck landing as interim measure. Production from N5500 with first deliveries N5501-16 to No. 801 Squadron, Donibristle, Feb., 1939, in light grey finish. **Sea Hurricane**: R.A.F. Hurricanes fitted for F.A.A., e.g. P2972, V6801, Z7055, etc. Those used for catapulting from merchant ships (F.A.A. or R.A.F.) were in standard fleet fighter finish with azure blue undersurfaces. **Seamew**: Standard; one, FN472, was used with U.S. insignia and R.A.F. fin flash! **Sea Otter**: Standard, JM and RD serial ranges. Also used by R.A.F. **Skua**: Prototypes K5178-9 in silver. Production L2867-3056 only, delivered in silver-grey. Temperate land scheme applied in 1939, sea scheme in 1940. Many variations 1939-40. L3007 had red diagonal stripes as an A.S.R. experiment. **Swordfish**: See also Part 2, Chapter 6. Various schemes applied 1939-40, but standard scheme 1941-42 as shown on page 104. Those numbered above V4288 built by Blackburn. W5992 (Mk. II) was one of the six of No. 815 Squadron led by Lt.-Comm. Esmonde (posthumously awarded the V.C.) that were all lost in the attack on the German cruisers *Scharnhorst*, *Gneisnau* and *Prince Eugen* during their dash through the Channel. LS423, another Mk. II, was coded K2G. **Walrus**: See also Part II, Chapter 6. Temperate land scheme applied in 1939 extending only to halfway down hull sides, extended to water-line in sea scheme by end of 1940. Used also by R.A.F. Representative serials: Mk. I, R6544 (Vickers-Armstrong built), R6583 (Saro-built); Mk. II, W3101, Z1768 and HD931. **Wildcat** (previously Martlet): Mk. I (various batches) AX824 and BJ507-9 were with No. 804 Squadron October, 1940. AL236-62 went to Donibristle 1940-41. Later Mk. IVs FN100-319 were in standard finish. Mk. V numbered from JV325 and Mk. VI from JV637 had high gloss blue-grey finish.

An Avenger leaving H.M.S. Fencer shows well the line dividing the two surfaces which can be seen to 'lift' to the main and tail planes. The dull red code letters have in this case been outlined in white. FN833 shown was a Mk I of the FN750-949 batch. Mk. IIs were numbered from JZ301, Mk. IIIs from JZ635 and Mk. IVs from KE540.

The familiar Tiger Moth with a finish typical of many R.C.A.F. trainers. However, in this instance, the normal red centre of the roundel and red leading section of the fin flash was in orange, for the aircraft did in fact belong to the South African Air Force.
Many of these 'Tigers' were ex-R.A.F., for example, S.A.A.F. Nos. 2256 and 4707 were ex-R.A.F. Nos. T6715 and T7672 respectively.

The magnificent contribution by the Commonwealth Air Forces can be viewed from three aspects so far as markings are concerned. Firstly aircraft provided by and used in the service of each Commonwealth country; markings varying according to the service. Secondly, aircraft provided under the Empire Air Training Scheme, and thirdly aircraft used in squadrons serving under R.A.F. Commands. Although this last aspect was the Commonwealth's major contribution in the war against Germany and Italy, it is not dealt with here, for the aircraft and markings were consistent with the R.A.F. Command under which they served. Many of their squadrons have been mentioned in the preceding chapters.

Australia

Up until early 1942 when the Japanese swept through S.E. Asia, a silver finish had been common in the R.A.A.F. with a yellow overall for trainers. Typical was the Wackett trainer in its yellow finish with 'A' type roundels in fuselage and wing positions. Serials, e.g. A3-88 in 9 in. figures were marked in black just aft of the roundel and repeated in 18 in. figures under the wings. The number 88 was repeated forward on the fuselage side; this was in factory finish and not just a unit marking.

Camouflaged in British schemes were Hudsons and Catalinas diverted from R.A.F. contracts (see Chapter 9) in America and Ansons, Battles and 127 Oxford IIs shipped from Britain in standard trainer camouflage.

National markings followed R.A.F. lines very closely until 1942, but then, in the same way as the Americans (evacuated from the Philippines to Australia) who were omitting the red disc from their insignia, so the Australians dispensed with red and used the roundel shown on page 133. Camouflage was now generally applied in a manner similar to M.A.P. patterns, but using the shades shown on the R.N.Z.A.F. Warhawk, page 158. This is no mere approximation, but the exact shades, as the R.N.Z.A.F. used Australian manufactured dopes and paints. Operational aircraft had this scheme but trainers, as in the U.K., retained their yellow undersurfaces.

Most famous of R.A.A.F. operational aircraft was the Australian-built Beaufort. A9-184 of No. 100 Squadron returned from a raid on Gasmato in July, 1943, even after its ailerons had been shot away, and A9-486 named 'Scotty's Homing Pigeon' survived 139 operations. Code letters were used for operational squadrons marked in R.A.F. style, A9-623 being A.KT (port side). Serialling followed the system explained on page 88 and serial prefixes are tabulated in Appendix IV. Some interesting examples are: A19-148 and A19-163 ex-R.A.F. Beaufighters XIc JL946 and JM164, A28-40 of No. 22 Squadron coded DU, A39-3 impressed Beechcraft C17L ex-VH-UXP and A72-75 a Liberator BIV in bare metal finish at an O.T.U.

New Zealand

Service aircraft in New Zealand, as in Australia, had a general silver finish except for trainers in an overall yellow up to 1941. That year several Hudsons arrived in British temperate land scheme camouflage from America (ex-R.A.F. AE490, AE494-504) and then, following the Japanese attack, a camouflage was instituted generally. This consisted of irregular patches of light green and earth as displayed on page 158 with a fawn, officially described as light earth, sometimes replacing the earth shade shown. Undersurfaces were in three shades, an azure blue being most common, with the other shades of light grey or a greyish mauve as alternatives. Trainers, too, were camouflaged at this time, but an increased accident rate and little immediate danger from bombing in the homeland, led to a reversion to the overall trainer yellow by 1943.

Roundels followed R.A.F. practice, Type 'A' being general up to 1942, when Types 'A1' or 'B' came in for drab surfaces. The change to 'C' types was effected in 1942 and was used until May, 1943, when the N.Z. Air Department instructed that red was no longer to be used and blue of a light shade was substituted. White rectangles were added to give a marking similar to that of United States aircraft operating in close co-operation. Several R.N.Z.A.F. squadrons were in fact under United States operational command. Generally, the blue in R.N.Z.A.F. roundels was in a lighter shade than in R.A.F. roundels and those used in 1943-45 are illustrated on page 133.

Squadron code letters marked R.A.F. fashion were introduced from early 1942 as follows: Squadron Nos. 1(SJ), 2(UH), 3(JV), 4(YZ), 5(OT), 6(XX), 8(PA), 14(HQ), 15(JL) and 16(XD). For security reasons they were banned in October, 1942, and the last two or three letters of the serial number were then marked on the fin, both as an individual number and as a unit marking.

Walrus flying boats used for training in a white finish were the only trainers 1943-45 not in yellow. Four ancient

Singapores arrived in New Zealand from Singapore late 1941. These had a temperate land scheme and sky undersurfaces. Destined for No. 5 Squadron, they bore the code 'OT'. Four Sunderland IIIs (including ML792-3) served the R.N.Z.A.F., 1944-45, in their original Coastal Command finish. Using a U.S. Navy finish of blue uppersurfaces and light blue undersurfaces were Avengers, Catalinas, Dauntlesses and Venturas. Transport aircraft, Dakotas and Lodestars, had standard American olive drab and neutral grey finish in general, although a few in 1945 had a bare metal finish.

The Warhawk illustrated on page 158 was a standard fighter/ground attack aircraft in the Force. Warhawks bore the elaborate identity markings shown and because the outline of its tail was similar to the Japanese Tony *they were painted white and in some cases left in bare metal.* This was in accordance with an American South-West Pacific Area Order. Some Warhawks bore unit codes in various colours when these were again permitted in 1944. Codes, however, were not generally reintroduced, Catalinas of Nos. 5 and 6 Squadrons being the only other types to bear them, as PA and XX respectively, during 1944-45.

Serialling continued in the blocking system mentioned in Part 2. Representative serials are: NZ118 Vincent, NZ289 Oxford I (ex-P2043). N573 an impressed Beech C.17L previously ZK-AEU, NZ631 Fairey IIIF, NZ741 Tiger Moth, NZ2001 Hudson, NZ3260 Warhawk, NZ4042 Catalina, NZ4518 Ventura and NZ5648 Corsair.

Canada

The plains of Canada became a vast training area for the R.A.F. and for Canada's own R.C.A.F. which by the end of the war was the fourth greatest air power of the world.

Three distinct colour schemes prevailed in the R.C.A.F. A silver or white for communications and reconnaissance aircraft; yellow overall for trainers, and a British temperate land scheme for operational fighters and bombers. The adoption of a British scheme was probably influenced by the numbers of R.A.F. aircraft constructed in the Dominion and finished in standard R.A.F. schemes.

The marking of roundels followed R.A.F. lines as regard their composition and proportions, but they were positioned as a rule further outboard on the wings than on R.A.F. aircraft where one-sixth of the span inboard was the ruling. The change-over to Type 'C' roundels in 1942 applied to the R.C.A.F., but not with immediate effect.

Only for aircraft moving to an operational area was it compulsory. Another reason was that it would have meant scrapping many 'A' type roundels already manufactured! Lest the reader regard this as a misprint, it should be explained that many roundels were made of plastic and affixed to the fabric. The white of the roundel in these cases actually bore a trademark! Some aircraft stationed in Western Canada bore S.E.A.C. type roundels.

Unit codes were allotted to operational squadrons or flights, marked yellow or white in R.A.F. fashion. One distinction from the R.A.F. method with R.C.A.F. codes was that the letters were underlined in the same colour as the coding. Goblin 344 for example was RE.W of No. 118 Squadron. These interesting biplane fighters had an uppersurface in temperate land scheme including the fuselage sides; undersurfaces in British 1939 style were port side black and starboard side white, applying to both main planes. Under the lower wing reading in opposite directions in black (starboard side) and white (port side) was the serial number in 2 ft. figures. Roundels were not marked on the undersurface and Type 'A' on fuselage sides gave way in 1940 to Type 'A1'. The complete fin was striped in red, white and blue.

In training units codes were not used and individual letters or numbers were not always necessary as many schools had the serial numbers presented in large black letters on the fuselage sides. On the other hand, Battles shipped from England, with R.A.F. size serials, needed large identification figures. Those at No. 9 Bombing and Gunnery School, Mont Joli, had numbers, 40, 71, 129, etc.

Serials are a feature of R.C.A.F. aircraft; they invariably appeared on the underside of the wings half chord size. On the fuselage sides most operational aircraft had normal sized serials, but on training and communications aircraft it was often as large as practicable, usually just aft of the fuselage roundel. Compared with R.A.F. serials of the period, perhaps the most noticeable thing was the absence of any prefix letters. Hundreds of R.A.F. aircraft were built in Canada and the U.S.A. and many more were being shipped from Britain for use in Canada. Upon this basic difference, *prefix or no prefix to the serial,* could R.A.F. and R.C.A.F. property be identified. This was complicated by transfers, e.g. Hurricanes built in Canada for the R.A.F. as AG299 and AG310 became respectively 1378 and 1362 in the R.C.A.F. Some twenty-five others in the AG batch were similarly diverted.

A feature of R.C.A.F. aircraft in Canada was the marking of serial numbers under the wings even on operational aircraft, and the placing of wing roundels well outboard. This is apparent on these Canadian-built Lysanders.

The four main training types must be mentioned. Their general finish was yellow overall, 'A' type roundels in all positions and an anti-glare black forward of the cockpit or cabin. The ubiquitous Tiger Moth was represented by the D.H.82C, the Canadian-built version, usually found with a black enamelled cowling. Serials 1136, 1209, 4035, 4400, 4971 (19 E.F.T.S.), 5142, 5800, 5999, 8935, show how widely spread the production batches were. Some of the early Ansons, e.g. 6153 were in temperate land scheme camouflage, but later machines had the standard finish. 7366 was the 1,000th Anson produced by Federal Aircraft of Canada and later Mk. Vs by the firm had serials running beyond 12,459. Early Harvards diverted from British contracts in 1939 had R.A.F. style trainer camouflage of that year, but from 3,001 onwards standard yellow overall prevailed. They were supplemented by hundreds of R.A.F. Harvards built for use under the Empire Air Training Scheme in Canada. Cornells were used to supplement and eventually replace the Tiger Moths as primary trainers. 1,642 were built in Canada to a standard finish, and a large number came from America. Mk. Is EW349-360 went to Trenton, EW370-409 and EW476-490 to Winnipeg and EW426-475 to Calgary, in 1944. FT542-831 were the first Mk. IIs that were built to replace Stearman PT-27 trainers being returned to the U.S.A. All subsequent to FT542 were Mk. IIs.

South Africa

The first concern of the Union was the security of the African continent: thus the S.A.A.F. units operated mainly along the North African coasts and against the Italians in East Africa. The S.A.A.F. also trained thousands of airmen under the Empire Scheme. We are not directly concerned here with those S.A.A.F. units operating under R.A.F. Command, to which Chapter 8 applies, but to those aircraft directly under S.A.A.F. Command. In the main, S.A.A.F. serialled aircraft, like R.C.A.F. machines, could be identified by the absence of prefix letters.

Training and communications aircraft in the Union were often in overall silver or training yellow finish together with British aircraft still in a temperate land scheme. For units taking their aircraft northwards into action a tropical land scheme was usual, but before this became general, circa 1941, several unorthodox schemes could be noticed.

Roundels were of the 'A' type in general but the colours were different and the implications of this are political. Instead of red, the centres were officially orange, in deference to the Dutch element of the Dominion, but with many aircraft supplied by Britain, their red centres were retained. Unit codes were not general except under R.A.F. command. Serials were marked under the wings on non-operational types and in the normal fuselage position. On trainers the fuselage serial marking was enlarged for identification purposes.

A representative selection of S.A.A.F. serials will no doubt be of interest to the enthusiast: 231-3 Lodestars ex-R.A.F. AX685-7, 439-41 Hornet Moths; 647, a dark green camouflaged Junkers Ju 86, previously a South African Airways civil airliner with its new number roughly painted in white aft of the fuselage roundels; 661 a Junkers Ju 52/3m from the same source; 1371 Lodestar in standard ambulance markings; 1680 Maryland II ex-R.A.F. AH421; 1876 Audax; 2537 Mohawk ex-R.A.F. BJ536; 4394 Anson ex-R.A.F. LT352; 4999 York, Field Marshal J. C. Smuts's personal aircraft, ex-R.A.F. MW107; 6066 Ventura; 6820 Dakota, and 7038 Harvard.

The blocking system described in Part 2 continued without regard for a chronological/numerical sequence. A typical example is 2601-3000 reserved for Miles Masters transferred from the R.A.F., including all those numbered between T8914 and T8999 and many from the AZ102 to AZ856 range.

To Oxfords used in South African schools goes the credit for the most outstanding markings and intentionally so, for they were used in Beam Approach practice. Their yellow finish was embellished by green or black diagonal bands around the fuselage and triangles in the same colours on the wings. 3794 of No. 26 Air School, Pietersberg, was an example.

Southern Rhodesia

In August, 1939, three Rapides, three Harts and three Audax left for their war station in Kenya. The remaining equipment was left for training and of this, some was taken over by No. 237 Squadron, R.A.F. A S.R.A.F. communications squadron remained, functioning in close co-operation with Rhodesia and Nyasaland Airways. Meanwhile hundreds of Rhodesians had left their homeland to serve the R.A.F. in the U.K. It was the official policy to concentrate Rhodesians into Nos. 44 and 266 Squadrons of the R.A.F. for which representative markings are respectively: Lancaster I (standard Bomber Command finish for late 1942) R5740 KM.O and Typhoon Ib (standard A.D.G.B. finish early 1944) MN683 ZH.R.

To return to Rhodesia, destined to provide facilities for a training group in the Empire Air Training Scheme, May, 1940, saw the opening of the first school. No. 25 Elementary Flying Training School equipped with Tiger Moths in standard R.A.F. trainer finish of 1939. They were in fact initially Nos. R4781, R4786-4797 and R4810-4829, straight from the production line, followed by T5430-3 and T5454-7. Later came ninety-four from the DX437/716 range, built in Australia with the distinction that these were not camouflaged, but yellow overall. Serials were not marked large, but in standard 8 in. size. Unusual was the fact that the prefix letters DX were obliterated and in some cases 'MC' was substituted. The reason for this still remains a mystery to the writer. Serials appeared in the normal trainer-type way, under the wings.

'Tigers' at No. 28 E.F.T.S. bore individual numbers on the nose (DX) 544 was '4'. Around the fuselages, about 18 in. aft of the roundel, was a 12 in. band in red and white dicing, to distinguish the unit. The choice of colours and the nature of the marking can be traced to a certain Flying Officer Danes in this unit who had served in No. 56 Squadron. If the reader glances at page 85 he will see a connection.

The markings of the Cornell show how truly integrated was the Empire Air Training Scheme. Arriving in 1944 to re-equip E.F.T.S.'s they were finished in yellow overall, with a black patch forward of the cockpit. Roundels were strangely in half normal size, positioned well outboard on the wings. Serials on the fuselage side were in 15 in. black figures in the Royal Canadian Air Force range! Canadian built to R.A.F. Lease/Lend requirements to numbers such as FV207 and FV210, they were taken over by the R.C.A.F. as 15103 and 15106 respectively and served in Rhodesia bearing these numbers. These two aircraft changed their identity yet again. Permanently grounded, they were renumbered in the Rhodesian series of instructional airframes, becoming, again respectively, 0024M and 0022M. Other Cornells, such as FV534, flew in their original R.A.F. allocations.

Many Harvards were used mostly in yellow overall contrasting with Oxfords also used for advanced training which had been shipped from the U.K. in standard R.A.F. trainer camouflage. At No. 33 Flying Instructors School representative aircraft types in use throughout the training group were held on charge. Examples there were: Oxfords X7317, AR846 and BG301; Harvard II AJ746, Harvard IIAs, EX526 and EX822; Cornell 15083.

A link with the following chapter, a part of No. 28 E.F.T.S. was devoted to training personnel of the Royal Hellenic Air Force.

India and Burma

The aircraft of the Indian Air Force both in India and Burma were so closely identified with the R.A.F. that their markings were in the main covered by Chapter 9. Serving operationally in Air Command, South East Asia, mid-1944 were five Indian Air Force Squadrons, Nos. 1, 4, 6 and 9 with Hurricanes replaced partly by Spitfires later, and No. 8 with Vengeances.

The Hurricanes shipped from the United Kingdom and used first for operational training had the usual sky fighter band and spinner. These markings were retained during training, but upon becoming operational the fighter bands were painted out, as the Japanese used a similar marking, and in place the white identification stripes described in Chapter 9 were applied to all I.A.F. operational fighter and ground attack aircraft.

Coastal patrol was a duty undertaken earlier by ancient Wapitis in silver finish with black fuselage decking. They were assisted by impressed A.W. Atlanta airliners, these were DG450 ex-G-ABTL, DG451 ex-G-ABTI, DG452 ex-G-ABTJ, DG453 ex-VT-AEF and DG454 ex-VT-AEG. Twelve Douglas D.C.2s were ordered by the Indian Government and registered from VT-AOU, these were taken over as Indian Air Force transports DG468-479. Many of the impressed aircraft mentioned served at the 104 I.A.F. stations in India, particularly as trainers. No less that eighty-eight Tiger Moths alone were impressed in India. R.A.F. serial allocations were used and retained throughout.

'Tigers' are associated with the small Burmese Volunteer Air Force that provided a communications flight when the Japanese threatened Rangoon. Numbered from Z-01 and originally in a silver finish these Tiger Moths were hastily camouflaged for operations. Their fate in the fall of Rangoon cannot be traced.

A Dauntless in light green and earth camouflage bears the distinctive blue and white insignia of the R.N.Z.A.F. 1943-46. Instead of unit or individual letters the last two numbers of the serial number are repeated in yellow on the fin. Above this is a red, white and blue fin flash in miniature, a common feature of R.N.Z.A.F. aircraft.

CAMOUFLAGE PATTERN EXAMPLES AS RECOMMENDED BY THE MINISTRY OF AIRCRAFT PRODUCTION

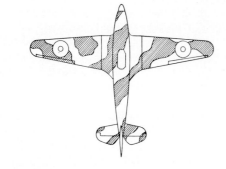

PATTERN No. I. Single Engined Monoplanes.

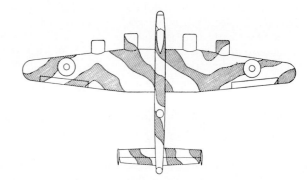

PATTERN No. 4. Four Engined Monoplanes.

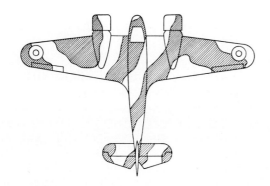

PATTERN No. 2. Twin Engined Monoplanes
of less than 70' span.

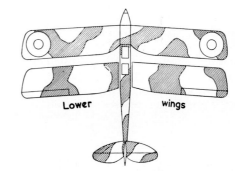

PATTERN No. 5. Single Engined Biplanes.

PATTERN No. 3. Twin Engined Monoplanes
of more than 70' span.

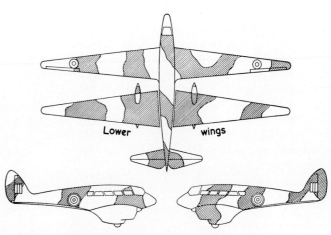

PATTERN No. 6. Twin Engined Biplanes.

N.B. Shaded portions show the darker areas where two colours are used in a disruptive pattern. Division between the upper and lower surfaces varied according to the aircraft type and the period as explained in text

132

MISCELLANEOUS MARKINGS–BRITISH AND ALLIED AIR FORCES 1939-46

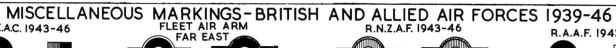

S.E.A.C. 1943-46

FUSELAGE AND WINGS

FIN

FLEET AIR ARM FAR EAST

Pacific Area 1945-6

Far East 1944-5

R.N.Z.A.F. 1943-46

Alternatives
(Without yellow outline on light surfaces)

R.A.A.F. 1943-46

FUSELAGE AND WINGS

FIN

BRITISH AND BRITISH COMMONWEALTH AIRCRAFT NATIONAL IDENTITY MARKINGS

☐ WHITE ■ DARK BLUE ▥ LIGHT BLUE ░ YELLOW

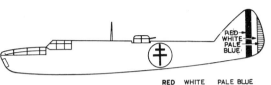

RED WHITE PALE BLUE

RED   WHITE   PALE BLUE WHITE RED

BLENHEIM IV OF LORRAINE SQUADRON N.AFRICA 1941-2

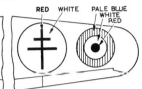

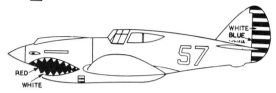

WHITE BLUE

RED

WHITE

57

WHITE BLUE

TOMAHAWK I OF AMERICAN VOLUNTEER GROUP. CHINESE/AIR FORCE 1941-2

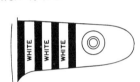

WHITE WHITE WHITE

SPECIAL IDENTITY MARKING – TYPHOON AND TEMPEST 1942–44
Black and white stripes on undersurface only

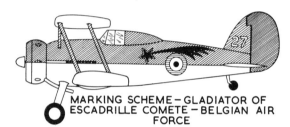

MARKING SCHEME–GLADIATOR OF ESCADRILLE COMETE–BELGIAN AIR FORCE

NATIONAL MARKINGS OF THE ALLIES

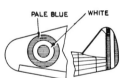

PALE BLUE   WHITE

GREECE–ARMY

DARK BLUE

GREECE–NAVY

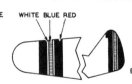

WHITE BLUE RED

NORWAY

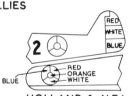

RED WHITE BLUE

2

BLUE

RED ORANGE WHITE

HOLLAND & N.E.I. Pre 1939

BLACK ORANGE

2

HOLLAND & N.E.I. 1939-46

INDIVIDUAL INSIGNIA R.A.F.

HURRICANE OF No 242 SQN

BEAUFORT U.K.

1234567890

SOVIET AIR FORCE STYLE OF INDIVIDUAL AIRCRAFT NUMBERS

INDIVIDUAL INSIGNIA R.A.F.

GLADIATOR MIDDLE EAST

WELLINGTON U.K.

NATIONAL EMBLEMS USED BY ALLIED SQUADRONS SERVING WITH THE R.A.F.
(Positioned on fuselage sides close to pilot's position and conditioned not to exceed 100 square inches in area)

RED
WHITE
BLUE

CZECH
(Pre-War National Aircraft Markings)

WHITE
WHITE

POLISH
National

BLUE RED WHITE

NORWEGIAN
(Flag)

BLUE WHITE   WHITE

GREEK
(Ensign and Standard)

ORANGE

BLACK

DUTCH
National
(Aircraft Markings)

YUGOSLAV
(Arms)

RED WHITE

FRENCH
(Cross of Lorraine)

BLACK YELLOW RED

BELGIAN
(Flag)

133

Fairchild M-62 trainers of 'Little Norway' in Canada bore Royal Norwegian Air Force colours on the rudder and around the wings. Presentation markings on some of these aircraft were Nos. 163 'Spirit of Little Norway', 169 'March of Time' (a popular war-time film series), 171 'Minnesota', 179 'Denmark' and 183 'State of New York'.

China

From 1937 the Sino-Japanese war had been raging in Manchukuo, but not until Japan became a common enemy did China receive much help from the Allies. In 1942 under Lease/Lend, 144 Vanguards were diverted from the R.A.F. (BW serials) to China together with Bostons and Hudsons such as FH387. Many ex-U.S.A.A.F. aircraft followed. They were given Chinese national markings (see page 150).

Czechoslovakia

Czechoslovakia was overrun in 1938 by political moves even before she had a chance to defend herself, but the Czech spirit was such that thousands fought with the French forces in 1939-40 and then with the British against Germany. Forming four R.A.F. squadrons, their aircraft had standard R.A.F. finish with the Czech emblem on the side of the fuselage.

Poland

It was in honouring an agreement over Poland that Britain went to war, but we could do little to prevent their annexation. Little known is the fact that Britain shipped about a hundred aircraft to Poland many Battles and also eleven Hurricanes, N2322-4, 2327, 2347-8, 2358 and 2392-5, but they were too late. In three weeks the Polish Air Force, in their standard olive drab and grey finish, with the Polish red and white emblem, were shot out of the sky.

Many Poles escaping to France fought on and No. 145 Polish Group was formed using firstly MS406 fighters in French Air Force markings. When France too fell, these Poles came to Britain and no less than twenty Polish squadrons were formed with the R.A.F. squadron numbers of No. 300 upwards. By the Anglo-Polish Agreement of August, 1940, they used aircraft in standard R.A.F. markings, bearing the previous Polish Air Force national marking as an emblem.

Norway

A brave fight against overwhelming odds disposed of Norwegian aircraft, Gladiators (e.g. ex-R.A.F. N5920) Fokker CVs and Heinkel He 115s, in a few days of 1940. Fortunately some staunch Norwegians escaped to form squadrons in the R.A.F. Their aircraft proudly bore the Norwegian flag as an emblem.

In Canada, after Norway's fall, a camp known as 'Little Norway' was set up, equipped by aircraft orders placed in America before the German invasion. These aircraft were given standard Norwegian markings as shown. No national marking appeared on the fuselage sides, but instead a large serial number. A new range of numbers was introduced for 'Little Norway' with block allocations as follows: 1-100 Northrop N-3PB, 101-200 Fairchild M-62, 201-300 miscellaneous types, 301-400 Douglas 8A and 401-500 Curtiss 75A Hawk. An exception to the Norwegian markings, Northrop N-3PB seaplanes serving in Iceland with No. 330 Squadron bore R.A.F. markings with a 'Little Norway' number above the fin flash; No. 12 was coded GS-D.

France

Pre-war French fighters were usually in silver or grey and a dark green was used for night bombers. Camouflage was generally introduced in 1938 with a pattern as shown on page 86, but with colours that varied to include dark blue and buff. National markings remained unchanged from the 1914-18 war, except that in the spring of 1940, French roundels were applied to the fuselage sides as a result of British representation. Serialling, too, remained unchanged; aircraft were serialled from No. 1 for each type, the marking appearing in the rudder striping. On the underside of the wings a unit and serial identity marking was given on army co-operation aircraft, marked in black on light undersurfaces or white on a dark surface. Identification numbers (letters were rarely used) sometimes appeared on fins and unit insignia on the fuselage sides.

French naval aircraft were in light grey finish with fuselage decking and the uppersurfaces of wings in a darker grey. The Navy's anchor symbol appeared on the roundels and rudder stripes. Additional to the rudder stripes, the tail elevators were often similarly striped. Identification markings appeared on the fuselage sides, such as E55 on the hull side of a Breguet Bizerte. Some French Navy seaplanes in 1940 bore 'sharks-teeth' markings, thus, as far as can be traced, the French originated this striking marking.

After the French collapse, aircraft escaping to British

134

territory proudly displayed a red Cross of Lorraine in a roundel size white circle painted on the fuselage side. Such 'escapees' were given a R.A.F. serial, examples are: AX672 Potez 63-11 No. 670 in dark green and light blue camouflage, AX675 MS406CI No. 827 in French fighter scheme and AX679 Potez 29 No. 99 in silver finish. A Lorraine Squadron was formed in North Africa; R.A.F. Blenheims such as R3877 were initially allotted in August, 1940. Later the Lorraine Squadron flew Bostons from Britain with a small white Lorraine Cross on a red shield identifying the unit. No. 340 Squadron was the first Free French fighter squadron formed in Britain, flying Spitfire Vs. From 9th February, 1942, a small Cross of Lorraine was marked by the cockpit of these Spitfires (see also Chapter 3).

Belgium

The Belgian Air Force was shot out of the sky by the Luftwaffe in a few days of 1940, but not before they had accounted for many German aircraft. Standard fighter finish was a brown uppersurface and light grey to white undersurface. On biplanes the finish was as illustrated (page 133). Roundels, marked on the fuselage and wing positions were rather smaller than usual if R.A.F. roundels be taken as the criterion. Rudder striping was discontinued about 1937.

An insignia was used for each Wing and each escadrille within that wing bore the marking with a different background colour, e.g. the Firefly fighters of No. 7 Fighter Wing of Chievres, (re-equipping with Fiat Cr 42s) bore the Cocotte (folded paper horse, see C.11 on page 50) insignia. Nos. 7, 8, and 9 Escadrille had respectively a red, blue and green background for this white marking.

Belgian Hurricanes (ex-R.A.F. L1918-20, L2040-4, etc.) had a uniform brown camouflage, with small Belgian roundels and service numbers in white on the fin or rudder. Battles were similarly camouflaged except for black instead of grey undersurfaces. Numbers such as '66' were marked on the rudder and underneath the wings in white 'T' and '66' on starboard and port sides respectively.

Firefly and Feroce biplanes in silver with black fuselage decking were used for operational training. They bore 3 in. Fairey factory numbers at the rear of the fuselage, e.g. A.F6078 (Service No. 87) was used personally by H.M. King Leopold III. A.F stood for Avions Fairey.

Holland

Dutch Army and Navy aircraft met the same fate at the same time as Belgian aircraft. Operational Dutch Army aircraft were camouflaged in an irregular pattern of dark green and khaki with grey undersurfaces. A large serial number appeared in white centrally on the fuselage side, allotted in blocks of numbers. Examples: 213 Fokker DXXI, 310 Fokker GI, 705 Fokker CX, 851 Fokker TV, etc. National markings changing in 1939 applied to the

undersurfaces of the wings, optional on the uppersurfaces, and well to the rear on fuselage sides.

Naval aircraft were mostly in silver-grey, with numbers usually in black on the fuselage sides, prefixed by a letter varying for each type of aircraft, e.g., F-1 Fokker CXIV-W training seaplane, S-20 Fokker SIX, etc. perhaps the best known were the Fokker T8-W seaplanes. During the 'Five-day war' in 1940, R-1, R-3, R-6 to R-11 eluded the Germans and escaped to Britain, where they received R.A.F. camouflage and markings with numbers AV958-965. A Dutch 9 in. equilateral triangle appeared on the nose. They flew 135 sorties. Later a Dutch squadron, No. 320 was formed with Ansons and Hudsons, then Mitchells.

Netherlands East Indies

The N.E.I. Air Corps was administered separately from the Army Air Corps in Holland, only national markings showing a common policy. Bombers such as the Martin 139W were, in 1939, in olive drab fuselages and cowlings with colonial white planes, both upper and lower surfaces. When the 1939 change-over to the triangular national marking was effected, the olive drab was extended overall. Fighters by 1940 were in a similar finish but with pale grey or azure blue undersurfaces. Lockheed 212A reconnaissance aircraft were delivered in a bare metal finish, with the old type national markings but without rudder striping. Large black numbers L201-212 appeared aft of the fuselage roundels. When they were camouflaged, the serials appeared in white half-size figures (9 in.) on the fuselage side.

Serial prefix letters were indicative of the type of aircraft, usually the initial letter of the manufacturer. Examples during 1939-42 were: B-3119 Brewster 339 Buffalo, C-310 Curtiss 75A Hawk, CW-359 Curtiss Wright CW21B, FCX-461 Fokker CX, LT911 Lockheed Lodestar, M-502 Martin 139W and M-551 Martin 166.

Greece

Greek aircraft had a brown/green camouflage in 1941 concealing a previous silver finish. Their national insignia is shown on page 133. Army markings applied to Potez 63s, Hs 126s, Breguet XIXs and also ex-R.A.F.

Mortal enemies, a Spitfire and a Focke Wulf Fw 190 fly side-by-side having a common bond— their Turkish national markings. The original camouflage style of their respective Service has been retained, but touched up to obliterate their original nationality and serial markings.

Battles (P6607-13) and twelve Blenheims (including ex-P6897-8). Navy markings applied, amongst other types, to ex-R.A.F. Ansons N5155, N5160, etc.

After the collapse three Hellenic squadrons were formed within the R.A.F., No. 13 using firstly Ansons, then Blenheims, bearing a flag insignia (page 133) by the cockpit. A Hurricane squadron in the Middle East marked this on the nose of their aircraft and also painted the spinners in blue, white and blue, the Royal Hellenic colours.

Yugoslavia

The pre-war markings of Yugoslav service aircraft are shown in colour on page 52. By 1941, the silver grey had been replaced by a brown and green on the uppersurfaces. Rudder striping as illustrated on page 52 gave way to a fin flash with horizontal striping. Several British-built aircraft were used in their short but bitter struggle in 1941. Hurricanes, e.g. ex-R.A.F. L1751 and L1837 were bearing Nos. 205 and 291 on their fuselage sides in Yugoslav service. Some fourteen Blenheims were in this Service, R.A.F. ex-L6827 was temporarily registered as a Yugoslav civil aircraft in 1940 for transit. On arrival its civil identity YU-BAL changed to Service No. 54.

Having shown British aircraft to be in Yugoslav service, we pass to Yugoslav aircraft in British service. Yugoslavia fell, but the Slav spirit was not broken; several aircraft were flown out from this Balkan country to Egypt. They included Do22 seaplanes in grey with irregular patches of blue bearing large black numbers on the fuselage side—306-309 later to become AX709-712 of the R.A.F. Other 'escapees' were two Savoia S79s 3702 (AX705) and 3714 (AX704) and a Dornier Do 17 3348 (AX707). Yugoslav civil Lockheed Electras YU-SAV, YU-SDA and YU-SBB became respectively R.A.F. aircraft AX669-771.

By arrangement with Tito the R.A.F. built up a Yugoslav element as part of the Balkan Air Force, starting off with training in all-yellow Tiger Moths bearing the new Yugoslav emblem instead of R.A.F. roundels, but retaining British numbers, e.g. NM149.

Russia

Considering the size of the Red Air Force and its contribution towards the defeat of Germany, this small section may not appear to do justice to that Union. The reason is two-fold, information, even historical information, on Russia's fighting services is difficult to obtain and their markings were so standardised as to preclude the necessity for lengthy description.

National markings were the well-known red star, sometimes outlined in yellow or black. They were positioned as shown on page 158, with the star on the tail overlapping both fin and rudder. Stars on the fuselage sides and undersides of wings were the invariable positions, with a tail star usual, and those on the uppersurface of the wings seemingly optional.

Camouflage was seasonal, snow camouflage being illustrated on page 158. The greyish-white was relieved sometimes by scarlet patches on the wings, presumably to assist search aircraft after a forced landing. These patches would be covered with white canvas sheeting at dispersal points. Summer camouflage varied in shades of green with light grey undersurfaces. A dappled green was often used on an overall neutral grey. Unit markings were not apparent, but individual numbers (never letters) were often carried aft of the fuselage star, or on the fin or rudder. They were in most cases obviously hand-painted. Only in very few instances were aircraft embellished, except where the pilot was acclaimed a 'Red Hero'. This entitled him to put his name by the cockpit.

Thousands of American and British aircraft were supplied to Russia under Lease/Lend. They left the U.S.A. in olive drab and neutral grey with red stars already marked, except in the case of R.A.F. aircraft diverted to Russia that were shipped still in R.A.F. markings over which red stars were hurriedly stencilled. Examples are Bostons AL303-316 and Kittyhawks FS100-269.

Turkey

Although Turkey did not enter the war until late, her potential strength and friendliness meant much throughout. British types supplied to Turkish orders in olive green and light blue undersurfaces, bearing the red square of Turkey, with a white border, were Hurricanes (e.g. L2032), Ansons (e.g. N9948), Blenheims and Lysanders; the latter bearing the Turkish Nos. 3101-3130. Britain's faith in Turkey is also evinced by the many R.A.F. aircraft handed over to her from the Middle East, initially in British camouflage, e.g. Beaufort I DX 144, Blenheim V EH 341, Spitfire VB ER 277 and Tomahawk IIB AN281.

A red star over the roundel on this Hurricane II shows that it has been taken over by the Russians. All the Hurricanes used by No. 151 Wing R.A.F. in Russia were similarly handed over. In addition, hundreds of Hurricanes were shipped direct to Russia for the Soviet Air Force, e.g. Nos. AP670-714, AP732-779, BN725-758 DR391-394, etc.

American Air Forces

American Army aircraft having occasion to enter the war zones September 1939 to December 1941 usually carried a large neutrality marking such as the U.S. Flag. This Liberator brought Mr. W. A. Harriman on a supply mission to Singapore shortly before the Japanese struck. There was then no further need for this marking!

United States National Insignia

Pre-war the United States marked their star insignia only on the wings of service aircraft. An additional indication of national identity on Army aircraft was a striped rudder symbolising the stripes of the United States Flag. The Navy too adopted this, but it was discontinued on camouflaged aircraft in February 1941 and on all aircraft in June 1942. From October that year and subsequently, four standard positions have been used for the national insignia; on each side of the fuselage, on the uppersurface of the port wing and the undersurface of the starboard wing. This unbalanced presentation facilitated identification, particularly in view of the balanced presentation of national insignia on the wings of both German and Japanese aircraft.

Experience in the Pacific war led to a modification of the insignia. The red centre could be to easily confused at a distance with the Japanese blood-red disc—the 'meatball' as it was dubbed. Orders were promulgated for the

red centre to be deleted on August 18th, 1942, the same day as the rudder striping was dropped. These changed markings are illustrated on page 147. Now the marking was a white star in a circumscribed blue circle, but it did not satisfy the Proving Ground at Eglin Field. At a distance it merged into an indistinguishable circle as did also the Japanese disc and the German cross, particularly when outlined in white. Apparently shape is more important than colour, for Eglin Field advocated that two white bars be marked each side, the whole being outlined in red. It was deemed to be 60 per cent. more easily recognised —but the basis of this calculation is a bit obscure! This marking was adopted officially on June 29th, 1943, but it had a psychological drawback, by the fact that it contained red—and red was anathema in the Pacific area as the colour of the Japanese identity marking. On September 17th, 1943, orders were given for the red to be replaced by a blue outline.

THE UNITED STATES ARMY AIR FORCE

Camouflage and General Finish

The British reader must appreciate that a reference to pre-war in this chapter is any time up to December 7th, 1941, when the Japanese made their devastating attack on Pearl Harbor without the formality of a declaration of war. If American awareness of that threat be judged by the precautions taken to provide security measures such as camouflaging aircraft at stations within striking distance of Japanese bases, then America could be said to have been totally unprepared. Authoritative documents, however, show that America was aware of Japanese preparations for war, but that their strength had been grossly underestimated and in any case it was considered that war would not come before mid-1942. Perhaps this explains why some pursuit squadrons late in 1941 had gaudy colour schemes with coloured fuselages and wings. Unfortunately that was not all.

The World's largest day bomber, the Boeing B-17

Fortress (B-17C, B-17D and B-17E versions) equipped the 19th Bombardment Group (Heavy) assigned to the Philippines in the Autumn of 1941. On Clark Field their shining bare metal finish was visible from forty miles out over the sea and one pilot even reported picking up the reflection of a Fortress in the pineapple plantation cum-airfield at Del Monte, seventy miles from the base. They were an excellent navigational aid—to the Japanese too. Within a few hours of the Pearl Harbor attack the Philippine airfields were being pounded—and they were over 2,000 miles *nearer* Japan than Pearl Harbor. Not only were the American planes uncamouflaged, but there was no suitable paint available. It was a critical situation. G.I. stores were searched and eventually some green paint was found which gave a finish one pilot described as 'liverish'. Unfortunately this paint was not matt, but gloss and as a camouflage it was therefore ineffectual. Finally in desperation, palm fronds were decked over the machines for concealment on the ground. It took ten truck-loads of palm fronds to camouflage each Fortress. Oh! for a drum of olive drab!

With Pearl Harbor disorganised by bombing, the shipping route was disrupted and as far as is known, no suitable camouflage paint was forthcoming. The Philippines were abandoned and most of the remaining aircraft were moved to Java, which in turn was evacuated for Australia. There are these significant figures for bomber losses on Java: lost by enemy action in the air—6, lost by accident—6, lost on the ground by enemy attack—26. A few drums of olive drab at the right place and time might well have saved a million dollars. Yet, ironically, in earlier war games in the States, camouflage had been used.

As late as March, 1942, B-18 bombers acting as transports in Northern Australia were still in pre-war finish, but by now production aircraft in America were already being delivered in camouflage and with the help of the R.A.A.F. in supplying khaki and khaki-green paints and dopes for the remnants of the aircraft of F.E.A.F., the operational aircraft of the United States donned war paint.

From production, operational aircraft were then finished in camouflage. At first a 'sand and spinach', coloured and patterned similar to the British temperate scheme but with less contrasting shades of brown and green. By 1942 however, an olive drab was standard uppersurface finish and undersurfaces were usually in neutral grey or azure blue for European and Pacific theatres respectively. All surfaces were in non-reflecting paints and the two surface shades merged into each other. The area covered by upper and lower surface shades followed British practice very closely. As early as July, 1942, the Kansas Modification Centre were applying dusty pink upper and azure blue lowersurfaces to B-25 Mitchells for operations in North Africa. Later a brown was usual for this area as shown on page 122. Various experimental schemes were tried; B-25 130115 had a cloud camouflage of neutral grey applied to uppersurfaces, with a creamy white undersurface extending half-way up the fuselage sides, meeting the grey in a wavy line along the length of the fuselage. Night fighter and intruder aircraft were in an overall black, but unlike British practice, a gloss black was often used.

Superiority over the enemy was eventually evinced by the discarding of camouflage. The advantage was that a smooth bare metal finish gave a slight improvement to the speed. B-26 Marauders set the style in the Pacific. They made their debut in olive drab and neutral grey by attacking Rabual during April, 1942. Just over a year later their paint was being scraped off and from mid-1943 until early 1944 when they were withdrawn from the Pacific Area, they were known as the 'Silver Fleet'. Other types followed suit and with the abandoning of camouflage came much more colour for unit insignia and individual emblems. One portion remained drab; the area in front of the pilot, usually the top of the nose of the machine was painted either black or olive drab to reduce glare and distracting reflections. In the case of an aircraft like the P-38 Lightning, it was necessary to treat similarly the inboard sides of the engine cowlings.

Practically the whole of the Twentieth Air Force based in the Marianas had uncamouflaged B-29 Super Fortresses and in clear finish, but with all insignia removed, one of these, 'Enola Gay' of the 509th Composite Group, dropped the bomb that changed the conception of war—the Atom Bomb. It was accompanied on that fateful day over Hiroshima by B-29 42-7353 'The Great Artiste' (page 140) which accompanied also, a few days later, on 9th August, 1945, the B-29 'Bock's Car' that dropped the second atomic bomb, this time on Nagasaki. And so ended the war. The same B-29s that had bombarded Japan then brought succour to thousands of our men in Japanese prisoner-of-war camps, with the words P.W. SUPPLIES painted under their wings.

Operational Markings

Special identification markings, additional to national insignia, were necessary with certain aircraft. The P-51 Mustang had identification bands in the same manner as R.A.F. Mustangs (see Chapter 6) to avoid confusion with the Me 109. P-47 Thunderbolts had similar bands in white. In the Pacific Area 1944-45, P-47s with a bare metal finish had blue identification markings as illustrated on page 150, those serving with the 35th Pursuit Group used pre-war rudder striping as a formation marking. To avoid confusion with the Japanese Tony, Warhawks in camouflage had their complete tail marked in white from aft of the leading edge of the tailplane.

Shark's teeth markings were not confined to fighters as will be seen on this B-25G Mitchell. It will be noticed that there is no clear-cut division between the upper and lower surfaces. The marking of the serial across the fin and rudder in yellow was a typical presentation.

Conspicuous against a white background, the Fiat Cr 42 biplane, a standard Italian fighter of 1940, had a camouflage designed for North African airfields.

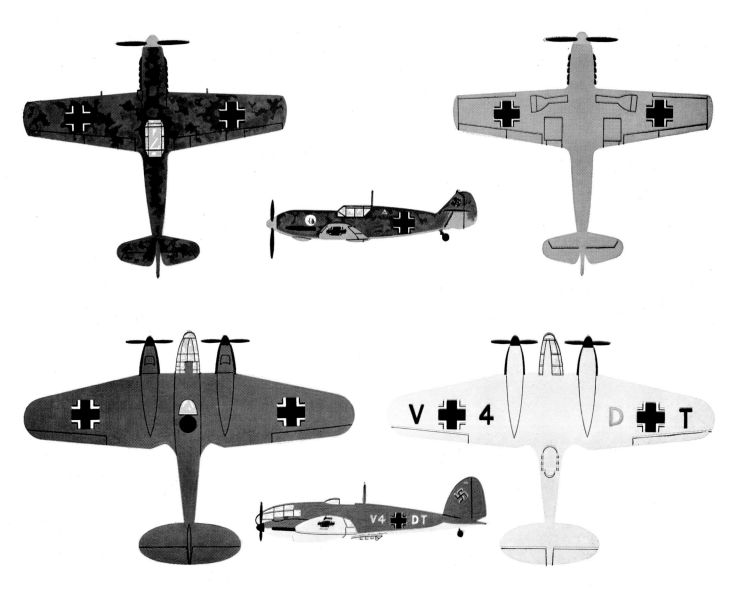

The Messerschmitt Me 109 of the 1940-41 period shows an offensive camouflage, for concealment over sea and in the air, without regard for concealment at its base for which there was little need at that time. The Heinkel He 111 is in Luftwaffe day-bomber camouflage, with formation markings.

The United States Twentieth Air Force had B-29 (Super-Fortresses) based on five great airfields in the Marianas. Two of these fields were on Tinian Island where these colour photographs were taken and here reproduced by kind permission of Dr. R. Wallace Teed.

To North Field, Tinian in June, 1945 came the 509th Composite Group to drop the first atomic bombs. On both missions, to Hiroshima and Nagasaki, the bombing aircraft was accompanied by 'The Great Artiste' shown here.

All the emblems are of B-29s of the 58th and 313rd Bombardment Groups based upon Tinian except for the marking borne by a C-54 transport (bottom left) that plied these Pacific Islands. What could be more appropriate than—'Island Hopper'?

Unofficial but condoned markings on operational aircraft were score or tally markings. The small bomb silhouette is well known, appearing usually in yellow or white on drab finish or black on metal finish. Fighter-bombers in particular, 'sported' at times row upon row of these markings. A rising sun flag or a black cross were the pilots' conventional markings for each Jap or German plane downed. Other silhouettes showed bridges, locomotives, flak towers or V1 flying bombs to record successful missions. Less obvious was a sitting duck silhouette implying a decoy mission and the silhouette of a camel repeated for each trip 'over the Hump'—over the Himalayas.

Non-Operational Aircraft

Blue fuselages with yellow wings was the usual trainer scheme up to 1940 when a bare metal finish became usual Trainers had various school schemes and varied as illustrated later. Individual identification was often by a 3-digit number. Luke Field for example, of the West Coast Training Centre, allotted blocks of one hundred numbers, 100-199, 200-299, etc., for each of its squadrons, all prefixed by 'X' as a Luke Field identification. Various colour schemes were used by the training squadrons often conforming to a Field or Centre directive. Conspicuous of the training aircraft were the radio-controlled target planes in their officially specified overall 'fire-truck red'.

Serialling

The fin was the normal position for the functional serial, although with small fins it extended across both fin and rudder, as for example 215135 on a Talyorcraft L-2A, with (port side) 21 on the fin and 5135 on the rudder. On some training aircraft it was sometimes placed centrally at the rear of the fuselage. It contained the last digit of the fiscal year appropriation, thus in the L-2A 215135 previously mentioned, the 2 stood for 1942 and 15135, the 15,135th aircraft ordered in the Fiscal Year 1942. Although the functional serial was presented in this way the true serial 42-15135 appeared in small letters on the fuselage side.

Unit Markings

American squadron insignia have a character of their own and several are illustrated in this book. There is an underlying sense of humour and many are caricatures, but nevertheless in perfectly good taste. Unit insignia were submitted to the U.S. Assistant Chief of Air Staff who had the assistance of a Heraldic Consultant. Regulations conditioned such markings to simplicity to avoid marking difficulties and to a visibility of 150 yards. No numbers, geographical locations or parts of the U.S. flag were permitted. In combat units, squadron markings were not officially permitted in operational zones.

Some airfields had their own markings, Bolling Field, Washington, used an appropriate marking depicting the Capitol.

Individual Markings

These are too numerous and varied to survey, but a representative selection are illustrated. Voluptuous females and comic characters embellished the aircraft, particularly in combat units. Others bore 'slick' names, pithy remarks or just a girl's name. Examples are: 'Miss Behavin'', 'Iza Vailable', 'Sweet Pea' and on B-17E 42-97061—'Ike' with a coloured portrait of General Eisenhower.

THE UNITED STATES NAVY

General Finish

Operational naval aircraft had a standard finish of a deep blue merging to an undersurface grey or azure. The blue, officially a 'sea-blue' was often in a semi-gloss. On folding-wing carrier aircraft, the undersurface portion of the wing that folded upwards was camouflaged in the uppersurface sea-blue, to merge with the colour of the carrier's deck. There was a general tendency to have slightly larger national insignia than on U.S.A.A.F. aircraft; the shade of difference being that where the Army used a 40 in. stencil, the Navy would apply the next highest denomination, i.e. 45 in. Where the Navy used an operational blue camouflage, the star of the insignia would be painted off-white. The precise shade being specified as a light grey obtained by mixing one part of insignia white with one part of neutral grey.

Patrol flying-boats had three distinct schemes, but common to all was the marking of the U.S. insignia each side of the nose of the hull. A dark blue topside extended well down the hull sides to merge with a light grey. This was the general finish, but several search boats in the North Atlantic area had an all-white finish and conversely, those operating at night an all-black finish. Catalinas so finished in black were appropriately named 'Black Cats'.

Some flying-boats had additionally a U.S. Star on the hull sides aft of the mainplanes and some naval patrol

A feature of United States Navy flying-boats was their national insignia displayed on the nose of the hull. The unit marking indicates that this all-white Mariner is No. 1 of Patrol Squadron 211.

finish in service. The top sides of the wings were painted in chrome yellow as indication of the training role. Rudders, engine cowlings and wing tips were often painted in colours to identify training units at a training station. Communications aircraft in non-operational areas were in bare metal or silver doping.

Identification Markings

The words U.S. NAVY appeared on naval aircraft in clear or yellow finish (see Part 2, Chapter 9) but not on camouflaged aircraft. Pre-war squadron markings were still used in many American-based units, e.g. 74 P3 in white on the nose of a Mariner indicating aircraft No. 3 of Patrol Squadron 74. These markings were, however, discarded in combat zones, because of their revealing nature. Typical of combat area individual and formation markings were letter/number combinations L17, L18, L19, etc., in 30 in. white letters forward of the U.S. star on the fuselage sides.

Serials from 1941 onwards were presented in the very reduced size of 1 in., until then they were presented as shown on page 87. The serialling system was a simple one. The same consecutive 'A' series used during the 1914-18 war continued, although the prefix letter 'A' was rarely marked after 1930. When 9999 was reached in 1936, a new series started at 0001, but owing to the expansion programme it had reached 9999 again by 1941. As a number of 1936 aircraft were still in service, a repetition of another 0001-9999 series might have led to identification difficulties; the allocation of numbers therefore continued progressively from 10,000 upwards—and they still do.

Naval aircraft designations, presented as shown on page 87, up to 1941 were, like the serial numbers, reduced in 1941 to 1 in. lettering. The designation system is explained on page 151.

Unit badges were used in non-operational areas, Utility Squadron VJ-2 using that symbol of utility—a safety pin!

Marine and Coast Guard aircraft both came under naval administration and were marked as for U.S. Navy aircraft according to their role. In light finish the words U.S. MARINES or U.S. COAST GUARD appeared as appropriate at the rear of the fuselage sides.

bombers, e.g. Lockheed PV-1s in late 1942, had usual sea-blue/light grey finish with the U.S. star insignia on both sides of the fuselage at the nose and mid-fuselage positions, besides at port and starboard sides on both upper and lower wing surfaces.

A dark blue, known as 'midnite' blue, was introduced for night-fighting aircraft and was later extended to other night-operational aircraft. The same regulations regarding an off-white star insignia applied.

General Finish—Non-Operational Aircraft

Primary trainers in the U.S. Navy were colloquially known as 'yellow perils' by their overall chrome yellow finish. Advanced trainers were delivered in a bare metal finish but it could hardly be described as a bare metal

AMERICAN AIR FORCES AND FORMATIONS OTHER THAN OF THE U.S.A.

Squadrons known as Eagle Squadrons were formed in the R.A.F. from American volunteers before America came into the war. The first squadron, No. 71 (Eagle) Squadron R.A.F., used initially Masters in trainer finish, then Spitfire Vs in standard R.A.F. Fighter Command finish.

An American Volunteer Group was formed in the Chinese Air Force. Tomahawks were chiefly used marked as shown on page 133. Ninety-eight Tomahawks (AK466-8, AK471-3, etc.) were diverted for A.V.G. use.

Brazil declared war on Germany and Italy, 22nd August, 1942, and a Brazilian squadron served with the Twelfth Air Force in Italy using P-47s. At home P-36 and P-40 fighters were used for training in Brazilian national markings, see page 150. Brazilians had presented Britain with a bomber, named BRITANNIA, and in 1945 Britain reciprocated by presenting the Brazilian Government with a Lancaster.

Mexico joined the war 29th May, 1942. AT-6 and Finch trainers, Lodestars and Dauntlesses were used at home in Mexican national markings (page 150). The 201st Fighter Squadron of the Mexican Expeditionary Air Force served in the S.W. Pacific Area, using P-47s in bare metal finish with American insignia on the fuselage sides, but with the triangular Mexican insignia on the wing positions and with rudders striped in Mexican colours as illustrated. U.S.A.A.F. serials appeared on the fin, e.g. 433738.

The Allies were helped in other ways, too, by Mexicans, and Fairchild M-62 trainers of Little Norway bore witness to this by presentation markings, e.g. No. 181 was Mexico I and Nos. 141, 151, 161 and 177 were EL GAUCHO I to IV respectively.

French Air Force Marauders in 1945 operating with the U.S.A.A.F. had typical U.S. markings but with the tri-colour roundel replacing the blue star and white circle. Dutch Air Force Mitchells in the S.W. Pacific carried the Dutch orange triangle and white serials such as N5-124 on the fuselage sides.

THE UNITED STATES ARMY AIR FORCES IN BRITAIN

Britain as a Base

Shortly after America's entry into the war, plans were made to base in the British Isles strategic and tactical elements of the U.S.A.A.F. Initially assigned were the 1st Fighter Group flying P-38s, the 31st Fighter Group with P-39s and the 97th Bombardment Group with B-17E Fortresses. However, before these units arrived, the 15th Bombardment Squadron was formed using ex-R.A.F. Bostons, e.g. Z2200, which retained R.A.F. finish but with U.S. insignia added. After training at Molesworth the squadron flew its first operation from Swanton Morley on the Fourth of July, 1942, thereby being the first U.S.A.A.F. unit to do battle in Europe. Meanwhile the 31st and 52nd Fighter Groups moved into Atcham and High Ercall. They received reverse Lend/Lease in the form of Spitfire VBs which retained their ocean grey and dark green camouflage and 'sky' trimmings. An anomaly was, that although a U.S. star insignia replaced the British roundel, the R.A.F. fin flash was usually retained.

On 23rd June, 1942, the first of many Boeing B-17 Fortresses set out for England by way of Greenland. The first to arrive at Prestwich was B-17E-BO, 19085, 'Jarring Jenny', on 1st July, 1942. In the first big movement, forty-nine B-17s, fifty-two C-47s and eighty P-38s were despatched arriving here in July. The first B-17 Group, the 97th, was completely equipped by 27th July at Grafton Underwood and was ready for operations the following month; then, on the first suitable day, 17th August, eighteen B-17s set out from Grafton to attack the railway yards at Rouen and commence the great campaign carried out by day, against targets in Europe.

The 'Heavies'

The United States Eighth Air Force, as this British-based force was designated, expanded rapidly. The first Fortresses to arrive were camouflaged with light and dark green uppersurfaces with patches of brown resembling the British 'dark earth'. Their undersurfaces carried a coat of pale greyish blue and the bold, black inscription U.S. ARMY in addition to the national insignia under the starboard wing. On their fins appeared the customary U.S.A.A.F. serial number in a yellowish-orange and on the noses of many were painted cute captions and quite often an eye-taking scene! Most famous was B-17E 19023 'Yankee Doodle' in which Brigadier-General Ira Eaker led the first famous raid on Rouen. Others were 19038 'Baby Doll' and 19047 'Birmingham Blitzkrieg'.

During September the 92nd, 97th, and 301st Bombardment Groups were operating and a new bomber had joined the Force, the B-24 Liberator. They were from the beginning in the camouflage scheme that became standard in the Eighth Air Force, olive drab uppersurfaces and dark grey undersurfaces. By the end of September white horizontal bars which some B-24s carried on their rudders were the first formation markings to appear on U.S. aircraft in the European Theatre. During November, B-24s appeared with short yellow diagonal stripes on the lower parts of their fins.

By this time the first B-17Fs had arrived in Britain coloured olive drab and dark grey and they participated in the Lille attack of 9th October, 1942, along with B-24Ds making their first operational sorties from Britain. One of the first B-17F units, the 91st Bombardment Group formed at Bassingbourn, may be taken as an example to show the manner in which the markings on the B-17s of the 1st Bombardment Wing developed. Initially in camouflage the B-17Fs had yellow fin serials with an individual aircraft-in-squadron letter below, 'T' being 25077, a B-17F-30-BO. Some like 'O' 24524, a B-17F-20-BO, had a yellow surround to their U.S. insignia on the fuselage, to bring this marking more into line with British practice. By November six groups were operational and some means of identifying individual squadrons during operations was needed. Following R.A.F. practice VIII Bomber Command issued two-letter symbols to each squadron of Fortresses during December, OR being allocated to the 322nd Squadron, part of the 91st B.G. These letters were applied ahead

Many British aircraft were used in American Service; here is one of 350 Spitfires handed over to the U.S.A.A.F. in 1943. Representative serials were Mk. VCs BS161, EE794 and EF529. Other aircraft handed over were 120 Mosquitos, Master II AZ672, Proctor I P6321, Kittyhawk II FL273, etc. Note in this case the British fin flash has been retained.

of the national insignia in yellow in this instance, with an individual letter aft. The fin serial and individual letter remained. Another squadron carried the letters TK followed by the individual letter aft of the insignia. During February, 1943, the 323rd Squadron applied its unit letters completely aft of the insignia with the individual letter adjacent the tail.

It was during July that the striking white group marking on the fin came into use, initially on the B-17s of the 1st Air Division. The large symbols were placed above the serial number on the fin of each aircraft in each group and upon these appeared a unit letter. The 92nd B.G. had a black letter 'B' on its triangle which itself was outlined in black as on B-17F-45-DL 23105 NV.N, whilst the 351st B.G. of the 1st Air Division had a yellow letter 'J' on its fin tips even before the triangle symbol was adopted. A second change to national insignia came in during July when the new type national marking with white bars was introduced; being outlined first in red and later in blue. Even so, some B-17Fs were still operating at this time with their U.S. insignia outlined in yellow, e.g. 24524 'The Eagle's Wrath' with some thirty-five missions to its credit. This particular Fortress had its squadron letters 'OR' aft of the U.S. insignia and the individual letter ahead. A few of the first B-17Gs, now in use, had grey stars to their U.S. markings. Whilst a white group marking without any outline and a black formation letter became standard, many irregularities occurred. For instance B-17F-55-BO 29921 the famed 'Oklahoma Okie' DF.Z of the 324th Squadron, 91st B.G., carried blue letter 'A's on its white fin triangles, repeated as was usual, above the starboard wing tip. Likewise B-24E 27014 of the 44th B.G. carried blue 'A's. Fortresses of the 92nd and 306th B.G.s later had their group marking repeated under the port wing.

As early as July, 1943, a few B-17s in natural finish had joined the Eighth Air Force and were operational. Absence of camouflage conferred a little extra speed and slightly reduced production man-hours. The need for camouflage

to give concealment from air attack whilst grounded no longer existed, and so, from March, 1944, more and more bombers came to Britain unpainted. Those aeroplanes already camouflaged often remained so, right up until VE-Day. On the bare metal finish, which could well be described as silverish, the aircraft serial number and lettering was in black, likewise the fin and wing tip symbols, carring white or silver letters. The B-17G-25-VE, 297674, WF.A of the 305th B.G. (G in triangle) was typical in this respect, whereas B-24J, 440052, EE.O of the 389th B.G. (C in circle) retained camouflaged fins and the older colours for its markings, whilst the rest of the aircraft was silver. The B-24s had, since receiving squadron letters, carried them aft of the fuselage insignia with the individual letter only on the fins, as a general rule.

The 457th B.G. which arrived at Glatton at the beginning of 1944 was one of the first to operate its four squadrons without squadron code letters. Although these letters had been allocated, the squadrons identified themselves instead by coloured spinners, as did some other groups. The practice of employing coloured markings already in use by the Ninth Air Force was extended in May, 1944, to the B-24s of the 2nd Bombardment Division, which dispensed with tail group markings in favour of coloured outer fin and rudder surfaces. The 467th B.G., previously 'P' in a circle, was amongst the first units to receive these new markings. By D-Day nearly all the B-24s operating had the new markings, a variety of colours and combinations being used. Squadron letters remained as before, also the group letter symbol above the starboard wing tip. Typical was 'RT' Squadron of the 446th B.G. which could be seen to carry a deep-yellow tail over which ran a black horizontal band, the aircraft's individual letter appearing on this in yellow.

D-Day markings, the A.E.A.F. stripe, did not apply to the 'heavies' of the Eighth Air Force, even though B-24s delivered a dawn assault on D-Day.

In the closing weeks of June, 1944, the Fortresses appeared wearing bright colours on their fins and sometimes tailplanes and wing tips. One of the first to display them, the 398th B.G. at Nuthampstead, retained its group symbol on a red background the width of the fin triangle, extending from the tip to the base of the fin. A red chord-wise band encircled the tailplane, excluding the elevators. Later the complete tailplane, less elevators, was in red with the mainplane tips also in this colour. The 91st and 381st B.G.s carried similar markings since they belonged to the same Combat Wing. A few units dispensed with their group markings when the colours were introduced, 'G' in a square used by the 385th B.G. being replaced by a red and white chequered fin and rudder, with red tailplanes and a red band chord-wise around the wing. These coloured markings on Fortresses, Liberators and also Marauders were in use up to VE-Day. A typical B-17G was 297061 LL.B 'General Ike' carrying standard colours of the 91st B.G. on its silver finish.

No account of the changing markings on bombers would be complete without reference to the brightly attired lead-ships used to assist in the forming up in the air of groups and wings prior to their missions. At first 'weary' B-24Ds were employed gaily decked, one in black and yellow vertical and horizontal bands. Later B-24H and B-24J Liberators were employed, examples being those of the 458th B.G., the front fuselages of which carried black and white checks, whilst the rear was camouflaged and carried a yellow band. Another B-24H in silver was heavily marked in red lightning flashes.

As the war came to an end some bombers were to be seen with their squadron letters under the port wing tip in black on silver, or yellow on camouflaged aircraft. Some Fortresses, unarmed retained their unit markings but were used for transport duties as CB-17s along with a few B-24s, their turrets being replaced by transparent castings. By August, 1945, the Eighth Bomber Command was little more than a memory.

The 'Mediums'

Of the twin-engined bombardment types, North American B-25C Mitchells were the first to arrive. They were initially finished in olive drab with U.S. ARMY in black on their greyish-blue undersurfaces. Some months later, in March, 1943, the Martin B-26B Marauder joined the Eighth Air Force in the 3rd Bombardment Wing, the 322nd B.G. being the first to operate the new type. Their first operation, after very low flying practice, was delivered on May 14th against a target near Ymuiden. Then followed the disastrous operation when one aircraft breaking away to an abortive sortie revealed the approach of ten others which were shot down. The B-26s were then confined to medium altitude attacks. The olive drab and grey B-26s carried grey squadron letters and yellow fin serials, 117961 ER.M of the 322nd B.G. being one of the first to arrive here. By June the B-26Bs had been supplemented by later types carrying extra guns and the 322nd were by this time using as squadron letters DR, ER, PN and SS.

An administrative change came about in the Autumn of 1943 when the U.S. Ninth Air Force in North Africa handed over its aircraft to the U.S. Twelfth Air Force and moved its H.Q. to England. That November their B-26 Marauders appeared wearing the coloured tactical markings illustrated. Its strength too was increased by Douglas A-20G bombers at the beginning of 1944. When D-Day came, A.E.A.F. stripes were appropriate to all aircraft of the Ninth, this was applied a few days before the assault. It may well have been an optical illusion which led one observer to report that these bands on A-20G 7G.W from Hadstock seen on 24th June, 1944, had red instead of black on the part of the A.E.A.F. stripes marked above the wings. Towards the end of June the first of the A-26 Invaders arrived to replace the A-20s; most of these were in silver finish.

Fighter Aircraft

The 1st and 14th Fighter Groups which arrived in Britain in August, 1942, operated Lockheed P-38E and P-38F Lightnings. They were coloured in olive drab and light-bluish-grey with U.S. ARMY on their undersurfaces. Within a few months they had departed for North Africa to join the Twelfth Air Force.

About October, 1942, the first Bell P-39 Airacobras appeared with the 350th F.G. at Duxford. These aircraft diverted from the R.A.F.'s order were in some cases in dark green and dark earth camouflage with duck egg blue undersurfaces and had their American insignia outlined in

British and American markings ings in the same formation show the close affinities between the R.A.F. and the U.S.A.A.F. It has not been ascertained whether the number '88' was marked by someone in a hurry or someone who had over-indulged! Interchanges with Bostons resulted in some displaying U.S.A.A.F. serials, but with R.A.F. roundels, whereas some others had R.A.F. serials with United States insignia. An equipment accounting officer's headache!

yellow, as did BX-288. Some had a yellow individual letter on their nose or a two-digit number. A fair proportion carried R.A.F. serials, AP282 and BX365 amongst them.

The third type of fighter to appear was the Republic P-47C Thunderbolt, examples of which reached England in November, 1942, and by April, 1943, had equipped the 4th, 56th and 78th Fighter Groups. They arrived coloured olive drab and dark grey with a yellow fin serial. A yellow surround to the U.S. insignia was added in many cases and forward of the fuselage insignia a white two-figure number was positioned, 16295 being '95'. To render the Thunderbolts readily identifiable a white horizontal band was painted across the fin and rudder. During March, white chord-wise bands appeared on the tailplane and around the front of the engine cowling. The markings of the 78th Fighter Group were typical although it was not until May that the Group adopted the white nose. Squadron letters appeared in white, WZ.N of the 84th Squadron, a P47C-2-RE, being 16228 and having the yellow surround to its insignia.

In September, the first North American P-51B Mustangs appeared, in olive drab and dark grey, later adorned by white bands placed as were those on the Thunderbolts, and white spinners. As a fighter the P-51B flew its first mission on 1st December and on 15th January, 1944, it made its debut as an escort fighter. Meanwhile, on 15th October, a few Lockheed P-38 Lightnings had become operational. Olive drab with grey undersurfaces, they carried white code letters aft of the U.S. marking such as CY.S on 267066.

Fighters in the Eighth Air Force acquired coloured markings about March at about the same time as uncamouflaged fighters appeared in numbers. With a bare metal finish, or silver as it was colloquially but incorrectly called, markings previously white were applied in black, likewise squadron letters and serial numbers as in the case of P-51B-15-NA 106767 QP.E., of the 4th Fighter Group. Some of the camouflaged fighters had coloured markings, e.g. P-47D-10-RE 275174 which bore the usual white identification bands, the squadron letters ahead of the insignia on the fuselage in the manner B7-T, had a yellow cowling. These markings were retained until the end of the war, with the addition in the Autumn of 1944, of coloured rudders to distinguish each of the squadrons within a group as well as squadron code letters.

During June, 1944, many fighters had 'A.E.A.F. stripes' amongst them some of the newly arrived P-47D-25 and P-51D fighters just entering operational service. Some groups added irregular colours to their aircraft like the high gloss blue uppersurfaces seen on the P-51Bs and P-51Ds of the 361st Fighter Group at Bottisham, for example on P-51D-50-NA 413763 E9-O. By August the fin-filleted P-51-5-NA was in service and by November, the 339th Fighter Group had made one of the first 2-seat conversions of a P-51D on 413918, named 'Grusome Twosome'. This aircraft was in bare metal finish and had a red and white spinner.

Early in 1945, fin-filleted P-51Bs were about, likewise 'war-weary' fighters with WW inscribed above their fin serials as on P-51C-5-NT 103601 HL-L 'Little Dog'. As the war drew to a close the fighters like the bombers of the Eighth, proudly displayed identity letters beneath their wings, sometimes their wing number or squadron letters.

Transports, Trainers and Miscellaneous Types

The first American transports to be operated in Britain were Douglas C-47 Skytrains finished either in khaki and dark grey or olive drab and dark grey. During 1943 some of these could be seen to carry yellow letters ahead of their national insignia on the fuselage sides. Later large yellow two-digit numbers appeared just aft of the pilot's cabin windows, C-47A-40-DL 224056 having '63.' By May, 1944, the large nose numbers had given way to grey squadron letters such as 'SB', the aircraft's individual letter appearing on the fin above the serial. The C-47 was joined by the paratrooping C-53 of which amongst those in Britain during 1944, C-53D 268713 E5.L was unusual in having a red fin serial.

The second principal transport to serve in Europe was the Curtiss C-46A Commando which arrived to equip the 313th Group at Folkingham towards the end of 1944. They were camouflaged olive drab and grey and carried squadron letters placed as on C-47s.

A variety of smaller transports came to Britain led by some Piper L-4s as early as December, 1942, and were used for various tasks. They were in olive drab, often without a fin serial but instead a large individual letter on the fin. By 1945 silver L-4s such as 43648 were in use. Some R.A.F. Dominies were turned over to the U.S.A.A.F. in 1943 and at first retained their standard finish of temperate land scheme with yellow undersurfaces. Alconbury based in 1944, Dominie X7522 had by then a coat of olive drab and grey with a yellow 7522 on its fin in the manner of a U.S.A.A.F. serial.

Arriving in May, 1943, came the first of a batch of Cessna UC-78 Brasshats such as 278517 joined in June by the UC-61A, e.g. 314471, and in January by the UC-64 Norseman, e.g. 470238. An unusual fin serial on a UC-61A was 4314499, unusual in that only rarely did the full U.S.A.A.F. serial appear on the aircraft's fin. Additional transports serving in Britain were the L-5 Sentinel which arrived in 1944 and the UC-45A, one of which in 1943 was oddly clad in olive drab and yellow with U.S. ARMY on its undersurfaces. During May, 1944, a number of AT-6Ds arrived, one usually being based with each fighter group, bearing the group's colours and suitable letters.

Markings of Morale

'Autograph a Warplane' became something of a catch-phrase with Americans. A war-weary Fortress (12577) returning home to Roswell, New Mexico, after completing forty-eight missions from Britain was autographed by the personnel of the 303rd B.G. to which it belonged. Signatures were etched all over its fuselage.

This was no one-way affair, many aircraft, particularly bombers, arrived with hundreds of autographs, pencilled or etched. Sometimes these were of those who had built them, or to those who had bought War Bonds, this privilege had been granted. Bombers toured the States in 'Autograph a Bomber' campaigns to aid war organisations. It was not always a practical proposition to bring the aircraft and signee into contact and, viewed impassively, not desirable to have scribbling all over the finish. The North American Company solved this by a certificate, observed in several Mitchells in Britain, bearing names of War Bond subscribers.

UNITED STATES AIRCRAFT
NATIONAL INSIGNIA

RUDDER	WING	FUSELAGE SIDES, PORT UPPER AND STARBOARD LOWER WING

ARMY
1927-
1942

1927-1941

ALL SERVICES
1921-1942

N.B. Rudder striping was used on Navy planes 1941-42 and was re-introduced for a short period in 1946 for U.S.A.A.F. aircraft.

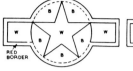

FROM AUGUST 18th. 1942

FROM JUNE 30th. 1943

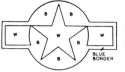

FROM SEPTEMBER 1943

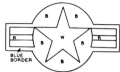

1947 ONWARDS

N.B. Although dates of promulgation are given in some cases, it does not necessarily mean that the changes came into immediate effect.

REPRESENTATIVE BOMBARDMENT SQUADRON MARKINGS

358th.

359th.

360th.

The Four Squadrons forming the 303rd Bombardment Group

427th.

REPRESENTATIVE FIGHTER SQUADRON MARKINGS

355 TH

PAGE COLOUR CODE
B=BLUE W=WHITE
R=RED   Y=YELOW
BLACK SHOWN IN BLACK

339 TH

U.S. NINTH AIR FORCE IX BOMBER COMMAND FIN MARKINGS BOMBARDMENT GROUPS 1944-1945

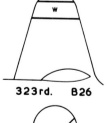

323rd.   B26

344th.   B26

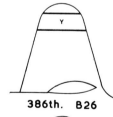

386th.   B26

387th.   B26

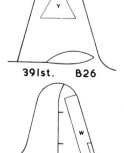

391st.   B26

394th.   B26

397th.   B26

409th.   A20

410th. A20

416th. A20

N.B. As applied to B26 aircraft in natural finish and A20 aircraft in camouflage.

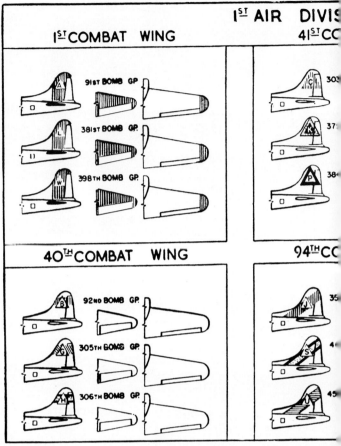

In 1943, when the strength of the Eighth Air Force was rapidly growing, it was decided that for ease of unit identification in the air, both operationally and when formating, a system of group markings should be introduced. Accordingly, a plan was drawn up whereby each division had a symbol and each group had a letter.

The symbols chosen were a triangle for the First Division, a circle for the Second Division and a square for the Third Division. In these symbols, which appeared on the fin and upper starboard wing tip of most aircraft, were the group letters, and beneath the group marking on the fin was the individual aircraft's serial number and squadron letter, also carried on the side of the fuselage.

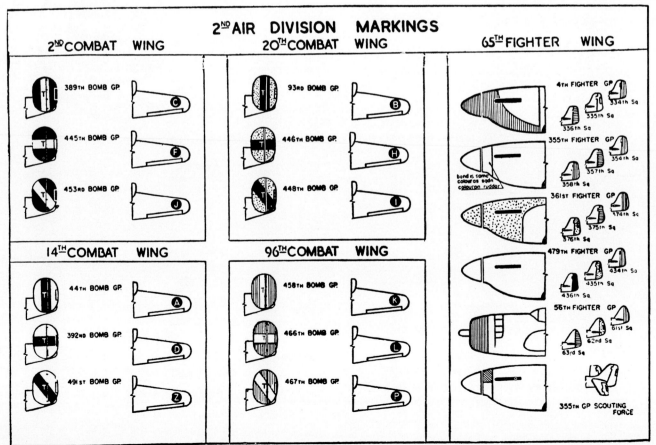

MARKINGS
WING

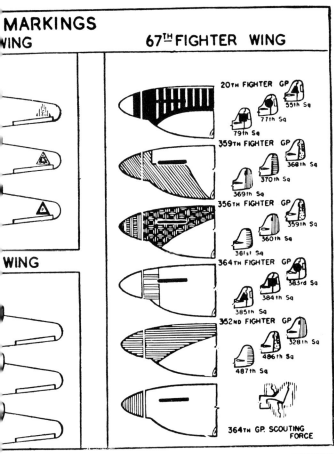

67TH FIGHTER WING

20TH FIGHTER GP.
55th Sq
77th Sq
79th Sq

359TH FIGHTER GP.
368th Sq
370th Sq
369th Sq

356TH FIGHTER GP.
359th Sq
360th Sq
361st Sq

364TH FIGHTER GP.
383rd Sq
384th Sq
385th Sq

352ND FIGHTER GP.
328th Sq
486th Sq
487th Sq

364TH GP. SCOUTING FORCE

These symbols did not show up well against the dull colours of Fortresses and Liberators, and some groups began to outline their own markings in colour. This eventually led, in late 1943, to the establishment of a complete colour marking system for the whole Air Force and, when the natural metal finish was adopted by the Americans, these colours presented themselves in startling brightness.

Fighters followed the bombers in their colour schemes by using coloured rudders and noses and they, too, in 1944 were discarding camouflage in favour of a bare metal finish.

Unit code letters were also allotted but were not always displayed. Some of these were 'bogey letters' designed to mislead enemy intelligence.

mark-
States
Force
Allied
Force
or the
tinent,
t apply
of this
marked
fighters
illustra-
B and
above,
typical
mation

made to
r perm-
all the
hese two

BLUE

YELLOW

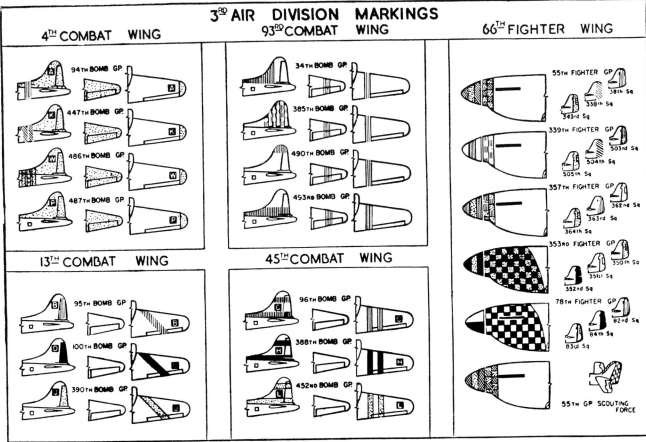

3RD AIR DIVISION MARKINGS

4TH COMBAT WING
94TH BOMB GP. A
447TH BOMB GP. K
486TH BOMB GP. W
487TH BOMB GP. P

93RD COMBAT WING
34TH BOMB GP.
385TH BOMB GP.
490TH BOMB GP.
493RD BOMB GP.

66TH FIGHTER WING
55TH FIGHTER GP.
38th Sq
343rd Sq

339TH FIGHTER GP.
503rd Sq
504th Sq
505th Sq

357TH FIGHTER GP.
362nd Sq
363rd Sq
364th Sq

353RD FIGHTER GP.
350th Sq
351st Sq
352nd Sq

78TH FIGHTER GP.
82nd Sq
84th Sq
83rd Sq

55TH GP. SCOUTING FORCE

13TH COMBAT WING
95TH BOMB GP. B
100TH BOMB GP. D
390TH BOMB GP. J

45TH COMBAT WING
96TH BOMB GP. C
388TH BOMB GP. H
452ND BOMB GP. L

AMERICAN AIR FORCES

U.S. INSIGNIA SIZES

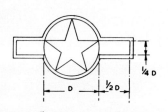

D = 20" minimum, 60" maximum in 5" denominations 20" to 60".

POSITION	LOCATION	SIZE
PORT WING UPPERSURFACE STARBOARD WING UNDERSURFACE	INBOARD BY ONE THIRD OF DISTANCE FROM THE WING TIP TO THE FUSELAGE.	30"– 60" DIAMETERS IN 5" DENOMINATIONS. DIA. SIZE USED WAS THAT NEAREST TO, BUT NOT EXCEEDING ¾ OF THE WING CHORD LESS AILERONS AT LOCATION.
FUSELAGE SIDES.	PLACED AS PRACTICABLE. WHERE POSSIBLE EQUI-DISTANT BETWEEN TRAILING EDGE OF MAINPLANE AND LEADING EDGE OF TAILPLANE.	20"–50" DIAMETERS IN 5" DENOMINATIONS. SIZE SELECTED AS APPROPIATE.
HULL SIDES.	WELL FORWARD, ON EACH SIDE OF HULL NOSE.	AS FOR FUSELAGE SIDES.

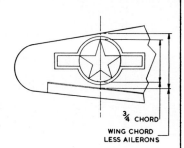

¾ CHORD

WING CHORD LESS AILERONS

AVENGER FIELD U.S.A.A.F.

EXAMPLES OF

U.S. TRAINING

AIRCRAFT

MARKINGS 1942

MOORE FIELD U.S.A.A.F.

CORPUS CHRISTI NAVAL AIR STATION U.S.N.

LUKE FIELD U.S.A.A.F.

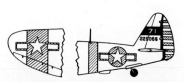

SPECIAL IDENTITY MARKINGS
P 47s PACIFIC AREAS
Blue markings on clear finish.
(Tail markings as for 35th. Pursuit Group.)

ELLINGTON FIELD
U.S. ARMY AT-6A
A.C. NO. 41-16774
CREW WEIGHT 400 LBS

A typical U.S.A.A.F. designation, serial and crew weight marking on the port side of all U.S.A.A.F. aircraft. The field name has been added in service.

RED
WHITE
GREEN

NATIONAL MARKINGS-MEXICO

Brazilian National Insignia.

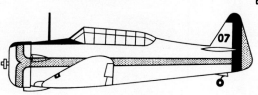

Fuselage Side.

BLUE   YELLOW   GREEN

EXERCITO

Upper Surface, Starboard Wing

Trainer Scheme. Brazilian Air Force.
Bare-metal finish. Insignia on upper and lower surface of wings, port and starboard sides.

150

UNITED STATES AIRCRAFT DESIGNATION MARKINGS

The U.S. Army aircraft designation was stencilled in 1 in. figures on the port side of the fuselage near the pilot's position. A typical example would be U.S. ARMY B-24D where the 'B' would stand for 'Bombardment'. This was known as the mission prefix and variations were as given in Table 'A'. The number '24' recorded the 24th bombardment type in U.S. Army service. 'D' recorded the fourth major modification to the basic design in alphabetical allotment. In 1942 the system was extended to show modifications other than basic design changes and also the manufacturer. Block numbers for modifications were allotted by the constructor in an arithmetical progression 5, 10, 15, etc., and the intermediate numbers were open for allotment as necessary by modification centres or service units. Thus in B-24J-86-CF the CF identified the manufacturer and factory, in a range of two code letters as per Table 'C'. The 86 showed seventeen modifications incorporated by this constructor and one subsequently.

The U.S. Navy designation appeared in 3-4 in. lettering on the fin, but it was reduced in size from 1941. Occasionally it was applied to the rear of the fuselage which is the present standard position. To take F2A-1 as a representative designation, the first letter denoted the mission (or role) as per Table 'B'. The number '2' represents the second fighter type by the manufacturer supplied to the Navy. Single letters, 'A' in this case, were allotted to manufacturers as per Table 'C'. Modifications to design are shown in a manner similar to mark numbers, thus the basic design is F2A-1 and changes shown as F2A-2, F2A-3, etc. In May, 1944, a suffix letter was added to show a changing role or special equipment, e.g. a PB4Y-2 converted for meteorological work would become PB4Y-2m.

TABLE 'A' — U.S. ARMY DUTY LETTERS

A — Attack; AT — Advanced Trainer; B — Bombardment; BT — Basic Trainer; C — Cargo and Personnel; CG —Cargo Glider; F — Photographic; L — Liaison; O — Observation; OA — Amphibian; OQ — Target (pilotless); P — Pursuit; PT — Primary Trainer; PQ — Target (piloted); R — Helicopter; TG — Training Glider.

TABLE 'B' — U.S. NAVY DUTY LETTERS

B — Bomber; BT — Bomber-Torpedo; F — Fighter; G — Transport (light); H — Ambulance; J — Utility; JR — Utility Transport; L — Glider; N — Trainer; O — Observation; P — Patrol; PB — Patrol Bomber; R — Transport (heavy); SB — Scout Bomber; SN — Scout Trainer; SO — Scout Observation; TB — Torpedo Bomber.

TABLE 'C'—MANUFACTURERS' SERVICE CODE LETTERS

Manufacturer	Army	Navy	Manufacturer	Army	Navy	Manufacturer	Army	Navy
Aeronca Aircraft Corp.	AE	R	(Santa Monica)	DO	D	Navy Dept. (U.S.N.)	—	N
Air Glider Inc.	AG	—	(Tulsa)	DT	D	Noorduyn Aviation	ND	—
Allied Aviation Corp.	—	A	Edo Aircraft Corp.	—	E	N. American (Dallas)	NT	J
American Aviation	—	R	Fairchild (Burlington)	FB	K	N. American (Inglewood)	NA	J
Atlantic Aircraft	—	A	Fairchild (Hagerstown)	FA	Q	N. American (Columbus)	NH	—
Atlantic-Fokker	—	A	Fleet Aviation	FE	—	N. American (Kansas)	NA	J
Babcock Aircraft	BB	—	Fleetwings Inc.	FL	—	Northrop Aircraft Inc.	NO	T
Beech Aircraft Co.	BH	B	Fletcher Aviation	FT	—	Northwestern Aero.	NW	—
Bell (Atlanta)	BA	—	Ford Motor Company	FO	R	Pennsylvania Autogiro	—	Z
Bell (Buffalo)	BE	L	Ford-Stout	—	R	Piasecki Corp.	PV	P
Bell (Fort Worth)	BF	—	Frankfort Sailplane	FR	—	Piper Aircraft	PI	E
Bellanca Aircraft Corp.	BL	E	G. and A. Aircraft	GA	—	Pitcairn Autogiro	—	P
Berliner-Joyce	—	J	General Aircraft	GE	—	Platt Le Page Aircraft	PL	—
Boeing (Renton)	BN	—	General Motors			Pratt, Read & Co.	PR	E
Boeing (Seattle)	BO	B	(Cleveland)	GC	M	Radioplane Corp.	—	R
Boeing (Wichita)	BW	—	(Detroit)	GM	M	Read-York Inc.	RD	—
Bowlus Sailplane	BS	—	Gibson Refrigeration	GN	—	Republic (Evansville)	RA	—
Brewster Aeronautical	—	A	Globe Aircraft	GF	G	Republic (Farmingdale)	RE	—
Bristol Aeronautical	—	Q	Goodyear Aircraft	—	G	Ridgeway Mfg. Co.	RI	—
Brieglebb Sailplane	BR	—	Great Lakes	—	G	Robertson Aircraft	RO	—
Budd Manufacturing	BU	B	Grumman Aircraft	GR	F	Ryan Aeronautical	RY	R
Canadian C. and F.	—	W	Hall Aluminium Corp.	—	H	Schweizer Aircraft	SW	S
Canadian Vickers	VI	V	Higgins Aircraft Corp.	HI	—	Sikorsky Mfg. Corp.	SI	S
Cessna Aircraft	CE	C	Hiller Helicopters	HR	E	Spartan Aircraft	SP	P
Chance-Vought	—	U	Howard Aircraft Corp.	HO	H	Sperry Gyroscope	—	S
Chase Aircraft	CA	—	Hughes Aircraft	HU	—	Stearman Aircraft Div.	—	S
Christopher Aircraft	CH	—	Interstate A. and E.	IN	R	Stearman-Hammond	—	H
Columbia Aircraft	—	L	Kaiser Cargo Inc.	—	K	Stinson Aircraft Corp.	—	Q
Commonwealth Aircraft	CM	—	Kaman Aircraft Corp.	KA	K	St. Louis Aircraft	SL	—
Consolidated Corp.	—	Y	Kellett Autogiro	KE	—	Taylorcraft Aviation	TA	T
Convair (Forth Worth)	CF	—	Keystone Aircraft Corp.	—	K	Temco Aircraft Corp.	TE	G
Convair (San Diego)	CO	—	Kinners Motors Inc.	—	K	Timm Aircraft	TI	T
Cornelius Aircraft	CR	—	Krieder-Reisner	—	K	Universal Products	UN	—
Culver Aircraft	CL	C	Laister-Kauffman	LK	—	Vega Aircraft Corp.	VE	V
Curtiss A and M Co.	—	C	Langley Aviation Corp.	—	L	Viking Aircraft	—	O
Curtiss-Wright			Lockheed (Burbank)	LO	O	Vought-Sikorsky	—	U
(Louisville)	CK	C	Lockheed (Marietta)	LM	—	Vultee (Downey)	VU	V
(St. Louis)	CS	C	Loening Aeronautical	—	L	Vultee (Nashville)	VN	V
(Buffalo)	CU	C	Martin (Baltimore)	MA	M	Vultee-Stinson	VW	—
De Havilland (Canada)	DH	—	Martin (Omaha)	MO	M	Waco Aircraft Co.	WO	W
Douglas (Chicago)	DC	D	Maxson-Brewster Corp.	—	R	Ward Furniture Co.	WA	—
Douglas (El Secundo)	DC	D	McDonnell (Memphis)	MM	H	Wichita Engineering	WI	—
(Oklahoma City)	DK	D	McDonnell (St. Louis)	MC	H	Willys Overland	—	W
(Long Beach)	DL	D	Nash-Kelvinator Corp.	NK	K	Wright-Aeroplane Corp.	—	W

ENEMY AIRCRAFT MARKINGS 1939-45

GERMAN NATIONAL MARKINGS
(Black and White as shown unless otherwise indicated)

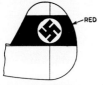

Rudder and Fin   Fuselage and Wings

PRE-WAR INSIGNIA

Wing and Fuselage Position Alternatives 1939-45
(Outlining usually in WHITE but occasionally in YELLOW)

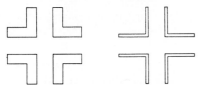   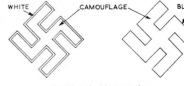

Wing and Fuselage Positions   Training Aircraft   General Form   Outlined Alternatives

N B. THE SWASTIKA WAS EXCLUSIVE TO THE TAIL (MARKED ON FIN OR OVER BOTH FIN AND RUDDER)

ROUMANIA 1939-43	ROUMANIA 1943-45	CROATIA	SLOVAKIA

  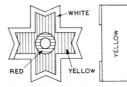 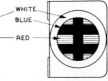

Wings and Fuselage   Rudder   Wings and Fuselage   Rudder   Various Positions   Rudder 1938-40   Rudder 1941-45
(Wings and Fuselage as for Luftwaffe)

HUNGARY 1939-41	HUNGARY 1941-45	BULGARIA

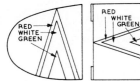

Wings   Rudder   Wings and Fuselage   Tailplanes   Wings   Fuselage   Rudder

ITALY	INDONESIAN FORCES 1945	JAPAN

     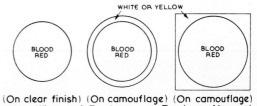

Wing   Fuselage (Well forward)   Rudder   Adaptation of Japanese marking   (On clear finish) (On camouflage)   (On camouflage)
Wings and Fuselage   Fuselage Alternative

REPRESENTATIVE ENEMY UNIT INSIGNIA

Luftwaffe Gruppe Markings (He III Ju 88 and Ju 87)   278th Squadriglia Regia Aeronautica   Luftwaffe Staffel Markings (All Me 109)

Germany and the German Satellites

The early type of German segment camouflage. Later straight, instead of curved, lines were used for the division of the different shades. A civil registration looks strange on this camouflaged Do 17z-o modified to Do 215v1 standard. The swastika is marked in a white disc on a red band around the fin.

National Markings

The national insignia of Germany carried on the aircraft of the *Luftwaffe* was the *Balkankreuz* (Greek Cross) generally referred to as the *Black Cross* and the *Hakkenkreuz*, symbol of Nazi Germany, the Swastika. For fuselage sides and wing positions the black cross was invariably used and the swastika was exclusive to the tail, being marked on the fin or placed centrally across fin and rudder. Variations were as illustrated.

These markings were first used from March, 1935, when the existence of the *Luftwaffe* was first revealed by Germany. Until that time it had been building in secret, since the Treaty of Versailles conditioned Germany to building only civil aircraft. Such types as the He 111, easily converted for bombing, were built as civil transports. They were identified by civil registration in the D (for *Deutsch*) series, that had started with a numerical series, changing to a normal alphabetical civil system in the 'thirties. D-AAAA to D-AZZZ were allotted to multi-engined transports, D-EAAA to D-EZZZ 'club' aircraft, D-IAAA to D-IZZZ touring aircraft—(Henschel Hs 123 dive-bombers came in this civil category!), D-OAAA to D-OZZZ, D-TAAA to D-TZZZ and D-UAAA to D-UZZZ to various classes of transport aircraft and D-YAAA to D-YZZZ for ultra-light aircraft.

Then, the black cross appeared in 1935 and for a time some aircraft bore both a civil registration and this national marking. For example, Hs 123 (Werke Nr 968) D-IKSW had the black cross interposed on the fuselage side in the manner D-1+KSW. Even more ominous than the revival of the black cross for wings and fuselage was the tail marking, a swastika in a white circle on a red field—representing the banner of the Nazi Party, that had appeared also on civil and sport aircraft from 1933 onwards.

Camouflage finishes necessitated abandoning the red field and white circle, but the swastika remained. It was then usual for both crosses and swastikas to be outlined in white to contrast against drab finishes.

General Finish

There were no general camouflage schemes in the *Luftwaffe* 1939-45. Administrative instructions concerning the position and nature of markings were issued to contractors but rarely repeated to field formations. Thus changes were effected on new production aircraft whilst those in service retained their earlier styles of markings.

A steel grey had been standard in the German Air Force of 1935 and that same year a segment camouflage was introduced for operational types. Grey, dark green,

This Me 109 with the Fliegerfuhrer Afrika *had a consistent sandy-brown uppersurface camouflage, with white half-metre band, spinner and wing tips. The 7 is its individual number in its unit,* Jagdgeschwader Nr 27.

mid-green and brown were the colours used in the pattern illustrated. It was usually so arranged, that a grey segment occurred on the fuselage sides to contrast against the black cross. This was a standard *Luftwaffe* scheme with grey or light blue undersurfaces and aircraft of *Luftflotte 1* so marked, opened the war by their violent attack on Poland.

Most other aircraft were in their factory schemes, maintained in service. In 1936 the German Air Ministry had invited tenders from the German paint industry for aircraft finishes. As a result the firm of Ikarol received the main contracts for paints and dopes. They were supplied to aircraft factories with a basic brown primer for all finishes, in the following basic shades: dark green known as 'camouflage green', silver with an aluminium base, light blue, white and sea-green; black, red, yellow, white and midgreen for code letters (limited issue), *caput mortum* or dead black to give its true translation, a non-reflecting black, and various tinted greys.

Dark green uppersurfaces and light blue undersurfaces was typical of most German bombers in the early war years. The *Luftwaffe* planned to operate by day and did—until our victory in the Battle of Britain convinced Goering that it was impracticable and this led to the hurried application of *caput mortum* to bomber undersurfaces for the 'Blitz' by night over Britain 1940-41. For the Battle of Britain itself, we have the recorded observations of a famous pilot, Wing Commander Roland Beamont, D.S.O., O.B.E., D.F.C. 'The air was thick with aircraft. Dark grey Ju 87s, dark green Me 110s with sky-blue bellies and pale green and silver Me 109s — all emblazoned with black crosses'.*

A product of the firm of Ruth of Hamburg opened up a completely new technique in aircraft camouflage. Varnish with a non-drying glyptal resin was applied over normal finish to give a temporary camouflage scheme for specific operations, that was easily removed. Temporary camouflage distempers were also widely used, for the *Luftwaffe*, even more than the R.A.F., was called upon to meet changing roles and in different theatres. Rigid descriptions cannot therefore be given, and for this reason the reader is provided with no less than seven views of German aircraft in full colour and the utmost care has been taken with their presentation. To give the story behind one of these paintings; page 122 shows a Do 217 M-1 that was hit by anti-aircraft fire over London on the night of 23/24th February, 1944. Although abandoned by the German

* 'Against the Sun', Edward Lanchbery.

crew who landed by parachute near Wembley, this aircraft went on to land intact at Cambridge. That well-known enthusiast Mr. M. J. F. Bowyer was early on the scene and spent three hours scribbling down its marking details and taking colour samples. It was an ugly brute and the night after drawing and painting it for record purposes, Mr. Bowyer confesses it gave him a nightmare. His painting and full description was made available to Mr. W. F. Hepworth, the artist of the colour work in this book, who has recaptured its sinister appearance.

In North Africa a light stone finish was general with a mottled dark brown sprayed on in blotches and undersurfaces were azure. On the Russian Front, German camouflage like that of the Russians tended to be seasonal, a light grey in winter and dark greens for summer.

Formation Markings

Formation letters were a feature of German aircraft from the official inception of the *Luftwaffe*. They appeared, usually in black upon each side of the fuselage cross. Pre-war a five letter system was used but this was reduced to a four letter system in the 1938 *Luftwaffe* reorganisation. In both systems, the letter appearing immediately after the black cross, reading from left to right, was the aircraft's individual letter within its *Staffel*. This letter was often emphasised, by presentation in white or yellow, e.g. with Henschel Hs 123s 52+A13, 52+B13 and 52+C13, the A, B and C were in white. These Hs 123s were *Luftwaffe* Nos. 968, 969 and 970 respectively and suggests that they were built specifically for their particular unit; a by no means unusual practice. To take a typical example, Do 217m-1 U5+DK, the 'U5' indicated 2 *Kampfgeschwader*, 'D' the individual letter in 2 *Staffel* indicated by 'K'. Usually these letters were proportioned and positioned as illustrated on page 139. Special allocations of

A Gruppe of Fw 200 Kondors operating far out over the Atlantic, used a symbol that implied encircling the world. This picture gives a good idea of division of surfaces, a grey-green above and light blue below.

radio call-sign letters were made for experimental aircraft;
V1+AA, V1+AB, V1+AC being allotted for progressive
development versions of the Me 262. Fighters in service
were generally excepted from this style of marking, having
instead a large single letter or number in a *Staffel* colour
marked either forward or aft of the fuselage cross. Another
type of formation marking was a white band, ½ metre wide,
around the rear of the fuselage.

Representative formation or factory letters on various
types were as follows: Ar 96 B1+AD, Ar 196A+11 (with
white band), Ar 240 GL+QA, Do 17 53+A25, Do 18
60+U5, Do 215 NO+TB, Do 217 DD+LF, FW 44
TQ.B1, FW 187 KG+JC, FW 190 TD+S1, FW 200
SG+KS, Go 244 4V+ES, He 51 60+A11, He 60 S6+
D15, He 70k 20+E1, He 115 GA+CT, He 177 DL+AQ,
Hs 126 L2+L37, Ju 52/3m 25+D38, Ju 86 33+D24,
Ju 87 SZ+KS, Ju 160 CE.KF., Ju 188 NP+KQ, Me 110
3C+GS, Me 210 NE+BH.

Special Schemes and Markings

Yellow was the colour used to make aircraft conspicuous where necessary. Target towing aircraft had yellow
wing tips and a yellow band around the fuselage. Unusual
aircraft such as French Loire-et-Oliver Leo 45 used for
communications were yellow overall. Training aircraft
were usually in grey or white finish, but to distinguish a
pilot making his first solo flight, a red streamer was affixed
to the wings or tail. After 1942, when the U.S.A.A.F.
were threatening Germany itself in daylight, many trainers
were given a dark green uppersurface. Some night-flying
aircraft, particularly Do 217s in Western Europe 1943-44,
were an overall black.

Sanitatsflugzeug (ambulance aircraft), usually Ju
52/3m or FW 58 transports, were an overall white with a
Red Cross of Geneva in normal black cross positions. On
the fin was the usual black *Hakenkreuz*. He 59 seaplanes in
this finish used on air/sea rescue were not acceptable to the
R.A.F. who forced down a machine so marked in the
Straits of Dover and in it was found photographic reconnaissance equipment that belied its markings.

Night-flying schemes varied considerably from a Ju 88g,

with light grey speckled with darker grey on the uppersurfaces and black beneath, to a He 219 painted half black
and half white.

Heinkel aircraft had HEINKEL in 6 in. letters on the
nose slightly below datum as part of the factory finish,
but with camouflage it was indistinct.

Numerous instructions were stencilled in black ½-1 in.
lettering on all surfaces. The serial number was invariably
in very small figures, usually placed on the fin. Often
confused with the serial number was the finishing scheme
specification marked at the rear of the fuselage, e.g. 3752/08
where the 3752 was the paint specification number and 08
the figure code for the shades used.

Gruppe or *Staffel* markings were quite common applied
to the nose or, in a few cases, the engine nacelles. A shield
form was common. The motifs varied considerably, an
umbrella in a gun-sight on the noses of a *Staffel* of Ju 88s in
1939 was almost certainly a hit at our Prime Minister, then
Mr. Neville Chamberlain, who was rarely seen without his
'brolly'. The significance of the silhouette of a pig on
Ju 87s one would like to think of as a sly, but apt, dig at
the *Luftwaffe's* chief—Goering, but in fact it was 'Jolanthe,'
a pig featured in pre-war German films. Individual markings were not so common as on British aircraft.

AIR FORCES OF THE GERMAN SATELLITES
Rumania

The Rumanian Air Force was the largest of the German
satellite forces, using German, Polish and Italian built aircraft as well as the Rumanian-built I.A.R.80. Perhaps the
most interesting to readers, were the British aircraft supplied
in 1939 before Rumania had allied herself with Germany.
Several Hurricanes, e.g. L2093-7 and nearly forty Blenheims, including L6696-6708, were supplied.

Camouflage was on German lines and their complicated national marking was simplified for operational aircraft on the Russian Front. Serial numbers were carried
on the fin in 10 in. white figures.

Hungary

The Hungarian Air Force was completely under
German direction and camouflage schemes were as for
German aircraft, except initially in the case of Italian
Cr 42 and Ca 135 bis aircraft which were supplied in the
usual green and brown of the Italian Air Force. Pre-war

markings were discarded in favour of a simple white cross on a black background. National colours were displayed on the rudders and tailplanes of non-operational aircraft.

Croatia

Germany created a Croatian Legion in late 1941 and supplied small numbers of Me 109G fighters and Do 17z bombers, to which Italy added some Fiat G.50 bis fighters. Initially *Luftwaffe* markings were used with the shield illustrated appearing on the nose and fin. Later this shield replaced the German crosses and it was embellished by a surrounding intertwined vine when presented as a crest on the nose of aircraft. Whatever bond this signified is not clear; it could hardly represent affinity with Germany, for the personnel of the Croat Air Force greatly disappointed the Axis partners—by deserting to join Tito.

Bulgaria

During 1944 the Bulgarian Air Force was in action against Russia in a defensive role using Dewoitine D 520 and Me 109G fighters supplied by the Germans in *Luftwaffe* camouflage to which national markings as illustrated were applied.

Slovakia

Smallest of the German Air Forces, the Slovak Air Force did not muster a hundred aircraft. At the beginning of the war a small unit operated in the Polish Campaign using Avia B.534 fighters in dark green camouflage, marked with German crosses, but with a large Slovak Cross on the

Grey streaking on a dull green finish was a camouflage pattern introduced by Germany late in the war, designed to blend with foliage. The Junkers Ju 88 tail gives a good impression of its application.

rudder instead of the usual swastika on the tail. A squadron of Me 109Es similarly marked operated on the Russian Front.

Finland

It is with regret that friendly Finland must be reviewed under this chapter. Her gallant defence lasting over one hundred days against the Red Air Force in 1939-40, won the admiration of the world and in the case of this country, material support.

At that time the Finnish Air Force had varied equipment. Operational aircraft were in a camouflage of dark green with grey undersurfaces. Finnish national markings appeared on the normal wing and fuselage positions, but there was no indication of nationality on the rudder, where an individual number was often marked. Finnish Air Force serials were marked large, usually 12 in. figures placed just aft of the fuselage insignia. Blocks of numbers were issued with a prefix of significant initial letters that varied for each different type. Typical are AN-101 Avro Anson, BW-363 Brewster Buffalo, FR-97 Fokker D-21 and R1-139 Blackburn Ripon. Assistance from Britain early in 1940 was evident by Blenheims still in shadow-shading with Finnish national markings and serials such as L9025, L9028, L9196, etc., replaced by those in the Finnish BL series. Similarly Lysanders R8991-9 entered the LY series and many Gladiators (N5584, N5706, N5722, etc.) the GL series.

When Finland joined Germany against Russia, JK, MT and ST identified respectively Ju 88s, Me 109Gs and Fi 156s diverted from the *Luftwaffe*. Other prefixes such as DB for DB-3, VH for I-16 and PE for PE-2 identified Russian aircraft put into service.

Vichy

French Air Force markings were retained by the Vichy Air Force, but to make their aircraft more conspicuous during Allied operations in North Africa, tailplanes and fins were striped in red. When German aircraft flew to Vichy-controlled Syria to exploit Raschid Ali's revolt mentioned below, Air Vichy Headquarters anticipating clashes between the *Luftwaffe* and R.A.F. over Syria, gave notice to the R.A.F. that by direction of the Wiesbaden Commission and by the express wish of Reichmarshal Goering, Vichy aircraft would be identified by chrome yellow colouring. This would cover all areas forward of the leading edge of the mainplanes and all areas aft of the leading edge of the tailplanes.

Iraq

When in April, 1941, the Iraqi politician, Raschid Ali, seized power a situation was created whereby a flying school fought an air force—No. 4 Flying Training School, R.A.F. Habbaniya, versus the Iraqi Air Force (the Royal title has been purposely omitted as it was not acting under the Regent's orders). Iraqi aircraft, mostly of British type, Hawker Nisrs, Gloster Gladiators and D.H. Dragons in silver finish included also Douglas 8A and Breda 65 attack-bombers. Markings were as illustrated on page 189.

N.B. A ½ metre wide yellow band encircling the rear of the fuselage was appropriate to all aircraft of the Rumanian, Hungarian, Croatian and Slovakian Air Forces operating under *Luftwaffe* command.

A Focke Wulf Fw190A (left) in a 1945 finish and a Fw190A3 (right) is shown as it appeared in late 1943.

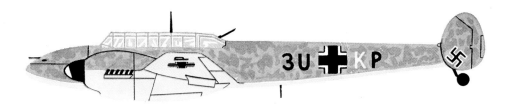

This Messerschmitt Me110E long range fighter has an off-set spinner marking, designed to distract enemy air-gunners.

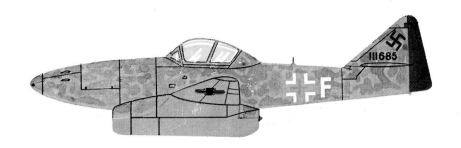

First operational jet-fighter of the Luftwaffe, the Messerschmitt Me262 shown here in day fighter finish, was also used at night.

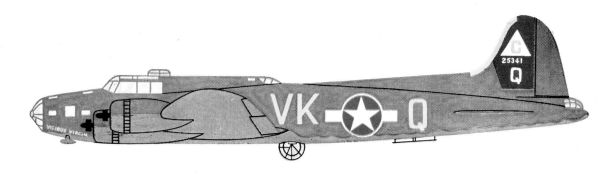

A Fortress as it appeared in early 1944 symbolises the day offensive of the 8th U.S.A.A.F. Later many of these bombers had bare-metal finishes.

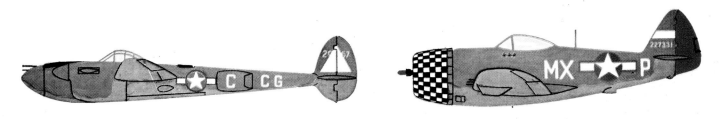

Escort fighters are represented by a P-38J Lightning of the 55th Fighter Group and a P-47 Thunderbolt of the 82nd Fighter Squadron.

WAR-TIME MARKINGS IN FOUR AIR FORCES 1944

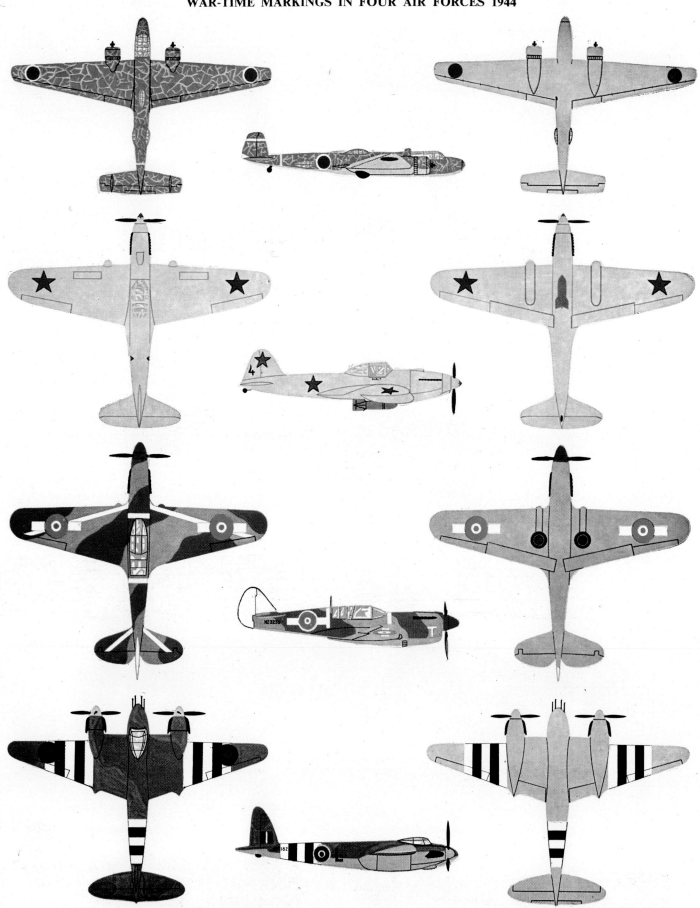

Here are seen the contrasts of a jungle camouflage on a Japanese Nell and the snow camouflage of a Russian Stormovik. Then follow a R.N.Z.A.F. Warhawk in elaborate identity markings of the Pacific area, and a Mosquito in the conspicuous A.E.A.F. stripes of June, 1944.

Italian and Japanese Aircraft

CHAPTER FIFTEEN

ITALIAN AIRCRAFT

National Markings

Fascist Italy used the *Fasces* as their national emblem. Three bundles of brown faggots with yellow binding that had a protruding axe blade were the peace-time markings, but for war a functional representation that could be stencilled on, in either black or white to contrast, was used. This was the wing marking, placed on the upper and lower surfaces, up to, but not exceeding, one-sixth of the span inboard. It was marked as large as practicable, comparable to R.A.F. roundel sizes, without overlapping control surfaces. Always the blades of the axes pointed outboard.

On the fuselage side near the pilot's position, but occasionally placed on the engine cowling was a miniature fasces in pre-war colours but with only one bundle of faggots, having the axe blade pointing forward. It was contained within a 30 cm. diameter circle.

When in 1940 the rudder marking changed from red, white and green striping to the white cross shown in the photograph, it was to avoid confusion with the markings of their new enemy—France, whose aircraft, as previously related, had red, white and blue rudder stripes. Later, in 1944-45, when some Italian Air Force units collaborated with the Allies, Italian markings of the early 'thirties were again used.

Camouflaged Schemes

The schemes of camouflage used earlier in the Spanish Civil War and illustrated on pages 92-3 were retained throughout, but the mottled scheme was by far the most common. This consisted of a mid-green base, with mottled browns sprayed on in blotches, and included yellow patches for those aircraft operating in, or destined for, North Africa. Undersurfaces were often in a light stone, although light blue and light grey were sometimes used.

Uppersurface camouflage extended completely down the fuselage sides, thus the whole side elevation of the fuselage was in the uppersurface colours. Engine cowlings, wheel spats and often spinners were included in the camouflage scheme. Concealment on the ground was evidently considered more important than in the air; the implication is that it was a camouflage scheme for defensive, rather than offensive roles. A dull green overall was applicable to the few night bombers used by the *Regia Aeronautica*.

Positioned in the white rudder markings of Italian aircraft was the Arms of the House of Savoy applied by a transfer. On the fin of this Reggiane Falcho appears the constructor's trade mark and below it a squadriglia insignia.

Markings

Most operational units of the *Regia Aeronautica* came under *Luftwaffe* command, who requested a special identity marking for Italian aircraft working in conjunction with them. This was a white band encircling the fuselage, $\frac{1}{2}$ metre wide on single-engined aircraft and 1 metre wide on twin- and multi-engined aircraft. It was positioned 1 metre forward of the leading edge of the tailplane.

A squadriglia marking, sometimes as a small silhouette on the white encircling band, or a more elaborate marking in colour on the fuselage side was common. Squadriglia and individual aircraft numbers such as 90-12 appearing in the white band of a Macchi 202 were common 1940-41, but appear to have been omitted, possibly for intelligence reasons, as the war progressed.

The Piaggio P108 was Italy's only four-engined bomber. Finish was dull green overall without the usual wing insignia. The usual white rudder cross was standard and with large aircraft the white fuselage band was one metre wide.

The camouflage of this Macchi 202 will be seen to include the spinner and to be marked partly over the usual white markings. The commander of this squadriglia is surely worthy of note He is aged 73! (5th from right.)

Serial numbers, allotted by the *Regia Aeronautica* in a separate series for each aircraft firm, were prefixed by the letters MM for *Matricula Militare* (Military Number) e.g. MM6032 on the rear of the fuselage of a Macchi 202 in 10 cm. figures. This marking in black or white was often preceded or headed by the aircraft type in lettering of the same height. Manufacturer's trade marks were a feature of aircraft newly delivered. Civil aircraft impressed into training schools re- tained their civil identity and markings, but a military serial was allotted and marked at the rear of the fuselage.

JAPANESE AIRCRAFT

National Markings

The Rising Sun was the national emblem of Japan with red rays spreading fan-wise, but it was the sun itself, represented by a blood-red disc that appeared on Japanese aircraft. This unvarying red disc or 'meat-ball' in the apt American colloquialism, was marked in the usual positions, fuselage sides and upper and lower surfaces of the wings. When applied to camouflaged surfaces it was usually outlined in white or yellow. In a few cases on the fuselage sides it was marked within a white or yellow square. Generally positioning of the red disc was comparable to R.A.F. practice, except that it was not uncommon for this Japanese emblem to be marked over control surfaces.

General Finish

For both Japanese Army and Naval aircraft a polished metal finish or white doped fabric had been usual. A transparent rust-resisting lacquer was applied producing a smooth surface. To this finish, camouflage was applied as necessary.

During 1938 in the Sino-Japanese War, camouflage had appeared on Japanese Army aircraft, applied only to the uppersurfaces of the wings in an attempt to conceal the unmistakable configuration of a conventional aeroplane, when parked on the open Manchurian airfields. It was a tactical field marking and camouflage was not then general.

Although Japan made meticulous preparations for an all-out war, camouflage was not stipulated as a general rule. Some Army bombers on Formosa and adjacent islands, however, had green uppersurfaces before Japan struck in December, 1941, but this was probably a precaution against extended air reconnaissance by American aircraft. When Japan struck it was with Japanese Navy aircraft in clear finish—or in brightly coloured schemes. In fact, during the attack on Pearl Harbour, Kates and at least one Jake were painted with red wings and yellow fuselages. Imperial impudence that was never to be repeated so blatantly. The sun was at its zenith.

With the Pacific War a few days old a navigator of a B-17c reported Japanese fighters unlike the silver ones he had previously noted, in that these had a pale green finish. Illogical as it may seem for Japan to don warpaint a few days after they opened the war, rather than a few

What a story these markings on this Japanese Mavis flying-boat tell. The eclipse of the rising sun is evident from the erased markings and the surrender cross marking. Indonesians have taken it over and marked on their red and white rectangle. The Dutch not recognising the Indonesia rising have added a strip of blue to the red and white fuselage marking!

Japanese aircraft — British Markings. The reason is explained by the initial letters they bear standing for Allied Technical Air Intelligence Unit, South East Asia. Aircraft so used were allocated a temporary identification number; a Tabby 3-2 for example was No. 27. It also bore an unofficial name on the nose— 'Fanny's Frolic'. The aircraft shown are Jacks, known to the Japanese as 'Raiden' (Thunderbolt). They bear non-standard red, white, blue and yellow roundels, whereas some other Japanese aircraft taken over had standard S.E.A.C. type roundels.

days before, there were no doubt subtle reasons. A camouflage scheme not having been general, its application prior to operations might have given warning of their attack. Surprise was Japan's object and surprise they achieved.

When Japan, having swept the Philippines and S.E. Asia, went on to attack Northern Australia, rising suns with orange rays were spread across the wing undersurfaces of some of the attacking aircraft, but it was the last time Japan could afford to flaunt such finishes. After that, a red lightning flash along the fuselage side was the only occasional embellishment worthy of note.

Functional schemes with green camouflage became usual, sometimes an even green over the uppersurfaces, or blotches of green on a silver-grey finish. This sometimes took the form of a frond camouflage; that is strokes of green to represent palm fronds. Navy aircraft also used this finish for their landplanes, but a sea-green was more usual. Little attention was paid to undersurface camouflage, the natural silver-grey finish with a transparent lacquer being most usual.

Formation and unit markings were simply white or coloured bands around the rear of the fuselage, or around the fin and rudder. Identification numbers such as YI-329 on a Nell (Mitsubishi 96) bomber, appeared across the fin and rudder in 10 in. figures. They were in black on light finishes and yellow or white on camouflage. Small ideographs

appeared in various positions giving instructions, such as the universal TRESTLE HERE (Kokora Noseru) marked in ideographs one above the other.

Special Markings

There was no doubting Japanese patriotism, even before hostilities many aircraft were presented to the nation. These aircraft had an inscription in ideographs to that effect on the fuselage side with a consecutive number series for each one presented. A Zeke (Navy O) was 872.

Most satisfactory of all markings were those decreed by the Allies when accepting the Japanese surrender, that the aircraft used by the Japanese emissaries should be in white with green crosses. The Rising Sun had set.

Japanese Satellites

Thai aircraft under Japanese control bore a white Siamese elephant cypher on a red field as their emblem in all standard positions, including the fin and rudder. Aircraft of the Manchurian Air Force 1942-45, bore a yellow disc insignia and yellow painted rudders, both tipped with four horizontal bands, coloured, from the top downwards: red, blue, white and brown.

A marking the world awaited in 1945, for it told of Japan's defeat. To comply with Allied orders that Japanese aircraft required to fly after their surrender would bear a white finish with green crosses, this Hickory in Java has had its camouflage paint scraped off and green crosses added. Originally its camouflage was a mid-green speckle applied to uppersurfaces and fuselage sides, leaving the undersurfaces in bare metal. An open door allows a glimpse of the interior which was finished in fawn and grey, with a green carpet matching green curtains.

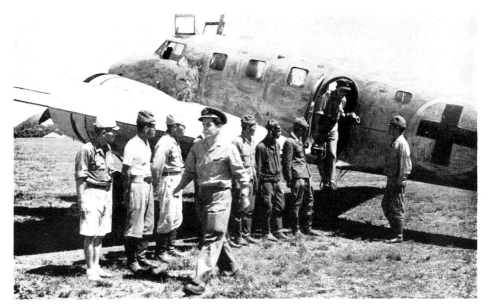

PART 4

CHAPTER ONE

Markings of the Royal Air Force 1945-54

The first signs of peace in aircraft markings were the re-introduction of serial numbers under the wings for all types, following the cessation of hostilities in Europe, mid-1945. To many aircraft, such as this Halifax G.T.3 of No. 190 Squadron, it was their only marking modification, between wartime operations—and the scrap heap!

Transition

The post-war years saw various stages in the transition in aircraft markings. By 1947, wartime camouflages were being discarded generally, all wood or fabric covered aircraft reverting to pre-war silver/aluminium finishes. This trend was stayed unhappily by the 'cold war'; expansion of the R.A.F. followed, and brought with it the use, again, of camouflage finishes consistent with operational readiness.

There were other changes too; the very configuration of the aeroplane was changing, necessitating in some cases a rearrangement of markings. The jet age led to the supersonic age where smooth finishes were required, not only to exact maximum performance by reducing drag, but to prevent the very paint from being torn from the surfaces at high speeds.

National Insignia

The roundel changed yet again in 1947. It was not a reversion to the pre-war type but to one of different proportions; the Type 'D' as illustrated on page 102. Bright red and bright blue were specified, but in 1947 these proprietary paints were in short supply and no longer did the services have priority. It was 1949 before the bright roundel colours became general. A feature of the new 'D' type was that it was applied in the same form to all surfaces and without any outlining.

There are three set sizes for this roundel, with the outside diameters of 54 in., 36 in. and 18 in. Their respective applicabilities were the same as for the old 'C' type roundel, see page 102. Exceptions were necessary for such types as the Venom or Vampire, where a thin twin-boom fuselage allowed only a very small roundel.

Fin flashes to correspond with the new roundels were introduced at the same time, with a standard 24 in. height and equal divisions of red, white and blue occupying a

length of 18 in., 24 in. and 36 in. for 18 in., 36 in. and 54 in. roundels respectively. For small triangular fins, this flash could be specially adapted, see illustrations.

Unit Markings

The wartime system of code letters was dropped in the main during 1949, but in 1954 some units still retained this system. Various methods were used in R.A.F. Commands as explained later. Unit badges, banned from presentation on aircraft during the war, were again permitted in 1950. There was a standard frame for all badges officially approved, but the device and motto varied according to the unit.

Towards the end of 1954, a number of stations were adopting a station marking on their aircraft. R.A.F. Binbrook for example having a red flash for its Canberra squadrons as shown on page 210.

Identification Markings

By the end of 1945, serialling by allocation had reached the series commencing VA. Late allocations showed many gaps, e.g. TN250-462 allotted to a batch of 150 Wellington G.R.14s with black-out blocks were all cancelled from production. For aircraft from post-war orders allocations continued progressively to VZ and then on to the WA-WZ series.

The positioning of the serial number in 8-in. digits on the rear of the fuselage followed the same wartime style. Reversion to the pre-war practice of marking the serial number under the wings of all R.A.F. aircraft recommenced mid-1945, using black or white as necessary to contrast.

Prototype markings, the wartime camouflage and yellow undersurfaces, gave way to manufacturers schemes and the yellow encircled 'P' for Prototype was dropped.

Over 150 enemy aircraft were brought to this country for technical evaluation. These were registered in a new

series, prefixed by the letters 'AM' or 'Air Min' for Air Ministry. Examples are AM17 Ar 232B, AM44 He 219A-7 and AM122 Bu 181C-3. Some of these aircraft were allotted serials in the normal range if required for flying trials, AM58 for example, a He 162A, was VH526. Several were sent to Commonwealth countries, e.g. Me 162s AM59 and AM62, Me 262s AM50, AM52 and AM80 to Canada; FW 190s AM10 and AM77 to South Africa and Me 262 AM81 to Australia.

Safety Precautions

Safety in flight, always carefully studied, has assumed a new importance. Markings such as TRESTLE HERE or STEP HERE designed to protect the aircraft from undue stresses are still as necessary, but to these have been added many others. Such unusual wording as DO NOT PAINT by an aperture, shows that the application of paint might affect a point where a good electrical contact was required. Propeller blades, normally black in colour, are still given 4 in. yellow tips to make their rotation more conspicuous and so warn persons in their vicinity.

There are now larger issues. To bale out of an aircraft at high speeds can be a physical impossibility and it is necessary, in case of emergency, to be shot out. This is literally so, a small charge being fired to shoot out the pilot's seat away from the aircraft, and the pilot thus free from his aircraft can descend by parachute. The danger is in an accidental ejection on the ground and for this reason all aircraft with ejection seats fitted must bear an indication on the fuselage side by the cockpit seat. This took the form of a 9-in. red equilateral triangle, introduced from 1949 when ejection seats first came into service.

In the event of a crash, rescuers are guided by instructions stencilled on the outside of the fuselage as may be seen on page 210. The silhouettes of fire extinguishers and hatchets show the stowage positions of these appliances. These markings are not for the benefit of trained rescue crews at airfields, who would know the rescue drills, but as a guidance to whoever might be first on the scene.

Miscellaneous Markings

Radome is a word recently introduced to our language for a radar head housing. On many fighters they appear prominently on the nose. Their colour, on service aircraft, is black.

Specialised equipment has led to many stencilled instructions for which 1 in. lettering is used. The paint scheme is indicated by a D.T.D. specification number, e.g. D.T.D.789. This appears on all major components, the D.T.D. standing for Directorate of Technical Development, a branch of the Ministry of Supply. Beneath this number a 'C' or 'S' indicates 'Cellulose' or 'Synthetic'. Part numbers in some cases, W/T markings in all cases where applicable and A.I.D. inspection stamps in every case, continue to be marked as before.

The Spitfires and Hurricanes as first-line fighters of 1938-1942 were replaced in the next decade by Meteors and Vampires. Here, Meteor N.F.11 night fighters display an immaculate finish, each with exactly the same camouflage pattern. The black-topped radome forward houses electronic detection equipment.

Bomber Command

Bomber Command is now the senior of the R.A.F. Commands. It still uses the Lincoln, basically similar to the wartime Lancaster, but the main force now has Canberras and the new 'V' bombers, Valiant, Victor and Vulcan in service. For bomber markings 1948-54 there has been a distinct difference between the piston-engined aircraft (Lancasters and Lincolns) on the one hand and jet-propelled bombers (Canberras) on the other.

The wartime night bomber camouflage remained only a few years after the war, although from mid-1945 bombers in this finish were displaying white serials under the wings positioned, usually, outboard of the engines. As the European war finished, so 'Tiger Force' was formed with the object of mounting a bomber force in the Far East. Lancasters modified for this task by Armstrong Whitworth Aircraft were designated B.1 (F.E.). They had white uppersurfaces which included the fuselage sides, spinners, fins and rudders. The undersurface, strict plan view, was matt black with white serials only. On the fuselage sides codes and serials were often in red but sometimes in black. Type 'C1' roundels of 4 ft. 6 in. diameter appeared on the fuselage side and Type 'C' on the uppersurface of the wings. This finish was still in limited use for some Lancasters and Lincolns well after the general changeover to 'D' type roundels. No. 35 Squadron with Lancaster B.1 (F.E.) bombers coded 'TL' visited the United States in 1945. Their aircraft individual letters and serial numbers were: 'A' Flight: 'A' SW315, 'B' SW313, 'C' TW657, 'D' TW872, 'E' TW879, 'F' TW880, 'G' TW869 and 'H' TW878; 'B' Flight: 'L' TW892, 'M' TW659, 'N' TW660, 'O' TW882, 'P' PA411, 'Q' PA414, 'R' TW890 and 'S' PA385.

In the summer of 1947 a new bomber finish became standard for Lancasters and Lincolns, that of medium sea grey uppersurfaces and spinners, with matt or semi-gloss black undersurfaces. The division between the surfaces was as for the wartime scheme. Code letters were usually in white and serials, white under wings, were often in red on the fuselage sides. A few Lancaster P.R.I.s had a bare metal finish.

The Canberras, the R.A.F.'s first jet bombers, after various schemes on prototypes, had a general very smooth silver or silver-grey finish. Up to 1952 several squadrons had Canberras camouflaged in a light slate grey and medium sea grey, with light blue undersurfaces; division of surfaces occurring along fuselage datum. A few had black undersurfaces, presumably for special night operations, and some P.R.3s, e.g. WE140, had azure blue and light grey for upper- and undersurfaces respectively. For night bombing a dark green and dark sea grey camouflage pattern was applied to uppersurfaces and a semi-gloss black underneath, from the levels of the main and tail planes downwards. With the silver finish, the detachable wing tip tanks have been used as a colour identification marking, e.g. B.2 WJ648 had red tanks, WK104 white tanks and WJ719 blue tanks. Washingtons, the American B-29s, used in the R.A.F., numbered in batches from WF434, retained their original U.S.A.F. bare metal finish, except for R.A.F. roundels and serial markings.

A feature of some Bomber Command aircraft from 1952 was the presentation of the serial number in large letters on the fuselage side. This followed the dropping of the unit-code and individual letter system. Some Lincolns, e.g. RA714, RE424, SX944 and WD148 had 30 in. digits, but later 24 in. became the standard height for this marking, just three times normal size. Marked in white on black and in black on all other surfaces, it was positioned just aft of the fuselage roundels.

Markings of Service Aircraft at Home 1945-54

Having illustrated the squadron markings of No. 23 Sqn. on Spads, Dolphins, Gamecocks and Demons, it is fitting that this progression is continued with their Vampire N.F. 10s of 1953 in standard night-fighter colours of the period. That the finish is gloss is evident from the reflections in the tailplanes.

Fighter Command

Fighter squadrons were quick to discard their camouflage; as early as June, 1945, with hostilities in Europe only over by a few days, No. 19 Squadron at Acklington had its Mustang F.4s in clear finish (e.g. KH858 QV.A and KM118 QV.X). Reversion to their pre-war squadron marking was not possible, because of the unit code letter positioning. So, No. 19 marked their blue and white checks around the nose, just aft of the spinner. Two years later their Hornets at Church Fenton were similarly adorned, this time on the nacelles. By 1947 fighter bands with sky spinners were no longer stipulated and No. 41 Squadron were able to mark their pre-war red band on to their Spitfire F.21s. It extended from the spinner, also in red, to the rear of the fuselage. Eight inches in width it was broken only by the necessary fuselage roundel.

There might well have been a new era of brightly coloured fighters, but for two limiting factors. Firstly, the high gloss finish, so essential at high speeds, made embellishments covering a large area impracticable on jet-propelled aircraft; secondly, events had overtaken policies and Russia, so recently an ally, became a threat to European security. Camouflage was re-introduced.

In 1947, the first post-war camouflage scheme was specified for night fighters. Day fighters for a few years remained in silver, which is in itself an air-to-air camouflage. Whatever schemes were used a high gloss became necessary for all fighter aircraft, as the piston-engined types gave way to full replacement by 'jets'. This was the era of the Meteor and Vampire.

For the few day fighter Spitfire and Hornet squadrons remaining, dark green and dark sea grey similar to the late wartime scheme was specified, but with a dark sea grey, replacing the lighter sky or ocean grey spinners. The Meteors and Vampires differed slightly by having light slate grey and medium sea grey, but all had light blue undersurfaces. Night fighters had dark green and dark sea grey with medium sea grey undersurfaces. The few piston-engined night fighters to which the finish applied had medium sea grey spinners. Division of upper and lower surfaces took place approximately along fuselage datum line level, being raised or lowered to meet centrally the leading and trailing edges of the main and tail planes.

Early in 1953 a standard scheme was introduced for all home-based fighters. Uppersurfaces were a standard dark green and dark sea grey with silver undersurfaces for day fighters, dark sea grey undersurfaces for night fighters and medium sea grey undersurfaces for the new all-weather fighters. Roundels were not marked on the undersurfaces of night fighters, otherwise national identity locations were standard. Serials appeared under the wings in the manner shown on the Hunter, but in the case of night fighters it was relatively inconspicuous in 16 in. black figures against the dark sea grey. Positioning was central on the wings outboard of the nacelles.

A standard scheme for fighter squadron markings was planned in 1949. Its application is a subject in itself, to which pages 185-188 have been devoted, to give the reader a pictorial representation, in colour, of a representative sixty-two fighter squadrons.

Many special markings have been applied in air exercises and several exceptions have occurred. Certain fighters, particularly early Hornets and Vampires, were given 'B' type roundels with corresponding red/blue fin flashes. This style was abandoned in 1947, but as late as 1954, a Vampire so marked was still to be seen.

Coastal Command

Coastal Command, enjoying for once the equipment

Cheat lines, anti-dazzle panels, identification letters and serial number on the fin (338 for WJ338) are markings typical of Handley Page Hastings, shown here ready for routine flights to the Far East. WJ338 is of interest, as one of the very few R.A.F. aircraft to have been behind the Iron Curtain. It flew to Moscow in 1953 to bring home British serviceman captured in Korea.

it needed in 1945, had to hand back on the cessation of hostilities its Liberators and Fortresses under the Lease/Lend agreements. Again it was in the unhappy state of using aircraft designed for other purposes, but which, with differing equipment and changed markings, served on coastal duties. The Lancaster was a typical example.

A small striking force was maintained, using Beaufighters and the new Brigands, some in a completely all-white finish. However, the bulk of the aircraft left in the Command, up to mid-1947, retained their wartime camouflage. Then, in common with other Commands changing their schemes, the aircraft of 'Coastal' were changed. Uppersurfaces then became a medium sea grey, fuselage sides remained their same matt white, but undersurfaces became a glossy white. Application of the uppersurface shade was to strict plan view, giving almost the appearance of a white aeroplane in side elevation. Spinners and engine cowlings were completely white, serials under the wings in black and slate grey on the fuselage side. This applied mainly to Shackletons and Lancasters. A new identification system was introduced within the Command, using two letters only, one to denote the unit and the other individual identity. On the finish described they were in light slate grey. WL742, a Shackleton M.R.2, had a 54 in. 'Z' on the nose and a 'B' of similar size aft of the serial at the rear of the fuselage. Examples of earlier Lancasters similarly finished were A.B SW376, B.B RE206, etc.

In 1954 some Shackletons appeared in a new finish of overall medium sea grey, with black spinners and all lettering in white. Typical was VP268 with Y.C. on each side of the roundel or VP266 of 120 Squadron with a white 54 in. 'A' on each side of the nose, repeated on the fuselage aft of the fuselage door position.

Hastings (Met) 1 used by the Command for meteorological duties, had a medium sea grey finish extending down to a level with the roots of the mainplane and curving sharply upwards to meet the tailplane leading edge. No code markings were carried; serial examples are TG567 and TG624.

Transport Command

The trend towards white and silver finishes mentioned in Part 3 continued for transport aircraft. It should be appreciated by the reader that large aircraft, such as heavy transports, can be several hundred pounds in weight heavier after the application of paint finishes. For an aircraft whose efficiency is judged by payload, a lightweight aluminium finish was therefore logical, combined with a heat reflecting white paint applied to the top of the fuselage.

It is with identification markings that we find complications, particularly in the immediate post-war years. As mentioned in Part 3, a new four-letter code was introduced into the Command. This took effect from September, 1945, a typical example being aluminium-finished Lancastrian VD238, bearing OKZS in 24 in. black letters along

Additional to the yellow bands of trainers, this Chipmunk T.10, bearing the crest of Cambridge University Air Squadron, wears also a red-centred light blue band of the squadron colours. This unit re-formed post-war with all-yellow Tiger Moths, later changing these for Chipmunks.

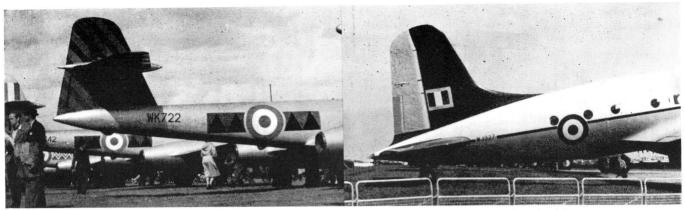

Tell-tale tails. The stripes of a leader's tail on a Meteor F.8 (No. 601 Sqn.) and the red fin and tailplane of a Hastings C.2 are for an entirely different reason; one to denote a leader and the other to make a conspicuous marking to assist search aircraft in the event of a forced landing in barren territory. To contrast the fin flash, it has been outlined in yellow on the Hastings.

the fuselage side. These letters were, in fact, the aircraft's radio call-sign and each of the four letters had a significance. Taking OKZS again, for a letter-by-letter break-down; the first 'O' was constant and denoted the series. The second letter related to the aircraft type, 'K' standing for Lancastrian. (Where possible it was the initial letter of the aircraft type, but 'L' had already been allotted for Liberators). 'Z', as the third letter, varied according to the unit, letters 'A' to 'Y' related to various R.A.F. units and 'Z' to R.A.F. aircraft on loan to British Overseas Airways Corporation. The final letter, 'S' in our example, was the individual letter of the aircraft within its unit. To recapitulate by a further example; Transport Command (O), Yorks (Y) of No. 511 Squadron (C) serial-numbered MW141, MW198, MW178 and MW192, bore the individual letters, V, W, X and Y, respectively. It therefore follows that their respective fuselage side markings were: OYCV, OYCW, OYCX and OYCY. The individual letters were repeated on the nose of these Yorks.

Following the 'O' system came a new movements system, the 'M' code, designed to fit into the new civil aviation radio network, then reviving. As far as markings were concerned, it meant a 'M' suffix to the 'O' series code.

Before leaving the code systems of the early post-war years, the special markings borne by R.A.F. transports on the Vienna service should be mentioned. Operating between Croydon and Vienna via Munich, they bore

initial letters appropriate to their itinerary, followed by an individual number, e.g. CVM-120. It served as a special identity marking for Customs clearance.

Hastings have been the mainstay of the Command for long-distance transportation. These had an aluminium finish with the fuselage top painted white, coloured cheat lines following the line of fuselage datum, a black anti-dazzle portion sloping downwards from the pilot's cabin, and the three digits of the serial number repeated in 18 in. figures above the fin flash. Another marking dates from the Korean war, when Hastings were operating from Korean and Japanese airfields together with transport aircraft from several nations, who all marked their service on their aircraft. The R.A.F. have followed suit and Hastings may be seen with— =ROYAL AIR FORCE TRANSPORT COMMAND= in 10 in. lettering placed centrally on the long fuselage a foot above the cabin windows.

The Command has on several occasions hired civil aircraft from private companies. These have been marked appropriately with roundels and allotted R.A.F. serials. Examples are York G-AHFB taken on as WW499 on one occasion, and WW 586 on another, Viking G-AHOW as XD636, Dakota G-AMSF as XF646 and Tudor G-ACRI as XF739. Such markings do not however apply to aircraft on normal charter.

Flying Training

By 1954 flying training was standardised on the Provost

Tails again! Only a small roundel can be positioned on a Vampire and even the standard size fin flash cannot be marked in full. In the background the 8 in. fuselage serials of the Washington B.1's are 'lost' against their massive bulk, but they are repeated, in large size, on their fins.

TI, Vampire T11 and Meteor T7 and for navigational training, the Valetta. Their finish was to a standard set in 1947, an overall silver with yellow bands replacing a trend towards the pre-war overall yellow. These bands encircled the rear of the fuselage and were chord-wise around each wing. They were positioned, as a general rule, centrally between the fuselage roundel and the tailplanes and centrally between the wing roundel and wing root on the mainplanes. Their width varied in 2 ft., 3 ft., and 4 ft. sizes according to the size of the aircraft. A rough ruling would be for single-, twin- and multi-engined aircraft respectively. It was not usual for the bands to be marked over control surfaces, thus the ailerons were excluded from the chord-wise wing band.

This scheme was a trainer finish, not only a Flying Training Command finish. It therefore applied to the aircraft of Home Command, which were practically all Chipmunk T.10s, used by the Reserve Squadrons. To some operational types too, in their operational finish, the yellow training bands did, in some cases apply. It applied also to training gliders used by the Air Training Corps under R.A.F. tuition.

Like Transport Command, it was in the immediate post-war years that complicated coding systems were to be found. By 1954, the eleven flying training schools used their own system of individual identification by neat black letters or figures, with the unit itself represented by the unit badge, forward on the fuselage sides. It was not so, 1946-50.

In 1946 a four letter code system was promulgated for training units. The last letter in each case related to an individual aircraft within a unit; it was therefore usual to group the first three letters together, with the fuselage roundel providing the division for the final letter. A few units, apparently regarding this as an unbalanced presentation, positioned the letters, two each side of the roundel. The first letter signified the Command, and applied as follows: F—Flying Training Command, R—Reserve Command and T—Technical Training Command.

A variety of types 'sported' 'F' codes, for which the allocation FAA to FZZ was made, letters being allotted alphabetically to units, starting with FAA to FAG for aircraft at 19 F.T.S. Thus individual aircraft would be marked FAA.A, FAA.B, FAA.C, etc. Examples: Anson NK564 FDY.J (Airfield Controller's School), Meteor T.7 VW450 FD.JR (Central Flying School) Lancaster NX779 FGA.B (Empire Air Armament School).

'R' Codes for Reserve Centres and Schools, needed only RC and RS at first to denote the series, with the third letter representing the school, e.g. D was 12 R.F.S. Filton. Unusual with this unit, was the use of individual numbers, instead of letters, as shown by Anson T.21 VV323 RCD.1. When in 1949 Reserve A.O.P. Flights were formed, they received the allocation ROAA-ROZZ. Thus Reserve Command (R) A.O.P. Flight (O) No. 1951 (C) aircraft serialled VX121, VW993, TJ340, etc., were ROC-A, ROC-B, ROC-C, etc. University Air Squadrons originally having allocations from FLAA were re-allotted letters from RUAA upon transfer from Flying Training to Reserve Command.

'T' Codes for Technical Training Command were different in that the second and third letters related to their station. Thus Anson AX636 TDE.A was machine 'A' at Debden (DE) in T.T. Command (T). Similarly Anson TX187 THA.E was 'E' of Halton.

During this era, several aircraft of the Empire Air Navigation School at Shawbury became news by their long-distance and record-breaking flights. They were given, not inappropriately for navigational training, the names of celestial bodies and they qualify for special mention here, by virtue of the fact these names were marked on the nose of their fuselages. Lancaster B1 (modified) PD328 was undoubtedly the most famous, culminating in its record-breaking flight to Australia in August, 1946. Finished in silver, with 'C' type roundels fully outboard on its wings, it bore all four letters of its 'F' code, FGFA, aft of the fuselage roundels. The unit badge of the cardinal points appeared under the pilot's position and forward of this, the name *Aries*. Later, Lincoln B.2s, RE364 and RE367 were *Aries II* and *Aries III* respectively.

Target-towing aircraft retained the conspicuously black and yellow undersurfaces, but with the invariable rule that from 1947 roundels were always displayed on this surface and the black diagonal lines were broken to allow normal serial presentation on the undersurface. At the same time, silver replaced the camouflage and yellow training bands applied to the fuselage and upper surface of the wings. This finish applied to many Beaufighters in the T.T.10 version; it also applied to aircraft used for parachute testing experiments, even to a Lancaster—PD119, a Mk. I (Special), used on this work.

Air Observation Post aircraft appeared in silver during 1947, but they reverted to their wartime finish of overall dark green/dark earth in 1950. This extended even to the spinner, but normal roundels were used and all markings (e.g. Auster A.O.P. 9 serialled WZ665) were in white. This same scheme applied to helicopters used by the Army and also to military gliders, but with the exception in the latter case, that undersurfaces were black for operational training and target-towing colours for initial training.

Photographic Reconnaissance Aircraft

The markings of P.R. aircraft became standardised in the post-war years. Standard roundels were made applicable, with the exception that they were not marked on the undersurfaces. Serials were presented in the normal manner. It was, however, the standard post-war finish itself that fluctuated. At first, 1945-46, a cerulean blue overall was general, changing in 1947 to a high speed silver finish overall. This later gave way to a camouflage of medium sea grey uppersurfaces and azure undersurfaces, but by 1952, an overall high-speed silver was again re-appearing, to become the standard finish for P.R. aircraft in 1954.

Prototype and Miscellaneous Aircraft

Prototype military aircraft produced to Ministry of Supply contracts are normally required to be finished in silver, with standard roundel and black serial markings.

Considerable latitude is, however, permitted in the general finish by constructors, particularly for events such as the annual British Society of Aircraft Constructors Display at Farnborough. Naturally, it is in the interests of the constructing firm to present the smoothest possible finish to exact maximum performance and in the choice of finishes there are certainly more attractive, if not functional, schemes than service camouflage. Roundels and serials normally remain standard, but that leaves scope enough. The year 1953 saw a big advance in brighter colours for prototypes. 'Flight' had this to say of the 1953 Farnborough Display—'Colour is the keynote: we cannot recall any comparable occasion upon which so many aircraft, civil and military, have been so vividly painted . . .' The Avro delta-wing experimental aircraft could be most easily identified apart by their colours; 707A (WD280) was red, 707A (WZ736) was orange, 707B (VX790) was azure and 707C (WZ744) was silver. Boulton Paul had their P.111 in a lurid yellow with a black cheat line and the prototype Hunter WB188 was an overall scarlet, that made the standard red of the roundels appear insipid. This is to mention but a few. We applaud this 'new look'.

Provisional Registrations

Provisional registrations were issued by the Ministry of Transport and Civil Aviation to aircraft on trial or awaiting delivery. G-7-1 a private venture Meteor is an example; 'G' denoted the series, '7' the manufacturer and '1' the licence number. 'G' allocations were as follows: G-1, Armstrong Whitworth; G-2, Blackburn; G-3, Boulton Paul; G-4, Portsmouth Aviation; G-5, De Havilland; G-6, Fairey; G-7, Gloster; G-8, Handley Page; G-9, Hawker; G-10, Reid and Sigrist; G-11, Avro; G-12, Saro; G-13 not allotted; G-14, Short Bros. and Harland; G-15, V.-A. (Supermarine); G-16, Vickers-Armstrong; G-17, Westland; G-18, Bristol; G-19, Heston; G-20, General Aircraft; G-21, Miles; G-22, Airspeed; G-23, Percival; G-24, Cunliffe Owen; G-25, Auster; G-26, Slingsby; G-27, English Electric; G-28, B.E.A.; G-31, Scottish Aviation; G-33, Flight Refuelling; G-35, F.G. Miles; G.37, Rolls Royce; G-39, Folland; G-41, Aviation Traders; G-43, Edgar Percival.

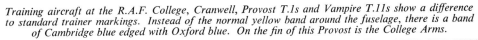

Training aircraft at the R.A.F. College, Cranwell, Provost T.1s and Vampire T.11s show a difference to standard trainer markings. Instead of the normal yellow band around the fuselage, there is a band of Cambridge blue edged with Oxford blue. On the fin of this Provost is the College Arms.

Post-war Hurricane. Although thousands of wartime aircraft went to the scrapheap, some went to new masters. Here is LF422 in Portuguese insignia (see under starboard wing) and fin flash (faintly visible). It was Portugal that supplied Hurricanes in 1952 for the filming of 'Angels One Five', when e.g. Portuguese Hurricane No. 600 coded MP.R became R.A.F. K1694 US.X in the Film. (K1694 being an anachronism as it was appropriate to the much earlier Bulldog IIA).

Prima facie, this picture might well be of an Allied Expeditionary Air Force aircraft of 1944, per the 'Invasion Stripes' on the wings and fuselage. Actually its serial number would prove this wrong, as it is of a Sea Fury F.B.11. A 1,000-lb. bomb is being fitted ready for take-off from H.M.S. Ocean operating in Korean waters during 1952. The identification markings were for recognition purposes to the various United Nations formations in the area. No more fitting marking could have been conceived than that with which British and American aircraft had borne as a common marking eight years earlier, for the liberation of Europe.

Post-war Spitfire. The Spitfire F.24 was the final, and entirely post-war version of that famous fighter. Similar to the F.22 it differed by having a strengthened undercarriage and by an increased fuel tankage. Markings at this time had not changed for day fighters since the war, except for the serial under the wings. PK713, shown here in October 1946, is an early production model.

The Royal Air Force Overseas

Brigands replaced Beaufighters in No. 84 Squadron during 1949 for continuing operations against the bandits in Malaya. This Brigand of that unit, has standard Bomber Command finish, but with white spinners. An individual letter appears on the nose and fuselage side, e.g. Brigand RH776 was 'K'.

R.A.F. Markings Overseas

The basic difference in the structure of R.A.F. Commands at home and overseas is that, whereas at home bombing, fighting, maritime, transport and training aircraft each have their separate Commands; overseas, all classes of R.A.F. aircraft come under the one Command. These are the Middle East Air Force, the Far East Air Force and the 2nd Tactical Air Force. They are Air Forces separately administered from Commands at home. It therefore follows, the special schemes or markings, promulgated in in Overseas Commands, may embrace all classes of aircraft. In practice, the general schemes of Chapter 2 applied.

At two places 'home schemes' applied overseas, firstly Gibraltar, a Coastal Command station and secondly the airfields in Rhodesia forming the Rhodesian Air Training Group. Aircraft in the latter formation had standard Flying Training Command finishes, but their own aircraft identification marking system. Ansons of No. 3 Air Navigation School, Thornhill, were Z-A (NK475), Z-B (NK944), Z-C (DJ563), etc. When this Group closed in 1953, twelve Harvards in trainer finish formed No. 1340 Flight for operations against the Mau Mau in Kenya.

The Far East

There was little encouragement to discard camouflage in the Far East after the War. Japan had been defeated, but not all invaded countries welcomed back their former administrators; indeed, in the Netherland East Indies they were resisted. To assist the Dutch Nos. 60, 155 and No. 656 (A.O.P.) Squadrons served under Air Headquarters, R.A.F., Batavia, in these Dutch possessions during 1946. Their aircraft were in wartime finishes; individual examples known to have served in the N.E.I. are Mosquito F.B.6 RF942 and Auster A.O.P. 5s NJ739, NJ741, RT537, TJ192, etc. Several Japanese aircraft acquired by the Indonesians were seized and were given R.A.F. roundels. By 1947, our forces were withdrawn.

The Far East Air Force based in Singapore and Malaya, Hong Kong and Ceylon was gradually bought to a peacetime establishment. By late 1946 the S.E.A.C. roundels

had been completely replaced by the 'C' type, with corresponding fin flashes. The 1947 changes at home slowly took effect in the Far East, by the end of 1947 most Dakotas were in bare metal finish, but not all. As late as 1948, the writer noticed KN212 still awaiting, with several others, a paint-scraping. Trainers in the Far East, Tiger Moths and Harvards, had at this time an all-yellow finish. Codes or individual letters did not apply, instead, the serial number at the rear of the fuselage was presented in 12 in. figures. A silver overall applied to communications aircraft and Anson C.19 VL299 so finished in 1948, bore the letters ACSEA on the fin (Air Command, South East Asia). Unorthodox markings were displayed on a Spitfire P.R. 19 at this time. One of the first operational aircraft in the command to have a high-speed silver finish, it had 'C' type roundels and fin flash of the smallest size and the serial, PM574 was placed some 8 in. higher than its normal position. Another roundel anomaly was Vampire F.3 VG703 with red and blue roundels and flashes on its silver finish. This aircraft was incidentally on tropicalisation trials.

Operational aircraft Mosquitos, Beaufighters and Hornets were, in general, finished consistent with schemes at home. Heavy bombers, taking part in actions against the Malayan bandits have come from R.A.F. Bomber Command or from the Royal Australian Air Force (see Chapter 5).

Army aircraft have proved their worth in the Malayan jungles. From 1947 Austers were in a silver finish, examples being A.O.P. VIs VF500 and VF501. Later these were in overall dark green and dark earth. Helicopters, of which Dragonfly H.C.2 WF309 was the first to arrive in Malaya, were similarly finished. With a Command that embraces the temperate climate of Hong Kong with the tropic climes of the Malay Peninsula, there are bound to be varying finishes.

Middle East

The finishing scheme for R.A.F. aircraft in the Middle East can be quite easily summed up by silver finish, standard roundel and serial presentation. It is a fact, that far higher temperatures are experienced at most R.A.F. Middle East

Stations, than in the Far Eastern stations of Singapore and Malaya, which are much nearer to the Equator. A heat-reflecting silver finish is therefore general, with such normal variations as the yellow bands of trainers and black and yellow undersurfaces for target-towing aircraft.

There were few irregularities or variations. Valetta C.2s could perhaps be mentioned as unusual, in that yellow was the colour of some of their anti-dazzle panels, instead of the usual black. Further, it extended aft into a cheat line, running the length of the fuselage, just above cabin window level.

The present scheme of silver dates back from 1947, following the run-down of hundreds of aircraft left over from the war. Wartime tropical camouflage of dark earth and middle stone, ceased to be applied even before the war ended and 1945-46, temperate land scheme or bare metal were common finishes. Unit code letter marking faded out and was not replaced by a Command scheme. It could be said that in consequence aircraft of the Middle East Air Force looked bare. Certainly the Proctors of M.E.A.F. Communications flight in standard trainer finish (silver with yellow bands), having their serials NP232 and RM175 as their only identification marking, appeared bare compared to aircraft in trainer finish in the United Kingdom, at a time when the cumbersome 'F', 'R' and 'T' codes were in use. Operational squadrons, e.g. Vampire F.B.5 squadrons, carried squadron badges on the nose. Presentation did not exceed 1 ft. in height and it was flanked, from 1949 onwards, with bars of the unit colours.

Europe

Just after the war finished our R.A.F. units in Germany, were re-organised into the British Air Forces of Occupation (B.A.F.O.) consisting of Nos. 2, 3, 4, 14, 16, 21, 26, 33, 69, 80, 98, 107, 302 (Polish), 305 (Polish), 308 (Polish), 317, 349 (Belgian), 350 (Belgian) and 652 Squadrons. Their aircraft were still in wartime finish and unit codes, which were retained, together with sky spinners and bands for fighters, up until mid-1947. One exception from their wartime finish was the marking of serials under the wings.

Passing from the conventional to the unconventional many ex-*Luftwaffe* aircraft were to be found, still in German finish, but with R.A.F. roundels and serials as their credentials. Field Marshal Lord Montgomery, it may be remembered, often used a German Fi 156 *Storch*; R.A.F. Fi 156s

VH754 and VH756 were attached to Supreme Headquarters. For high-ranking R.A.F. officers Fi 156s VH752-3 of B.A.F.O. Communications Flight were available. Also for communications, several Bu 181 *Bestmann* light mono-planes were acquired, *Luftwaffe* Nos. 120502, 120508, 120518 and 120222 becoming VM227, VM243, VM772 and VM231 respectively. In larger numbers, involving runs of numbers such as VN113 to VN139, Si 204Ds were taken on charge and the larger and ubiquitous Ju 52/3m was represented by several numbers between VN709 and VN756.

The post-war situation in Europe led to B.A.F.O. becoming a Tactical Air Force (2nd T.A.F.). Aircraft finishes followed closely those of the Home Commands. All classes of aircraft were stationed in Europe except heavy bombers, but the latter were often visitors and Lincoln B.2 RF342 it may be remembered was lost there, shot down by a Russian Mig 15.

Aircraft of Transport Command abounded in and out of Berlin's airfields in the Allied Zones, 1948-49, when Operation Plainfare, the Berlin Air Lift took place. No special markings, except for a large fin number, are associated with the operation, although, in a rather different way, transient markings such as smudges of coal dust on aircraft, were both unusual and significant.

Unit code letters faded out and in 1950 they were being replaced by squadron colours in fighter squadrons. When first introduced some 2nd T.A.F. stations were employing a station emblem, marked on the fin of their aircraft. By 1952, R.A.F. fighters were given dark sea grey and dark grey as standard fighter finish, this was effected throughout 2nd T.A.F. Undersurfaces however differed from the scheme at home, being P.R. blue for all under-surfaces except night and all-weather fighters. Night fighter was already an obsolete term, as new types took the role of all-weather fighters, with a finish compromising night and day as shown in Chapter 2.

The Sabre deserves special mention as a mainstay of 2nd T.A.F. in 1954. They were originially delivered under a Mutual Aid Pact that initially concerned 370 Sabres from Canadian production. Their Canadian serials were changed for R.A.F. numbers, e.g. XB678 was R.C.A.F. 19564. Delivered in bare metal finish, they displayed a mass of closely stencilled instructions all over. 2nd T.A.F. soon settled this by putting their standard fighter finish over; presumably someone noted the instructions first!

Chipmunks, Harvards and Ansons were the chief types of aircraft used by the Rhodesian Air Training Group in standard trainer finish. They bore R.A.T.G. numbers as shown. When this formation closed down, Harvard T.2B FT392, '64' of R.A.T.G. became 'G' of No. 1340 Flight operating against the Mau Mau. It bore the name 'Gremlins Castle'.

Aircraft of the Royal Navies

Changing roles mean changing code numbers. Here is a Mosquito T.3 of Bawdy, as revealed by BY on the fin; with the unusual coding 000 as a trials aircraft and with 422 as a standard trainer. Absence of the words ROYAL NAVY above the serial suggest this aircraft was handed over by the R.A.F. and was not built specially for the Fleet Air Arm.

National Markings—Fleet Air Arm

Basically the same as R.A.F. national markings, aircraft of the Fleet Air Arm showed some differences in the manner of presentation. The changeover to 'D' type roundels and corresponding fin flashes in 1947 followed R.A.F. practice, but the following year, the Navy ceased to mark fin flashes on their aircraft, leaving the fin clear for ship/station code letters.

The Navy had no occasion to use the largest size (54 in.) roundel and 36 in. became the largest size in naval use. Positioning was standard, on the fuselage sides and upper and lower surfaces on the wings for all classes of aircraft, but the actual location on the wing undersurfaces varied from the R.A.F. standard, in that they were presented farther outboard. On some Firefly and Sea Fury aircraft, these roundels were fully outboard. The object of this, was to allow a clear and a reasonably large serial presentation under the wings. The difference in location was not always appreciated, as one could rarely see upper and lower surfaces both at the same time—except when, in the case of folding-wing types, the wings were folded upwards and a comparison could easily be made. The disparity could be quite surprising, when so revealed. Apart from this, the normal regulations that roundels would not be marked over control surfaces applied.

General Finish—Fleet Air Arm

The various wartime finishes remained officially in force until 1st October, 1946, when naval aircraft were divided into two classes for markings, to take effect for new aircraft immediately, and, for aircraft in service, as and when re-finishing became necessary. Metal-clad aircraft were to have extra dark sea grey uppersurfaces extending three-quarters down the fuselage sides, to meet sky undersurfaces; fabric-covered aircraft were to be silver.

In less than a year, there were further modifications, appearing at the same time as the R.A.F. 1947 changes, suggesting inter-Service co-operation, no doubt co-ordinated by the Ministry of Supply. Non-operational naval types, trainers, target-tugs and communications aircraft conformed to the general finish given to R.A.F. aircraft in the same class. Operational aircraft, excluding Mosquitos, retained their same colours of extra dark sea grey and sky, but the uppersurface grey was applied only to plan view and mainplane leading edges. The undersurface sky then included the fuselage sides and fins and rudders complete.

Aircraft supplied under Mutual Security Aid have retained their 'midnite blue' United States Navy finish. These are of three types, Douglas Skyraider A.E.W. 1s, Hiller HTE-2s (twenty supplied for helicopter training) and Sikorsky HO4S-3 helicopters. It should be mentioned that Neptunes supplied also under M.S.A. were retained in this same finish, but these long range reconnaissance aircraft in British service were exclusive to R.A.F. Coastal Command.

Unit and Identification Markings—Fleet Air Arm

Serials were displayed under the wings from late 1945, in much the same way as on R.A.F. aircraft; the presentation of this number at the rear of the fuselage however, remained half R.A.F. size, i.e. 4-in. figures. In the latter position, the words ROYAL NAVY in 4 in. lettering were still marked. A recent practice has been to present the wording in larger size, but this did not apply up to 1954.

In late 1954 the words ROYAL NAVY began to appear in large letters upon fuselage sides in addition to the small presentation of this wording above the serial number. Dragonfly H.R.3 WN496 coded 981 of Ford (FD) is seen to be so marked.

Late in 1945, a completely new identification system was introduced using three-digit numbers placed on the fuselage side. These figures, varied in size from 2 to 3 ft. in height, according to the aircraft and were positioned either forward or aft of the fuselage roundels as convenient. The first figure in each case was significant of the class of aircraft, e.g. 100-199, 200-299 and 300-399 related to single-, two- and three-seat aircraft types respectively. In combination with the numbers, letters on the fin denoted the aircraft's unit, single letters relating to aircraft carriers and two letters signifying a shore-base. These were: A—H.M.S. *Indomitable*, B—H.M.S. *Indefatigable* and H.M.S. *Bulwark*, C—H.M.S. *Implacable* and H.M.S. *Centaur*, D—H.M.S. *Collossus* and H.M.S. *Illustrious*, F—H.M.S. *Formidable*, G—H.M.S. *Victorious* and H.M.S. *Glory*, J—H.M.S. *Eagle*, K—H.M.S. *Terrible*, O—H.M.S. *Ocean* and H.M.S. *Ark Royal*, P—H.M.S. *Triumph*, R—H.M.S. *Glory*, T—H.M.S. *Theseus*, V—H.M.S. *Venerable*, W—H.M.S. *Warrior*, Y—H.M.S. *Unicorn* and Z—H.M.S. *Albion*.

As far as possible shore station fin code letters had some phonetic significance, examples are CH for Culham, EV for Evanton, FD for Ford, GN for Eglinton, HF for Hal Far (Malta), JZ for Edzell, etc. JO for Wigtown is difficult to explain and so is VM for Worthy Down. Typical examples, with identification markings given in serial number, fuselage number and fin code letter(s) order, are: Attacker F.1 WA506 116/J, Firebrand T.F.5 EK694 100/A, Firefly F.1 MB616 227/LM (Lossiemouth), Hornet P.R.22 VZ655 005/FD, Mosquito T.R.33 TW250 543/FD, Seafire F.17 SX297 170/CW, Sea Fury F.B.11 WJ288 158/CW (Culdrose) and Sturgeon T.T.2 TS484 590/FD. Markings were in black on sky or silver surfaces and in white on midnight blue.

Squadron or ship crests were carried well forward as illustrated. In many F.A.A. units, the rank and name of the crew members were marked in 1-2 in. letters along the top of cockpit sides.

Royal Australian Navy

Aircraft finishes in the Royal Australian Navy were the same as for the Royal Navy. Firefly A.S.6 and Sea Fury F.B.11 aircraft were mainly used. These had normal serial markings having been in fact diverted from the Royal Navy. As would be expected, the letters R.A.N. replaced the normal wording above the serial. Later some aircraft also had NAVY in large letters along the fuselage sides. National markings are as for Fleet Air Arm aircraft of the Royal Navy.

Identification markings appeared in a manner similar to Royal Naval aircraft, NW being the fin marking for R.A.N. Air Station, Nowra, N.S.W. H.M.A.S. *Sydney* operating its Fireflies and Sea Furies in Korean waters, was allotted by coincidence, the fin letter 'K'—the national fin marking for South Korean aircraft.

Royal Canadian Navy

The largest of the Commonwealth Navies too, followed Royal Naval patterns and colours for general finishes. Here too, many Seafires, Fireflies and Sea Furies were to be seen with their original serials allotted in the U.K., conditioned by the 4 in. wording ROYAL CANADIAN NAVY (the last word forming a second line) placed above. National markings were as for the R.C.A.F., not as for the Royal Navy.

Fin code letters were not always used, but 'X' was allotted to H.M.C.S. *Magnificent*. Identification letters, following R.N. practice were marked on the fuselage side, balanced on the other side of the roundel by the word NAVY in up to 36-in. letters, e.g. NAVY*132 (* = roundel) on the fuselage side. Instead of serials, these markings were marked on the wing undersurfaces in the manner NAVY ↑ 132 (↑ = fuselage and direction of travel).

The F-84 Thunderjet was widely used in Korea, and here two squadrons of United States Air Force Thunderjets display their unit markings and Buzz Numbers.

In a ' midnite ' blue finish the Panther was used by both the U.S. Navy and the U.S. Marines. Here Panthers are shown on the deck of a United States aircraft carrier and a Cougar at a naval base.

A U.S. Naval study in blue and red for a Cutlass and Sikorsky S-51 helicopter respectively. Below is a Boeing KC-97G with red ' Arctic markings ' and under the tail boom of another American transport, is a British Auster A.O.P.6.

Showing two camouflage schemes and the method of displaying fighter squadron markings in the Royal Air Force are a Hunter F.2 of No. 257 Squadron (left) and a Meteor F.R.9 of No. 2 Squadron (right). These colour photographs are all from the M. J. F. Bowyer collection.

On the left are Canadian-built Sabres F-86E of No. 439 Squadron, Royal Canadian Air Force and on the right, a Javelin F(AW)1 with a black radome and roundel well forward, shows the trend of markings in the future.

The U.S.A.F. in Britain is represented here by a F-86D and a F-84G above. Below is the Royal Navy's Gannet A.S.1 in typical colour scheme and a Firefly U.8 displaying the colours of an unmanned aircraft, cream and red.

 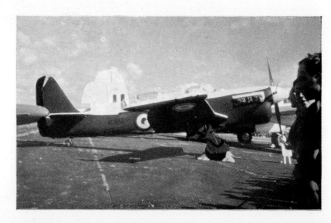

Commonwealth Air Forces

The bomb silhouettes on these Lincoln B.30s of No. 1 Squadron, Royal Australian Air Force, represent bombing missions against Communist bandits in Malaya, from their Singapore base. These aircraft are Australian-built, Nos. A73-1 to A73-5 being erected from parts pre-fabricated in Britain and Nos. A73-6 upwards being airframes built entirely in Australia.

National Markings

Most of the Commonwealth Air Forces, as will be seen from page 184, displayed red, white and blue roundels to show their affinity with Britain. Understandably, South Africa must represent, by orange, her Dutch community, for the country is essentially a Union. The new Air Forces of India, Pakistan and Ceylon, are of countries who have so recently acquired independence, that a national, rather than a Commonwealth expression, is to be found in their markings.

There has been a trend to incorporate a symbol within the British roundel, first introduced by Canada during 1946 in using a red maple leaf instead of a red disc as the centre of the roundel. South Africa followed suit in late 1950, with an orange springbok replacing the orange centre. The Royal Rhodesian Air Force adopted three assagai as representative of the three main territories concerned in the Central African Federation. At the time of writing, it is noted that Australia has displayed a kangaroo form on a R.A.A.F. D.H. Beaver.

Fin flashes are usual to all Commonwealth Air Forces. Canada it will be noted still retains the 'C' type flashes which were given up in other Services during 1947. India, not to be outdone with changing configurations, marks a fin flash at the rear of her helicopters (W.S. S-55s) and an I.A.F. roundel in the centre of the nose.

General Finish

Silver or bare metal is the general finish throughout the Commonwealth Air Forces, using, chiefly, British specifications for finishing schemes. Exceptions are a number of camouflaged fighters in both the Indian and Pakistan Air Forces. South Africa, while using Sabres in bare finish in Korea, had their Venturas at home in camouflage. Neptunes used by both the R.C.A.F. and R.A.A.F. were retained in U.S. Navy "midnite" blue. Embellishments were not usual, but in 1949, R.C.A.F. Vampires of No. 442 (City of Vancouver) Reserve Squadron, coded BU, had 'bat's head' markings on the nose, rivalling the 'shark's teeth' markings of wartime.

Identification Markings

Each Commonwealth Air Force has its own system of identification markings. The R.C.A.F. used a wartime code letter system, e.g. Sabre F86E 19152 was BT.C, with the radio call-sign VR-BRC marked under the wing in accordance with a post-war policy. This extended throughout the Force and to aircraft of the Canadian Army, such as Sikorsky S-51 9604 marked with VC-BVS. By 1952, some units, particularly fighter squadrons, had the last three letters of the serial number for individual identity, e.g. a CF100 Mk. 3, No. 18134 bore SA*134 on the fuselage side; SA being No. 445 Squadron. Almost conversely, other aircraft, such as a Chipmunk T.30 bore the call-sign VC*GPY on the fuselage side and in the normal full serial position over the fin flash was 185 (for 18185). Undoubtedly, this was a transitional period for R.C.A.F. markings.

Code letter or numbers were not usual in the Royal Australian Air Force, identification being purely by serial number, which has varied only by the allocation of blocks of numbers, instead of invariably starting at No. 1 after the 'A Number' prefix, e.g. Mosquito B.16s were numbered from A52-601 although A52-1 to A52-600 had not been fully allocated. New Zealand followed her same serialling system and used unit codes, KW being No. 5 (Maritime) Squadron equipped with Sunderland M.R.5s. The same applied in South Africa where a Sunderland was coded RB in a S.A.A.F. unit. With the latter Force however, the serialling system re-started circa 1950. Under the old system Harvards 7636, 7637 and 7642 were some of the highest numbers recorded. They were incidentally connected—literally! At the Rhodes Centenary Air Display in 1953, they gave a performance of aerobatics, linked together by cord. In the new system blocks of three digit numbers were initially allotted, e.g. Vampire F.B.5s were numbered from 201.

The SR serials, e.g. SR107 for a Vampire F.B.9 in the Southern Rhodesian Air Force, became a RRAF series, officially taking effect from October, 1954, when the new title Royal Rhodesian Air Force was conferred, following the Central African Federation. Thus SR107 became RRAF 107.

The Indian, Pakistan and Royal Ceylonese Air Forces use 8 in. serials positioned as on R.A.F. aircraft, examples being ID593 Vampire N.F.10, R4030 Vickers-Supermarine Attacker and CA302 Balliol T.2 respectively. Only India had a separate series for naval aircraft, these having the words INDIAN NAVY in 8 in. lettering above the serial. Auxiliary Air Force units in Hong Kong and Malaya use R.A.F. aircraft in their standard service finishes.

The large size of the Service markings on this F-84F Thunderstreak has caused the Buzz number to be relegated to the rear. The serial number is presented in three forms, as 52-6570 in small figures by the cockpit, as 26570 on the fin and as FS-570 in the Buzz number.

The United States Air Force

By the American National Security Act of 1947, the bulk of the United States Army Air Force was re-designated the United States Air Force. America at last had an independent air force. Its first task was outlined as the organisation, training and equipping of Air Force units for the conduct of prompt and sustained aerial combat operations. A high standard of operational readiness was in fact soon obtained—and not without provocation. Yet, camouflage of aircraft had not been considered advisable. The reason can be conjectured. In meeting its tasks, mobility was the keynote. Camouflage relates to local geography, but the mobility achieved by U.S.A.F. Combat Commands outstripped such considerations. Perhaps now camouflage of aircraft is even considered archaic, although it is possible that, in a tactical role in specific areas, a camouflage suited to the terrain would be applied. This did not, however, happen in Korea. A bare metal finish, offering a smooth, continuous low-drag surface was universal in the U.S.A.F.

Before the re-designation, a few U.S.A.A.F. aircraft seen with pre-war rudder markings led to reports that America was reverting to pre-war national markings. It was not so. Red however, was again brought into the insignia, as shown on page 147.

Another identification marking of a different kind was introduced late in 1945, becoming known as the 'Buzz number'. The word suggests the original purpose of the marking. 'Buzzing' was low or close flying, usually without authorisation. By presenting a large number, in black on bare-metal, yellow or white on camouflage, and red on black finishes, marked both sides of the fuselage and port lower and starboard upper wing surfaces; an observer might well be able to take an offender's number. Partly for this reason, British aircraft displayed serials under the wings but on U.S.A.F. aircraft, the serial was rarely presented in positions other than the fuselage 'name-plate' and fin. However, the 'Buzz number' bore a relation, both to the serial number and the aircraft type. A typical example was P-80B Shooting Star 45-8480 (58480 fin serial) which bore the Buzz number PN-480. 'P' denoted the role, 'Pursuit', as in P-80B. Each different type within the pursuit

class had a different second letter, e.g. PA for P-38 Lightnings, PE for P-47 Thunderbolts, PF for P-51 Mustangs, etc., and PN was for P-80 Shooting Stars. The letters I and O were not used. Numbers, quite simply, as will be seen from the example above, were the last three figures of the serial number. It was possible, however, for more than one aircraft of the same type, to have the same last three letters to the serial number. When this happened an 'A' suffix was given to the first duplication, a 'B' suffix to the second and so on. One F-84E Thunderjet had the Buzz number FS-558-D.

With American aircraft, it is difficult to treat the subject of aircraft markings separately from that of aircraft designations, for they are so inter-related. In June, 1948, the U.S.A.F. changed the designations of some categories of aircraft. 'Pursuits', for example, became 'Fighters'. It followed that in a P-80 Shooting Star becoming a F-80 Shooting Star the PN of the Buzz number would become FN. That was so in theory, but within eight weeks of the new designations becoming effective, the second letters were re-allotted to take into account earlier types that had now gone out of service and new types coming in. To have more than twenty-four fighter types would have upset the system (N.B. Twenty-six letters to the alphabet less I and O not used). In the case of the P-80 Shooting Stars becoming F-80s, before FN replaced PN in practice, the new letters FT were assigned. It applied similarly to many other aircraft types.

At about the time of this change, the Buzz numbers ceased to be marked on the wings, being replaced by the familiar letters U.S.A.F. Also, from these 1948 changes, new letters for Buzz numbers were assigned only to light bomber, fighter and training types, in fact, those aircraft types most likely to indulge in 'buzzing'.

For the first year after the war, many U.S.A.A.F. aircraft were still to be seen in some form of camouflage, as a relic from the war. A B-29A-109-BW Superfortress (521752) at Marham, visiting on 'Operation Ruby' in the summer of 1946; still had undersurfaces, including fuselage sides below wing root level in anti-searchlight black; above this was a normal bare metal finish. Even as late as 1950 a few C-47s were still in wartime camouflage and one still retained A.E.A.F. stripes at that time!

Most of the significant markings on this Boeing B-50A are grouped about the tail. A triangular formation marking reveals the unit and the serial and Buzz number show the individual identity of the machine and gives an indication of its basic type.

As in the R.A.F., it is the fighter squadrons of the U.S.A.F. that are permitted embellishment in a unit scheme. The 20th F.B. Wing for example had its F-84G Thunderjets in lightning flashes of yellow, red and blue for the 55th, 77th and 79th Squadrons respectively. Wing-tip tanks where carried or applicable were often painted in different colours for each squadron within a wing.

To aircraft in special roles, overall colour schemes *did* apply, such as night interdictor aircraft based in Europe, an individual example being B-26C-40-DL in an overall glossy black with the serial, 435583 on the fin in red. Radio-controlled aircraft had an overall fire-truck red and whether manned or unmanned, carried normal insignia and serials, even Buzz numbers 1945-48! Partial finishes, apart from formation markings or adornment, were not usual, except in the case of transport aircraft for personnel or V.I.P.'s, where a heat-reflecting white was given to the top of the fuselage, sometimes including the fin.

Safety and rescue have engendered both markings and marking schemes. Rescue aircraft, in the U.S.A.F. had a yellow band some 2-3 ft. wide around the fuselage, aft of the insignia. This band was edged in black of some 3-4 in. thickness. The word RESCUE appeared on the fuselage side and under the wings, sometimes on a yellow panel, edged in black. Helicopters of rescue flights had the same kind of yellow band with the word RESCUE on the fuselage sides. On the port side of a H-19A, however, the large door on this side necessitated an abbreviation to RCUE.

Both the U.S.A.F. and the R.A.F. have taken precautions in recent years, to render conspicuous aircraft committed to flying over barren territory, particularly the Arctic wastes. In consequence, the markings have become known as 'Arctic markings'. They concern usually the tail; the uppersurfaces of the tailplane and the fin and sometimes additionally the uppersurface of the wing panels outboard of the ailerons at their inset point.

United States Army

When the U.S.A.A.F. became the U.S.A.F. some liaison and observation aircraft were retained. New aircraft were purchased through the U.S.A.F. and thereby the same serialling system applied. Standard finish was olive drab, with U.S. ARMY in yellow on the fuselage sides and on the wings in port lower and starboard upper positions. The same wording appeared above the fin serial also in yellow, as on L-19A-CE 15007. Most of these helicopters were in olive drab, but some communications aircraft such as U-1 Otters (built by de Havilland of Canada) had a silver finish and red tails and wing tips as 'Arctic markings' for operating in the Far North. Standard national insignia and positioning applied.

In standard United States Navy "midnite" blue finish and white unit markings, this HUP-2 helicopter gives a 'worms-eye-view' of aircraft markings. With this view in mind a national insignia, it will be noticed, is placed on the undersides.
Similar Piasecki helicopters used by the U.S. Army as H-25A 'Army Mules' were finished in overall olive drab, with serials (e.g. 116572) placed on the fuselage sides, just aft of the pilot's cabin.

This F-84E Thunderjet has its Buzz Number on the nose and a close scrutiny of the photograph reveals that it was previously presented in a different size. It was used by a squadron commander and is shown as it appeared during 1952 in Britain.

United States Navy

Wearing national insignia identical to the U.S.A.F., the United States Navy differ in their standard finish for operational aircraft, which is an overall "midnite" blue with white serial and identification markings. Non-operational naval aircraft are mostly in bare metal finish, although special finishes may be applied for certain duties. A Convair PB4Y-1 used in guided weapons experiments was yellow overall. This aircraft had a lage number, 309, on the fuselage aft of the insignia and NAMU in large letters on the fin, indicating its unit, the Naval Aircraft Modification Unit.

After the war the wording U.S. NAVY again appeared aft on the fuselage in about 4 in. lettering on all aircraft and the rear of the fuselage became the post-war position for the designation and serial number. An identification marking scheme, issued under U.S. Navy Directive ACL 156-46 became generally effective in 1947. Under this scheme, tail letters on fin and rudder, were 36 in. in height and rather smaller individual numbers appeared on the fuselage sides, usually forward of the insignia. Both were in white on dark finishes and in black on light finishes. To take a particular example, a Curtiss SC-1 in "midnite" blue, had CE on the tail and 2 on the fuselage side. These were combined to give 2-CE as the marking under the port wing and on the uppersurface of the starboard wing. This indicated the second aircraft (2) of the cruiser (C) U.S.S. *Pasedena* (E), in a system where B and C would be battle-ships and cruisers respectively and each individual ship within its class would have an arbitrary allotment of a letter of the alphabet, to appear after the 'class' letter. The battleship allocations started with A for U.S.S. *Iowa* and therefore its attached aircraft were identified from 1-BA.

Aircraft carriers had either a single or two-letter marking on the fins of their aircraft, significant of the carrier's name, e.g. M for U.S.S. *Midway* and SA for U.S.S. *Saipan*.

The U.S. Navy Fleet Air Wings, shore based, but operating as fleet support units, had similarly marked identification letters in a slightly different system. Of the two letters on the tail, the first indicated the wing and the second, the individual squadron within the wing. In 1947, the six Navy Fleet Air Wings had allocations as follows: 1st (Marianas) A, 2nd (Hawaii) B, 3rd (Panama Canal Zone) C, 4th (Washington) D, 5th (Virginia) E, and 14th (California) S.

Naval Air Reserve aircraft in 'midnite' blue or natural finish came within the system, but yet again, their two fin letters had a differing significance. The first letter in each case denoted the base, as follows: B—Atlanta, C—Columbus, D—Dallas, E—Minneapolis, F—Oakland, H—Miami, J—Jacksonville, K—Olathe, L—Los Alamitos, M—Memphis, P—Denver, R—New York, S—Norfolk, T—Seattle, U—St. Louis, V—Glenview, W—Willow Grove, X—New Orleans and Z—Squantum. Second letters denoted the class of aircraft, following the Navy's aircraft designation letters, i.e. A—Attack, F—Fighter, P—Patrol, R—Transport, T—Trainer and U—Utility.

With the creation of a U.S.A.F., the Navy took to marking NAVY in large letters on the fuselage sides. Many fighter squadrons reverted to pre-war styles of squadron markings. Squadron VF211 with North American FJ-3s had red and white chequered tails with large white numbers 101. 102, 103, etc. By 1954 several fighter squadrons had their aircraft in a natural finish.

The fin-marking system lapsed in many areas, possibly for security reason; but at home, bases were revealed in the most open way, e.g. under the large presentation of NAVY, base names such as NIAGARA FALLS or LOS ANGELES would appear in about 8 in. lettering. In operational units, however, large three-digit numbers on fuselage sides or each side of the nose, provided the tactical recognition markings for the area. A feature of naval reserve aircraft is an orange band around the fuselage.

United States Marines

Markings and finishes of U.S. Marine aircraft were based on those of the U.S. Navy, with the obvious difference that where the Navy put NAVY the Marines put MARINES. As an integral part of the U.S. Fleet, they came into the Navy's tail marking system. Two letters were used, the first indicating the command and the second the squadron within the command of each fleet marine force. As an example, the force known as Marine Air Atlantic used the letter 'L'. The 20th Marine Squadron in this command was allotted the letter 'T', thus the fin markings of its Grumman F7F-3Ns was 'LT'. As this squadron was a land-based unit, its fin letters were underlined, a practice exclusive to Marine units.

Most widely used of N.A.T.O. fighters was the F-84 Thunderjet shown here with markings and code of a Royal Norwegian Air Force squadron. Another F-84 in this service coded H-PX, retained its original United States Air Force serial on the fin —110918.

Collective Security

The potential threat from the East had to be met by alliance in the West. Firstly Britain's bonds with France were cemented by the Treaty of Dunkirk in 1947 to provide against a revival of a militant Germany. By 1948, the cold war had commenced and Western Union, a military alliance of the the Benelux countries, France and Britain resulted. Fifty-four ex-R.A.F. Lancasters, delivered from 1951 to the French Naval Air Arm *Aeronavale* under this Union were serialled WU-1 to WU-54. The WU, standing for Western Union, was the first aircraft marking indicative of the policy of collective security in the West. By that time however, alliance was on a far larger scale in a far wider sphere; the United States, Canada, Britain, France, Italy, Belgium, the Netherlands, Norway, Denmark, Portugal, Iceland and Luxembourg had signed the North Atlantic Treaty in 1949. In 1952, Greece and Turkey also acceded making a total of fourteen countries, of which all but two, Iceland and Luxembourg, had air forces. Where N.A.T.O. countries had air force units integrated, such as in the 2nd Allied Tactical Air Force, normal national markings were retained and so far no overall N.A.T.O. symbol or N.A.T.O. formation marking has yet appeared on any aircraft. In this chapter the markings of European Air Forces in N.A.T.O. are reviewed.

France

Natural finish was general throughout the French Air Force (*Armee de l'Air*) except for a few army liaison types in olive brown. The familiar French roundels were displayed in all six standard positions and surprisingly, rudder striping was maintained; only in a few cases had it given way to fin flashes. The width of the division of colours was for practical purposes equal, but some were marked to the letter of the law, in that the proportions as well as the colours were those of the Tricolour—90:99:111 for blue, white and red respectively.

Immediately after the war many ex-*Luftwaffe* aircraft were taken over by the French including 154 Bu181s for communications. Many ex-R.A.F. aircraft, 242 Spitfires, 185 Wellingtons, 64 Halifaxes, 141 Ansons also went to the French. In many cases their original finish was retained. Vampire F.B.5s acquired later had a silver finish with French roundels replacing those of the R.A.F. and rudder stripes in place of fin flashes. Original R.A.F. serials were retained and French unit codes were marked each side of the nose, A-DU being VV726 and D-DU was VZ221.

A typical fighter unit in 1952, the 10th *Escadre de Chasse* of Villacoubly had some twenty P47 Thunderbolts in bare metal finish still with their American serials on the fin, 420027, 420367, etc. Also attached to the unit were two Goelands and two Morane 472s. The famous *Cigogne Escadrille* was revived and being attached to the 2nd Fighter Wing at Dijon its Dassault MD450 *Ouragans* bore the coding 2-EA, 2-EB, 2-EC, etc., in 30 in. black letters below the cockpit. Forward of this, measuring some 3 ft. from beak to feet, was the same stork emblem borne by SPA3 in 1917-18 (see page 50).

Constructors' numbers appeared as before in the top of the rudder stripes and were accepted for service identity. Sometimes the number was repeated on the fuselage sides, as on three Morane 472s, No. 328, No. 362 and No. 418. An interesting distinction in serialling was that prototypes were numbered No. 01, No. 02 *et seq.* and production aircraft No. 1, No. 2 *et seq.* A number of French aircraft carried letters, similar to French civil registrations. They were in fact radio call-signs, associated with the civil registrations, in that whereas the letters F-AAAA to F-PZZZ were reserved for civil aircraft, F-RAAA to F-ZZZZ were reserved for *Groupement des Moyens Militaires de Transport Aerien*, F-TAAA to F-TZZZ for *Commandement Superior des Ecoles*, F-UAAA to F-UZZZ to *Defense Aerienne du Territoire* and F-ZAAA to F-ZZZZ prototypes.

Naval aircraft were a deep blue overall, a scheme applied to the forty-eight Seafires used in the reconstituted *Aeronavale*. As previously mentioned fifty-four Lancasters were supplied for general reconnaissance in a royal blue overall finish. Serials appeared in 10 in. figures under the French fin flash with its anchor device. Their numbers WU-01, WU-02, WU-03, etc., were ex-R.A.F. NX613, SW297, RT697, etc., respectively. Sunderlands used by this arm remained in their R.A.F. white finish and Neptunes in their U.S. Navy "midnite" blue. Where radio call-signs were marked, the allocation F-XAAA to F-YZZZ applied.

Belgium and the Netherlands

The Royal Belgium Air Force used standard silver finish for its Meteor F.8s and R.A.F. (1952 style) camouflage for its

Meteor N.F.11s, with Belgian roundels and flashes in the Brabant colours replacing the red, white and blue of R.A.F. aircraft. Serials, marked as on R.A.F. aircraft, were in the Belgian series, examples of which are EF48, EG49 and EN3 for a Meteor F.4, F.8 and N.F.11 respectively. Transport aircraft bear their serials above the fin flash and radio call-signs marked each side of the fuselage roundel. Silver finished Pembrokes serialled RM-1 to RM-12 were call-signs OT-ZAA to OT-ZAL respectively.

Examples of serial prefix letters that varied according to type were: D Dominie, H Harvard, ID Hunter, K Dakota, and KX Skymaster. Finishes in the R.Ned.A.F. were silver at first for fighters such as Meteor F.8s and F-84G Thunderjets and yellow for trainers. Identity was by code letters marked each side of their national insignia, e.g. a Spitfire F.9 was H*9 and two Meteor F.4s of No. 323 Squadron were Y9*5 and Y9*8. Serials were marked on the fin, e.g. Y9-11 was I-23 and S8-2 was I-171. Squadron codes for the later Meteor F.8s were as follows: No. 322, W3; No. 323, Y9; No. 324, P3; No. 325, R4; No. 326, I9. Naval aircraft finishes were similar to those of the country of their origin. Royal Naval finishes for Fireflies and Sea Furies, but with a dark glossy blue replacing the extra dark sea grey. Neptunes and Sikorsky S-55s retained U.S. Navy "midnite" blue. At the rear of the fuselage of all naval aircraft in 6 in. letters appeared the words KON MARINE and identity markings were similar to those of their Air Force, e.g. a Sea Fury was G*43.

Norway and Denmark

As soon as Germany was defeated a Norwegian Spitfire squadron serving with the R.A.F. flew to Norway in full national markings as illustrated on page 134. These were later discarded for the more conventional markings as illustrated on page 184. Silver or natural finishes are usual. A R.Norwegian A.F. Dakota, retaining its U.S.A.F. fin serial 315613, was coded BW*K (*=Norwegian insignia) and bore the words DET KONGELIGE NORSKE FLY-VAPEN above the cabin windows.

Denmark used camouflage for operational aircraft and a silver or bare metal finish for other aircraft. Identification throughout was by the presentation of the serial number in 12 in. letters aft of the fuselage roundels, e.g. 493 Meteor F.8, 672 B-17 Fortress. Post-war allocations were in blocks of numbers, e.g. Oxford T.2s 201+, Harvard T.2Bs 301+, Harvard T.3s 351+, Spitfire L.F9/16s 401+, Spitfire P.R. 11 451+, Meteor N.F.11 501+, etc.

Italy

The general finish in the Italian Air Force is quite simply silver, with Italian roundels in the standard six positions. Unit identity is a conventional code system marked each side of the roundel, e.g. S.2*66 on a Harvard and S.3*26 on a Fiat G.59-4A. Presentation of the serial in only 2 in. figures is at the rear of the fuselage; five Vampire F.B.5s delivered in March, 1950, were MM6000 to MM6004.

Camouflaged aircraft were used in the early post-war years. Examples are ex-R.A.F. Baltimore Vs FW419, FW439, FW584, FW592, FW649 and FW660, that changed their roundels from red, white and blue to green, white and red in the summer of 1946.

Turkey, Greece and Portugal

Olive green was usual in the Turkish Air Force but many Lockheed T-33s and F-86 Sabres, some ex-R.A.F. and R.C.A.F. were kept in bare metal finish. The Royal Hellenic Air Force even retained Buzz numbers on ex-U.S.A.F. aircraft; F-84 Thunderjet 19695 bearing FS-695-D on the nose whilst wearing the azure and white markings of Greece. Portugal too, has maintained a bare metal finish on her Thunderjets which bore such widely separated serials as 501 and 5102 in black 8 in. figures above the Portuguese Air Force fin flash.

Portugal is Britain's oldest ally by the Anglo-Portugese Treaty of 1373, still recognised as one of the treaties committing this country to military action. British aircraft have found favour in Portuguese service, in fact, Portugal was the first foreign power to have Spitfires. A number of wartime aircraft ended up in Portugal, e.g. Blenheim IVs R3830 and Z5762, Blenheim Vs AZ986-7, Mohawk IV AX882, Hudson VI FK714, etc. Some of these have been sought post-war by film companies for re-marking, to take part in war films.

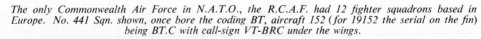

The only Commonwealth Air Force in N.A.T.O., the R.C.A.F. had 12 fighter squadrons based in Europe. No. 441 Sqn. shown, once bore the coding BT, aircraft 152 (for 19152 the serial on the fin) being BT.C with call-sign VT-BRC under the wings.

Markings behind the Iron Curtain

Standard fighter in the Soviet Air Force 1949-54 was the Mig 15, of which it is estimated some 17,000 were built in Russian, Polish and Czech factories. An advanced trainer version, the U-Mig15 is here shown in Czech Air Force markings. An unspecified number were recently reported bearing the green and white insignia of Egypt.

The Red Air Force

The Russian Air Force was part of the Red Army, divided into two air fleets, one in the East and the other in the West, each entirely independent. Naval aircraft came under the naval commands of Arctic, Baltic, Black Sea and North Pacific areas. A strategic bomber and transport force came, operationally, directly under the Supreme Defence Council. All service aircraft bore the same unvarying red star as their national identity marking, outlined in yellow or white on dark finishes. Positioning remained as detailed in Part 3, Chapter 12.

Individual markings remained in unrevealing two or three digit numbers, but on a few aircraft, particularly transports; long serial numbers, of the nature 01255125, have been observed on the fin in some 8 in. digits. Their significance is not known, but it is possible they break down into parts, for example, one digit denoting the Five Year Plan under which the aircraft was ordered. It might be worth noting that 1946-50 was the 4th Five Year Plan and 1951-55 the 5th. Possibly, another digit or digits relates to the State Factory Number in which it was constructed.

A dark green and dark brown in a disruptive pattern for uppersurfaces and fuselage sides with undersurfaces in grey was usual in the immediate post-war years, giving way to an even dark green above and a bare metal finish below. Later, many fighters appeared in a completely unpainted metal finish, but which appeared to have a transparent varnish, probably for protective purposes.

Few Russian aircraft ever leave that vast Union to permit a close examination. An exception was forty YaK-3 fighters presented to France after the war. These aircraft, as used by the *Normandie Escadrille* in Russia, had a dark green and dark brown finish, French roundels and rudder striping and additionally, spinners in a blue, white and red roundel marking (red outermost). Other, later aircraft have been extracted less willingly for evaluation. A Mig 15 that fell in the sea off Korea was recovered by a joint Anglo-American salvage effort. It carried North Korean insignia, but no serial. There were, however, small letters to indicate that it had been built in State Factory Zabod 1, Kuybyshev, in 1948. An American £35,000 offer for a Mig 15, persuaded Ro Kun Sak, a North Korean pilot,

to 'drop in' with No. 8170 to Kimpo Air Base. Re-marked with United States insignia and allotted the serial 7616 (significance unknown) it was tested in America, later bearing the Buzz number TC-616.

Russian Satellites

It is with Russian satellite countries that markings have shown transition. The national markings of Hungary, Rumania and Bulgaria have been subordinated to the Red Star as shown on page 184. Polish and Czech markings do not yet show Soviet autocracy, but one wonders how long they will be permitted this individuality. Czechoslovakia did make a start post-war with British equipment, an agreement being signed in Prague during February, 1947, for seventy-two Spitfires, twenty-four Mosquito F.B.6s, three Austers and an Anson—then the Iron Curtain clamped down.

Sometimes the curtain rises unwittingly. Two Russian fighters landed on R.A.F. airfields in Germany by mistake, but, having realised their error they made off without so much as a 'hello'! In March, 1953, however, a Mig 15 of the Polish Air Force landed on Bornholm Island, Denmark. It had a polished metal finish with the Polish insignia appearing on the wings, fuselage sides and on the fin. Instead of being in its usual red and white, only the red portions of the insignia were marked. This, it is understood, is now the standard method of presentation on aircraft with bare metal finish. Some of the older piston-engined types such as the PE-2, had white spinners, centred in red, to match the insignia colours.

Red China

Russian aid to China is by no means new. As far back as 1937, thirty SB-2 bombers and several I-15 fighters formed an independent unit in the Sino-Japanese war, but using Chinese markings. They were then the white sun in a blue sky marking first adopted by Dr. Sun Yat-Sen as the national flag of China, but now applying only to the Chinese Nationalist Air Force on Taiwan (Formosa). On the vast mainland of China, the service aircraft of the Peoples Republic of China, Mig 15, La 9, and La 11 fighters, I128, Tu2 and Tu4 bombers, bear now a red star, with red band background.

WORLD AIR FORCES INSIGNIA

COMMONWEALTH AIR FORCES

CANADA (R.C.A.F. and R.C.N.)

Wings and Fuselage (1946 Limited Use)   Fin Flash   Wings and Fuselage (From 1947)

AUSTRALIA (R.A.A.F. and R.A.N.)
FROM 1947 AS PER R.A.F.
NEW ZEALAND (R.N.Z.A.F.)
FROM 1947 AS PER R.A.F.
SOUTH RHODESIA (S.R.A.F.)
1947 to 1954 AS PER R.A.F.
(See page 102 for dimensions)

SOUTH AFRICA (S.A.A.F.)

Wings and Fuselage (Up to 1950)   Fin Flash   Wings and Fuselage (From 1950)

INDIA   **PAKISTAN**   **RHODESIA AND NYASALAND (R.R.A.F.)**   **CEYLON (R.Cey.A.F.)**

       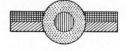

Wings and Fuselage Fin Flash 1947-1948 Flash   Wings and Fuselage (1948 onwards)   Wings (Without yellow borders on clear surfaces)   Fin Flash   Fuselage   Fuselage Sides (otherwise as for R.A.F.)   Wings and Fuselage   Fin Flash

EUROPEAN AIR FORCES OF WESTERN ALLIANCE

FRANCE   **BELGIUM**

 (Army)   (Navy)

Wings and Fuselage   Rudder or Fin Flash   Wings and Fuselage   Rudder or Fin Flash   Wings and Fuselage   Fin Flash

NETHERLANDS   **PORTUGAL**   **NORWAY**

Wings and Fuselage   Fin Flash   Rudder (old style)   Wings and Fuselage   Fin Flash (new style)   Rudder and chordwise around wings (Pre 1948)   Wings and Fuselage (From 1948)

DENMARK   **TURKEY**   **GREECE**

Wings and Fuselage   Fin Flash   Wings and Fuselage   Rudder (old style)   Fin Flash (new style)   Fin Flash   Wings and Fuselage

COMMUNIST AIR FORCES

UNION OF SOVIET SOCIALIST REPUBLIC   **POLAND**   **KOREA**   **BULGARIA**   **OUTER MONGOLIA**   **PEOPLES REPUBLIC OF CHINA**

Wings. Fuselage and Tail   Wings, Fuselage and Fin Flash   Wings Fuselage and Tail   Wings and Fuselage   Rudder Wings, Fuselage or Fin and tail from 1954   Wings, Fuselage and Tail   Wings and Fuselage

HUNGARY   **CZECHOSLOVAKIA**   **RUMANIA**

Wings and Fuselage   Rudder   Wings, Fuselage and tail from late 1954   Wings and Fuselage   Fin Flash   Wings, Fuselage and Tail   Rudder   Wings and Fuselage

GREEN   RED   BLUE   WHITE   BLACK   ORANGE   YELLOW   GOLD   AZURE   SAFFRON

N.B. LEFT SIDE OF RUDDER OR FIN FLASH IS TOWARDS NOSE OF AIRCRAFT

STANDARD MARKING SCHEME IN USE TODAY FOR FIGHTER SQUADRONS OF THE ROYAL AIR FORCE AND THE ROYAL AUXILIARY AIR FORCE

This, and the following three pages, of coloured insignia give a representative selection of fighter squadron markings of aircraft serving in Fighter Command in this Country, with the 2nd Allied Tactical Air Force in Western Europe, and in the Middle East and Far East Air Forces.

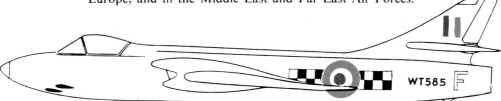

A Hunter F.I of 43 Squadron R.A.F. Fighter Command

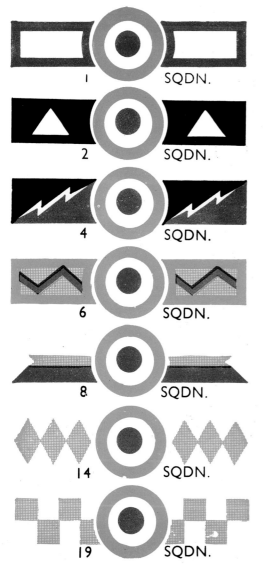

Squadron markings are not heraldic designs like unit badges, but usually have some connection with the history of their unit. These paintings provide an interesting comparison with earlier ones of R.A.F. fighter squadron insignia in 1934. The chief difference is that whereas pre-war the fighters bore their markings along the length of the fuselage and often with associated markings on the top-wing, they are now confined to a standard frame marked each side of the fuselage roundels.

Traditionally in the R.A.F., brightly coloured insignia have been exclusively to fighter aircraft. Our fighter strength is now considerably greater than in the 'thirties; the formation of some fighter units dating back only to the recent war. Even so, some old-established squadrons are wearing bright colours for the first time, an indication

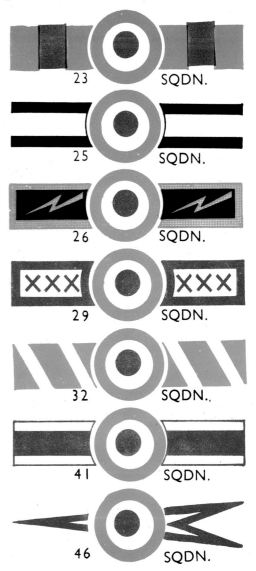

Additional to a squadron insignia, each machine usually bears an individual identification letter. On No. 43 Squadron Hunters this appears as shown above, at the rear of the fuselage, other examples in this unit being 'D' (WT618), 'G' (WT622) and 'S' (WW645). Some Hunter squadrons are now placing their insignia, without the roundel, on the side of the nose of their machines.

185

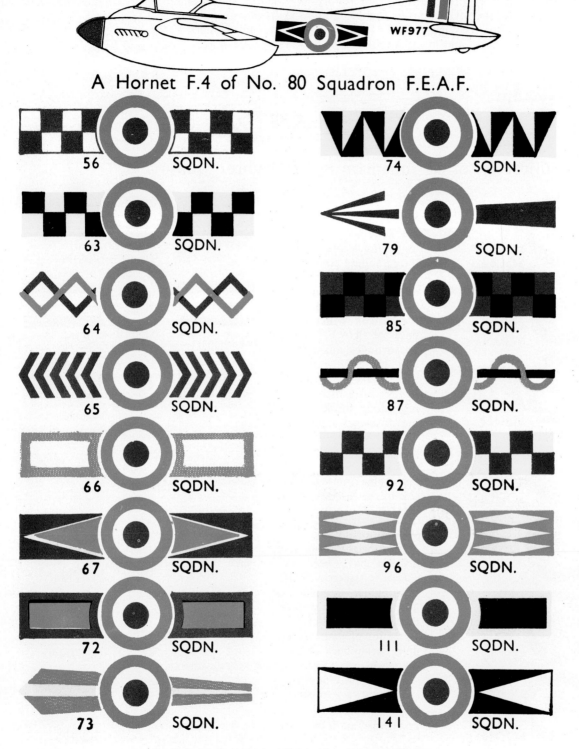

A Hornet F.4 of No. 80 Squadron F.E.A.F.

56 SQDN.
63 SQDN.
64 SQDN.
65 SQDN.
66 SQDN.
67 SQDN.
72 SQDN.
73 SQDN.
74 SQDN.
79 SQDN.
85 SQDN.
87 SQDN.
92 SQDN.
96 SQDN.
111 SQDN.
141 SQDN.

Last of the piston engined fighters in service, the Hornet was used by Nos. 33 and 80 Squadrons in Malaya until recently. The tall tail fin accommodates easily the fin flash and an individual letter. Flight identification markings take the form of a colour-coded spinner. Hornets in Malaya were not camouflaged, having an aluminium finish. Serial numbers were in the 'WB' and 'WF' series.

of changing roles. P
Squadrons on arm
No. 8 Squadron wi
course come into th
with these duties hav
aircraft, this type h
fighter-bomber and t
has been changed;
duty now qualifying

It is perhaps surp
the oldest squadrons
the Air Battalion, R
their long-standing a
blue, the colours of t
No. 3 was in fact all g

Some markings sh
First World War. N
equilateral triangle in
related on page 12, w
seen that this connec
insignia is new to
army co-operation
corporates two ' flash
with wireless telegra
significance of No.
becomes obvious wh
destruction of 225 er
of 1918 earned the uni

Markings are occas
the two black bars o
their pre-war marking
finish between the
standard frame, the s
white and complete
border. In the case
arrowheads were la
and a black border

The reason for th
always apparent, in
an arbitrary selectio
symbolic. No. 208
Squadron, Royal Na
Army Co-operation S
Middle East, and ind
origin and its long ass
desert are symbolise
blue and yellow.

Black is unpretent
chosen for squadron
camouflage is still in
Squadron's insignia
marking that appea
Duxford during the
not unsuited, to cont
doped finish.

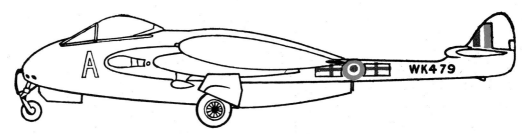

A Venom F.B.I of No. 145 Squadron 2nd A.T.A.F.

s. 2, 4, 6, 14 and 26
ration duties and
ombers did not of
of fighters. Now,
vay to close support
superseded by the
f several squadrons
g element in their
fighter colours.

t Nos. 1, 2 and 3,
in May, 1912, from
eers, did not depict
by adopting red and
of Royal Engineers.
a thin white border.

ssociation with the
uadron had a white
cn unit markings, as
troduced. It will be
remains. Although
quadron, a pre-war
new marking in-
resent an association
ments in 1914. The
uadron's markings
ppreciated that the
aft in eight months
of ' Tiger Squadron'.

odified, for example
Squadron, based on
the normal aircraft
conform with the
veen is now painted
ed with the black
153 Squadron, the
ed to turn inward
d.

of colours is not
s it may have been
thers are certainly
n (formerly No. 8
ervice), served as an
or many years in the
still there. Its naval
with the sands of the
squadron colours of

hardly likely to be
present times when
he black in No. 111
e to perpetuate a
he unit's Siskins at
s. Then black was
a bright aluminium-

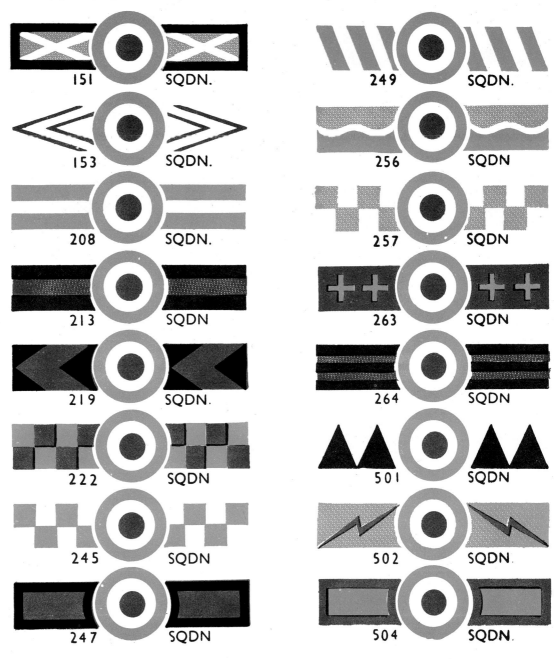

151 SQDN.	249 SQDN.
153 SQDN.	256 SQDN
208 SQDN.	257 SQDN
213 SQDN	263 SQDN
219 SQDN.	264 SQDN
222 SQDN	501 SQDN.
245 SQDN	502 SQDN.
247 SQDN	504 SQDN.

The configuration of Vampires and Venoms make a different layout of markings necessary and individual letters are marked on the nose of the aircraft. Venom F.B.I's of No. 6 Squadron in the Middle East carry a unit badge on the nose with a miniature of the squadron colours as a background. Machines serving in this unit are WE435 ' X ', WE453 ' V ', WE 454 ' D ', etc.

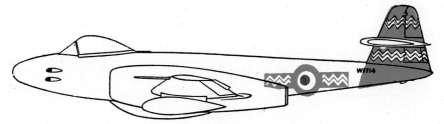

A Meteor F.8 of No. 500 Squadron R.Aux.A.F.
(Squadron Commander's Aircraft)

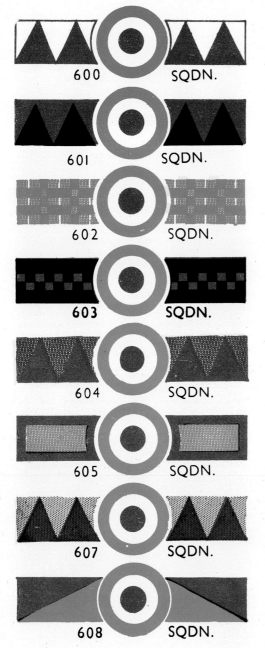

No. 87 Squadron showed originality by representing their badge, a serpent, by a green undulating line, but to No. 29 Squadron must undoubtedly go the credit for the most significant marking—'XXX,' the brewers' mark for 'Extra Strong.'

Squadrons shown with numbers of 500 and upwards were Royal Auxiliary Air Force units. Some of these revived their pre-war marking, but new, with an apparent connection with Scotland, are the markings of No. 602 (City of Glasgow) and No. 612 (County of Aberdeen) Squadron.

It should be noted that No. 501's insignia varied in service and that the checks on No. 603's were changed to blue and red. As the original colours of No. 604 did not contrast well, they were usually marked in red and yellow and on No. 605's aircraft a thin light blue line was sometimes used to separate the two colours.

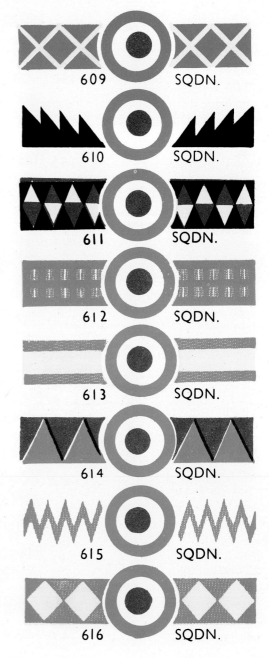

Most squadron commanders have a distinguishing marking on their aircraft, often a striped or chequered tail. In No. 41 Squadron, for example, the red bar of the squadron marking is extended up the fin on the C.O's aircraft. Whatever distinguishing mark is used, it is logical for it to appear on the tail, in order that all the members of a formation can easily recognise their leader's aircraft.

WORLD AIR FORCES INSIGNIA
FOREIGN AIR FORCES FROM 1945

AFGHANISTAN

Wings and Fuselage | Fin or Rudder

ARGENTINA (ARMY)

Wings and Fuselage | Fin or Rudder

ARGENTINA (NAVY)

Wings and Fuselage | Fin or Rudder

BOLIVIA

Wings and Fuselage | Rudder

BRAZIL

Wings and Fuselage | Fin or Rudder

BURMA

Wings and Fuselage | Fin Flash

CHINESE NATIONALIST

Wings and Fuselage | Rudder

CHILE

Wings and Fuselage | Rudder

COLOMBIA

Wings and Fuselage | Rudder

CUBA

Wings and Fuselage | Rudder

DOMINICA

Wings and Fuselage | Rudder

ECUADOR

Wings and Fuselage | Rudder

EGYPT

Wings and Fuselage | Fin Flash

ETHIOPIA

Wings and Fuselage

FINLAND

Wings and Fuselage (Post 1947)

GUATEMALA

Wings and Fuselage | Rudder

HAITI

Wings and Fuselage

HONDURAS
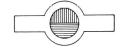
Wings and Fuselage | Rudder

INDONESIA

Wings and Fuselage | Fin Flash

IRAN

Wings and Fuselage | Fin Flash

IRAQ

Wings and Fuselage | Fin Flash | Wing Under surfaces

IRELAND (EIRE)

Fuselage and Wing Upper surfaces

ISRAEL

Wings and Fuselage

JAPAN

Wings and Fuselage

JORDON

Wings and Fuselage | Fin

LEBANON

Wings, Fuselage and Fin Flash | Rudder

MEXICO

Wings and Fuselage | Rudder

NICARAGUA

Wings and Fuselage | Rudder

PANAMA

Wings and Fuselage

PARAGUAY

Wings Fuselage | Rudder

PERU

Wings and Fuselage | Rudder

PHILIPPINES

Wings and Fuselage

SALVADOR

Wings and Fuselage | Rudder

SOUTH KOREA

Wings and Fuselage | Fin

SPAIN

Wings | Rudder

SWEDEN

Wings and Fuselage

SWITZERLAND

Wings and Fuselage | Rudder

SYRIA

Wings and Fuselage | Fin Flash

THAILAND

Wings and Fuselage | Rudder

URUGUAY

Fuselage (Army and Navy) | Rudder (Army) | Wings (Navy) | Rudder (Navy)

VENEZUELA

Wings and Fuselage | Rudder

YUGOSLAVIA

Wings and Fuselage | Rudder or Fin Flash

GREEN | RED | BLUE | WHITE | BLACK | ORANGE | YELLOW | GOLD | AZURE

N.B. LEFT SIDE OF RUDDER OR FIN FLASH IS TOWARDS NOSE OF AIRCRAFT

C54s of the 61st Group. This had a dual significance; as well as a conspicuous marking to assist search aircraft in the event of forced landing, it signified, in the case of the 61st Group, that the aircraft were conveying live ammunition. Unit badges appropriate to roles were newly adopted. The 6th T.C.S. had a snorting bull's head each side of the nose of their C-54s, with the inscription 'Bully Beef Express'. In common with other transports the full designation of the unit was written along the nose-wheel trapdoors—6th Troop Carrier Squadron.

Mission silhouettes were again marked. Some fighters having their nose literally covered with bomb silhouettes. One U.S. Marine Panther having no less than 400 of these in white on its "midnite" blue finish. In the 374th Troop Carrier Wing, donkey silhouettes were marked for each mission completed by their C-54s. Fuel drops were recorded by oil-drum markings on the sides of C-119s. Personal emblems again adorned fuselage sides and the choice of subject in a decade, had changed little. Presentation, however, showed a subtle difference, where a conventional style bathing suit had been usual in 1942-45, a 'bikini' sufficed in 1952!

U.S.A.F. C-47 347965 bearing the words THE VOICE on the nose, showed another aspect of operations, psychological warfare. A highly amplified loudspeaker would exhort the enemy with such slogans as—'Surrender or die'. (Although unusual, the method is not new; the R.A.F. in 1935 used Valentia K2345 for broadcasting.)

Commonwealth Aircraft

The R.A.F. was represented by two squadrons of Sunderland M.R.5s, Nos. 88 and 209, plying between Korea and Japan in an immaculate white maritime finish. Examples are SZ577 and RN277 bearing the individual letters 'A' and 'D' respectively. Hastings in standard Transport Command finish were frequent visitors conveying personnel and stores to and from the United Kingdom. Commanded and piloted by Army personnel, Auster A.O.P.6s of Nos. 1903 and 1913 Independent A.O.P. Flights spotted for the Commonwealth Brigade. They bore standard A.O.P. camouflage, an individual identity being VF622 coded TS.U. This was not the first time Austers had served the United Nations Organisation. Several years earlier A.O.P.6 VF503 in silver finish had its R.A.F. roundels painted out and the words UNITED NATIONS painted on the side of the fuselage. This was in connection with the Palestinian troubles of 1948.

The Fleet Air Arm was represented by aircraft of the various carriers of the Royal Navy operating in Korean waters; H.M.S. *Ocean*, H.M.S. *Theseus*, H.M.S. *Triumph* and H.M.S. *Unicorn*. The last-named acting as a supply

United States Aircraft

Of the United Nations, participating to resist Communist aggression in the Korean War, the United States of America made by far the largest contribution. Aircraft of the United States Air Force, United States Navy and Marines engaged, showed finishes no different from those at home. Coloured squadron markings and Buzz numbers as shown on page 175, were typical of fighters and fighter-bombers in their bare-metal finish. Camouflage in the U.S.A.F. applied only to some C-46 transports which had retained an earlier olive drab uppersurface and to light spotter and liaison types for which olive drab was standard.

Fighter and attack aircraft all bore Buzz Numbers for individual identification, but transports, for which this practice had been dropped, each bore the last three digits of their serial numbers marked large on each side of the nose, without the type-letter prefixes. Examples are 128 on 9128 and 195 on 9195, two C-119s, which bore respectively the wording GREEN HORNETS and PACKET RATS on their long tail-fin fillets.

Many transports had red tails, certainly most of the

and repair ship. In all some twenty-seven naval aircraft were lost and 140 damaged. To the ships named, should be added H.M.A.S. *Sydney* of the Royal Australian Navy. Fireflies and Sea Furies were the main operational aircraft types used and to provide an additional identification marking for United Nations units, black and white stripes, similar to the A.E.A.F. stripes of 1944 were marked.

Australia was also well represented by No. 77 Squadron using firstly Mustangs and then Meteor F.8s. The Meteors were in standard silver finish with R.A.A.F. serials in the A77 range. It is evident that these were not numbered consecutively as of a total ninety-eight delivered to the R.A.A.F., two in Korea were numbered A77-728 and A77-851. The last three numbers were repeated in 18-in. digits on the nose, as an individual marking. Apart from the standard R.A.F. type roundels, fin flash and ejection seat warning, the only unusual feature was the pilot's name or nickname, by the side of the cockpit, e.g. A77-446 as Pilot Officer K. Murray's aircraft was 'Black Murray'.

South Africa's No. 2 Squadron too, first went into action in Korea with Mustangs, serialled from No. 301. Later the unit re-equipped with bare-metal finished F86F Sabres bearing 12 in. serials, numbered from 601. South African (post-1950 type) roundels were used with a 24 in. wide orange-white-blue fin flash extending 5 ft. up the fin in line with the leading edge. Large individual identity letters appeared on the fuselage side, just aft of the cockpit, 'B' being S.A.A.F. No. 603.

Royal Canadian Air Force transport aircraft were often observed on Korean airfields, particularly North Stars of the well-known batch numbered 17501-17525.

Aircraft of Other Nations that were United

United Nations Forces would have been an empty phrase, but for the support given by many other nations of U.N.O. Greece sent Flight 13 of the R.H.A.F. to Korea, where its silver Dakotas served the 374th Wing of the U.S.A.F. They were marked with the Greek azure and white roundels in the normal positions and additionally on the centre of the nose. This was to bring them in line with aircraft of the 374th Wing, that normally had a formation marking on the nose. Above the cabin windows in 12 in. lettering was the inscription: ROYAL HELLENIC AIR FORCE. Individual numbers 36 in. high, 1 to 10 appeared just aft of the cabin windows.

Other aircraft were to be seen with the words ROYAL THAI AIR FORCE above the cabin windows. Fin serialled,

silver Dakotas, 293045 and 293629 being two such examples. Standard Thai roundels were carried, but the flash was marked on the rudder and not on the fin. A Dakota bearing the coding ZU.7 marked each side of the Dutch insignia, showed participation by yet another nation. Although Turkey's main contribution was by her magnificent infantry at least one Piper L-18B, bore Turkish markings in Korea.

South Korean Aircraft

P-51D Mustangs supplied by the U.S.A. were the main operational air weapon of the South Korean Air Force. A few miscellaneous aircraft were used including an ex-Japanese Army Type 95 training biplane. Standard South Korean insignia applied, but not until late in the war did the 'K' fin marking become general.

Strangely, these markings had an interesting sequel in England. It happened on the 11th March, 1954, at Prestwich when the movements board showed 'R.A.F. Commander from Kefflavick E.T.A. 18.50'. A discerning enthusiast, knowing full well that no Commanders were in R.A.F. Service, roused the local spotters. As they gathered to witness the arrival, the board was corrected from R.A.F. to Korean Air Force. Disbelief turned almost to howls of derision—and then the Aero Commander 520 serialled 503 on the fin arrived—with South Korean Air Force insignia. It had a highly buffed finish, a dark green anti-dazzle panel and from this two green cheat lines trailing aft. It was one of three S.K.A.F. Nos. 501-503, being ferried to Korea.

North Korean Aircraft

The North Korean Air Force left little doubt that North Korea has become a Russian satellite country. A red star in a circumscribed red circle within a blue ring was their adopted, or enforced marking. Their aircraft came mainly from Russian sources. Russia and the Peoples Republic of China did not enter the Korean war officially, but as well known, many 'volunteers' from these two countries participated. As far as aircraft were concerned, the subterfuge of North Korean markings was used.

From combat reports, Mig 15s in Korea had three distinct finishes. One camouflage scheme was two shades of green, a dark-green and a mid-green for uppersurfaces with light blue undersurfaces. In another scheme the same blue undersurface was used with a disruptive pattern for uppersurfaces of copper and blue. Major J. A. Jaraba of the U.S.A.F. on the other hand reported very highly polished Mig 15s with red noses.

Although the Peoples Republic of China and Russia did not officially participate in the Korean war, the North Korean Air Force was undoubtedly assisted by these two powers. The United Nations Command was restrained from bombing Chinese airfields where Mig 15s in the peculiar camouflage illustrated were stationed.

191

A Vickers F.B. 5a 'Gun-bus', the second presented by Bombay. *The third aircraft presented by Rhodesia, a Martinsyde G.102 Elephant.*

REPRESENTATIVE PRESENTATION AIRCRAFT 1914-1918

Type	Serial	Presentation Details	Type	Serial	Presentation Details
B.E.2c	2667	Malaya XVI Menang	F.E.2D	A6547	Australia No. 13
B.E.2E	A3100	Malaya No. 10 Malacca Chinese	F.E.2D	B1897	Australia No. 14
Bristol F.2B	D8065	Australia No. 24	R.E.8	A3654	Australia 19, Victoria 1
Camel	B3865-70	Basutoland Nos. 1-6	S.E.5A	C6424	Australia 41, Victory Scout
Camel	B3877-80	Basutoland Nos. 7-10	S.E.5A	D6940	Parish of Ince
Curtiss J.N.4	C138	City of Toronto	S.E.5A	D6967	Horwich
Curtiss J.N.4	C254	Mercer	S.E.5A	E254	Marple
D.H.4	A7483	Australia No. 5, N.S.W. No. 4	S.E.5A	E256	Lamberhurst
D.H.5	A9357	Malaya No. 33	Short 827	3063-5	Britons Overseas Nos. 1-3
D.H.5	A9415	Australia No. 5, N.S.W. No. 7	Short 827	3067	Hong Kong Britons
D.H.5	A9432	Australia No. 16, N.S.W. No. 15	Short 827	8220	New York Britons
D.H.9	F1222	Australia 26, Queensland 2	Sopwith	N5427	Philippine Island Britons
F.E.2B	5201	Bombay No. 1	Triplane	N5440	Britons in Siam
F.E.2B	6341	Zanzibar No. 1	Sopwith	N5479	Britons in Spain
F.E.2B	6365	Mauritius No. 2	Triplane	N5494	Peking Britons No. 1
F.E.2B	6928	Malaya No. 12	Sopwith 1½	9378	Poverty Bay, N.Z.
F.E.2B	6933	Malaya No. 17	Strutter	9383	Britons in Japan
F.E.2B	6945	Rajpipla	Sopwith 1½	9395	Tientsen Britons
F.E.2B	6951	Kedah No. 1	Strutter	9405	Britons in Egypt No. 1
F.E.2B	7027	Australia No. 1	Sopwith 1½	9654	Rio de Janeiro Britons 1
F.E.2B	7686	Australia No. 2	Strutter	9667	Tientsin Britons No. 2
F.E.2B	A5447	Australia No. 5	Sopwith 1½	9722	San Paulo Britons No. 1
F.E.2B	A5478	Gold Coast No. 10	Strutter	9739	Britons in Egypt No. 2
F.E.2D	A6360	Australia No. 10	Sopwith 1½	9744	Britons in Italy No. 1
F.E.2D	A6361	Australia No. 11	Strutter	N5084	San Paulo Britons No. 2

Two presentations of identical type, D.H.5 Scouts, show a marked difference in presenting the serial numbers. HONG KONG No. 8 is typical of the Aircraft Manufacturing Company built batch A9163-9362 and DUNGARPUR of the Darracq built batch A9363-9562. This provides a perfect example of 'manufacturing characteristics' referred to in Part 1.

No. 65 (East India) Squadron received its name following the presentation of eight Spitfires to the unit from the East India Fund. Each Spitfire bore an inscription by the cockpit.

Presented by the Bellows Fellowship this Westland Whirlwind of No. 263 Squadron bears by the cockpit the word BELLOWS, and beneath it a pair of bellows has been painted within an elliptical surround.

REPRESENTATIVE PRESENTATION AIRCRAFT 1939-1945

Type	Serial	Presentation Details	Type	Serial	Presentation Details
Cornell	141	El Gaucho Nos. I-IV	Hurricane	Z3500	Aden II
Cornell	151	respectively of 'Little	Hurricane	Z3595	British Honduras
Cornell	161	Norway' Royal Norwegian	Hurricane	Z3900	Women's Voluntary Services
Cornell	177	Air Force	Hurricane	BN795	Our John
Hampden I	AD719	Instanbul	Oxford	P8833	Nurse Cavell
Hurricane	V7607	Hyderabad City	Spitfire II	P7736	Cambridgeshire
Hurricane	V7649	The Paigahs	Spitfire II	P7744	Bow Street Home Guard
Hurricane	V7650	Secunderabad City	Spitfire II	P8175	Baltic Exchange II
Hurricane	V7651	Salar Jung	Spitfire II	R7193	Silver Snipe
Hurricane	V7652	Jagirdars I	Spitfire V	X4912	Sutton Coldfield
Hurricane	V7653	Jagirdars II	Spitfire V	BM124	Queen Salote
Hurricane	V7654	Bahamas II	Sunderland III	DV198	Gillingham
Hurricane	V7773	Surrey	Typhoon IA	R8200	Island of Britain
Hurricane	V7774	Cheltenham Queen	Wellington Ic	R1719	British Guiana II
Hurricane	V7775	Sussex	Wellington Ic	R1721	Jodhpur
Hurricane	V7776	Spirit of the R.F.C.	Wellington Ic	R1722	Corakhpur
Hurricane	V7777	Go To It (Ford Motors)	Wellington Ic	T2877	British Guiana I
Hurricane	V7779	Alma Baker F.M.S.	Wellington Ic	T2879-81	Ceylon Nos. I-III
Hurricane	V7780	Alma Baker Malaya	Wellington Ic	T2884	Fiji
Hurricane	V7795	Alma Baker Australia	Wellington Ic	T2885	Gold Coast
Hurricane	V7796	Alma Baker New Zealand	Wellington Ic	T2886	Ashanti
Hurricane	Z2703	Croydon	Whirlwind I	P7055	Bellows-Argentina No. 1
Hurricane	Z2815	Loughborough	Whirlwind I	P7056	Pride of Yeovil
Hurricane	Z2882	Garfield Weston VI	Whirlwind I	P7116-21	Bellows-Argentina Nos. 2-7
Hurricane	Z3436	Kalhiwar	Whirlwind I	P7122	Bellows-Uruguay No. 1

Two D.H.89 ambulances, Z-7258 and Z-7261 were presented by the 'Women of the Empire' and by the 'Women of Britain' as their inscriptions indicate.

Markings of the Military Aerostats 1907-1954

A close-up of a blimp reveals it for what it was—a gas bag made up, in this case, of some 2,500 separate pieces o aluminium doped proofed fabric. Only under the nose is its identity N.S.4 revealed. The N.S. series were the largest British non-rigid airships and were used 1916-18 for anti-submarine patrols and in 1919 for mine-spotting. One, the N.S.11 was lost with its crew of eight in July, 1919, off Salthouses during a mine-spotting patrol. Lightning was the presumed cause of the disaster.

The Aerostats

In the foregoing pages, 'aircraft' has been taken to be the military aerodynes, that is the heavier-than-air craft—aeroplanes, gyroplanes, helicopters and gliders. We are now concerned with the aerostats, the lighter-than-air craft—balloons and airships. Their markings were in the main confined to national insignia and individual identity. Practically all nations using airships had similar systems of designation, that of prefix letter(s) and a number. The letters were sometimes significant, such as N.S. for North Sea, or, an alphabetical allotment for each different type. Numbers were usually consecutive from No. 1. In some cases, individual names were used.

Changes in temperature affected trim and therefore camouflage was often sacrified for a heat-reflecting finish, usually an aluminium dope, producing a silver finish. National markings became general in 1915; France using her roundel as early as September, 1914, following the regretable accident in the early days of the war, when French Territorial troops shot down their own airship *Dupuy-de-Lome*.

British

Observation kite balloons used by the R.F.C./R.A.F. 1914-18, normally had a khaki-green envelope and small black serial identity numbers, those of Drachen type being A1 to A75 and S1 to S46 for those built by Airships Ltd. and C. G. Spencer Ltd., respectively. Little further use was made of balloons until the 1939-45 war, when barrage balloons were again used. These were in a silver-grey proofed fabric—still to be seen acting as efficient rainproof car covers! No national identity markings were considered necessary as the ownership was obvious—except, apparently by an old Cockney lady, who remarked when the balloons were raised in September, 1939—'If them Germans think they can scare me by sitting up there in them ruddy balloons, they've got another think coming!'

The markings of blimps 1914-19 (see Appendix Four) had an aluminium dope, with an additional aluminium varnish, over their proofed fabric. Designation markings showed one main difference from aircraft serialling; a replacement airship would bear an 'A' suffix, e.g. the replacement airship for the S.S.14 was S.S.14A.

Airships were used by the British Army until November, 1913, when they were handed over to the Admiralty. The *Astra Torres, Beta, Gamma, Delta* and *Eta* then became H.M. Airships Nos. 16 to 20 respectively. This was in a series reserved for rigid airships that had started with No. 1 in 1908. Later the prefix R for Rigid was added, as on the post-war R23.

No. 9, making the first flight on the 27th November, 1916, may be taken as typical of British airship markings, 1914-18. The number appeared in 12 ft. figures on each side of the envelope, fore and aft. Rudders and elevators were striped in blue, white and red and roundels appeared on the fins. Four roundels on the envelope were placed:— one at middle top dead centre, two others in line with it at 120° spacing and the fourth central on the nose. Fin and envelope roundels at 15 and 18 ft. diameter respectively were the largest insignia borne by aircraft. All piping was to a strict R.N.A.S. colour code:—Petrol—red, air—yellow, oil—black, and water—blue.

Post-war came the famous rigids such as the R34, first airship to cross the Atlantic. Economies, however, led to the R.A.F. giving up its airships. R33, similarly marked to No. 9 described above, lost its service identity, to bear the civil registration G-FAAG in the civil airship series. It was as civil aircraft that the R100 and R101 were built, and with the tragic end of the latter airship, went any thought of re-introducing airships into the British Services.

Germany

The Zeppelin, a type of rigid airship, was the terror weapon of the First World War. Germany had faith in their airships, and they were used by both Army and Navy. Each Service had its own numbering system, complicated by the fact that German airships were often referred to by their constructor's number. The main builders, Parseval (*Luftfahrzeug G.m.b.H.*), Zeppelin (*Luftschriffbau Zeppelin G.m.b.H.*), and Schütte Lanz numbered their airships from P1, L.Z.1 and S.L.1 respectively. They were given Service numbers on being taken over. As a typical example, Zeppelin Works Nos. LZ24 and LZ25 became L3 (German Navy) and ZIX (German Army) respectively.

Naval airships, mostly of Zeppelin type, were numbered from L.1. This appeared in some 12 ft. figures, forward on the sides of the envelope. A black cross patée was positioned amidships, each side of the envelope at 120° from top dead centre in section. The envelope was of rubberised single-ply cotton, sometimes with a natural colour or an aluminium doping. Variations were an overall cream finish by *Cellonstaffabrik G.m.b.H.* as applied to L.15, or, in the case of LZ.77, a fabric of an ultramarine shade, with a pattern of closely printed black dots.

German Army kite balloons operating at the war fronts, usually had a dark green fabric, with a black cross patée outlined thinly in white, centrally positioned.

America

The United States used both an alphabetical and a significant letter system for airship type identification. As a general rule, the former system for production types and the latter for experimental types. An 'A' series was in use 1917 and wartime production included thirty-three

of a 'B' series (B1-B33), followed in 1919 by orders for a 'C' series (C1-C15). The system progressed, but it was not the invariable rule to have the numbers conspicuously marked. Nationality in some cases was represented by a rudder flash; a square with vertical red, white and blue stripes, red leading. Kite-balloons used in France bore the A.E.F. roundel.

Progressing to large rigid airships, the U.S. Navy in the early 'thirties had a silver giant 785 ft. long. The wording, U.S. NAVY, normal star insignia of the period and in relatively small letters, the name AKRON, were presented on the envelope. Aft, the rudders were striped in red, white and blue. A sister-ship, the Macon, was similarly marked. The tragic loss of the Akron with 73 lives, followed by an accident to the Macon, sealed the future for the large rigid airship.

Some naval airships bore the prefix 'Z' to their identity marking. 'Z' was the U.S. Navy designation letter for lighter-than-air craft, in the same way the 'V' was the prefix letter for naval aeroplane designations, albeit rarely used. Thus ZR on the envelope would indicate 'Airship Rigid' or ZMC 'Airship Metal Clad'.

The U.S. Army gave up its Airship Service in 1937, handing over its two airships at that time, TC13 and TC14, to the Navy. During the recent war, small patrol airships were still used by the U.S. Navy, bearing the U.S. insignia appropriate to the period. They still apparently have a use today, with their marking as the point of their existence. At Lakehurst an airship had these words marked large on the envelope—JOIN THE U.S. NAVAL AIR RESERVE.

Other Countries

French airships in the 1914-18 war were marked similar to British, the point being that we followed the French example. Italy used her red, white and green colours for roundels and rudder striping, but considered a heat-reflecting aluminium doping too conspicuous and applied instead a drab paint. Identification numbers on the envelope were prefixed by significant letters, e.g. G for *Grande* (Large), M for *Medio* (Medium), P for *Piccolo* (Small) or V for *Veloce* (Fast). Russia had several airships 1910-17 with a type or individual name on the cab or envelope, an example being *Kommissiony* in 1910.

Most of the S.S.Z. type blimps (S.S. for Submarine Scout) had their identity clearly marked on the envelope, with full stops occupying a square foot! In addition to the national identity markings of roundels and rudder stripes, a White Ensign flutters underneath between the cab and the fin.

BRITISH RIGID AIRSHIPS 1911-1930

No.	Type or Name	Remarks	No.	Type or Name	Remarks
R1	Vickers 'Mayfly'	Launched 22.5.11, Wrecked 24.9.11	R24	R23 Class	Beardmore (Inchinnan) built
R2	Willows	Envelope used for S.S.1	R25	R23 Class	A.W. (Selby) built
R3	Astra Torres	Purchased from France	R26	R23 Class	Vickers (Barrow) built
R4	Parseval	German-built	R27	R23X Class	Beardmore (Inchinnan) built
R5-7	Parsevals	Vickers-built	R28	R23X Class	Cancelled
R8	Astra Torres	Obsolete May 1916	R29	R23X Class	A.W. built
R9	Vickers (Barrow)	Based at Howden	R30	R23X Class	Cancelled
R10	Astra Torres	Envelope used for C.1	R31	R31 Class	} Built by Short Bros., Bedford,
R11-13	Forlanini	Not delivered	R32	R31 Class	} on Schutte-Lanz principles
R14-15	R9 Type	Cancelled	R33	R33 Class	A.W. built } Based on
R16	Astra Torres	}	R34	R33 Class	Beardmore-built } L.33
R17	Beta	} Ex-Army airships numbered	R35	R33 Class	Cancelled } Zeppelin
R18	Gamma	} in R series on transfer to	R36	Enlarged R33	Scrapped 1927
R19	Delta	} R.N.A.S.	R37	Enlarged R33	Cancelled
R20	Eta	}	R38	Enlarged R33	Built at Cardington for U.S.A.
R21-22	—	Cancelled	R39-40	Project	Cancelled
R23	R23 Class	Vickers (Barrow) built	R80	Special Class	Vickers (Barrow) built
			R100	Civil Class	Airship Guarantee Co.-built
			R101	Civil Class	Government-built, Cardington

BRITISH NON-RIGID AIRSHIPS 1914-1919

Type	Detail	Identification Markings		Remarks
		Range	Where Marked	
Coastal	Standard East Coast Patrol Type 1917	C1 to C27 Ca to Ce	On fabric of the cab	32 built. 1 (Ce) for France, 4 (Ca-Cd) for Russia, 27 for R.N.A.S. C26 interned in Holland after forced landing 13.12.17
C Star	Improved Coastal	C*1 to C*26	On plywood sides of cab	Coastal type modified. Star added to marking to indicate modifications—thus *
S.S.	B.E.2c Type (All 70 h.p. Renault except S.S. 23 with 80 h.p. Renault)	S.S.1 to S.S.26 (S.S.10A, S.S.10B, S.S.23 replacement aircraft)	} On envelope and/or on sides of cab	Nos. S.S.4, 5, 6, 10B, 11 and 22 to Italy, Nos. 21 and 26 to France. S.S. 23 and S.S. 24 to American Forces. Remainder used by R.N.A.S. S.S.1 was destroyed by fire
S.S.	Maurice Farman Type	S.S.28 to S.S.39 (S.S.39A replacement aircraft)	}	S.S.34 fitted with Nieuport Seaplane Floats
S.S.	Armstrong Whitworth Type	S.S.40 to S.S.47		S.S.43, 44, 45, 46, 47 to Italy, S.S.48, 49 to France
S.S.P.	Similar to Coastal	S.S.P.1 to S.S.P.6	} Normally on envelope	6 only. S.S.Z type considered superior
S.S. Twin	Experimental S.S.	S.S.T.1 to S.S.T.14	}	Limited use. First model built April 1918
S.S. Zero	Standard Patrol Craft 1917-18	S.S.Z.1 to S.S.Z.77	}	S.S.Z21 and 22 to France, S.S.Z23 and 24 to U.S.A.
North Sea	North Sea Patrol	N.S.1 to N.S.16	On envelope	N.S.1, 2 and 5 wrecked. N.S.14 to U.S. Forces

* Star marking as shown, e.g. C*12

BRITISH SERVICE AIRCRAFT SERIAL NUMBER ALLOCATIONS 1912-1954

Serial Nos.	Period	Allotment	Remarks
1-200	1912-14	Admiralty	13 and 191 to 198 not allotted. 147-8 cancelled.
201-400	1912-14	R.F.C.	Numbers allotted by Royal Aircraft Factory, Farnborough, Hants.
401-600	1912-14	R.F.C.	Central Flying School, Upavon, aircraft. E.g. 436 Deperdussin.
601-800	1912-14	R.F.C.	Originally reserved for experimental aircraft.
801-1600	1914-15	R.N.A.S.	1417-22 and 1448-9 not allotted. 1424-35 and 1497-508 cancelled.
1601-3000	1915	R.F.C.	2735, 2737, 2929, 2933, 2934, 2973, 2982 and 2984 tranferred to R.N.A.S.
3001-4000	1915	R.N.A.S.	3073-3092 and 3345-3594 reserved for aircraft from the U.S.A.
4001-5000	1915	R.F.C.	4043-4, 4336-7, 4524-6 and 4570-2 transferred to R.N.A.S.
5001-5200	1915	R.F.C.	Nieuport and Morane aircraft purchased in France by G.H.Q., B.E.F.
5201-8000	1915	R.F.C.	5564-5 and 6324-7 transferred to R.N.A.S.
8001-10000	1915-16	R.N.A.S.	8112-7, 8238, 8243, 8424-5, 8427-8 and 9213-32 transferred to R.F.C.
A1-A115	1916	R.F.C.	A1-40 F.E.2D, A41-65 F.E.8, A66-115 R.E.8.
A116-A315	1916	R.F.C.	Morane, Nieuport and S.P.A.D. aircraft purchased in France by G.H.Q., B.E.F. E.g. A208 Nieuport 16, A268 Morane Parasol.
A316-A6600	1916	R.F.C.	A324, A334, A345, A1284-7, A1326-9, A1382-5, A1769-72 and A1790-1 transferred to R.N.A.S. A3021-3 and A5800-99 not allotted.
A6601-A6800	1916	R.F.C.	Morane, Nieuport and S.P.A.D. aircraft purchased in France.
A6801-A9999	1916	R.F.C.	A7043-50 and A8693-9 transferred to R.N.A.S., A8957-62 reserved for Aerial Targets. A9000-99 and A9813-978 re-numbered in 'N' series.
B1-B700	1917	R.F.C.	B381-400 reserved for ex-R.N.A.S. aircraft.
B701-B900	1917	R.F.C.	Rebuilt machines by No. 1 (Southern) A.R.D., Farnborough.
B901-B1500	1917	R.F.C.	B1351-400 ex-R.N.A.S. S.P.A.D. S.7 and Avro 504 aircraft.
B1501-B1700	1917	R.F.C.	Morane, Nieuport and S.P.A.D. aircraft purchased in France.
B1701-B3450	1917	R.F.C.	B1901-50 ex-R.N.A.S. Curtiss J.N.4 trainers.
B3451-B3650	1917	R.F.C.	Nieuport and S.P.A.D. aircraft purchased in France by G.H.Q., B.E.F.
B3651-B4000	1917	R.F.C.	Last fifty numbers reserved for experimental aircraft, e.g. B3996-4000 A.W. Quadraplane and aircraft transferred from Admiralty.
B4001-B4200	1917-18	R.F.C.	Rebuilt machines by No. 2 (Northern) A.R.D., Coal Aston, Sheffield.
B4201-B6730	1917	R.F.C.	B4351-400 cancelled. 25 in B4651-850 range transferred to R.N.A.S.
B6731-B7130	1917	R.F.C.	Aircraft purchased in France by G.H.Q., B.E.F. Numbers over B7000 not taken up. Mostly S.P.A.D. S-7s.
B7131-B7730	1917	R.F.C.	B7131-480 Camel, B7481-580 Pup, B7581-680 D.H.9 and B7681-730 R.E.8.
B7731-B8230	1917-18	R.F.C.	Rebuilt machines by No. 1 (Southern) A.R.D., Farnborough.
B8231-B8830	1917	R.F.C.	B8781-320 re-allotted after cancellation of an order for 50 Avro 504J.
B8831-B9030	1917-18	R.F.C.	Rebuilt machines by No. 3 (Western) A.R.D., Yate, nr. Bristol. Included B8962 Radio Target and B8844 Caudron C.IV.
B9031-B9999	1917-18	R.F.C.	B9431-75 reserved for experimental aircraft. B9911-30 and B9970-89 ex-R.N.A.S. aircraft.
C1-C2300	1917-19	R.F.C./R.A.F.	Canadian-built (mainly Curtiss J.N.4) for R.F.C./R.A.F. (Canada).
C1-C9999	1918	R.F.C.	C1701-50 cancelled. C3481-486, C4277-300, C4541-50 and C8652-60 reserved for experimental aircraft. C7901-8000 re-numbered N7000-7099 in R.N.A.S. range. C9986-9999 not used.
D1-D9999	1918	R.F.C.	D3276-3325 re-numbered N6900-6949, D3836-910 cancelled. D7401-500 not used.
E1-E9999	1918	R.F.C./R.A.F.	R.A.F. allocations from E1601 onwards. Some orders cancelled.
F1-F9999	1918	R.A.F.	Several orders cancelled after the Armistice, 11th November, 1918.
G1-200	1916-19	—	Ministry of Munitions series for captured enemy aircraft.
H1-H9999	1918	R.A.F.	Many orders cancelled from November, 1918, onwards.
J1-J9999	1918-28	R.A.F.	Many orders cancelled 1918-19 in J1-6584 range.
K1000-K9999	1928-36	R.A.F./F.A.A.	Fleet aircraft included from K2774. Some numbers cancelled, e.g. K8005-7 and K9056-175. 52 aircraft re-numbered within the series.
L1000-L9999	1937	R.A.F./F.A.A.	Blocks of numbers omitted for security reasons from L7273 onwards.
M1-M7000	1921-54	R.A.F.	Instructional airframes permanently grounded. 'M' appears as a suffix.

Serial Nos.	Period	Allotment	Remarks
N1-118	1915-18	R.N.A.S.	Experimental seaplanes or ship-board aircraft. Numbers 2, 3, 6, 7, 11-13, 20-25, 33-35, 51-52, 62-63 and 99 not used.
N119-N299	1918-28	R.A.F.	Experimental naval aircraft. Numbers from N256 up, not used.
N300-N499	1916	R.N.A.S.	Development aircraft. N300 only taken up for a Sopwith Baby (Blackburn-built).
N500-N999	1916-18	R.N.A.S.	Experimental landplanes. Series ended at N546. N510 and N513 cancelled. N526-31 handed back to Italy. N519-520 not built.
N1000-N2999	1916-18	R.N.A.S	Production seaplanes. N1720-39 re-numbered B9970-89. N1890-959 not allotted. N1160-79, 1291-9, 1340-59, 1570-9, etc., cancelled.
N3000-N3999	1916-18	R.N.A.S.	French-built aircraft. Series ended at N3400. N3105-69 cancelled.
N4000-N4999	1916-18	R.N.A.S./R.A.F.	Production Flying Boats. R.A.F. from N4601 onwards. Some orders cancelled and some numbers not allotted, e.g. N4050-4059.
N5000-N8999	1916-18	R.N.A.S./R.A.F.	Production landplanes. R.A.F. from N7100 onwards. Several orders cancelled, e.g. N7200-99 and N7300-49 for Camels.
N9000-N9300	1918	R.A.F.	Production seaplanes, mostly Fairey III B/C and Short 184.
N9301-N9999	1918-26	R.A.F.	General naval aircraft. Fleet Air Arm formed as part of R.A.F. in 1923.
N1000-N9999 (Second Series)	1937-38	R.A.F./F.A.A.	Included 400 aircraft from U.S.A. Admiralty gained control of Fleet Air Arm in 1937. 30 Ansons delivered direct to Australia.
P1000-R9999*	1939	R.A.F./F.A.A.	Included 251 from U.S.A. P2045-59 renumbered NZ1201-15.
R1000-R9999*	1939	R.A.F./F.A.A.	Several orders cancelled. Nos. R1810 and R1815 duplicated.
S1000-S1865	1926-30	R.A.F.	Fleet Air Arm and service aircraft equipped to fly over water.
T1000-T9999*	1939	R.A.F./F.A.A.	Included Hudsons from U.S.A. Some transfers to R.A.A.F. A19 series.
V1000-V9999*	1939	R.A.F./F.A.A.	Included Hudsons from U.S.A., and cancellations, e.g. V8920-69.
W1000-W9999*	1939	R.A.F./F.A.A.	Some orders cancelled. Included several batches of impressments.
X1-X25	1918	R.A.F.	Experimental aircraft. Not all were built, e.g. X21-24 were cancelled.
X1000-X9999*	1939-40	R.A.F./F.A.A.	Some 2,000 numbers cancelled. Included batches of impressments.
Z1000-Z9999*	1940	R.A.F./F.A.A.	Purchases from U.S.A. included. Some orders cancelled.
AA100-AZ999	1940	R.A.F./F.A.A.	AA100-AE442 and AP385-AZ999—British contracts with blocks of numbers omitted. AE443-84, AV951-AW183 and AX657-999 impressed aircraft and miscellaneous acquisitions. AE485-AP384 British Direct Purchase in U.S.A. and Canada.
BA100-BZ999	1940-41	R.A.F./F.A.A.	BA100-BV999 with blocks of numbers omitted and several reservations for impressed aircraft. BW100-BZ999 allotted to British Purchasing Commission in U.S.A. and Canada. BW778-827 re-numbered FP475-524.
DA100-DZ999*	1941	R.A.F./F.A.A.	DA and DB not used. DG450-549 reserved for aircraft impressed in India. Included re-numbered Hurricanes in DG and DR range.
EA100-EZ999	1941	R.A.F./F.A.A.	EA not used. EB100-ES999 had blocks of numbers omitted. ET100-EZ999 were American lease-lend.
FA100-FZ999	1941-42	R.A.F./F.A.A.	Lease-lend allocation. FM100-999 reserved for Canadian production.
HA100-HZ999	1942	R.A.F./F.A.A.	HA not used. HB100-HD776 lease-lend. HD777-HZ999 had blocks of numbers omitted. HK807-HL540 and HM486-594 reserved for miscellaneous acquisitions.
JA100-JZ999	1942	R.A.F./F.A.A.	JA100-JR999 had blocks of numbers omitted. JE, JH and JJ series were not used. JS100-468 were Canadian-built and JS469-JZ999 American lease-lend.
KA100-KZ999	1942-43	R.A.F.	KA and KB Canadian-built lease-lend. KD to KP311 U.S.A.-built lease-lend. KP312-KV300 not used. KV-KZ British contracts with blocks of numbers omitted and cancellations, e.g. KV480-893.
LA100-LZ999*	1943	R.A.F./F.A.A.	Included Mohawks taken over in India and batches of impressments.
MA100-MZ999*	1943	R.A.F./F.A.A.	Indian impressments in range MA919-62.
NA100-NZ999*	1943	R.A.F./F.A.A.	The combination NC was used, but the combination NZ was not.
PA100-PZ999*	1943-44	R.A.F./F.A.A.	Several orders cancelled. Included Seafires re-numbered from Spitfires.
RA100-RZ999*	1944	R.A.F./F.A.A.	Several orders cancelled for Spitefuls, Lincolns, Tiger Moths, etc.
SA100-SZ999	1944	R.A.F./F.A.A.	SA-SK cancelled lease-lend allocations.
TA100-TZ999*	1944	R.A.F./F.A.A.	Many orders cancelled, e.g. Horsas allotted TT367-974.
VA100-VZ999*	1945-46	R.A.F./F.A.A.	A number of ex-Luftwaffe aircraft included.
WA100-WZ999	1947-50	R.A.F./F.A.A.	Included aircraft supplied under M.D.A.P.
XA100-	1950-	R.A.F./F.A.A./A.A.C.	Current series. Allocations up to XP (1961).

* Blocks of numbers omitted for security reasons.

AUSTRALIAN TYPE NUMBER SERIES 1920-1954

Type No.	Aircraft Type	Remarks
A1	D.H.9A	First Series 1919
A1	Hawker Demon	Second series 1934
A2	S.E.5A	First series 1919
A2	Supermarine Seagull V	Second series 1929
A3	Avro 504K	First series 1919
A3	C.A.C. Wackett	Second series 1938
A4	D.H.53	First series 1925
A4	Avro Anson I	Second series 1938
A5	Supermarine Southampton	First series 1926
A5	Westland Wapiti I	Nos. 1-8, 1929 order
	Westland Wapiti IIA	Nos. 9-28, 1931 order
	Westland Wapiti IIA	Ex-R.A.F. aircraft, Nos. 29-34
A6	D.H.9	First series 1919
A6	Avro Tutor/Cadet	Ex-R.A.F. and Impressments
A7	D.H.60G/60M/60X	Australian and British-built
A8	D.H.50	One only. First series
A8	Bristol Beaufighter 21	Australian-built Nos. 1-364
A9	Bristol Beaufort	Nos. 1-746 various Marks
A10	Fairey IIID	Originally ANA 1-6
A11	Auster	1-40 Mk. III, 200-201 Mk. VI
A12	Bristol Bulldog	1-8 ordered 1929
A13	Link Trainer	U.K. supplied
A14	Tugar LJW7 Gannet	No. 1 only
A15	Miles Magister	1 for trials in 1938
A16	Lockheed Hudson	1-50 Mk. I. From 51 Mk. IV
A17	D.H.82 Tiger Moth	1-20 U.K., 21-3 and 674-691 impressed, 24-673 and 692 plus Australian/British built
A18	Short Empire	Impressments
A19	Bristol Beaufighter	British-built
A20	C.A.C.3 Wirraway	Nos. 1-757 allotted
A21	D.H.94 Moth Minor	Nos. 1-42 allotted
A22	Fairey Battle	Allocation not known
A23	C.A.C. Woomera	3 of 3 versions
A24	Consolidated Catalina	Lease/Lend
A25	Airspeed Oxford	Many delivered, R.A.F. serials
A26	Short Sunderland III	Nos. 1-9 allotted
A27	Vultee A-31 Vengeance	400 ordered, 34 delivered
A28	Douglas A-20 Boston	Lease/Lend supplies
A29	Curtiss P-40	Lease/Lend
A30	Douglas DC-2	Nos. 1-14, all impressed
A31	D.H.86B	Nos. 1-8, all impressed
A32	Percival Vega Gull	Nos. 1-3, all impressed
A33	D.H.89 Dragon Rapide	Nos. 1-7, all impressed
A34	D.H.84 Dragon	87 built, 11 impressed
A35	Douglas Dolphin	No. 1 only. Impressed
A36	Fairchild 24	Nos. 1-4, all impressed
A37	Miles aircraft types	Nos. 1-6, all impressed
A38	Stinson Reliant	No. 1 only, ex-VH-UXL
A39	Beech 17 series	Nos. 1-3, all impressed
A40	Cessna C.34	No. 1 only, ex-VH-UYG
A41	D.H.83 Fox Moth	Nos. 1-4 only, all impressed
A42	Lockheed Vega	No. 1 only, ex-VH-UVK
A43	D.H.90 Dragonfly	No. 1 only, ex-VH-UXS
A44	Junkers G.31/W.33	Nos. 1-2 only, impressed
A45	Ford 4ATC/5ATE	Nos. 1-2 only, impressed
A46	C.A.C. Boomerang	Nos. 1-250 allotted
A47	N.A. B-25 Mitchell	Lease/Lend deliveries
A48	V.S. Kingfisher	12 at least supplied
A49	Dornier Do24	Impressed ex-Netherlands East Indies, 1942
A50	Ryan STM-2	
A51	Brewster F2A-2 Buffalo	
A52	D.H.98 Mosquito	1-212 F.B.40, 301-327 P.R.41, 601-619 B.16, 1001 F.2, 1002-1012 T.3, 1050-1071 T.43
A53	Bell P-39 Airacobra	Few supplied—Lease/Lend
A54	Waco YQC-6	Loaned by D.C.A.
A55	Lockheed Lightning	Transferred from U.S.A.A.F.
A56	Republic P-43 Lancer	Transferred from U.S.A.A.F.
A57	Gliders (all types)	No. 1 D.H. E.G.2
A58	Supermarine Spitfire	1-300 Mk V, 301 plus Mk VIII
A59	Vega Ventura	Lease/Lend deliveries
A60	Hawker Hurricane	Allocation only
A61	Northrop Delta	One only, loaned by D.C.A.
A62	C.A.C.15	No. 1001 only
A63	Link Ground Trainer	Modified version
A64	V.S. Vigilant	Lease/Lend deliveries
A65	Douglas DC-3 Dakota	Over 100 L/L deliveries
A66	Avro Lancaster	Special delivery
A67	Lockheed Lodestar	Limited L/L deliveries
A68	C.A.C. 17/18 Mustang	1-80 Mk 20, 81-200 Mk 21
A69	Curtiss A-25 Shrike	10 transferred from U.S.A.A.F.
A70	Martin Mariner	12 tranferred from U.S.N.
A71	Noorduyn Norseman	Nos. 1-14 all ex-U.S.A.A.F.
A72	Consolidated Liberator IV	Nos. 1-200 plus, Lease/Lend
A73	Avro Lincoln B.30	Nos. 1-73
A74	Avro York	One only
A75	Percival Proctor	Ex-Royal Navy
A76	Boeing B-29	One only for evaluation
A77	Meteor F.8/T.7	98 delivered
A78	D.H. 100 Vampire F.2	41 British-built
A79	D.H. 100 Vampire	Australian production
A80	Sikorsky S.51	Three ordered in 1951
A81	Bristol Freighter	Acquired for Woomera range
A82	Vickers Viking	Ministry of Supply order
A83	D.H.102 Sea Hornet	Ministry of Supply order
A84	E.E.Co. Canberra	201-248 B.20. Other blocks allotted for T.21, B.22
A85	C.A.C.22 Winjeel	Nos. 364 and 618 prototypes, No. 401 plus production
A86	Hawker P.1081	Project only
A87	Vickers Valetta	Ex-R.A.F.
A88	Winged targets	R.F.D. Winger Target
A89	Lockheed P2V-5	Supplied from U.S.A.
A90	Percival Prince C.1	Nos. 1-3
A91	Bristol Sycamore	Used on H.M.A.C. *Sydney*
A92	Jindivik (Project B)	Pilotless target aircraft to M.o.S. specification
A93	Pika (Project C)	
A94	North American F-86	Australian-built
A95	D.H.C. Beaver	One, No. 201
A96	Convair 340/440	For V.I.P. transport

Royal Air Force Unit Code Letters 1939-1945

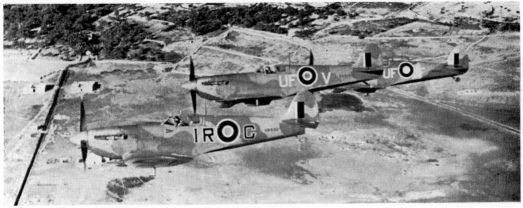

An exception to code letters denoting a unit, was the personal initials used by Wing Leaders, here Wing Commander Ian R. Gleed, D.S.O., D.F.C. is accompanied by Spitfires coded 'UF' which the tables will show to be No. 601 Squadron.

Code	Year(s)	Unit	Code	Year(s)	Unit	Code	Year(s)	Unit	Code	Year(s)	Unit
AA	40-45	75 Sqn.	5A	45	329 Sqn.	CA	44-45	189 Sqn.	DY	39-45	102 Sqn.
AB	43-44	1557 R.A.T.F.	7A	45	614 Sqn.	CE	43	5 L.F.S.	DZ	40-45	151 Sqn.
AC	44-45	138 Sqn.	8A	43-45	298 Sqn.	CF	44-45	625 Sqn.	D4	44-45	620 Sqn.
AD	39	60 Sqn. India	BA	41-45	277 Sqn.	CJ	44-45	203 Sqn.	4D	44-45	74 Sqn.
AD	39-43	11 Sqn.	BB	41-45	27 O.T.U.	CM	44-45	107 O.T.U.	6D	45	631 Sdn.
AD	44-45	251 Sqn.	BD	42-45	43 O.T.U.	CM	45	1333 (T) C.U.	8D	45	220 Sqn.
AE	41-45	402 Sqn.	BE	41-45	8 O.T.U.	CR	44-45	162 Sqn.	EA	39-45	49 Sqn.
AE	45	1409 Flt.	BF	39	14 Sqn.	CT	43-45	52 O.T.U.	EB	39-45	41 Sqn.
AF	40-45	607 Sqn.	BF	42-45	54 O.T.U.	CX	45	14 Sqn.	EC	45	Odiham
AF	40-45	A.F.D.U.	BG	45	660 Sqn.?	C6	44-45	51 Sqn.	ED	41-45	21 O.T.U.
AH	42-45	332 Sqn.	BH	39	215 Sqn.	C7	44-45	1 F. Pool	EE	41-45	404 Sqn.
AJ	43-44	617	BH	40-45	300 Sqn.	C8	43-45	640 Sqn.	EF	39	15 Sqn.
AK	39	213 Sqn.	BK	39	115 Sqn.	6C	45	P.R.D.U.	EF	41-45	232 Sqn.
AK	39-45	213 Sqn.	BJ	40	1680 Flt.	7C	44-45	296 Sqn.	EG	42-45	487 Sqn.
AK	43-45	1674 H.C.U.	BJ	41-44	271 Sqn.	DA	39-44	210 Sqn.	EH	41-45	55 O.T.U.
AL	39	79 Sqn.	BL	39-45	40 Sqn.	DB	42-45	411 Sqn.	EH	45	3 T.E.U.
AL	43-45	429 Sqn.	BL	43-45	1656 H.C.U.	DD	39	45 Sqn.	EJ	43-45	C.C.F.I.S.
AM	42-45	14 O.T.U.	BM	44-45	433 Sqn.	DD	44-45	22 O.T.U.	EK	44-45	1656 H.C.U.
AN	39	13 Sqn.	BN	39-42	240 Sqn.	DE	44-45	61 O.T.U.	EL	42-45	181 Sqn.
AN	42-44	417 Sqn.	BN	44	1401 Flt.	DF	44-45	B.D. Flt.	EM	41-45	207 Sqn.
AP	44-45	130 Sqn.	BP	41-43	457 Sqn.	DG	39	150 Sqn.	EN	45	27 O.T.U.
AP	43	186 Sqn.	BP	44-45	459 Sqn.	DG	42-44	155 Sqn.	EO	42-45	15 O.T.U.
AQ	41-45	276 Sqn.	BQ	39-41	600 Sqn.	DG	42-45	228 Sqn.	EP	40-45	104 Sqn.
AR	41-42	309 Sqn.	BQ	41-44	451 Sqn.	DH	44-45	1664 H.C.U.	EP	45	84 Gp. C.F.
AR	42-43	460 Sqn.	BQ	43-45	550 Sqn.	DJ	39	612 Sqn.	EQ	39	57 Sqn.
AS	42-45	166 Sqn.	BR	43-45	184 Sqn.	DK	45	158 Sqn.	EQ	41-45	408 Sqn.
AT	42-45	60 O.T.U.	BS	39	148 Sqn.	DL	39	54 Sqn.	ER	45	1552 R.A.T.F.
AU	43-45	421 Sqn.	BS	42-45	1651 H.C.U.	DL	40-45	91 Sqn.	ES	44-45	541 Sqn.
AV	41-42	121 Sqn.	BS	44-45	160 Sqn.	DN	42-45	416 Sqn.	ET	44-45	662 Sqn.
AW	39	504 Sqn.	BT	39	113 Sqn.	DP	39	30 Sqn.	EU	42-43	26 O.T.U.
AW	40-45	42 Sqn.	BT	42-45	30 O.T.U.	DP	43-45	193 Sqn.	EV	43-45	180 Sqn.
AX	41-45	413 Sqn.	BU	39-45	214 Sqn.	DQ	41-43	95 Sqn.	EW	39	47 Sqn.
AY	39	110 Sqn.	BW	39	58 Sqn.	DR	45	1555 R.A.T.F.	EW	41-45	307 Sqn.
AY	40-45	17 O.T.U.	BX	40-43	86 Sqn.	DT	40-41	257 Sqn.	EX	43-45	199 Sqn.
AZ	40-45	234 Sqn.	BX	44-45	666 Sqn.	DT	43-45	192 Sqn.	EY	39	233 Sqn.
AZ	43-45	627 Sqn.	BY	42-44	23 O.T.U.	DU	39	70 Sqn.	EY	39-45	78 Sqn.
A2	44-45	514 Sqn.	BY	44-45	59 Sqn.	DU	40-45	312 Sqn.	EY	43-44	80 Sqn.
A3	43-45	1653 H.C.U.	BZ	39	107 Sqn.	DV	43	237 Sqn.	EZ	45	1380 (T) C.U.
A4	43-45	115 Sqn.	BZ	43-45	82 O.T.U.	DV	44-45	129 Sqn.	E7	44-45	570 Sqn.
A5	43-45	3 L.F.S.	B4	43-44	282 Sqn.	DW	39-45	610 Sqn.	3E	44-45	100 Gp. C.F.
2A	45	St. Eval	B9	43	1562 Flt.	DX	40-42	245 Sqn.	4E	44	1687 B.D.T.F.
4A	45	2 Gp. C.F.	7B	43-45	595 Sqn.	DX	41-45	57 Sqn.	8E	44-45	295 Sqn.

Code	Year(s)	Unit	Code	Year(s)	Unit	Code	Year(s)	Unit	Code	Year(s)	Unit
FA	42-45	281 Sqn.	GS	43	83 O.T.U.	IO	42-43	41 O.T.U.	KN	39-45	77 Sqn.
FB	42-45	24 O.T.U.	GT	42-45	156 Sqn.	IP	45	B.C.I.S.	KO	39-41	2 Sqn.
FD	39	114 Sqn.	GU	39	18 Sqn.	IQ	44-45	150 Sqn.	KO	41-45	115 Sqn.
FD	44-45	1695 H.C.U.	GV	39	103 Sqn.	I2	44-45	48 Sqn.	KP	39	226 Sqn.
FE	42-45	56 O.T.U.	GV	42	134 Sqn.	I4	43-45	567 Sqn.	KP	41-45	409 Sqn.
FF	42-45	132 Sqn.	GV	43-45	1652 H.C.U.	I5	45	1381 (T) C.U.	KQ	43-45	13 O.T.U.
FG	44	335 Sqn.	GW	41-45	340 Sqn.	I8	44-45	440 Sqn.	KR	45	61 O.T.U.
FH	42-45	15 O.T.U.	GX	41-43	415 Sqn.	I9	44-45	575 Sqn.	KT	39	32 Sqn.
FH	43	46 Sqn.	GZ	39	611 Sqn.	2I	44-45	443 Sqn.	KU	39-41	47 Sqn.
FH	45	53 Sqn.	GZ	39-45	32 Sqn.	8I	45	A.P.S.	KU	43-45	457 Sqn.
FI	43	279 Sqn.	G2	45	19 Gp. C.F.	9I	44-45	326 Sqn.	KW	39-45	615 Sqn.
FJ	39	37 Sqn.	G5	43-45	297 Sqn.	JA	43-45	1652 H.C.U.	KW	40-42	267 Sqn.
FJ	42-45	261 Sqn.	G7	45	B.C.F.U.	JC	45	11 Gp. C.F.	KW	42-45	425 Sqn.
FJ	43-44	164 Sqn.	G9	44-45	430 Sqn.	JE	39	610 Sqn.	KX	40-43	311 Sqn.
FK	39	209 Sqn.	3G	44-45	14 OT.U.	JF	44-45	3 Sqn.	KX	44-45	529 Sqn.
FK	40-45	219 Sqn.	5G	44-45	190 Sqn.	JG	40-45	17 O.T.U.	KY	44-45	242 Sqn.
FL	42-45	81 Sqn.	6G	44-45	233 Sqn.	JH	41-45	317 Sqn.	KZ	42-45	287 Sqn.
FM	41-45	257 Sqn.	9G	44-45	441 Sqn.	JI	43-45	514 Sqn.	K7	43-45	6 O.T.U.
FN	41-45	331 Sqn.	HA	39-45	218 Sqn.	JJ	44-45	274 Sqn.	2K	43-45	1668 H.C.U.
FQ	42-45	32 O.T.U.	HB	40-43	239 Sqn.	JM	41-45	20 O.T.U.	8K	43-45	571 Sqn.
FS	43-45	148 Sqn.	HC	44-45	512 Sqn.	JN	44-45	75 Sqn.	9K	45	1 T.T.U.
FT	39-45	43 Sqn.	HC	45	241 Sqn.	JO	39	62 Sqn.	LB	39	34 Sqn.
FU	42-45	453 Sqn.	HD	42-45	466 Sqn.	JO	43-45	463 Sqn.	LB	41-45	28 O.T.U.
FV	39	230 Sqn.	HE	39	605 Sqn.	JP	39	21 Sqn.	LD	41-45	250 Sqn.
FV	40-45	13 O.T.U.	HE	39-45	263 Sqn.	JP	43-45	32 O.T.U.	LE	39-41	242 Sqn.
FV	41-42	205 Sqn.	HF	43-45	183 Sqn.	JQ	40-42	2 A.A.C.U.	LE	43-45	630 Sqn.
FX	45	234 Sqn.	HH	42-45	175 Sqn.	JS	41-45	16 O.T.U.	LF	39-41	38 Sqn.
FY	39	4 Sqn.	HJ	39-42	100 Sqn.	JT	41-45	256 Sqn.	LG	39-40	108 Sqn.
FY	39-45	611 Sqn.	HK	42-45	F.L.S.	JU	39	202 Sqn.	LG	45	13 Gp. C.F.
FZ	39	65 Sqn.	HL	39	26 Sqn.	JU	39-45	111 Sqn.	LJ	39	211 Sqn.
F2	44-45	635 Sqn.	HM	42-45	136 Sqn.	JV	40-45	6 Sqn.	LK	39-45	87 Sqn.
F3	44-45	438 Sqn.	HM	44	1677 B.D.T.F.	JW	39	44 Sqn.	LK	43-45	578 Sqn.
8F	43-45	105 O.T.U.	HN	40-45	93 Sqn.	JW	45	A.F.D.U.	LL	44-45	1513 R.A.T.F.
8F	45	1381 (T) C.U.	HP	40-41	247 Sqn.	JX	40 45	1 Sqn.	LN	39-42	99 Sqn.
GA	39	208 Sqn.	HP	45	A.F.D.U.	JZ	42-45	57 O.T.U.	LN	44-45	83 Gp. C.F.
GA	40-45	112 Sqn.	HQ	43-45	56 O.T.U.	J6	44	1521 R.A.T.F.	LO	39-45	602 Sqn.
GA	41-45	16 O.T.U.	HR	40-44	9 O.T.U.	J9	43-45	1668 H.C.U.	LP	42-44	8 O.T.U.
GB	39	166 Sqn.	HS	39-41	37 Sqn.	5J	44-45	126 Sqn.	LQ	41-45	405 Sqn.
GB	39-45	105 Sqn.	HS	41-45	260 Sqn.	9J	44-45	227 Sqn.	LR	39	56 Sqn.
GE	39-43	58 Sqn.	HS	41-45	109 Sqn.	KA	39	9 Sqn.	LR	44-45	1667 H.C.U.
GE	43-45	349 Sqn.	HU	39	220 Sqn.	KB	39	142 Sqn.	LS	39	61 Sqn.
GF	43-45	56 O.T.U.	HU	41-45	406 Sqn.	KB	43-45	1661 H.C.U.	LS	39-45	15 Sqn.
GG	39	151 Sqn.	HV	45	East Kirby	KC	43-45	617 Sqn.	LT	39	7 Sqn.
GG	43-45	1667 H.C.U.	HW	43-45	100 Sqn.	KD	42-45	30 O.T.U.	LT	41-45	22 O.T.U.
GI	43-45	622 Sqn.	HX	41-45	504 Sqn.	KE	40-41	229 Sqn.	LU	39	101 Sqn.
GK	39	80 Sqn.	HX	41-45	61 O.T.U.	KE	41	C.A.M.S.	LU	42-43	M.S.F.U.
GL	40	5 Gp. Pool	HY	39	88 Sqn.	KG	39	502 Sqn.	LV	44-45	57 O.T.U.
GL	41-43	185 Sqn.	H3	44-45	111 O.T.U.	KG	39-42	204 Sqn.	LW	39	607 Sqn.
GL	45	1529 R.A.T.F.	H4	43-45	1653 H.C.U.	KG	41-42	3 O.T.U.	LW	43	318 Sqn.
GM	39	55 Sqn.	H7	44-45	346 Sqn.	KG	45	1380 (T) C.U.	LX	41-42	Sch. of A.C.
GM	41	42 O.T.U.	3H	43-45	80 O.T.U.	KH	41-45	403 Sqn.	LX	42-45	54 O.T.U.
GN	40-45	249 Sqn.	4H	44-45	142 Sqn.	KH	45	11 O.T.U.	LY	39	149 Sqn.
GO	42-45	129 Sqn.	6H	44-45	96 Sqn.	KJ	39	16 Sqn.	LY	40-41	P.D.U.
GO	45	A.F.D.U.	6H	44-45	1688 B.D.T.F.	KJ	40-45	11 O.T.U.	LY	41-43	1 P.R.U.
GP	44-45	1661 H.C.U.	IC	43-44	623 Sqn.	KK	40-45	15 O.T.U.	LZ	39-45	66 Sqn.
GR	39-40	64 Sqn.	IF	44-45	84 O.T.U.	KK	44-45	333 Sqn.	LZ	40-41	1421 Flt.
GR	40-43	301 Sqn.	II	41-42	116 Sqn.	KL	39	269 Sqn.	L5	43-45	297 Sqn.
GR	43-44	1586 S.D.F.	II	44-45	59 O.T.U.	KL	39-41	54 Sqn.	L7	44-45	271 Sqn.
GR	44-45	301 Sqn.	IK	45	B.C.I.S.	KM	39	205 Sqn.	L8	44-45	347 Sqn.
GS	41-42	330 Sqn.	IL	44-45	195 Sqn.	KM	39-45	44 Sqn.	L9	44-45	190 Sqn.

Code	Year(s)	Unit	Code	Year(s)	Unit	Code	Year(s)	Unit	Code	Year(s)	Unit
5L	45	187 Sqn.	NR	39-43	220 Sqn.	PG	39	608 Sqn.	QV	39-45	19 Sqn.
7L	44-45	59 O.T.U.	NS	41-45	52 O.T.U.	PG	44-45	619 Sqn.	QW	45	1516 R.A.T.F.
MA	42-45	161 Sqn.	NS	44-45	201 Sqn.	PH	39-45	12 Sqn.	QX	39	50 Sqn.
MB	39	52 Sqn.	NT	41-45	29 O.T.U.	PJ	39	59 Sqn.	QX	41-43	233 Sqn.
MB	44-45	236 Sqn.	NU	44-45	1382 (T) C.U.	PJ	42-43	130 Sqn.	QX	45	C.C.C. Flt.
MD	42-43	133 Sqn.	NV	39	144 Sqn.	PK	41-45	315 Sqn.	QY	39-45	235 Sqn.
ME	42-45	488 Sqn.	NV	39-45	79 Sqn.	PL	39	609 Sqn.	Q6	45	1384 (T) C.U.
MF	39	108 Sqn.	NW	41	33 Sqn.	PL	39-45	144 Sqn.	4Q	43-45	C.C.F.A.T.U.
MF	43-45	280 Sqn.	NW	43-45	286 Sqn.	PM	39	20 Sqn.	RA	39	100 Sqn.
MF	44-45	F.L.S.	NX	41-45	31 Sqn.	PM	42-45	103 Sqn.	RA	41-45	410 Sqn.
MG	40-45	7 Sqn.	NY	43-45	1665 H.C.U.	PN	39	41 Sqn.	RB	39	66 Sqn.
MH	39-45	51 Sqn.	NZ	40-42	304 Sqn.	PN	41-42	252 Sqn.	RC	44-45	5 L.F.S.
MJ	45	1680 Flt.	N4	44-45	281 Sqn.	PN	41-45	1552 R.A.T.F.	RD	41-45	67 Sqn.
MK	39-41	500 Sqn.	5N	45	38 Gp. C.F.	PO	39	104 Sqn.	RE	45	A.F.D.U.
ML	44-45	132 O.T.U.	9N	44-45	127 Sqn.	PO	39-42	46 Sqn.	RF	39	204 Sqn.
MN	42-45	350 Sqn.	OA	39-45	22 Sqn.	PO	42-45	467 Sqn.	RF	40-44	303 Sqn.
MP	39-45	76 Sqn.	OA	43-45	342 Sqn.	PP	39	203 Sqn.	RF	45	1510 R.A.T.F.
MQ	39-45	226 Sqn.	OB	45	45 Sqn.	PQ	44-45	2 T.E.U.	RG	44-45	208 Sqn.
MR	39	97 Sqn.	OD	39-40	80 Sqn.	PQ	45	206 Sqn.	RH	39-45	88 Sqn.
MR	42-45	245 Sqn.	OD	43-45	56 O.T.U.	PR	39-45	609 Sqn.	RJ	39	46 Sqn.
MS	39	23 Sqn.	OE	39	98 Sqn.	PS	40-45	264 Sqn.	RL	44-45	279 Sqn.
MT	39	105 Sqn.	OE	44-45	661 Sqn.	PT	41-42	62 Sqn.	RM	41-43	26 Sqn.
MT	41-45	122 Sqn.	OF	39-45	97 Sqn.	PT	43-45	420 Sqn.	RN	39-45	72 Sqn.
MU	39-45	60 Sqn.	OG	43-45	1665 H.C.U.	PU	44-45	187 Sqn.	RO	40-45	29 Sqn.
MV	39	600 Sqn.	OH	42	120 Sqn.	PV	41-45	275 Sqn.	RP	43-45	288 Sqn.
MV	42-45	63 O.T.U.	OJ	39-45	149 Sqn.	PW	39	224 Sqn.	RR	39	615 Sqn.
MW	39-42	217 Sqn.	OK	42-45	450 Sqn.	PW	42-45	57 O.T.U.	RR	41-43	407 Sqn.
MY	39	27 Sqn.	OK	44-45	3 G.R.S.	PY	44-45	1527 R.A.T.F.	RS	42-45	157 Sqn.
MY	42-45	278 Sqn.	OL	39-45	83 Sqn.	PZ	40-41	53 Sqn.	RS	42-45	30 Sqn.
M4	44-45	587 Sqn.	OM	39-45	107 Sqn.	PZ	41-43	456 Sqn.	RT	41	114 Sqn.
M5	44-45	128 Sqn.	ON	41-45	124 Sqn.	P3	43-45	692 Sqn.	RU	41-45	414 Sqn.
M6	45	83 Gp. C.F.	OO	39-42	13 Sqn.	P4	43-45	153 Sqn.	RV	43-45	1659 H.C.U.
M7	44-45	41 Gp. C.F.	OO	43-45	1663 H.C.U.	P5	43-45	297 Sqn.	RW	42-45	36 Sqn.
M9	45	1653 Flt.	OP	39	3 Sqn.	P6	43-45	489 Sqn.	RX	39	25 Sqn.
2M	44-45	520 Sqn.	OP	40-45	11 O.T.U.	2P	43-45	644 Sqn.	RX	43-45	456 Sqn.
4M	43-45	695 Sqn.	OQ	43-44	52 O.T.U.	9P	44-45	85 O.T.U.	RY	42-45	313 Sqn.
7M	45	1 P.T.S.	OQ	44-45	172 Sqn.	QA	40-43	224 Sqn.	RZ	41-45	241 Sqn.
9M	44	1690 B.D.T.F.	OQ	44-45	F.L.S.	QB	42-45	424 Sqn.	R2	43-45	P.A.U.
NA	39	1 Sqn.	OR	45	B.C.D.U.	QC	44-45	168 Sqn.	R4	43-45	A.P.S.
NA	43-45	428 Sqn.	OT	42-44	B.D. Flt.	QD	39	42 Sqn.	5R	44-45	33 Sqn.
ND	41-45	236 Sqn.	OU	41-45	485 Sqn.	QD	42-45	304 Sqn.	6R	43-44	41 O.T.U.
NE	39	63 Sqn.	OV	43-45	197 Sqn.	QD	44-45	654 Sqn.	9R	44-45	229 Sqn.
NF	41-45	138 Sqn.	OW	42-45	426 Sqn.	QE	39	12 Sqn.	SA	42-45	486 Sqn.
NG	39-45	604 Sqn.	OX	39	40 Sqn.	QE	45	C.F.E.	SB	42-45	464 Sqn.
NH	39	38 Sqn.	OY	39	11 Sqn.	QF	43-45	N.T.U.	SD	39-45	501 Sqn.
NH	43-45	415 Sqn.	OY	40-43	48 Sqn.	QG	43-45	53 O.T.U.	SE	41	95 Sqn.
NH	44	119 Sqn.	OZ	39	82 Sqn.	QJ	39	616 Sqn.	SE	43-45	431 Sqn.
NI	45	451 Sqn.	OZ	44-45	179 Sqn.	QJ	40-45	92 Sqn.	SF	39	39 Sqn.
NJ	39	207 Sqn.	O1	44-45	2 Sqn.	QL	41-43	413 Sqn.	SF	41-45	137 Sqn.
NJ	43	274 Sqn.	O5	44-45	B.S.D.U.	QM	42-45	254 Sqn.	SG	41-44	9 O.T.U.
NK	41-45	118 Sqn.	O9	45	S.F.C.S.	QN	39	5 Sqn.	SH	39	240 Sqn.
NL	43-45	341 Sqn.	2O	45	84 Gp. C.F.	QN	41-45	28 O.T.U.	SH	39-41	216 Sqn.
NM	39	76 Sqn.	5O	43-45	521 Sqn.	QO	39-44	3 Sqn.	SH	41-45	64 Sqn.
NM	41-43	268 Sqn.	6O	44-45	582 Sqn.	QO	43-44	432 Sqn.	SJ	41-44	21 O.T.U.
NN	40-44	310 Sqn.	PA	42-45	55 O.T.U.	QQ	39	83 Sqn.	SK	42-45	165 Sqn.
NO	39	85 Sqn.	PB	39	10 Sqn.	QQ	43-45	1651 H.C.U.	SL	42-43	13 O.T.U.
NO	41-45	320 Sqn.	PB	42-45	26 O.T.U.	QR	39	223 Sqn.	SM	40-45	305 Sqn.
NP	43-45	158 Sqn.	PD	39	87 Sqn.	QR	39-45	61 Sqn.	SN	40-43	152 Sqn.
NQ	39	43 Sqn.	PD	44-45	303 Sqn.	QS	43-45	620 Sqn.	SO	39-42	145 Sqn.
NQ	43-45	24 Sqn.	PF	42-45	43 O.T.U.	QT	39-44	142 Sqn.	SP	40-43	400 Sqn.

Code	Year(s)	Unit	Code	Year(s)	Unit	Code	Year(s)	Unit	Code	Year(s)	Unit
SQ	39	500 Sqn.	UH	41-45	21 O.T.U.	WG	42-45	26 O.T.U.	YG	39-43	502 Sqn.
SR	39-45	101 Sqn.	UJ	41-45	27 O.T.U.	WH	42-44	330 Sqn.	YH	39-45	21 Sqn.
SS	45	1552 R.A.T.F.	UL	39-41	608 Sqn.	WJ	40-45	17 O.T.U.	YI	43-45	423 Sqn.
ST	41-45	54 O.T.U.	UL	43-45	576 Sqn.	WL	41-43	612 Sqn.	YO	40-45	401 Sqn.
SV	39	218 Sqn.	UM	43-45	626 Sqn.	WM	41-45	68 Sqn.	YP	39-45	23 Sqn.
SV	43-45	1663 H.C.U.	UM	44-45	152 Sqn.	WN	42-45	527 Sqn.	YQ	39	217 Sqn.
SW	40-45	253 Sqn.	UO	40-45	19 O.T.U.	WO	39	604 Sqn.	YQ	39-45	616 Sqn.
SW	43-44	1678 H.C.F.	UO	41-42	154 Sqn.	WP	39-45	90 Sqn.	YS	44-45	271 Sqn.
SY	39	139 Sqn.	UP	42-45	605 Sqn.	WQ	39-45	209 Sqn.	YT	39-45	65 Sqn.
SY	43-45	613 Sqn.	UQ	39-41	211 Sqn.	WR	41-44	248 Sqn.	YW	39	601 Sqn.
SZ	41-45	316 Sqn.	UR	39	84 Sqn.	WS	39-45	9 Sqn.	YW	43-45	1660 H.C.U.
S6	44-45	Gp. C.F.	US	39	28 Sqn.	WT	39	35 Sqn.	YX	39	614 Sqn.
S8	44-45	328 Sqn.	US	39-45	56 Sqn.	WT	39-40	142 Sqn.	YX	41-45	54 O.T.U.
4S	45	R.W.E.	UT	39	51 Sqn.	WV	40-41	18 Sqn.	YY	45	1332 (T) C.U.
5S	43-45	691 Sqn.	UT	43-45	461 Sqn.	WX	41-45	302 Sqn.	YZ	43-45	1651 H.C.U.
9S	45	M.A.E.E.	UU	44-45	61 O.T.U.	WY	44	28 O.T.U.	YZ	45	617 Sqn.
TA	40-45	4 O.T.U.	UV	39	77 Sqn.	WZ	39	19 Sqn.	Y2	44-45	442 Sqn.
TB	44	77 Sqn.	UV	41-43	460 Sqn.	W2	44-45	80 Sqn.	Y3	43-45	518 Sqn.
TB	45	51 Sqn.	UW	43-45	55 O.T.U.	W4	44-45	G.P. Flt.	2Y	43-45	345 Sqn.
TC	44-45	170 Sqn.	UX	39	214 Sqn.	3W	43-45	322 Sqn.	3Y	44-45	577 Sqn.
TD	42-43	126 Sqn.	UX	45	C.F.E.	8W	44-45	612 Sqn.	6Y	44-45	171 Sqn.
TE	39	53 Sqn.	UY	40-45	10 O.T.U.	9W	43-45	296 Sqn.	9Y	44-45	132 O.T.U.
TE	42-43	1401 Flt.	UZ	41-45	306 Sqn.	XA	42-43	489 Sqn.	ZA	39	31 Sqn.
TF	41-45	29 O.T.U.	U3	45	R.W.E.	XB	42-45	224 Sqn.	ZA	39-45	10 Sqn.
TH	42-45	418 Sqn.	U4	44-45	667 Sqn.	XB	44	2 T.E.U.	ZB	43-45	1658 H.C.U.
TJ	41-45	52 O.T.U.	U7	44-45	A.D.L.S. Flt.	XC	43-45	26 Sqn.	ZD	40-45	222 Sqn.
TK	43-45	149 Sqn.	6U	45	415 Sqn.	XD	39-45	139 Sqn.	ZE	39-40	52 Sqn.
TL	40-45	35 Sqn.	9U	43-45	644 Sqn.	XE	42-43	123 Sqn.	ZF	40-45	308 Sqn.
TM	39	111 Sqn.	VA	39-41	113 Sqn.	XF	44-45	19 O.T.U.	ZG	40-45	10 O.T.U.
TM	39-40	111 Sqn.	VA	42-45	125 Sqn.	XG	40-45	16 O.T.U.	ZH	39	501 Sqn.
TM	44-45	504 Sqn.	VC	44-45	655 Sqn.	XH	45	218 Sqn.	ZH	40-45	266 Sqn.
TN	39	33 Sqn.	VE	39-41	110 Sqn.	XJ	40-41	261 Sqn.	ZJ	40-44	96 Sqn.
TN	42-45	30 O.T.U.	VF	39	99 Sqn.	XJ	40-44	13 O.T.U.	ZK	39	24 Sqn.
TO	39	228 Sqn.	VG	39	210 Sqn.	XK	44-45	46 Sqn.	ZK	39-45	25 Sqn.
TO	42-45	61 O.T.U.	VG	43-45	285 Sqn.	XL	45	1335 (T) C.U.	ZL	39	77 Sqn.
TP	39-40	73 Sqn.	VI	43-45	169 Sqn.	XM	42-45	182 Sqn.	ZL	43-45	427 Sqn.
TP	44-45	198 Sqn.	VL	42-43	167 Sqn.	XM	44-45	652 Sqn.	ZM	39	185 Sqn.
TQ	39	102 Sqn.	VN	39-45	50 Sqn.	XN	42-44	22 O.T.U.	ZM	39-43	201 Sqn.
TQ	39-41	202 Sqn.	VO	42-45	98 Sqn.	XO	42-45	57 O.T.U.	ZN	39-45	106 Sqn.
TR	43-44	59 Sqn.	VR	43-44	419 Sqn.	XP	42-45	174 Sqn.	ZO	43-45	196 Sqn
TS	44-45	657 Sqn.	VT	39	216 Sqn.	XQ	39	64 Sqn.	ZP	39-44	74 Sqn.
TT	43-45	1658 H.C.U.	VT	40-44	84 Sqn.	XQ	45	86 Sqn.	ZQ	44-45	A.F.D.U.
TU	42	1 T.T.U.	VT	45	1556 R.A.T.F.	XR	40-42	71 Sqn.	ZR	44-45	1333 (T) C.U.
TV	43-45	1660 H.C.U.	VU	39	36 Sqn.	XS	39	106 Sqn.	ZS	44-45	48 Sqn.
TW	40-45	141 Sqn.	VU	44-45	246 Sqn.	XT	39-45	603 Sqn.	ZT	39	602 Sqn.
TX	40-45	11 O.T.U.	VX	39-43	206 Sqn.	XT	43-45	1657 H.C.U.	ZT	44-45	258 Sqn.
TY	42-45	24 O.T.U.	VY	39-45	85 Sqn.	XU	39	49 Sqn.	ZU	43-45	1664 H.C.U.
5T	44-45	233 Sqn.	VZ	43-45	412 Sqn.	XU	43	7 Sqn.	ZV	41-43	19 O.T.U.
6T	44-45	608 Sqn.	V6	45	615 Sqn.	XV	42-43	2 Sqn.	ZW	39	48 Sqn.
7T	44-45	196 Sqn.	V7	45	192 Sqn.	XY	43	90 Sqn. (C Flt.)	ZX	43-45	145 Sqn.
8T	44-45	298 Sqn.	V8	43-45	570 Sqn.	XY	44-45	186 Sqn.	ZX	43-45	55 O.T.U.
UA	40-42	269 Sqn.	V9	44-45	502 Sqn.	X3	44-45	111 O.T.U.	ZY	42-45	247 Sqn.
UB	41-45	455 Sqn.	2V	44-45	18 Gp. C.F.	X6	44-45	290 Sqn.	ZZ	45	220 Sqn.
UB	43-44	164 Sqn.	4V	44-45	302 F.T.U.	X9	44-45	517 Sqn.	Z2	44-45	437 Sqn.
UB	44-45	63 Sqn.	5V	44-45	439 Sqn.	9X	44	1689 Flt.	Z5	41-45	462 Sqn.
UD	41-42	452 Sqn.	WB	45	B.C.I.S.	YB	39	29 Sqn.	Z9	44-45	519 Sqn.
UF	39-45	601 Sqn.	WC	44-45	309 Sqn.	YB	39-45	17 Sqn.	4D	45	74 Sqn.
UF	43-45	24 O.T.U.	WD	39	206 Sqn.	YD	41-43	255 Sqn.	4Z	44-45	B.C.C.F.
UG	39-41	16 Sqn.	WF	44-45	525 Sqn.	YE	43-45	289 Sqn.	7Z	45	1381 (T) C.U.
UG	43-45	1654 H.C.U.	WG	41-42	128 Sqn.	YF	42-43	280 Sqn.	8Z	43-45	295 Sqn.

R.A.F. SQUADRON AND UNIT BADGES

Squadron badges, or the crest at the centre of the badge, have appeared on aircraft from the 'twenties onwards as illustrations throughout this book show. Here, every R.A.F. Squadron Badge, authorised up to 1955 is presented and additionally, the badges of certain flying units, and for some Commonwealth Air Force Squadrons.

In most cases crests are symbolic of the unit. The Fox, Elephant, Camel and Hind reflect earlier equipment with aircraft of that name in the case of Nos. 12, 27, 45 and 90 Squadrons respectively, and the Puma of No. 99 Squadron recalls Puma-engined D.H.9s. A maple leaf (No. 5) and a Springbok (No. 26) symbolises the association these squadrons had with Canadian and South African forces in the 1914-18 War.

Many crests are symbolic of the squadron's role, a bat almost certainly reflects night-fighter or night-intruder operations; perhaps more subtle is the retriever of No. 276 Squadron, appropriate indeed to an Air-Sea Rescue squadron. Another A.S.R. squadron, No. 283, clearly indicate their wartime role and base with a lifebuoy and a Maltese Cross.

Air Ministry Photographs, Crown Copyright Reserved

XV SQUADRON ROYAL AIR FORCE — AIM SURE

XVI SQUADRON ROYAL AIR FORCE — OPERTA APERTA

XVII SQUADRON ROYAL AIR FORCE — EXCELLERE CONTENDE

18 SQUADRON ROYAL AIR FORCE — ANIMO ET FIDE

SQUADRON ROYAL AIR FORCE — POSSUNT QUIA POSSE VIDENTUR

20 SQUADRON ROYAL AIR FORCE — FACTA NON VERBA

21 SQUADRON ROYAL AIR FORCE — VIRIBUS VINCIMUS

XXII SQUADRON ROYAL AIR FORCE — PREUX ET AUDACIEUX

23 SQUADRON ROYAL AIR FORCE — SEMPER AGGRESSUS

XXIV SQUADRON ROYAL AIR FORCE — IN OMNIA PARATI

XXV SQUADRON ROYAL AIR FORCE — FERIENS TEGO

26 SQUADRON ROYAL AIR FORCE — N WAGTER IN DIE LUG

27 SQUADRON ROYAL AIR FORCE — QUAM CELERRIME AD ASTRA

XXVIII SQUADRON ROYAL AIR FORCE — QUICQUID AGAS AGE

29 SQUADRON ROYAL AIR FORCE — IMPIGER ET ACER

30 SQUADRON ROYAL AIR FORCE — VENTRE A TERRE

205

47 SQUADRON ROYAL AIR FORCE
NILI NOMEN ROBORIS OMEN

48 SQUADRON ROYAL AIR FORCE
FORTE ET FIDELE

49 SQUADRON ROYAL AIR FORCE
CAVE CANEM

50 SQUADRON ROYAL AIR FORCE
FROM DEFENCE TO ATTACK

51 SQUADRON ROYAL AIR FORCE
SWIFT AND SURE

52 SQUADRON ROYAL AIR FORCE
SUDORE QUAM SANGUINE

53 SQUADRON ROYAL AIR FORCE
UNITED IN EFFORT

LIV SQUADRON ROYAL AIR FORCE
AUDAX OMNIA PERPETI

55 SQUADRON ROYAL AIR FORCE
NIL NOS TREMEFACIT

56 SQUADRON ROYAL AIR FORCE
QUID SI COELUM RUAT

LVII SQUADRON ROYAL AIR FORCE
CORPUS NON ANIMUM MUTO

58 SQUADRON ROYAL AIR FORCE
ALIS NOCTURNIS

59 SQUADRON ROYAL AIR FORCE
E UNO DISCE OMNES

60 SQUADRON ROYAL AIR FORCE
PER ARDUA AD AETHERA TENDO

LXI SQUADRON ROYAL AIR FORCE
PER PURUM TONANTES

62 SQUADRON ROYAL AIR FORCE
INSPERATO

79 SQUADRON ROYAL AIR FORCE — NIL NOBIS OBSTARE POTEST

80 SQUADRON ROYAL AIR FORCE — STRIKE TRUE

81 SQUADRON ROYAL AIR FORCE — NON SOLUM NOBIS

82 SQUADRON ROYAL AIR FORCE — SUPER OMNIA UBIQUE

83 SQUADRON ROYAL AIR FORCE — STRIKE TO DEFEND

84 SQUADRON ROYAL AIR FORCE — SCORPIONES PUNGUNT

85 SQUADRON ROYAL AIR FORCE — NOCTU DIUQUE VENAMUR

86 SQUADRON ROYAL AIR FORCE — AD LIBERTATEM VOLAMUS

87 SQUADRON ROYAL AIR FORCE — MAXIMUS ME METUIT

88 SQUADRON ROYAL AIR FORCE — EN GARDE

89 SQUADRON ROYAL AIR FORCE — DEI AUXILIO TELIS MEIS

XC SQUADRON ROYAL AIR FORCE — CELER

91 (NIGERIA) SQUADRON ROYAL AIR FORCE — WE SEEK ALONE

92 (EAST INDIA) SQUADRON ROYAL AIR FORCE — AUT PUGNA AUT MORERE

93 SQUADRON ROYAL AIR FORCE — AD ARMA PARATI

94 SQUADRON ROYAL AIR FORCE — AVENGE

209

CXI SQUADRON ROYAL AIR FORCE
AD STANTES

112 SQUADRON ROYAL AIR FORCE
SWIFT IN DESTRUCTION

113 SQUADRON ROYAL AIR FORCE
VELOX ET VINDEX

114 SQUADRON ROYAL AIR FORCE
WITH SPEED I STRIKE

115 SQUADRON ROYAL AIR FORCE
DESPITE THE ELEMENTS

116 SQUADRON ROYAL AIR FORCE
PRECISION IN DEFENCE

117 SQUADRON ROYAL AIR FORCE
IT SHALL BE DONE

118 SQUADRON ROYAL AIR FORCE
OCCIDO REDEOQUE

119 SQUADRON ROYAL AIR FORCE
BY NIGHT BY DAY

120 SQUADRON ROYAL AIR FORCE
ENDURANCE

121 (EAGLE) SQUADRON ROYAL AIR FORCE
FOR LIBERTY

122 (BOMBAY) SQUADRON ROYAL AIR FORCE
VICTURI VOLAMUS

123 (EAST INDIA) SQUADRON ROYAL AIR FORCE
SWIFT TO STRIKE

124 (BARODA) SQUADRON ROYAL AIR FORCE
DANGER IS OUR OPPORTUNITY

125 (NEWFOUNDLAND) SQUADRON ROYAL AIR FORCE
NUNQUAM DOMANDI

126 SQUADRON ROYAL AIR FORCE
FOREMOST IN ATTACK

SQUADRON 143 ROYAL AIR FORCE — VINCERE EST VIVERE

SQUADRON 144 ROYAL AIR FORCE — WHO SHALL STOP US

SQUADRON 145 ROYAL AIR FORCE — DIU NOCTUQUE PUGNAMUS

SQUADRON 146 ROYAL AIR FORCE — PERCUTIT INSIDIANS PARDUS

SQUADRON 147 ROYAL AIR FORCE — ASSIDUE PORTAMUS

SQUADRON 148 ROYAL AIR FORCE — TRUSTY

SQUADRON 149 ROYAL AIR FORCE — FORTIS NOCTE

SQUADRON 150 ROYAL AIR FORCE — ΑΙΕΙ ΦΘΑΝΟΜΕΝ

SQUADRON 151 ROYAL AIR FORCE — FOY POUR DEVOIR

(HYDERABAD) SQUADRON 152 ROYAL AIR FORCE — FAITHFUL ALLY

SQUADRON 153 ROYAL AIR FORCE — NOCTIVIDUS

SQUADRON 154 ROYAL AIR FORCE — HIS MODIS AD VICTORIAM

SQUADRON 155 ROYAL AIR FORCE — ETERNAL VIGILANCE

SQUADRON 156 ROYAL AIR FORCE — WE LIGHT THE WAY

SQUADRON 157 ROYAL AIR FORCE — OUR CANNON SPEAK OUR THOUGHT

SQUADRON 158 ROYAL AIR FORCE — STRENGTH IN UNITY

159 SQUADRON ROYAL AIR FORCE — QUO NON QUANDO NON

160 SQUADRON ROYAL AIR FORCE — API SOYA PARAGASAMU

161 SQUADRON ROYAL AIR FORCE — LIBERATE

162 SQUADRON ROYAL AIR FORCE — ONE TIME ONE PURPOSE

164 (ARGENTINE BRITISH) SQUADRON ROYAL AIR FORCE — FIRMES VOLAMOS

165 (CEYLON) SQUADRON ROYAL AIR FORCE — INFENSA VIRTUTI INVIDIA

167 SQUADRON ROYAL AIR FORCE — UBIQUE SINE MORA

168 SQUADRON ROYAL AIR FORCE — RERUM COGNOSCERE CAUSA

169 SQUADRON ROYAL AIR FORCE — HUNT AND DESTROY

170 SQUADRON ROYAL AIR FORCE — VIDERE NON VIDERI

171 SQUADRON ROYAL AIR FORCE — PER DOLUM DEFENDIMUS

172 SQUADRON ROYAL AIR FORCE — INSIDIANTIBUS INSIDIAMUR

174 (MAURITIUS) SQUADRON ROYAL AIR FORCE — ATTACK

175 SQUADRON ROYAL AIR FORCE — STOP AT NOTHING

176 SQUADRON ROYAL AIR FORCE — NOCTE CUSTODIMUS

177 SQUADRON ROYAL AIR FORCE — SILENTER IN MEDIAS RES

200 SQUADRON ROYAL AIR FORCE — IN LOCO PARENTIS

201 SQUADRON ROYAL AIR FORCE — HIC ET UBIQUE

202 SQUADRON ROYAL AIR FORCE — SEMPER VIGILATE

CCIII FLYING BOAT SQUADRON ROYAL AIR FORCE — OCCIDENS ORIENSQUE

204 SQUADRON ROYAL AIR FORCE — PRÆDAM MARI QUÆRO

205 SQUADRON ROYAL AIR FORCE — PERTAMA di-MALAYA

206 SQUADRON ROYAL AIR FORCE — NIHIL NOS EFFUGIT

CCVII SQUADRON ROYAL AIR FORCE — SEMPER PARATUS

208 SQUADRON ROYAL AIR FORCE — VIGILANT

209 SQUADRON ROYAL AIR FORCE — MIGHT AND MAIN

210 SQUADRON ROYAL AIR FORCE — YN Y NWYFRE YN HEDFAN

211 SQUADRON ROYAL AIR FORCE — TOUJOURS A PROPOS

212 SQUADRON ROYAL AIR FORCE — A MARI AD ASTRA

213 SQUADRON ROYAL AIR FORCE — IRRITATUS LACESSIT CRABRO

214 SQUADRON ROYAL AIR FORCE — ULTOR IN UMBRIS

CCXV SQUADRON ROYAL AIR FORCE — SURGITE NOX ADEST

234 SQUADRON ROYAL AIR FORCE — IGNEM MORTEMQUE DESPUIMUS

235 SQUADRON ROYAL AIR FORCE — JACULAMUR HUMI

236 SQUADRON ROYAL AIR FORCE — SPECULATI NUNTIATE

237 (RHODESIA) SQUADRON ROYAL AIR FORCE — PRIMUM AGMEN IN CÆLO

238 SQUADRON ROYAL AIR FORCE — AD FINEM

239 SQUADRON ROYAL AIR FORCE — EXPLORAMUS

240 SQUADRON ROYAL AIR FORCE — SJO-VORDUR LOPT-VORDUR

241 SQUADRON ROYAL AIR FORCE — FIND AND FOREWARN

242 (CANADIAN) SQUADRON ROYAL AIR FORCE — TOUJOURS PRET

243 SQUADRON ROYAL AIR FORCE — SWIFT IN PURSUIT

245 SQUADRON ROYAL AIR FORCE — FUGO NON FUGIO

247 (CHINA-BRITISH) SQUADRON ROYAL AIR FORCE — RISE FROM THE EAST

248 SQUADRON ROYAL AIR FORCE — IL FAUT EN FINIR

249 (GOLD COAST) SQUADRON ROYAL AIR FORCE — PUGNIS ET CALCIBUS

250 (SUDAN) SQUADRON ROYAL AIR FORCE — CLOSE TO THE SUN

251 SQUADRON ROYAL AIR FORCE — HOWEVER WIND BLOWS

SQUADRON 271 ROYAL AIR FORCE
DEATH AND LIFE

SQUADRON 272 ROYAL AIR FORCE
ON ON

SQUADRON 274 ROYAL AIR FORCE
SUPERO

SQUADRON 275 ROYAL AIR FORCE
NON INTERIBUNT

SQUADRON 276 ROYAL AIR FORCE
RETRIEVE

SQUADRON 277 ROYAL AIR FORCE
QUÆRENDO SERVAMUS

SQUADRON 278 ROYAL AIR FORCE
EX MARE AD REFERENDUM

SQUADRON 279 ROYAL AIR FORCE
TO SEE AND BE SEEN

SQUADRON 280 ROYAL AIR FORCE
WE SHALL BE THERE

SQUADRON 281 ROYAL AIR FORCE
VOLAMUS SERVATURI

SQUADRON 283 ROYAL AIR FORCE
ATTENDE ET VIGILA

SQUADRON 284 ROYAL AIR FORCE
FROM THE DEEP

SQUADRON 285 ROYAL AIR FORCE
RESPICE FINEM

SQUADRON 286 ROYAL AIR FORCE
PRESIDIA NOSTRA EXERCEMUS

SQUADRON 287 ROYAL AIR FORCE
C'EST EN FORGEANT

SQUADRON 288 ROYAL AIR FORCE
HONOUR THROUGH DEEDS

220

349 (BELGIAN) SQUADRON ROYAL AIR FORCE — STRIKE HARD STRIKE HOME

350 (BELGIAN) SQUADRON ROYAL AIR FORCE — BELGAE GALLORUM FORTISSIMI

353 SQUADRON ROYAL AIR FORCE — FEAR NAUGHT IN UNITY

355 SQUADRON ROYAL AIR FORCE — LIBERAMUS PER CAERULA

356 SQUADRON ROYAL AIR FORCE — WE BRING FREEDOM AND ASSISTANCE

357 SQUADRON ROYAL AIR FORCE — MORTEM HOSTIBUS

358 SQUADRON ROYAL AIR FORCE — ALERE FLAMMAM

401 SQUADRON ROYAL CANADIAN AIR FORCE — MORS CELERRIMA HOSTIBUS

404 SQUADRON ROYAL CANADIAN AIR FORCE — READY TO FIGHT

407 SQUADRON ROYAL CANADIAN AIR FORCE — TO HOLD ON HIGH

409 SQUADRON ROYAL CANADIAN AIR FORCE — MEDIA NOX MERIDIES NOSTER

412 SQUADRON ROYAL CANADIAN AIR FORCE — PROMPTUS AD VINDICTAM

413 SQUADRON ROYAL CANADIAN AIR FORCE — AD VIGILAMUS UNDIS

415 SQUADRON ROYAL CANADIAN AIR FORCE — AD METAM

421 SQUADRON ROYAL CANADIAN AIR FORCE — BELLICUM CECINERE

422 SQUADRON ROYAL CANADIAN AIR FORCE — THIS ARM SHALL DO IT

423 SQUADRON ROYAL CANADIAN AIR FORCE QUÆRIMUS ET PETIMUS

426 SQUADRON ROYAL CANADIAN AIR FORCE ON WINGS OF FIRE

435 SQUADRON ROYAL CANADIAN AIR FORCE CERTI PROVEHENDI

436 SQUADRON ROYAL CANADIAN AIR FORCE ONUS PORTAMUS

438 SQUADRON ROYAL CANADIAN AIR FORCE GOING DOWN

450 SQUADRON ROYAL AUSTRALIAN AIR FORCE HARASS

453 SQUADRON ROYAL AUSTRALIAN AIR FORCE READY TO STRIKE

455 SQUADRON ROYAL AUSTRALIAN AIR FORCE STRIKE AND STRIKE AGAIN

460 SQUADRON ROYAL AUSTRALIAN AIR FORCE STRIKE AND RETURN

461 SQUADRON ROYAL AUSTRALIAN AIR FORCE THEY SHALL NOT PASS UNSEEN

463 SQUADRON ROYAL AUSTRALIAN AIR FORCE PRESS ON REGARDLESS

464 SQUADRON ROYAL AUSTRALIAN AIR FORCE AEQUO ANIMO

500 SQUADRON ROYAL AIR FORCE QUO FATA VOCENT

501 COUNTY of GLOUCESTER SQUADRON AUXILIARY AIR FORCE NIL TIME

502 ULSTER ~ SQUADRON AUXILIARY AIR FORCE NIHIL TIMEO

504 COUNTY of NOTTINGHAM SQUADRON AUXILIARY AIR FORCE VINDICAT IN VENTIS

223

511 SQUADRON ROYAL AIR FORCE — SURELY AND QUICKLY

512 SQUADRON ROYAL AIR FORCE — PEGASUS MILITANS

514 SQUADRON ROYAL AIR FORCE — NIL OBSTARE POTEST

515 SQUADRON ROYAL AIR FORCE — CELERITER FERITE UT HOSTES NECETIS

517 SQUADRON ROYAL AIR FORCE — NON NOBIS LABORAMUS

518 SQUADRON ROYAL AIR FORCE — THA AN TUCHAIR AGAINNE

519 SQUADRON ROYAL AIR FORCE — UNDAUNTED BY WEATHER

520 SQUADRON ROYAL AIR FORCE — TOMORROW'S WEATHER TODAY

525 SQUADRON ROYAL AIR FORCE — VINCIENDO VINCIMUS

527 SQUADRON ROYAL AIR FORCE — SILENTLY WE SERVE

540 SQUADRON ROYAL AIR FORCE — SINE QUA NON

541 SQUADRON ROYAL AIR FORCE — ALONE ABOVE ALL

544 SQUADRON ROYAL AIR FORCE — QUAERO

547 SQUADRON ROYAL AIR FORCE — CELER AD CAEDENDUM

570 SQUADRON ROYAL AIR FORCE — IMPETUM DEDUCIMUS

575 SQUADRON ROYAL AIR FORCE — THE AIR IS OUR PATH

657 SQUADRON ROYAL AIR FORCE
PER TERRAS PERQUE CAELUM

658 SQUADRON ROYAL AIR FORCE
VIDEMUS DELEMUS

659 SQUADRON ROYAL AIR FORCE
QUOVIS PER ARDUA

661 SQUADRON ROYAL AUXILIARY AIR FORCE
DESIGNO OCULIS AD CAEDEM

662 SQUADRON ROYAL AIR FORCE
OLETHRION OMMA

663 SQUADRON ROYAL AUXILIARY AIR FORCE
WE FLY FOR THE GUNS

664 SQUADRON ROYAL AUXILIARY AIR FORCE
VAE VISO

666 SCOTTISH SQUADRON ROYAL AUXILIARY AIR FORCE
SPECULATUM ASCENDIMUS

683 SQUADRON ROYAL AIR FORCE
NIHIL NOS LATET

684 SQUADRON ROYAL AIR FORCE
INVISUS VIDENS

691 SQUADRON ROYAL AIR FORCE
VOLAMUS UT SERVIAMUS

69 SQUADRON ROYAL AIR FORCE
POLUS DUM SIDERA PASCET

695 SQUADRON ROYAL AIR FORCE
WE EXERCISE THEIR ARMS

FIGHTER COMMAND COMMUNICATION SQUADRON ROYAL AIR FORCE
EVERYWHERE

MIDDLE EAST COMMUNICATION SQUADRON ROYAL AIR FORCE
WE TRAVEL THE HORIZONS

84 GROUP COMMUNICATION SQUADRON ROYAL AIR FORCE
IN NOBIS VINCULUM

Lions and Tigers: Equipment changes but crests remain the same. Here to prove this point in 1958 is the lion of No. 263 Squadron and the tiger of No. 74 Squadron on Hunter F.6 aircraft XE584 and XK136 respectively—and today (1961) the same tiger face adorns Britain's latest fighter—the Lightning.

Period	Uppersurface Finish	Undersurface Finish	Roundel Type 1.	Roundel Type 2.	Roundel Type 3.	Sqn. Code Colour	Other Features
Mar. '39-July '40	Shading in dark green and dark brown	Port side: Black Starboard side: Grey	B	Nil	B	Grey	Nil
July-Dec. 1940 (non-operational)	Shading in dark green and dark brown	Port side: Black Starboard side: Sky	B	Nil	A1	Grey	Fin stripes in red, white and blue
July-Dec. 1940 (operational)	Shading in dark green and dark brown	Light blue or Sky Type S	B	A	A1	Grey	Fin stripes in red, white and blue
Dec. '40-Sep. '41 (non-operational)	Shadow shading or M.A.P. Pattern No. 1 in dark green and dark brown	Port side: Black Starboard side: Sky	B	A1 / A	A1	Grey	Fuselage band and spinner in sky. Fin flash 24 in. × 27 in.
Dec. '40- Sep. '41 (operational)	Shadow shading or M.A.P. Pattern No. 1 in dark green and dark brown	Sky Type S only as from dawn 22nd April, 1941.	B	A	A1	Grey	Fuselage band and spinner in sky. Fin flash 24 in. × 27 in.
Sep. '41-June '42 (all day fighters)	M.A.P. Pattern No. 1 in dark green and ocean grey	Medium Sea Grey	B	A	A1	Dull Red	As above with yellow line along wings
June '42-Sep. '45	Ditto	Ditto	B	C	C1	Grey Sky or Dull Red	Ditto (Yellow line omitted from 1944).

Note—Roundel. 1 = Uppersurface. 2 = Undersurface. 3 = Fuselage Side.

FIGHTER SQUADRONS IN THE BATTLE OF BRITAIN

Sqn.	Equipment	Base	Code	Sqn.	Euipment	Base	Code
1	Hurricanes	Northolt	JX	222	Spitfires	Kirton-in-Lindsey	ZD
3	Hurricanes	Wick	QO	229	Hurricanes	Wittering	KE
17	Hurricanes	Debden	YB	232	Hurricanes	(2 flights) Turnhouse	EF
19	Spitfires	Duxford	QV			(1 flight) Sumburgh	EF
23	Blenheims*	Colly Weston	YP	234	Spitfires	St. Eval	AZ
25	Blenheims*	Martlesham	ZK	238	Hurricanes	Middle Wallop	—
29	Blenheims*	Digby	RO	242	Hurricanes	Coltishall	LE
32	Hurricanes	Biggin Hill	GZ	245	Hurricanes	Aldergrove	DX
41	Spitfires	Hornchurch	EB	247	Gladiators	Roborough	HP
43	Hurricanes	Tangmere	FT			(1 flight only)	
46	Hurricanes	Digby	PO	249	Hurricanes	Church Fenton	GN
54	Spitfires	Hornchurch	KL	253	Hurricanes	Turnhouse	SW
56	Hurricanes	Rochford	US	257	Hurricanes	Northolt	DT
64	Spitfires	Kenley	SH	264	Defiants*	('A' Flight) Ringway	PS
65	Spitfires	Hornchurch	YT	266	Spitfires	Wittering	ZH
66	Spitfires	Coltishall	LZ	501	Hurricanes	Gravesend	SD
72	Spitfires	Acklington	RN	504	Hurricanes	Castletown	HX
73	Hurricanes*	Church Fenton	TP	600	Blenheims*	Manston	ZO
74	Spitfires	Hornchurch	ZP	601	Hurricanes	Tangmere	UF
79	Spitfires	Acklington	NV	603	Spitfires	('A' Flight) Dyce	XT
85	Hurricanes	Martlesham	VY			('B' Flight) Montrose	XT
87	Hurricanes	Exeter	LK	604	Blenheims*	Middle Wallop	NG
92	Spitfires	Pembrey	QJ	605	Hurricanes	Drem	UP
111	Hurricanes	Croydon	JU	607	Hurricanes	Usworth	AF
141	Defiants*	Prestwick	TW	609	Spitfires	Middle Wallop	PR
145	Hurricanes	Westhampnett	SO	610	Spitfires	Biggin Hill	DW
151	Hurricanes	North Weald	DZ	611	Spitfires	Digby	FY
152	Spitfires	Warmwell	SN	615	Hurricanes	Kenley	KW
213	Hurricanes*	Exeter	AK	616	Spitfires	Leconfield	YQ
219	Blenheims*	Catterick	FK				

* Night flying units in night fighter camouflage by Oct. '40, all others in standard day finish.

The Future of Aircraft Markings

Markings of today. Emergency tools and first-aid kit stowage are clearly marked. Close by is the ejector seat warning.
The badge is of No. 9 Squadron. The two silver stars indicate an Air Vice-Marshal, and the red flash R.A.F. Station Binbrook.
The Union Jack is for a Royal occasion, the visit of H.M. the Queen and H.R.H. The Duke of Edinburgh to Nigeria in 1956.

Speculation on the future of aircraft markings is perhaps a fitting end to a work that has traced service aircraft markings from their inception. It is also the only part of this book not based on fact.

In the general trend towards 'press-button warfare' the pilotless missile for both defence and attack will undoubtedly replace the fighter and bomber. National identity markings would no longer be necessary as speeds would be too great to permit observation. Camouflage too, for the same reason would be unnecessary in flight and in the matter of concealment on the ground, it is possible that with the strategic concepts of atomic warfare, such tactical considerations would be out of place. Far better a dispersed launching site be the target of an atomic missile than a great metropolis. General finish would probably be conditioned by anti-friction considerations, a graphite finish thereby being a possibility.

Such weapons, unmanned and expendable would have the status of ammunition and it is unlikely handling crews would be sufficiently moved to apply any insignia. Nevertheless, they will be costly items of ammunition and no doubt identified by serial number. Initially it would seem logical that as far as the R.A.F. and U.S.A.F. are concerned, they would be numbered in the current series for aircraft. Warning markings might well be stencilled on, although a prosaic HANDLE WITH CARE would appear to be a gross understatement for a missile with an atomic warhead!

Guided weapons used for practice would probably be conspicuously coloured and for missiles where speeds would not be so great as to preclude a visual observation, two contrasting colours might well be used, to facilitate observation of any rotation in flight. For this very reason, German V2 rockets were painted in portions of black and white or red and yellow. Since practices would most likely be carried out over water, coloured dyes would perhaps be carried, to stain the water and so allow the point of fall it to be assessed. A case of an aircraft making its own marking! Another German idea.

There will of course be piloted aircraft for some time to come. Man has not yet found the means whereby his body may be scanned, transmitted electronically and re-formed at a receiving end—and even if he did, it might well be found that resuscitation after reformation was the prerogative of higher hands than his. Transport by aircraft is still the answer to the speedy conveyance of human beings.

The configuration of the D.H. Comet may be taken as a pattern for many years yet, a large streamlined form, lending itself to the marking of cheat lines, but with general markings of roundels and serials varying little from the lumbering Vickers Vernon of thirty years ago. Helicopters will be the short-range transports and mainly the concern of the Army for the rapid deployment of troops and weapons which will no longer be restricted by road blocks or rivers. In such a support role, the present scheme for aircraft of the Army Air Corps, dark brown and dark green overall, would appear to be the most appropriate scheme.

For the immediate future, indications are that the type of markings will remain much the same but that their positions will alter. The swept-back wings of the Hunter have conditioned the marking of the serial under the wings from the form WP213 to the two prefix letters having to be placed above the number in order that it might fit in at a reasonable size for low-flying identification. The Javelin with its delta wing form has caused the replacing of the serial at the rear of the fuselage—standard practice for forty years—to the side of the engine nacelle. This new configuration has also caused the national marking to be placed well forward on the protruding nose. In the U.S.A.F. this is already a common practice; no doubt the Soviet Air Force will soon follow suit.

One important factor does not seem to have been considered, that of a common marking for the North Atlantic Treaty Organisation countries. With twelve national air forces (two of the fourteen NATO countries have no aircraft) under an integrated command, some conspicuous common marking is surely desirable and might well be one of the markings of the future. It would certainly show solidarity. A replacement of national markings would not necessarily be entailed, but an additional marking similar to the Allied Expeditionary Air Forces black and white stripes used on D-Day is suggested.

Whatever markings come in the future, let us hope there will be plenty of aircraft with roundels of red, white and blue in the skies—even though they will be flying too fast to be observed. With our close affinities to friends across the Atlantic we shall surely be secure provided they are accompanied by others, bearing stars of white upon a circle of blue.

AIRCRAFT MARKINGS FOR BRITISH STANDARD DOPING SCHEMES 1914-1918

Aircraft Marking	Doping Scheme	Aircraft Marking	Doping Scheme
A.A.	Standard Collar Co. 'Armoid' A	E.B.	British Emaillite 'B'
B.*	Clarkes 'Britannia' Nitro-Dope	E.C.	British Emaillite 'C' (4 coats)
B.B.	Clarkes 'Britannia' B	E.C.2	British Emaillite 'C' (3 coats)
C.A.	Cellon Ltd. 'A'	E.C.2‡	British Emaillite Nitro-Dope (3 coats)
C.B.	Cellon Ltd. 'B'	N.A.	Siebe, Gorman & Co. 'Novellon' 'A'
C.C.	Cellon Ltd. 'C'	N.D.	Siebe, Gorman & Co. 'Novellon' 'D'
C.D.	Cellon Ltd. 'D'	R.A.	Royal Aircraft Factory 'A'
C.†	Cellon Ltd. Nitro-Dope	T.A.	British Aeroplane Varnish Co. 'Titanine' A
E.A.	British Emaillite 'A'	T.D.	British Aeroplane Varnish Co. 'Titanine' (Nitro) D

Notes.—Letters in black 1-in. to 2-in. characters on doped surfaces: * marked in black; † marked in red; ‡ marked in blue.

Dopes were altered several times owing to a shortage of certain solvents, necessitating a change in composition.

Nitro-dopes were mainly used from August, 1917, to February, 1918, due to a failure in the supply of cellulose acetate, for aircraft on home service or where danger from incendiary bullets did not arise, hence the additional coloured annotation.

Index of Aircraft Types

AMERICAN
Pages

Beech
C-45 Expeditor — 126–7
Bell
P-39 Airacobra — 101, 104
Boeing
B-17 Fortress — 106, 137, 143–5
B-29 — 138–140
B-29 (Washington) — 164, 167
B-50A — 179
F4F-4 — 90
KC-97 — 175
Brewster
F2A Buffalo — 123
SB2A Bermuda — 127
Cessna
L-19A Bird Dog — 179
UC-78 Brasshat — 146
Chance-Vought
F4U Corsair — 127
F7U-1 Cutlass — 175
Convair
B-24 Liberator — 123, 137, 141, 143–5, 180
PBY-5 Catalina — 110–1
Curtiss
C-46 Commando — 146
H-Boats — 36–8, 54
J.N.3/4 — 28–30, 41, 53
P-36 Mohawk — 124
P-40A-C Tomahawk — 114, 133
P-40D-K Kittyhawk — 104, 119–20
P-40L-N Warhawk — 129, 158
SO3C Seamew — 127
Douglas
A-20 Boston — 107, 120 145–7
A-26 Havoc — 101
AD-4 Skyraider — 173
C-47 Dakota — 122–4, 146, 191
C-54 Skymaster — 190
SBD Dauntless — 104, 127, 131
Fairchild
C-119 Packet — 190
PT-26 Cornell — 124, 130–1, 134
Great Lakes
TG-2 — 91

Grumman
F4F Martlet (see Wildcat)
F4F Wildcat — 125–7
F6F Hellcat — 127
F9F Panther — 175
TBF/TBM Avenger — 127, 174
Hiller
HTE-2 — 173
Lockheed
14 — 191
Hudson — 95, 109, 111, 128
Lodestar — 103
PV Ventura — 107
P-38 Lightning — 138, 143–6
P-80 Shooting Star — 178
Martin
A-22 Maryland — 103, 120
A-30 Baltimore — 120
B-26 Marauder — 5, 120, 122, 138, 144–5, 147
PBM-3 Mariner — 142
North American
AT-6 Harvard — 112–3, 130
B-25 Mitchell — 107, 138
F-86 Sabre — 172, 176, 191
P-51 Mustang — 115, 138, 146, 165
SNJ Texan — 150
Piper
L-4 — 146
Republic
P-47 Thunderbolt — 123, 138, 146, 181
F-84 Thunderjet — 175, 182
Sikorsky
S-51 — 175
Stinson
AT-19 Reliant — 127
Thomas Morse
Scout — 54
Vought-Sikorsky
SB2U-2 Chesapeake — 127
Vultee
A-31 Vengeance — 124
L-1 Vigilant — 116
Waco
CG-4A Hadrian — 124

BRITISH AND BRITISH COMMONWEALTH

Airspeed
Horsa — 96, 115
Oxford — 112–3
Armstrong Whitworth
Albemarle — 115
Atlanta — 131
Atlas — 72
F.K. series — 24, 30, 56
Siskin — 68
Whitley — 107, 111
Auster Aircraft
Auster — 115–6, 169–71, 175, 190
Avro
504 series — 25, 28, 31–3, 39 76
707 series — 169
Anson — 81, 87, 103, 109, 110, 171
Lancaster — 107–8, 164
Lancastrian — 167
Lincoln — 164, 169
Manchester — 108
Rota — 77
Shackleton — 166
Tutor — 76–7
York — 167
Blackburn
Baffin, Dart — 80
Iris, Perth — 81
Ripon — 80
Roc — 127
Shark — 80
Skua — 127
Boulton Paul
Defiant — 100
Overstrand, Sidestrand — 75
Bristol
Beaufighter — 101
Beaufort — 111, 128
Blenheim — 86, 94, 101, 105–7, 133
Bombay — 84, 120
Brigand — 171
Bulldog — 52, 68–70
Fighter — 21, 41, 46, 65, 71
Monoplane — 15, 46
Scout — 9, 13

C.A.C.
Wirraway — 130
De Havilland
2 — 13–14
4 — 26–7, 55
5 — 15–16, 56, 192
6 — 28–31
9 — 25–7, 33
9A — 27, 66, 71
10 — 27, 65
Chipmunk — 166–8, 172
Dominie — 146, 193
Hornet — 165, 186
Mosquito — 101, 107, 109, 120, 158, 173
Moths (Gipsy, Genet, etc.) — 76–7
Queen Bee — 80
Sea Fury, Sea Venom — 124
Tiger Moth — 77, 112–3, 124, 128, 130–1
Vampire — 165–7, 171, 181
Venom — 187
English Electric
Canberra — 164, 230
Fairey
1914-18 Seaplanes — 37
IIIF — 72–3, 80
Albacore — 125, 127
Barracuda — 127
Battle — 82–3, 105–6
Fawn — 72
Firefly — 127, 176, 190
Flycatcher — 67, 72
Fox — 79
Fulmar — 127
Gannet — 176
Gordon — 72–3
Hamble Baby — 36
Hendon — 75
Swordfish — 81, 104, 126–7
Fleet
Types 7 and 16 — 88–9
General Aircraft
Hotspur — 114
Gloster
Gamecock, Gauntlet — 68–9
Gladiator — 69, 98–9, 120, 127, 133
Grebe — 68

Javelin 101, 164–7, 176
Meteor 101, 164–7, 176, 188, 190
Grahame White
Type XV 29–30
Handley Page
0/100 and 0/400 25–6
Halifax 106–110, 162
Hampden 107, 111
Hastings 166–7
Hereford 107
Heyford 52, 74–5, 87
Hinaidi, Hyderabad 75
Hawker
Audax 66, 73
Demon 70, 82–3
Fury 52, 69, 70
Hardy 73
Hart 66, 73, 84
Hector 73
Henley 116
Hind 73
Horsley 75
Hunter 163, 176, 185
Hurricane 86, 97–100, 115, 119, 127, 136, 170
Nimrod, Osprey 80–1
Tempest 115, 133
Typhoon 113–5, 131, 133
Woodcock 67–8
Martinsyde
Elephant 15, 41, 192
Scout 13
Miles
Magister 113
Martinet 116
Master 112–3, 130
Monitor 116
Norman Thompson
N.T.2b 38
Percival
(now Hunting Percival)
Proctor 113, 172
Provost 169

Royal Aircraft Factory
B.E.2 series 9, 22–3, 28, 192
F.E. series 14, 19, 33
R.E. series 9, 23–4, 41
S.E.5/5A 11–12, 17, 33, 41, 55
Royal Navy Designs
Felixstowe Boats 2, 37–8, 81
Saro
Cloud 81
Lerwick 110
London 81
Short
S.38 29, 39
184 11, 36–7
320 10, 36
827 28, 36–7
Rangoon, Singapore 81
Stirling 107
Sunderland 110–1, 122, 129
Slingsby
Sky 168
Sopwith
1½ Strutter 21–2
Baby 35–7
Camel 16–7, 40
Cuckoo 38, 79
Dolphin 18
Pup 4, 16
Seaplanes 37
Snipe 18, 68
Triplane 15–6
Supermarine
Scapa 81
Seafire 127
Seagull 81
Sea Otter 127
Southampton 81
Spitfire 5, 8, 96–104, 110, 116, 120, 124, 135, 143, 170–1, 193, 200
Stranraer 81, 109
Walrus 81, 127
Vickers
'Gunbus' types 19, 56, 192
Valentia, Vernon 74

Victoria 74
Viking 167
Vildebeest 75, 87
Vimy, Virginia 74–5
Warwick 110
Wellesley 82
Wellington 107, 121
Wackett
Trainer 128
Westland
Lysander 114, 129
Wallace 72, 78, 83
Walrus 81
Wapiti 71–2
Westland-Sikorsky
Dragonfly 171, 173
Whirlwind 100–1, 193
Wight
Seaplanes 37

DUTCH
General 135, 182

FRENCH
General 47–50, 134–5
Breguet
14 34, 55
Bizerte 135
Caudron
GIII and GIV 25, 28
Farman
All types 28, 31, 47, 58
Franco-British Aviation
Flying-boats 38, 48, 58
Hanriot
H.D. types 48, 56–7
Morane Saulnier
M.S.406 86
Nieuport
1914–18 types 14, 47, 53–8, 63
Potez
Types 29 and 63 134–5
S.P.A.D.
S.VII 34

GERMAN
General 59–64, 152–7
A.E.G.
CIV 8
GIV 61
Bucker
Bu 181 172
Dornier
Do 17 92, 136, 153–4
Do 22 136
Do 217 122
Fieseler
Fi 156 Storch 172
Focke-Wulf
Fw 58 155
Fw 190 135, 155
Fw 200 154
Heinkel
He 51 93
He 111 139
He 219 155
Junkers
Ju 52/3m 130, 155, 172
Ju 86 130
Ju 88g 155
Messerschmitt
Me 109 139, 153
Siebel
Si 204 172

ITALIAN
General 57–8, 159–60, 182
Ansaldo
S.V.A. Scout 34
Caproni
Ca 101 93
Fiat
B.R.20 139
Cr 32 93
Cr 42 139
Savoia-Marchetti
S.M.79 93, 136
JAPANESE
General 158–161
RUSSIAN
General 136, 158, 183, 191

Abbreviations

A.A.C.	Army Air Corp	F.	Felixstowe	P.R.	Photographic Reconnaissance
A.A.C.U.	Anti-Aircraft Co-operation Unit	F.B.A.	Franco-British Aviation	P.T.S.	Parachute Training School
A.A.F.	Auxiliary Air Force	F.E.	Farman Experimental	R.A.A.F.	Royal Auxiliary Air Force or
A.C.	Army Co-operation	F.E.A.F.	Far East Air Force		Royal Australian Air Force
A.D.L.S.	Air Despatch Letter Service	F.K.	Frederick Koolhoren	R.A.T.F.	Radio Aids Training Flight
A.E.A.F.	Allied Expeditionary Air Forces	F.L.S.	Fighter Leader School	R.E.	Reconnaissance Experimental
A.E.F.	American Expeditionary Force	F.T.S.	Flying Training School	R.F.C.	Royal Flying Corps
A.F.D.U.	Air Fighting Development Unit	Gp.C.F.	Group Communications Flight	R.N.A.S.	Royal Naval Air Service
A.O.P.	Air Observation Post	G.R.S.	General Reconnaissance School	R.N.Z.A.F.	Royal New Zealand Air Force
A.P.S.	Armament Practice Station	G.T.S.	Glider Training School	R.W.E.	Radio Warfare Establishment
A.R.D.	Aircraft Repair Depot	H.C.U.	Heavy Conversion Unit	S.A.A.F.	South African Air Force
A.S.R.	Air Sea Rescue	I.A.F.	Indian Air Force	S.D.F.	Special Duties Flight
A.V.G.	American Volunteer Group	M.A.P.	Ministry of Aircraft Production	S.E.	Scouting Experimental
A.W.	Armstrong Whitworth	M.D.A.P.	Mutual Defence Aid Pact	S.E.A.C.	South East Asia Command
B.E.	Bleriot Experimental	M.E.A.F.	Middle East Air Force	T.A.F.	Tactical Air Force
B.O.A.C.	British Overseas Airways Corporation	M.O.S.	Ministry of Supply	T.C.U.	Transport Conversion Unit
		N.A.F.	National Aircraft Factory	T.E.U.	Tropical Experimental Unit
C.F.E.	Central Fighter Establishment	N.A.T.O.	North Atlantic Treaty Organisation	U.S.A.A.F.	United States Army Air Force
C/N	Constructor's Number			U.S.A.F.	United States Air Force
C.O.	Commanding Officer	O.T.U.	Operational Training Unit	U.S.N.	United States Navy
D.C.A.	Department of Civil Aviation	P.A.U.	Pilotless Aircraft Unit	V.S.	Vought Sikorsky

ERRATA

Page 103. Spitfire: The two shades of grey in the three drawings should be interchanged, i.e. the darker grey where it is shown is light grey and vice versa.

SPECIAL NOTE ON COLOURING

Shades varied in service as explained on page 94. The correct official shades for the Second World War, as issued by the Ministry of Aircraft Production, are featured on the opposite page.

COLOUR STANDARDS OF THE MINISTRY OF AIRCRAFT PRODUCTION

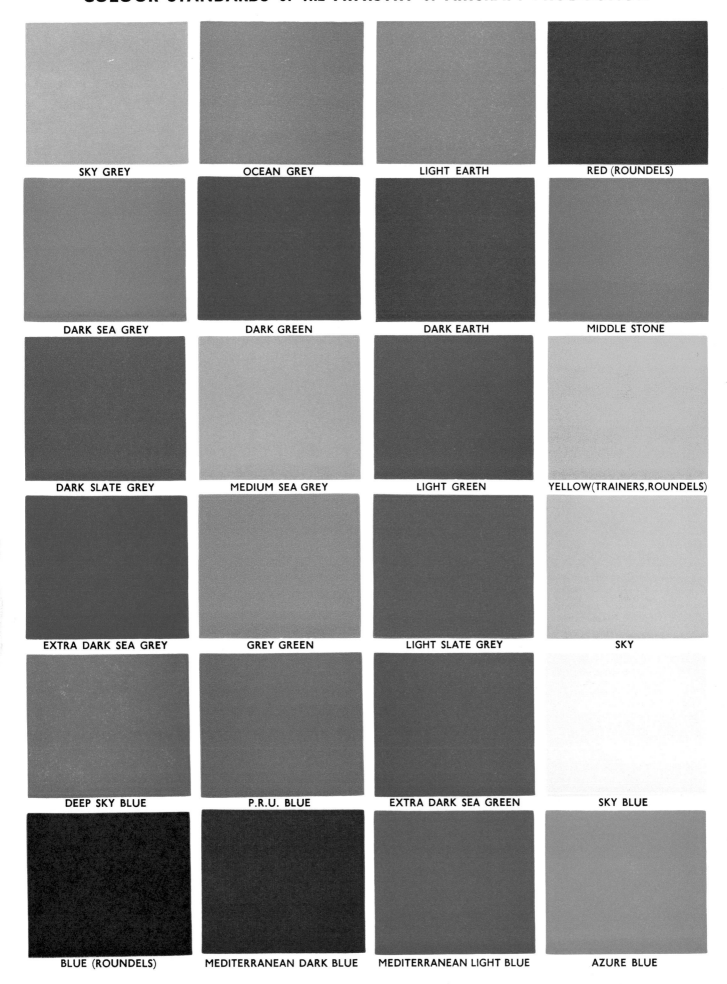

SKY GREY	OCEAN GREY	LIGHT EARTH	RED (ROUNDELS)
DARK SEA GREY	DARK GREEN	DARK EARTH	MIDDLE STONE
DARK SLATE GREY	MEDIUM SEA GREY	LIGHT GREEN	YELLOW(TRAINERS,ROUNDELS)
EXTRA DARK SEA GREY	GREY GREEN	LIGHT SLATE GREY	SKY
DEEP SKY BLUE	P.R.U. BLUE	EXTRA DARK SEA GREEN	SKY BLUE
BLUE (ROUNDELS)	MEDITERRANEAN DARK BLUE	MEDITERRANEAN LIGHT BLUE	AZURE BLUE